BESTSELLING BOOK SERIES

Grilling For Dummies®, 2nd Edition

Cheat Sheet

Grilling Times for Red Meat

Cut (Beef)	*Thickness/Weight*	*Grill Temp*	*Approximate Time*
Steak*	1 inch thick	Direct high	6–8 minutes
	$1\frac{1}{2}$ inches thick	Sear 8–10 minutes over direct high and then grill 4–6 minutes over indirect high	12–16 minutes
Skirt steak	$\frac{1}{4}$–$\frac{1}{2}$ inch thick	Direct high	4–6 minutes
Flank steak	$1\frac{1}{2}$–2 pounds, $\frac{3}{4}$ inch thick	Direct high	8–10 minutes
Kebab	$\frac{1}{2}$ inch cubes	Direct high	7–8 minutes
Ground beef patty	$\frac{3}{4}$ inch thick	Direct high	8–10 minutes
Rib roast (prime rib), boneless	5–6 pounds	Indirect medium	$1\frac{1}{4}$–$1\frac{3}{4}$ hours
Rib roast (prime rib), with bone	5–6 pounds	Indirect medium	$1\frac{1}{2}$–2 hours

** New York strip, porterhouse, rib-eye, T-bone, or tenderloin*

Cut (Lamb)	*Thickness/Weight*	*Grill Temp*	*Approximate Time*
Chop (loin, rib, shoulder, or sirloin)	$\frac{3}{4}$–$1\frac{1}{4}$ inches thick	Direct medium	8–12 minutes
Leg of lamb roast, boneless	5–7 pounds	Indirect medium	$1\frac{1}{4}$–$1\frac{3}{4}$ hours
Leg of lamb, butterflied	3–$3\frac{1}{2}$ pounds	Sear 10–15 minutes over direct medium and then grill 1–$1\frac{1}{4}$ hours over indirect medium	$1\frac{1}{4}$–$1\frac{1}{2}$ hours
Rack of lamb	1–$1\frac{1}{2}$ pounds	Direct medium	20–30 minutes

Grilling Times for Seafood

Type	*Thickness/Weight*	*Grill Temp*	*Approximate Time*
Crab (snow, legs)	2 ounces each	Indirect medium	5–8 minutes
Fish, steak	2 inches thick	Indirect medium	10–12 minutes
Fish, whole	1–2 pounds	Indirect medium	20–30 minutes
Scallops (raw, 6 to 8 count)	4–6 ounces	Indirect medium	5–8 minutes
Shrimp (raw, 6 to 8 count)	6 ounces	Indirect medium	5–10 minutes
Oysters	10–12 ounces	Indirect medium	5–10 minutes

Grilling For Dummies®, 2nd Edition

Cheat Sheet

Grilling Times for Pork

Cut	Thickness/Weight	Grill Temp	Approximate Time
Bratwurst, fresh	4–6 ounces	Direct medium	20–25 minutes
Pork chop, boneless or bone-in	$\frac{1}{2}$ inch thick	Direct high	5–7 minutes
	1 inch thick	Direct medium	8–10 minutes
	$1\frac{1}{4}$–$1\frac{1}{2}$ inches thick	Sear 6 minutes over direct high and then grill 4–6 minutes over indirect medium	10–12 minutes
Loin roast, boneless	$2\frac{1}{2}$ pounds	Direct medium	40–45 minutes
Loin roast, bone-in	3–5 pounds	Indirect medium	$1\frac{1}{4}$–$1\frac{3}{4}$ hours
Pork shoulder (Boston Butt), boneless	5–6 pounds	Direct low	$3\frac{1}{2}$–4 hours
Ribs, baby back	$1\frac{1}{2}$–2 pounds	Indirect low	$1\frac{1}{2}$–2 hours
Ribs, spareribs	3–5 pounds	Indirect low	$2\frac{1}{2}$–3 hours
Ribs, country-style, boneless	$1\frac{1}{2}$–2 pounds	Direct medium	12–15 minutes
Ribs, country-style, bone-in	3–4 pounds	Indirect medium	$1\frac{1}{2}$–2 hours
Tenderloin, whole	$\frac{3}{4}$–1 pound	Direct medium	15–20 minutes

Grilling Times for Poultry

Cut	Weight	Grill Temp	Approximate Time
Chicken breast, boneless, skinless	6 ounces	Direct medium	8–12 minutes
Chicken pieces, bone-in breast/wing	6 ounces	Indirect medium	30–40 minutes
Chicken pieces, bone-in leg/thigh	6 ounces	Indirect medium	40–50 minutes
Chicken, whole	$3\frac{1}{2}$–5 pounds	Indirect medium	1–$1\frac{1}{2}$ hours
Cornish game hen	$1\frac{1}{2}$–2 pounds	Indirect medium	30–45 minutes
Turkey breast, boneless	$2\frac{1}{2}$ pounds	Indirect medium	1–$1\frac{1}{4}$ hours
Turkey leg, bone-in	6–8 ounces	Indirect medium	20 minutes
Turkey, whole, unstuffed	10–11 pounds	Indirect medium	$1\frac{3}{4}$–$2\frac{1}{2}$ hours
Duck breast, boneless	7–8 ounces	Direct low	12–15 minutes
Duck, whole	$5\frac{1}{2}$–6 pounds	Indirect high	40 minutes

For more information about Wiley Publishing, call 1-800-762-2974.

Grilling FOR DUMMIES®

2ND EDITION

by Marie Rama and John Mariani

WILEY

Wiley Publishing, Inc.

Grilling For Dummies®, 2nd Edition

Published by
Wiley Publishing, Inc.
111 River St.
Hoboken, NJ 07030-5774
www.wiley.com

Published simultaneously in Canada

Library of Congress Control Number: 2009923065

ISBN: 978-0-470-42129-1

Manufactured in the United States of America

10 9 8 7 6 5 4 3 2

WILEY

About the Authors

Marie Rama is coauthor of *Cooking For Dummies.* She has worked as a professional pastry chef and recipe developer for numerous food companies and associations, including The McIlhenny Company and The United Fresh Fruit and Vegetable Association. Marie served as Director of Romance, Weddings, and Entertaining for Korbel Champagne and as a spokesperson for Sunkist Growers. She is a regular guest-chef on hundreds of TV and radio shows in the U.S. and Canada, and she lives with her husband, Mark Reiter, and their two sons, Nick and Will, in Bronxville, New York.

John Mariani is the author of several of the most highly regarded books on food in America today. His first book, *The Dictionary of American Food & Drink* (Ticknor & Fields, 1983), was hailed as the "American Larousse Gastronomique" and was chosen "best reference book on food for 1983" by *Library Journal*. It was later revised as *The Encyclopedia of American Food & Drink* (Lebahr-Friedman, 1999). His history of food service in the U.S., *America Eats Out* (William Morrow, 1991), won the IACP Award for best reference book. *The Dictionary of Italian Food & Drink,* the most comprehensive study of Italian food published in the U.S., was published in 1998 by Broadway Books. He is also coauthor, with Alex von Bidder, of *The Four Seasons: A History of America's Premier Restaurant* (Smithmark, 1999) and is coauthor with his brother Robert Mariani of a memoir entitled *Almost Golden* (Infinity, 2005), about growing up in the Bronx, New York. His latest book, with his wife Galina, is *The Italian-American Cookbook* (Harvard Common Press, 2000).

Mariani is currently food and travel correspondent for *Esquire;* wine columnist for Bloomberg News; dining columnist for *The Wine Spectator;* food columnist for *Diversion;* restaurant columnist for *Forbes* Magazine; and publisher/editor of the online newsletter *Mariani's Virtual Gourmet* (`www.johnmariani.com`). Mariani was born in New York City and received his B.A. from Iona College and his M.A. and Ph.D. from Columbia University. He lives in Tuckahoe, New York, with his wife, Galina, and two sons, Michael and Christopher.

Authors' Acknowledgments

There is a long list of people we would like to especially thank, who helped make this book possible.

To gather accurate information for the sidebars and icons in this book, we turned to many food experts and associations. We'd like to thank Susan Lamb Parenti and the National Cattlemen's Beef Association; Robin Kline and Ed Newman, consultants for the National Pork Producers Council; the American Lamb Council; and the National Institute of Fisheries. We are also grateful for the invaluable contributions of Donna Myers, editor of "*The BackYard BarbeQuer*" newsletter — after more than 25 years as spokesperson for the Barbecue Industry Association, Donna knows as much about grilling equipment, manufacturers, and techniques as anyone we know. And thank you illustrators extraordinaire, Liz Kurtzman and Rich Tennant.

We thank Galina Mariani for her creative and delicious recipe contributions to this new edition. We'd also like to thank the following manufacturers who generously donated our very reliable testing grills, grilling equipment, and accessories: Weber, Sunbeam, Char-Broil, Ducane, Jackes-Evans, and E-Z Fit Barbecue Parts and Accessories. We offer more information about these and other equipment manufacturers in Chapter 2.

We owe special, heartfelt thanks to our Project Editor, Kristin DeMint, and our Copy Editor, Jessica Smith. Throughout all these months, they kept us on track with their tireless devotion, editorial skills, and insightful questions. We also thank Acquisitions Editor Stacy Kennedy for her continuous, invaluable support and clear-sighted counsel.

And one final note: Marie would like to thank her friend, Ira Bart, who one perfect summer day, waved a two-inch-thick steak in front of his personally-designed brick grill and announced, "Marie, you ought to write *Grilling For Dummies.*" So, we did.

Publisher's Acknowledgments

We're proud of this book; please send us your comments through our Dummies online registration form located at `http://dummies.custhelp.com`. For other comments, please contact our Customer Care Department within the U.S. at 877-762-2974, outside the U.S. at 317-572-3993, or fax 317-572-4002.

Some of the people who helped bring this book to market include the following:

Acquisitions, Editorial, and Media Development

Project Editor: Kristin DeMint

(Previous Edition: Tere Drenth)

Acquisitions Editor: Stacy Kennedy

Copy Editor: Jessica Smith

(Previous Edition: Tina Sims)

Assistant Editor: Erin Calligan Mooney

Editorial Program Coordinator: Joe Niesen

Technical Editor: Patricia Santelli

Recipe Tester: Emily Nolan

Editorial Manager: Michelle Hacker

Editorial Assistant: Jennette ElNaggar

Art Coordinator: Alicia B. South

Photographer: T.J. Hine Photography

Food Stylist: Lisa Bishop

Cover Photo: © Jupiter Images

Cartoons: Rich Tennant (`www.the5thwave.com`)

Composition Services

Project Coordinator: Katherine Key

Layout and Graphics: Reuben W. Davis, Sarah Philippart, Christin Swinford, Christine Williams

Proofreader: John Greenough, Nancy L. Reinhardt

Indexer: Estalita Slivoskey

Publishing and Editorial for Consumer Dummies

Diane Graves Steele, Vice President and Publisher, Consumer Dummies

Kristin Ferguson-Wagstaffe, Product Development Director, Consumer Dummies

Ensley Eikenburg, Associate Publisher, Travel

Kelly Regan, Editorial Director, Travel

Publishing for Technology Dummies

Andy Cummings, Vice President and Publisher, Dummies Technology/General User

Composition Services

Gerry Fahey, Vice President of Production Services

Debbie Stailey, Director of Composition Services

Contents at a Glance

Introduction 1

Part I: Getting Ready to Show the Grill Who's Boss 7

Chapter 1: Mastering Grill-Speak 9
Chapter 2: Buying the Grill of Your Dreams (and Accessories to Boot) 21
Chapter 3: To Build a Fire 41

Part II: Adding Spice to Your Life 55

Chapter 4: Peeking Inside the Grilling Guru's Pantry 57
Chapter 5: Infusing Foods with Flavor: Marinades, Oils, and Rubs 73
Chapter 6: The Saucy Side of Grilling 91

Part III: For the Fanatics of the Classics 113

Chapter 7: Bun-Lovin' Burgers, Sausages, and Hot Dogs 115
Chapter 8: Swordplay: Grilling Kebabs and Satay 127
Chapter 9: Maybe Messy, Definitely Delicious: Ribs Worth Drooling Over 151
Chapter 10: Pair a Rotisserie with a Grill? Oh Yes, You Can 165

Part IV: Grilling Everything Under the Sun 179

Chapter 11: Beef: It's What Grills Were Made For 181
Chapter 12: Pork — The King of Barbecue 199
Chapter 13: Savoring the Peppery Meat of the Middle East: Lamb 215
Chapter 14: Birds of a Feather 231
Chapter 15: She Grills Seafood by the Seashore 259
Chapter 16: Not for Vegetarians Only: Vegetables and Side Dishes 285
Chapter 17: Grill to Go: Sandwiches, Pizzas, and Other Finger Foods 311
Chapter 18: Sweets Can Take the Heat, Too (And Cocktails Cool and Refresh) ... 325

Part V: The Part of Tens 335

Chapter 19: The Ten Commandments of Grilling 337
Chapter 20: Ten of Our Favorite Barbecue Joints 341
Appendix: Metric Conversion Guide 345

Index 349

Recipes at a Glance

Marinades

Hoisin Marinade and Basting Sauce 78
Spicy Soy and Cilantro Marinade 78
Spicy Cinnamon and Soy Marinade 79
Five Spice and Soy Sauce Marinade 80
Provençal Marinade 80
Moroccan Marinade 81
Lime and Cumin Marinade 81
Cuban-Style Mojo Marinade 82
Greek Marinade 82
Gingery Grilled Vegetable Marinade 83

Rubs

Hot and Sweet Spice Rub 86
Cajun-Style Steak Rub 86
Peppery Dried Herb Rub 87
Peppery Parsley Rub for Tender Steaks 88
Five Spice Asian Rub 88
Coriander and Fennel Rub 89
Middle Eastern Rub 90

Sauces

Roasted Garlic and Red Pepper Puree 92
Mushroom-Butter Sauce 93
Ginger Cream 94
Mustard and Rosemary Grilled Chicken Sauce 95
Tarragon Sauce 96
Creamy Asian Peanut Sauce 97
Raita 98
Creamy Horseradish Sauce 99
Tahini Dressing 99
Teriyaki Sauce 100

Condiments

Fresh Tomato Salsa 101
Roasted Sweet Pepper Salsa 102
Black Bean and Red Pepper Salsa 103
Sun-Dried Tomato and Basil Mayonnaise 104
Tomato Chutney 105
Summer Squash Chutney 106
Cherry and Pear Chutney 107
Tapenade 108
Guacamole 109
Barbecued Onions 110
Compound Butter 111

Burgers

Turkey Burger 118
Gorgonzola Hamburgers with Balsamic Onion Relish 119
Lamb Burger 120

Sausages

Grilled Kielbasa with Creamy Mustard Sauce 125
Grilled Italian Links with Caraway Sauerkraut 126

Kebabs

Artichoke, Mushroom, and Cherry Tomato Kebabs 130
Western Beef Kebabs with Red Peppers and Onions 132
Teriyaki Steak Kebabs 134
Apple and Tarragon Pork Kebabs 136
Pork Kebabs with Nectarines and Red Onions 137
Lamb and Eggplant Kebabs with Tarragon Marinade 138
Lemony Fresh Lamb Kebabs 140
Chicken Tikka 142
Mixed Grill Seafood Kebabs with Fresh Lemon Sauce 144
Sweet-and-Sour Shrimp Kebabs with Scallions 146
Satay with Peanut Dipping Sauce 148

Ribs

Just-Right Pork Ribs 155
Donna Myers's Baby Back Ribs with Sweet-Hickory Barbecue Sauce 158
Soul Food Pork Ribs 160
Korean Beef Short Ribs 163

Rotisserie

Rotisserie-Grilled Chicken 170
Lemon-Herb Gravy 173
Rotisserie Pork Spareribs 174
Rotisserie Boneless Pork Loin with Herbes de Provence 176

Beef

Grilled Steak 101 190
Texas Beef Barbecue 191
Chuck Steaks Marinated in Red Wine 192
Grilled Steak Salad 194
Grilled Tenderloin Au Poivre with Herb Butter Sauce 196

Pork

Lemony Tarragon Pork Chops 205
Grilled Pork Chops with Rosemary Oil 206
Apricot-Glazed Pork Chops 207
Caribbean Pork Chops 208
Brined and Grilled Loin O' Pork 209
Curried Pork Tenderloins 211
Soy-Marinated Pork Tenderloin with Asian-Flavored Vegetables 212
Coriander and Fennel Rubbed Pork Tenderloin 214
Grilled Chops with Orange and Rosemary 220

Lamb

Lamb Shoulder Chops with Yogurt and Curry Marinade 222
Western Lamb Steaks 224
Butterflied Leg of Lamb with Honey-Mustard Dressing 226
Rack of Lamb with Hoisin Marinade 228

Poultry

Lemon Chicken Breasts 234
Jerk-Seasoned Chicken Breasts 235
Spicy Chili Chicken Wings 237
Orange-Garlic Chicken Wings 238
Grilled Chicken Quarters with Barbecue Sauce 240
Grilled Lime Chicken with Onion Compote 241
Lemon-Cilantro Chicken with Garlic-Ginger Mayonnaise 242

Moroccan Chicken Legs and Thighs 243
Chicken alla Mattone 244
Brined and Grilled Chicken 246
Dry Poultry Rub for Brined Chicken 247
Grilled Turkey Tenderloins with Honey-Mustard Glaze 248
Dale Curry's Hickory-Smoked Whole Turkey 250
Rock Cornish Game Hens with Molasses-Rum Marinade 254
Whole Game Hens with Asian Flavors 256

Seafood

Grilled Swordfish Steak with Chipotle Salsa 263
Grilled Fish Steaks with Avocado and Citrus Salsa 264
Whole Grilled Trout with Thyme and Almond Butter Sauce 266
Flatfish Fillets Grilled on Lemon Slices with Mediterranean Skillet Sauce 269
Seasoned and Breaded Catfish Fillets with Basil Mayonnaise 271
Asian-Style Salmon Fillets with Vegetables 272
Smoked Salmon Fillet 275
Scallop Kebabs with Pineapple and Bacon 276
Grilled Clams and Mussels with Lemon Butter or Fresh Tomato Sauce 278
Grilled Soft-Shell Crabs 280
Pesto Shrimp in the Shell 281
Jimmy Schmidt's Grilled Barbecued Shrimp 283

Vegetables

Linguine with Goat Cheese and Grilled Asparagus 289
Garlic-Grilled Portobellos 294
Grilled New Potato Salad with Fresh Mint 298
Stuffed Summer Squash 299
Grand Marnier Grilled Sweet Potatoes 301
Grilled Tomatoes with Cumin Butter 303

Side Dishes

Couscous with Apples, Onions, and Raisins 304
Middle Eastern Rice 305
Tomato and Red Onion Salad 306
Orange-Ginger Coleslaw 307
Tabbouleh 308
Macaroni Salad with Sun-Dried Tomato Mayonnaise 309
Yogurt Cucumber Salad 310

Pizzas, Sandwiches, and Other Finger Foods

Sun-Dried Tomato and Mozzarella Cheese Pizza 313
Tomato Bruschetta 315
Best-Ever Fajitas 317
Mango and Cheese Quesadillas 319
Tortilla Towers 320
Open-Faced Grilled Eggplant and Goat Cheese Sandwiches 321
Gorgonzola and Fig Sandwiches 323

Fruits

Foil-Wrapped Baked Apples 327
Grilled Figs and Prosciutto 328
Grilled Bananas with Caramel Sauce 329
Grilled Pound Cake and Fruit with Brandy Sauce 330

Cocktails

Classic Daiquiri 331
Mojito Mojo 332
Frozen Mango Martini 332
Caipirinha 333
The Best Bloody Mary Ever 333

Table of Contents

Introduction 1

About This Book 2
Conventions Used in This Book 2
What You're Not to Read 3
Foolish Assumptions 3
How This Book Is Organized 4
Part I: Getting Ready to Show the Grill Who's Boss 4
Part II: Adding Spice to Your Life 4
Part III: For the Fanatics of the Classics 4
Part IV: Grilling Everything Under the Sun 5
Part V: The Part of Tens 5
Icons Used in This Book 5
Where to Go from Here 6

Part I: Getting Ready to Show the Grill Who's Boss 7

Chapter 1: Mastering Grill-Speak 9

Two Key Terms: Direct Grilling and Indirect Grilling 9
Searing food with direct, no-frills grilling 10
Staying away from the heat: Indirect grilling 11
Slow and Smoky: Barbecuing with Success 13
Even Slower than Barbecuing: Smoking 14
Dry smoking 15
Water smoking 15
A Whole Mess of Grilling Terms: A Griller's Glossary 16
Looking at a Few Guidelines before You Begin 18

Chapter 2: Buying the Grill of Your Dreams (and Accessories to Boot) 21

Choosing the Type of Grill You'll Shop For 22
Perusing your options 22
Comparing the two main types: Charcoal or gas? 24
What Do You Have to Offer? Looking at Grill Features 27
Playing with Tools and Toys 28
Kid in a grilling shop: Looking at basic grilling utensils 28
Surveying tools and toys for the serious griller 33
Caring for Your Grill 39
Oiling the grids 39
Cleaning the grill inside and out 39
Storing your grill 40

Chapter 3: To Build a Fire....................................... 41

Getting Your Grill Ready for Use 41
Fueling a Hunk of Burnin' Fire.. 42
Using propane with your gas grill.. 42
Going with the old standard: Charcoal briquettes 43
Grilling like a pro with natural lump charcoal 44
Adding hardwood chips or chunks 45
Arranging the Coal to Suit Your Fancy 47
Let There Be Flames: Igniting Your Grill.. 48
Your very best bet: An electric charcoal igniter.. 48
The runner-up: A chimney starter 50
Old-school style: A butane lighter 51
Controlling and Maintaining the Heat.. 52

Part II: Adding Spice to Your Life.............................. 55

Chapter 4: Peeking Inside the Grilling Guru's Pantry.............. 57

Adopting Some Kitchen Helpers: Bottled and Canned Goods................ 57
Condiment-ry, My Dear Watson.. 59
Flavoring Foods with Oil.. 61
Adding Tartness with a Splash of Vinegar 63
Sweeten the Pot: Using Sweeteners in Sauces and Marinades 63
Wine and Dine Me: Marinating and Basting with Wines........................ 64
Walking through a Griller's Herb Garden.. 65
Adding Zest with Fruits and Veggies.. 70

Chapter 5: Infusing Foods with Flavor: Marinades, Oils, and Rubs . . . 73

The March of the Marinades.. 74
Choosing your marinade ingredients.. 74
Preparing to marinate 76
Deciding how long to marinate your food 77
Using marinades for basting and finishing 77
Flavoring with Oils: The Slick Solution 84
Rub-a-Dub-Dub: Coating Foods with Dry Rubs 85

Chapter 6: The Saucy Side of Grilling 91

Adding Flavor with Warm Sauces.. 91
Chillin' Out: Working with Cold Sauces 98
Complementing Foods with Condiments 100
Salsas.. 101
Mayonnaise.. 103
Chutneys 104
Other condiments.. 108
Dressing Up Your Meal Using Compound Butters 110

Part III: For the Fanatics of the Classics 113

Chapter 7: Bun-Lovin' Burgers, Sausages, and Hot Dogs 115

Everyone Loves a Burger 115
Choosing your burger meat 116
Creating the mixture of ingredients 116
Preparing your patties for the grill 117
Topping your burger 121
Simple Sausages and Fancy Franks 122
Knowing how long to cook 'em 124
Loading up on toppings 125

Chapter 8: Swordplay: Grilling Kebabs and Satay 127

Ladies and Gentlemen — Choose Your Skewers! 128
Mastering the Skill of Grilling Kebabs 129
Putting Veggies on a Stick: The Fun Way to Eat Them 129
Kebabing for Beef 131
Porky Pig on a Stick 135
Lamb Kebabs — the Real Deal 138
Chicken Flying Full Mast, Half-Mast, All Over the Mast 141
Gone Fishin' and Sea Divin' (For Kebabs) 143
Please Satay for Dinner 147

Chapter 9: Maybe Messy, Definitely Delicious: Ribs Worth Drooling Over 151

Back, Spare, and Country-Style: Recognizing Pork Rib Varieties 152
The Many Ways to Grill Pork Ribs 152
Getting to Know Beef Ribs 162

Chapter 10: Pair a Rotisserie with a Grill? Oh Yes, You Can. 165

Grilling Off the Grid: A Primer on Rotisserie Cooking 165
Choosing the best meat for the mill 166
Keeping some general tips in mind 166
Heeding meat-specific rotisserie cooking tips 168
Let the Rotisserie Games Begin! 170

Part IV: Grilling Everything Under the Sun 179

Chapter 11: Beef: It's What Grills Were Made For 181

All You Need to Know to Grill a Mean Hunk of Beef 181
Grading beef 182
Naming the cuts of beef 184
Preparing and Grilling Your Steaks 187
Love them tender: Marinating meats before grilling 188
Grilling 'em up! 189
Giving Grilled Beef Roast a Chance 195

Chapter 12: Pork — The King of Barbecue 199
Hit Me with Your Best Cut 199
Here's the Rub: Flavoring Pork with Herbs and Spices 202
And This Little Pork Was Done Just Right 202
Chop, chop, who's there? 204
Brine 'n dine 208
Tenderloin is the night 210

Chapter 13: Savoring the Peppery Meat of the Middle East: Lamb 215
Lamb and Spice and Everything Nice: What You Need to Know 215
Surveying the cuts 216
Looking for lamb by country of origin (yes, it matters!) 216
Seasoning your lamb 218
Grilling your lamb with TLC 219
Licking Your (Lamb) Chops 220
The Lowdown on Lamb Shoulders 221
A Leg Up on Lamb 223
Grill roasting a leg 223
Grilling legs, steak-style 224
Butterflying, marinating, and grilling legs: A no-fail method 225
Racking Up Lamb for the Grill 228

Chapter 14: Birds of a Feather 231
Finger-Lickin' Chicken 231
Handling chicken with care 233
Grilling chicken breasts 233
Just wingin' it 236
Chowing down on chicken quarters 239
It's thigh time to grill some legs 243
Dishing up a whole chicken 244
Being Thankful for the Many Uses of Turkey 247
Game Birds Make for Healthy Eating 251
Comparing wild versus farm-raised game birds 251
Surveying game bird varieties 252

Chapter 15: She Grills Seafood by the Seashore 259
More Fish at Market, if Fewer Fish in the Sea 260
Cooking Fresh Fish by the Cut 260
Fish steaks: The thick and easy cut 261
Making heads and tails of whole fish 265
Being gentle with fillets 268
Holy Smoked Fish, Batman! 274
Mmm, Mollusks! Clams, Mussels, and Scallops 276
The Softest Swimmer in the Sea: Soft-Shell Crabs 280
Don't Call Me a Shrimp (But Do Feed Me Some!) 281

Chapter 16: Not for Vegetarians Only: Vegetables and Side Dishes 285

Updating Your Mom's Veggie-Cooking Technique 286
Simple seasoning (and brief marinating) is best 286
Exercising care while grilling 287
Simply Vegetables 288
Artichokes 288
Asparagus 289
Belgian endive 290
Broccoli 290
Brussels sprouts 291
Carrots 291
Corn 291
Eggplant 292
Garlic 293
Leeks 293
Mushrooms 294
Onions 295
Parsnips 296
Peppers 296
Potatoes 297
Squash 298
Sweet potatoes 300
Tomatoes 302
Not Grilled, but Still Good: Warm and Cozy Sides 303
Cool and Refreshing Sides 306

Chapter 17: Grill to Go: Sandwiches, Pizzas, and Other Finger Foods 311

Giving Pizza the Third Degree 311
Play dough perfect 311
Can you top this? 312
Adding charcoal and hardwood to the mix 314
Bring on the Bruschetta 315
Fixin' Fajitas and Fajita Fixins 316
Let Them Eat Quesadillas 319
Sandwich Face-Off 321

Chapter 18: Sweets Can Take the Heat, Too (And Cocktails Cool and Refresh) 325

Grilled Fruit? Oh Yeah! 325
Care for a Cocktail? 331

Part V: The Part of Tens 335

Chapter 19: The Ten Commandments of Grilling 337

Practice Patience with Your Fire 337
Organize Your Grill Space 337
Flavor Your Food 338
Don't Skimp on Fuel 338
Police the Fire! 338
Build a Fire with Different Hot Spots 339
Understand the Grilling Variables 339
Figure Out When Food Is Done 339
Sprint from the Grill to the Table 340
Relax! 340

Chapter 20: Ten of Our Favorite Barbecue Joints 341

Arthur Bryant's 341
Charlie Vergos' Rendezvous 341
Kreuz Market 342
Goode Company Texas Bar-B-Q 342
Carson's 343
Blue Smoke 343
Lexington Barbecue No. 1 343
Sconyers Bar-B-Que 344
Sonny Bryan's Smokehouse 344
Ono Hawaiian Foods 344

Appendix: Metric Conversion Guide 345

Index 349

Introduction

If your grilling experience is limited to flipping a few burgers on a kettle grill or roasting a hot dog on a branch over an open fire when you were a kid at camp, you've just scratched the surface of what can be a very exciting (and somewhat intimidating) way to cook. After all, you're dealing with an open fire, red-hot coals, and a certain amount of danger, not to mention the potential embarrassment of burning the heck out of a $10 steak.

What was once a backyard adjunct to the kitchen, the grill has become as essential an appliance as an oven, range, or microwave. The popularity of grilling shows on TV, the availability of new ingredients, bottled sauces and seasonings, and innovations to the grill itself show just how big grilling has become.

Grilling has become such a popular American pastime in the last decade that many people own two or more grills — a charcoal grill for weekend grilling, a gas grill for weeknight grilling, and maybe a hibachi or portable grill for tailgate parties or camping. Thus the need for a new edition of the original *Grilling For Dummies.*

Grilling For Dummies, 2nd Edition, takes you through the basics of grilling and then shows you the infinite possibilities of this terrific cooking technique. Even if you've done a certain amount of serious grilling out on the patio, this book can help you to refine your technique. It also introduces you to many foods that you may never have considered suitable for grilling, including vegetables and fruits. We also have updated the book to include new techniques and more information on grills, accessories, and the ingredients themselves — some of which weren't even available a decade ago. Finally, we try very hard to take the intimidation factor out of the process and replace it with a whole lot of fun.

We've noticed such a sharp increase in ethnic cooking done on the grill that we've added a lot more Mediterranean, Middle Eastern, and Asian recipes in this edition. We think it reflects current tastes. But we would love to hear from you, the reader, as to what you're interested in seeing and trying and tasting in a world of grilling that no longer starts at Memorial Day and stops after Labor Day.

About This Book

Grilling For Dummies, 2nd Edition, is a book that will make an expert grill master out of you — or at least make the exercise painless. But this isn't just a book of recipes or tips on how to buy a grill. The recipes and tips are all in here, but the book includes a great deal more.

Grilling has its own jargon and requires its own accessories. So we explain everything you need to know and buy to be successful with your grill. Grilling has been so popular in the past decade that the market has responded by improving features of basic grills and by providing a wider variety of grill options. Even though all these new features make the grilling marketplace a bit confusing, we ask you to relax because you have this book to help you! We show you the differences — and they are numerous and significant — among different grills and tell you what you can expect to pay for grills and grill accessories.

In the recipe chapters, we discuss the kinds of foods that are great on the grill and how to select them. The recipes range from classic to contemporary — all perfect for the grill. We give you some quick information in the Part of Tens, including ten ways to become a grill master, the ten best barbecue places in America, and ten tips on how to throw an outdoor party — which, in the end, is the best reason to grill.

We also include a section of color photos that shows you what some of our recipes look like. (This section is located in the center of the book.) These photos are so mouth-watering that you'll want to go directly to the recipes and start grilling.

You don't need to read this book straight through. In fact, we've deliberately arranged it so it works for those who already know a bit about grilling as well as for those who are just beginners. Depending on your admitted level of expertise, you may want to skip directly to the recipes (see Parts II, III, and IV), or you may want to start with Chapter 2 to find out more about the differences between gas grills and charcoal grills. Go right ahead: Read the book in any order you want. That's why this book looks and reads the way it does.

Conventions Used in This Book

Here are a few guidelines that'll help ensure your success with the recipes in this book:

- Pepper means ground black pepper unless otherwise specified.
- All butter is unsalted.

- Sugar is granulated unless otherwise noted.
- All temperatures are Fahrenheit.

In addition to the conventions we follow for the ingredients, we use a few other conventions to point out helpful info:

- We use *italic* to point out new terms that we define.
- We use **boldface** to highlight the keywords in a bulleted list or the action parts of numbered steps.
- We use `monofont` to point out Web addresses that you may want to check out for further information that we don't dive into here.

What You're Not to Read

Sidebars contain extra information, so you don't have to read them. They do, however, often explain some fun technique or issue in more detail, and you may find the information helpful. So skip over these paragraphs if you want, but know that you may be missing some gold nuggets of additional info if you do!

Foolish Assumptions

We're making certain assumptions about you, the reader, in this book. First of all, you obviously have a real interest in good cooking and grilling beyond the obvious burgers and hot dogs, so we gear this book toward you, the reader who really wants to take a little time to get the best results.

Although we never take our assumptions for granted, we believe that you're well aware of the dangers of working with an open fire. But we still continue to stress the safety rules throughout the book. If you wish to skip around this book for information, that's great. But we urge you to read every safety tip that you come across.

We keep our recipes as simple as possible in terms of their instructions, but we firmly believe that these recipes take grilling several steps higher than some of you may have thought possible. Even those with only basic cooking skills shouldn't have the slightest trouble following any recipe in this book. But if you've never done much grilling before, go step-by-step through our simple, classic recipes for items like steaks and burgers. Then try some simple seafood recipes, like a swordfish steak. By the time you master those recipes, you'll be able to reproduce anything in this book.

How This Book Is Organized

As with all the books in the *For Dummies* series, *Grilling For Dummies,* 2nd Edition, is arranged for maximum ease of use. We break down subjects into simple-to-understand units. We begin with a section we call a *part,* which is further broken down into chapters, within which we cover specific subjects and topics, often with lists for handy reference.

Part I: Getting Ready to Show the Grill Who's Boss

In this part, we go over everything you need to know to decide among the various kinds of grills on the market, their relative virtues and problems, their costs, and what all those grilling terms mean when you're ready to buy. We also provide a checklist of accessories.

This part also shows you the differences among hardwoods, charcoal, briquettes, self-igniting coals, flavoring woods, and any other fuel that makes for a good fire. This part also explains how to make a good fire for your particular intentions, whether you're grilling fish, barbecued ribs, or kebabs. We discuss the strategies of safely starting a fire and maintaining it for maximum effect, and then we make some recommendations about the best fire starters on the market, from electric coils to metal chimneys.

Part II: Adding Spice to Your Life

This is the part where you really start to cook. First, we help you stock your pantry with the kinds of foods and seasonings that make for great grilling. Anyone can slap a sirloin down on a grill, but this part suggests herbs, spices, rubs, and marinades that can add flavor and texture to your grilled foods. We also provide some delectable sauces on the side that add measurably not just to the grilled foods but to the other ingredients on the plate.

Part III: For the Fanatics of the Classics

Ready, set, grill! In this part, we cover old-fashioned favorites like burgers (there's more to a great burger than buying a frozen patty at the supermarket, you know), hot dogs, kebabs, ribs, and rotisseried foods. In Chapter 9, we also explain the distinctions between regular grilling and barbecuing (ribs, in particular), which can be easily accomplished at home with a little patience and a lot of time.

Part IV: Grilling Everything Under the Sun

This part takes you beyond the old-fashioned grilled foods and invites you to try a variety of recipes, including those for beef, pork, lamb, and chicken. We give you tips about how to buy the best cut for your purposes. This part also shows you that the grill is one of the most versatile cooking methods imaginable for adding flavor to seafood, vegetables, and even fruits. And if you've never considered making pizzas or other sandwiches directly over coals, we think that you'll be surprised by the possibilities. We even include recipes for some side dishes and our favorite cocktails to serve with the food that's coming off the fire.

Part V: The Part of Tens

We finish the book with some fun information that will make outdoor cooking even more enjoyable. Here, you get tips on ten crucial grilling guidelines as well as our personal pick of the best barbecue restaurants across the United States, where you may pick up a few pointers that even we missed.

At the end of this book, we include an appendix with a Metric Conversion Guide to help you quickly translate common abbreviations for cooking measurements and figure out how to change the recipe measurements to metric sizes.

Icons Used in This Book

This book uses icons that alert you to something you may not have thought of but that will help make outdoor cooking a lot easier and more pleasurable. Here's what they all mean:

This icon gives you tips on buying the best meats, seafood, vegetables, seasonings, and equipment.

These tips give helpful information about successful grilling techniques, from temperature control to ease of cleanup.

This icon highlights advice that we suggest you keep in mind as you're grilling.

All cooking involves a certain degree of danger, and safety should always be on the mind of anyone cooking outdoors over an open fire. This icon reminds you of ways to avoid personal injury or property damage.

Grilling itself is a pretty healthy way to cook, but this icon tells you how to further cut the fat from grilled foods.

In addition, the following types of text offer ways to stretch the recipes in this book:

> ***Vary It!*** When you're grilling, there's never just one way to prepare a recipe. So, we highlight ways that you can improvise and vary the preparation or the ingredients.
>
> ***Go-With:*** These give you ideas for side dishes to pair with tasty grilled main dishes; marinades and sauces that work well with your chosen meat; and grilled fruits and vegetables that go with delicious recipes throughout the book.

Where to Go from Here

If you're just starting out in the wonderful world of grilling, we recommend that you read the first several chapters — especially those on safety and technique — before proceeding to the recipes. If you're ready to start grilling, simply go to the chapter that discusses the food you want to prepare. Whatever your expertise level, remember that we've attempted to make everything about grilling as simple to understand as possible. We've sprinkled plenty of little tricks and bits of advice throughout the book — they're sure to increase your knowledge and expertise as you become more experienced. Our aim is to get you going if you're just beginning and to make you a master if you're already good at one of the most popular and enjoyable social activities that surrounds the enjoyment of good food and friends.

Part I
Getting Ready to Show the Grill Who's Boss

"I use old Duke to check my steaks. If it feels like Duke's tongue, it's rare; if it feels like his ear, it's medium; and if it feels like his butt, it's well done."

In this part . . .

Grilling has its own jargon, equipment, and strategies — all of which are completely different from traditional cooking. This part introduces you to the grilling basics: from a quick tutorial on Grill-Speak to guidelines on shopping for a grill and from tips for cleaning up those nasty bits of food and grease to sound advice for building a perfect charcoal fire — with or without wood chips. We also share a list of grilling gadgets and accessories that range from must-haves to nice-to-haves — many of them make perfect gifts for that special someone who lives to flip burgers on the weekends (as we do!).

Chapter 1

Mastering Grill-Speak

In This Chapter

- Grilling directly and indirectly
- Understanding the finer points of barbecuing
- Looking into the process of smoking
- Getting to know grilling terms and guidelines

Nothing — not roasting, not frying, not sautéing, and certainly not poaching — gives such wonderful, smoky flavor to food as grilling does. And because it's done outdoors, grilling is the most social of cooking techniques. For as long as man has known how great foods can taste when cooked over an open fire, grilling outdoors has been a social event that invites people to participate.

By some strange twist of fate, men seem to take to grilling like ducks to water. (Perhaps women have just let men think that they're better at it!) But we find that no matter who's doing the grilling, everyone has fun. Grilling brings the kitchen outdoors and often gathers friends, neighbors, and family members around the grill to share stories, watch the fire, and trade recipes.

Grilling over a charcoal fire is perhaps the most interactive of all cooking techniques. It demands that you respond like an athlete to the changes of a live fire. This intense interaction is one of the aspects of grilling that makes it so much fun. You have to play with and master the elements of fire, smoke, and heat — and this book shows you how (as well as how to use a gas grill).

But first, in this chapter, we start off with some translation for you — from Grill-Speak into everyday language.

Two Key Terms: Direct Grilling and Indirect Grilling

In your introduction to the language of grilling, we start you off with the two basic methods of grilling — direct and indirect.

Searing food with direct, no-frills grilling

Direct grilling means that the food is placed on the grill directly over the full force of the heat source, whether it's charcoal, hardwood, or gas. (See Figure 1-1.) Just about every food, from meats to vegetables, can be grilled directly over fire. Some foods, however, are better cooked over indirect heat, a great grilling technique that's introduced in the following section. Foods that are often grilled directly over the heat include hamburgers, hot dogs, pork chops, lamb chops, boneless chicken breasts, beef tenderloins, and all types of fish and shellfish.

Grilling over direct, intense heat sears the food, coating its exterior with a tasty brown crust that's loaded with flavor. Steamed or boiled foods don't have this flavor advantage, nor do foods that are stir-fried or microwaved. The techniques of sautéing, deep-frying, roasting, and broiling create this crusty effect, but grilling rewards you with a seared crust *and* the extra benefit of smoky flavoring that comes from the charcoal, wood chips, or hardwood chunks. And unlike sautéing and deep frying, grilling doesn't cook food in a layer of hot fat to produce this sear — you get all the benefits of a rich, brown crust with fewer calories.

Figure 1-1: The placement of coals depends on the type of grilling you're doing.

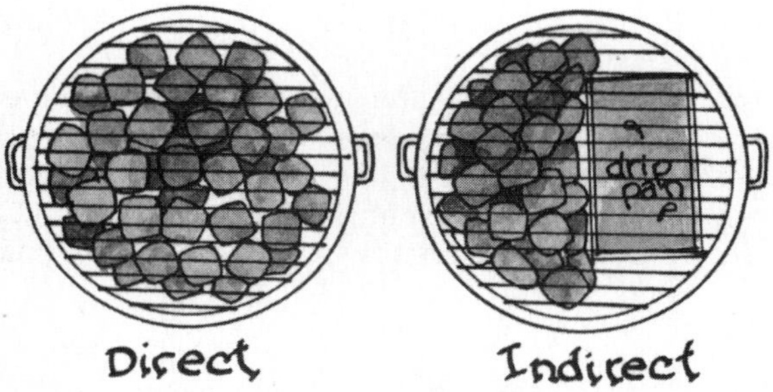

Direct grilling — the primary focus of this book — is a fast cooking technique that doesn't require elaborate finishing sauces. Simple marinades (covered in Chapter 5), salsas (discussed in Chapter 6), and condiments (also in Chapter 6) are all you need to complement directly grilled meat.

WARNING!

The primary difficulty with direct grilling is that you must watch your food closely to prevent it from burning.

On a charcoal grill, the coals should be spread in a solid layer that extends about 1 to 2 inches beyond the edges of the food. In all our recipes, the *grill grid* — the metal latticework you place the food on — is placed 4 to 6 inches from the heat.

We find that most foods are best grilled over medium heat because you have more control and end up with a nice brown crust without any nasty charring. However, fire temperatures vary according to what's being cooked. For example:

- You can sear $1\frac{1}{2}$-to 2-inch-thick steaks first over medium-high (or even high) heat and then finish cooking them over medium heat to end up with a crispy, brown crust and a rare to medium-rare center.
- Pork and chicken require moderate heat to give the interior a chance to cook completely. However, these foods can be started on a higher temperature, which gives them a nice crust, and then moved to grill slowly over an indirect fire to finish cooking through.

Direct grilling can be done with or without the grill cover. The recipes in this book always tell you when to cover the food. Covering the grill instantly traps and raises the heat and tends to increase the smoky flavor, especially if you're using wood chunks or chips. However, covering food also can increase the chance that you'll burn or overcook it, simply because you can't see the food. When direct grilling, sometimes it just makes sense to use the grill cover. We find that thick bone-in pork chops, for example, grill more evenly and better retain their succulence when grilled with the cover down.

When grilling directly in a covered grill, the vents — if you have them on your grill — are usually left open. Opening the vents allows more oxygen to enter the grill and increases the temperature of the coals. Closing the vents partially or totally has the opposite effect. So, if your fire is too hot and is browning food too quickly, either remove the cover or try closing the top grill vents.

Staying away from the heat: Indirect grilling

Indirect grilling grills foods slowly, off to one side of the heat source, usually over a drip pan in a covered grill (see Figure 1-1). If you want to use this technique, here's what you do:

- In a charcoal grill, place the food on the grill grid so that it's away from or to the side of the full force of the heat or fire. Arrange the lit coals around the drip pan or bank them to one side of the pan.
- In a gas grill with two burners, you ignite only one burner and place the food over the unlit burner. If your gas grill has only one burner, place

the food in an aluminum foil pan or on several layers of foil and grill over very low heat. Always preheat your gas grill with all burners on high and the lid down for about 15 minutes; then turn one of the burners off before cooking indirectly.

- Whether you're using a gas or charcoal grill, place a drip pan directly under the food. Often you fill the pan with water or another liquid, such as broth or apple juice, to add moisture and keep the slow-cooking food from drying out.
- Close the grill lid to cover the grill, trap the heat and smoke, and mimic the desirable effects of slow, oven roasting.
- To collect pan juices (especially with large roasts), place the food in a roasting pan and then set the pan on the grill.

When indirectly grilling on a charcoal grill, usually you can partially close both top and bottom vents to hold down the intensity of the fire. So be sure to clean out the ash catcher underneath a charcoal grill before starting the fire. Doing so allows the bottom vents to properly draw air over the coals. Remember to dispose of the ashes properly — in a sealed paper bag. The ashes are a great fertilizer for some trees and plants as well. (Think about how forests restore themselves after a fire.)

Indirect grilling has a multitude of advantages:

- **It slows down the cooking process.** How many times have you used direct grilling to cook chicken and ended up with skin charred beyond recognition and meat that's practically raw in the center? Indirect grilling takes care of that problem. Food is cooked in a covered grill by heat that never directly touches it. Indirect grilling is comparable to oven roasting.
- **Indirect cooking actually gives you two types of fires (or two levels of heat) in one grill.** You have a direct fire that can be used to sear food and an indirect fire to cook food slowly and thoroughly. For example, chicken, left whole or cut into pieces, can be first seared over the direct heat of the fire and then placed on the side over the drip pan without any direct heat. You then cover the grill to let the chicken finish cooking.
- **Indirect grilling eliminates the possibility of dangerous flare-ups.** Fat drips from the food into the drip pan, rather than onto the hot coals, lava rocks, or ceramic briquettes.

Indirectly grill any large cuts of meat or whole birds, poultry pieces, pork tenderloins, ribs, or large roasts for delicious results. In this book, we use the indirect cooking method for the following recipes: Just-Right Pork Ribs

(Chapter 9), Whole Game Hens with Asian Flavors (Chapter 14), Brined and Grilled Loin O' Pork, and Curried Pork Tenderloins (both in Chapter 12).

Slow and Smoky: Barbecuing with Success

Barbecuing is the technique of indirectly and slowly cooking large cuts of meat for a long period of time, over low heat, and with lots of hot smoke. Compare this to direct grilling, which cooks small, tender pieces of food at higher temperatures for shorter grilling times. You might say that the two techniques are almost opposites.

Barbecuing generally takes tough cuts of meat and cooks or breaks down connective tissue into tender morsels that practically fall apart. Foods that are barbecued often include beef brisket, whole hogs, pork ribs, and pork shoulder (which includes two pieces of meat — the Boston butt, which has the least amount of bone, and the picnic ham). These foods are perfect for barbecuing because they actually *demand* to be cooked for long periods in order to break down their stubborn tissues and release flavor. Fish and vegetables can also be barbecued, not to break down their already tender tissues, but to add smoky flavor.

SHOPPING TIP

Depending on the preference of the cook, barbecued food may or may not be seasoned. But many barbecuing chefs create elaborate rubs, basting sauces, and finishing sauces to enhance the flavor of foods. At your local supermarket, you can find a tremendous number of packaged and bottled dry rubs, seasonings, and marinades specifically for use on grilled and barbecued foods. It's also fun to pick up some of these products while visiting places like Texas, Arizona, North Carolina, and Florida for local varieties.

A *barbecue pit* refers to a solidly built, upright grill apparatus with a deep hold for the fuel. The term also can mean an actual pit dug into the ground and filled with heated stones, over which the food is cooked, creating a steaming process. Most of the smoky flavor you get from using a barbecue pit comes not from fat dripping on the coals or coils, but from smoldering wood. (Flip to Chapter 3 for more on wood chips and chunks.)

A common kettle charcoal grill can come close to duplicating the effects of a barbecue pit. Simply build a small, indirect fire and use a combination of good-quality charcoal briquettes and flavored wood chips or hardwood chunks.

You have to give the flavored smoke a chance to have an effect. Adding a handful of wood chips to a fire when grilling a piece of fish for a few minutes won't have much of an impact. But cooking the same piece of fish slowly and indirectly, adding a steady supply of presoaked wood chips as you go along, can produce excellent smoky flavor.

A few more techniques can help you turn your covered charcoal grill into a mini-barbecue pit. Consider the following:

- **Because the food is cooked indirectly, you'll need a drip pan under the food to catch the drippings.** (See Chapter 2 for more on drip pans.) If the food requires a long cooking time, more than 30 to 40 minutes, fill the pan with water, apple juice, beer, or another flavored liquid to add moisture and prevent the food from drying out as it slowly grills.
- **The grill must have a vented hood.** Keep the top vents partially closed to trap the smoke and decrease the supply of oxygen that fuels the fire. Position the lid so that the top vents are opposite the fire and directly above the food. This helps to draw the flavored smoke across your food. And don't lift the lid to peek — each time you do so, you release precious smoke and disrupt the cooking process.
- **Keep a supply of preheated coals next to the grill in a metal bucket.** Add a few every 40 minutes with long-handled tongs (see Chapter 2) to maintain the temperature of the fire. Lift the grill grid gently to add the hot coals, or use tongs to insert them into the space near the grid handles. Or add a few fresh briquettes to the edges of the fire every 20 to 30 minutes. When they're ashy, move them to the center of the fire.

Even Slower than Barbecuing: Smoking

The technique of *smoking* food differs from barbecuing because it uses even lower heat to slow down the cooking process. Food cooks for hours, and becomes infused with hot, aromatic smoke. The cooking temperatures for smoking foods range from 180 to 250 degrees. You can choose from two methods — dry or wet — and both can be duplicated on your kettle grill. However, if you do use your kettle grill, you should place a temperature gauge on the grill to monitor and keep the heat within the proper temperature range.

A 7-pound whole turkey or a 12- to 14-pound ham can take 9 hours or more to smoke. A 5- to 7-pound roast beef takes 5 to 6 hours to reach an internal temperature of 140 degrees. At many professional barbecue eateries and stores, beef and pork may be smoked for 12 hours or more at a very low heat.

Dry smoking

Dry smoking requires indirect cooking in a closed charcoal grill. The food is placed on the grill with the lid on top. Then the air vents are adjusted enough to lower the flames but still keep enough oxygen inside to allow the fire to burn and create smoke. This smoke, in turn, flavors the food while the low heat cooks it. The degree of smoking is based on personal taste and the kind of food to be cooked. Instead of using your kettle grill, you can buy a dry smoker — a contraption that looks like a horizontal barrel and, depending on its size, can cook up to 50 pounds of food at one time. The dry smoker has two chambers: one for the food, and one that vents heat and smoke into the cooking chamber.

If you've tried smoking but find that the smoke flavor is too intense for your taste, cover the food with foil about halfway through the cooking process.

Water smoking

Water smoking, also known as *wet smoking,* is an alternative to dry smoking. This technique involves placing a pan of water in the grill in order to maintain the moisture needed for moister, more succulent foods. Water smoking is an excellent method for delicate foods such as fish, shrimp, and lobster. It also does well with vegetables that would otherwise dry out quickly.

You can buy a water smoker if you don't want to use your kettle grill. Water smokers are now being made by most grill manufacturers, but two companies — Brinkmann and Meco — specialize in such equipment. Water smokers come in three varieties:

- **Charcoal:** This is the most popular and least expensive water smoker; however, charcoal must be replenished every hour for long-term cooking. Charcoal water smokers also tend to have peaks and valleys of heat as the coals burn down.
- **Electric:** This popular type of smoker plugs into an electric socket and offers consistent heat.
- **Gas:** This is the most expensive type of water smoker, but it's a cinch to use (and you don't have to be near an electric outlet to use it). A gas water smoker also provides consistent heat.

Water smoking is a very slow and easy method, but don't expect a crusty exterior on your food — which, for many people, including us, is the whole point of good grilling.

A Whole Mess of Grilling Terms: A Griller's Glossary

To help you wade through the Grill-Speak that you may hear when shopping for accessories — or from your neighbor down the street — we compiled the following glossary of terms. Use these, and you'll be a grilling guru in no time!

- **Baste:** To brush a seasoned liquid over the surface of food to add moisture and flavor.
- **Brazier:** An inexpensive, open charcoal grill with a grid that's usually just a few inches from the coals. A brazier is best for quick grilling. Some braziers may have a partial hood or cover to better retain heat. Braziers sometimes also come with rotisserie attachments.
- **Ceramic briquettes:** These briquettes are made of radiant materials and are used in gas grills to transfer heat from the burners and spread it evenly under the grill grid. Briquettes made of ceramic don't burn up like charcoal briquettes do. *Lava rock* and *metal plates* are an alternative to ceramic briquettes. They don't, however, give the smoky, charcoal flavor that many folks crave.
- **Charcoal briquettes:** The most common fuel for a live fire, manufactured from ground charcoal, coal dust, and starch. These materials are compressed into a uniform, pillow shape and packaged for sale in 5- to 50-pound bags.
- **Charcoal chimney starter:** A metal, cylinder-shaped container that's filled with newspaper and charcoal and used to quickly ignite a charcoal fire.
- **Charcoal grill:** A grill that uses charcoal as its principal fuel. A charcoal grill can be round, square, covered, uncovered, portable, or stationary. The most common type is a covered kettle grill.
- **Coal grate:** The rack that holds the charcoal in the firebox.
- **Drip pan:** A metal pan placed under the food to catch drippings when grilling indirectly.
- **Electric grill:** An indoor or outdoor grill whose heat comes from electric coils.
- **Fire starters:** Any number of gadgets or materials, such as the chimney starter, electric coil, wax or gel cubes, or compressed wood, used to ignite charcoal. (Flip to Chapter 3 for the lowdown on all these fire-starting gadgets.)

- **Firebox:** The underbelly or bottom of the grill that holds the fire or heat.
- **Flare-ups:** Flames caused by fat dripping onto hot coals or lava rock.
- **Gas grill:** A grill whose heating source is gas from a propane tank (or occasionally, a main gas line).
- **Grid:** The latticework of metal rods where you place your food on a grill is called a *grid,* or a *grill grid.* (Weber confuses things a little by calling this area the grate, which everyone else calls the metal piece on which the charcoal sits.) One grid is included with every grill.
- **Grill baskets:** Hinged, wire baskets that ease the grilling (and turning) of sliced vegetables, a delicate piece of fish, burgers, and other foods. Chapter 2 has more on accessories.
- **Hibachi:** A small, portable, uncovered grill that's often made of cast-iron. A hibachi is great for beach or tailgate grilling.
- **Kettle grill:** A relatively inexpensive, round charcoal grill with a heavy cover. It stands on three legs and is excellent for either direct or indirect grilling.
- **Lava rock:** This long-lasting natural rock results from volcanic lava and is used as an alternative to ceramic briquettes. The irregularly-shaped lava rock heats evenly in gas or electric grills. Unlike charcoal briquettes, it can be used over and over.
- **Marinate:** To soak food in a seasoned liquid mixture in order to impart flavor to the food before it's cooked. The steeping liquid, often made with herbs, spices, oil, and an acidic ingredient like lemon juice or vinegar, is called a *marinade.*
- **Natural lump charcoal:** The carbon residue of wood that's been charred in a kiln — usually found in the form of chunks. This is one heating source for charcoal grills. Natural lump charcoal gives you the smokiest flavor.
- **Roasting:** The process of cooking food in a pan in a closed-grill setup. By using indirect heat, you can roast an entire prime rib or turkey to perfection on a grill.
- **Rotisserie rod:** The spit or long metal skewer that suspends and rotates food over a grill's heat source.
- **Rub:** A concentrated, flavorful blend of dry or wet herbs, seasonings, and spices that's rubbed onto the surface of food before grilling.
- **Sear:** To cook food directly above relatively high heat in order to seal in juices and impart flavor, a brown color, and a slightly crusty surface.

Grilling Web sites to fire you up

If you can pull yourself away from your grill long enough, you may enjoy searching the Internet for tips and recipes for outdoor cooking. Here are some sites to get you started:

- **World Wide Weber** (`www.weberbbq.com`): The mouth-watering recipes at this site will send you scurrying to your grill. (And, of course, if you don't have one, the Weber folks tell you all about their products here.)
- **About.com** (`bbq.about.com`): This site links you to recipes, grilling books, cooking magazines, and videos. It also has updates on new barbecue and grill products and cookers.
- **USDA Guide to Grilling and Smoking Food Safety** (`www.fsis.usda.gov`): This site doesn't offer the attractive graphics of some other sites, but the information from the U.S. Department of Agriculture is a good, basic grilling guide. The site contains facts on defrosting, marinating, grilling away from home, and serving food safely.

- **Smoker box:** A small, perforated steel or cast-iron container that's placed directly on the lava rocks or ceramic briquettes of a gas grill. This box holds flavored wood chips and provides smoke.
- **Vent:** The holes in a grill cover or firebox that open and close like shutters. An open vent increases the oxygen and heat of a fire, while a closed vent does the opposite. Some grills don't have vents.
- **Wood chips and wood chunks:** Natural hardwood materials added to the fire to impart smoky flavor to food as it grills. Some of the best materials are hickory, mesquite, and grapevine trimmings.

Looking at a Few Guidelines before You Begin

Every cook has his or her preferences, so it's best to know ours before you begin sampling our recipes. Here are some guidelines:

- **All recipe cooking times are just estimates.** The wind, temperature of the air and the food, and the intensity of the fire all affect, sometimes radically, the amount of time needed to grill food.

  By testing gas grill thermometers, we've found that their temperature readings can be off by a great deal. Charcoal grills nearly always burn hotter and cook faster than gas grills. Our best advice is to experiment with your own grill and adjust the cooking times of our recipes accordingly.

- **Marinate all foods in the refrigerator in nonmetal or nonreactive containers like glass or ceramic.** Metal may impart an unpleasant flavor to the foods. Plus the acids in the food may cause a chemical reaction to the metal. Plastic, resealable bags are excellent for this purpose and take up less space than dishes. (Flip to Chapter 5 for more on marinating.)

- **Be careful with leftover marinade.** Never use leftover marinade as a finishing sauce unless you thoroughly boil the marinade for 15 minutes to kill any possible bacteria picked up from the raw food.
- **Don't bring food to room temperature.** Although some cookbooks say to bring your food to room temperature before cooking, with few exceptions, we don't recommend this tip for outdoor cooking. If the temperature is in the 80s or 90s, foods can spoil quickly.
- **Salt can add tremendous flavor and even a little texture to grilled food.** The optimum time to salt food is just before you place it on the grill. You can add more salt and sprinkle on the pepper (which should always be freshly ground) after you remove the food from the grill.
- **Oil your grids.** Before preheating a gas grill or building a fire (see Chapter 3 for how to do that), brush the grill grid with a vegetable oil, such as peanut or corn oil. This step helps to keep the food from sticking unpleasantly to the grill grid. Some grillers find it easier to use a nonstick cooking spray. Never brush or spray the grid while the grill is heating or after the fire has started, because this can cause dangerous flare-ups. The food itself should also be brushed with oil or marinade and basted, when necessary.

- **Stay safe!** Always read all safety information and every warning icon (like this one) in this book. Following the safety advice is absolutely essential if you want to have a pleasant grilling experience.

Chapter 2

Buying the Grill of Your Dreams (And Accessories to Boot)

In This Chapter

- Exploring various types of grills
- Considering the many grill features
- Deciding which accessories you really need
- Cleaning and storing your grill

Without a doubt, the most important grilling decision that you make is the type of grill you buy. Regardless of your needs or how you live and cook, you can find a grill that's just right for you. Today, you can buy big grills or small; basic grills or those with lots of bells and whistles; grills fueled by charcoal, gas, or electricity; or inexpensive grills that meet short-term needs or high-quality grills that are long-term investments, serving you well for many years.

Gas grills in particular have become more and more sophisticated over the last ten years. This increase in sophistication is due to consumer demands, which sparked many fancy innovations. Grills these days are not only sturdy, compact, and portable, but they're also crafted in finishes that range from shiny stainless steel to easy-to-clean porcelain enamel. And burner controls are much more flexible than ever before. You now get a much better, safer, more efficient grill for about the same money you would have paid a decade ago. And after you choose a grill, you can find an amazing assortment of accessories at your local hardware or kitchen store. How can you know what kind of grill and accessories will do the best job for you? This chapter helps answer that question.

Choosing the Type of Grill You'll Shop For

Ultimately, your decision to buy a grill depends on a few personal preferences: where you want to use it (outdoors or indoors), how much food you want to cook at one time, how much space you have to store it, how important convenience is to you, whether charcoal flavor is important to you, and how often you actually plan to use it.

Perusing your options

A *gas grill,* powered by low-cost propane from a cylinder, stores easily. It's also economically priced (starting around $130), easy to set up, easy to turn on, and easy to work with. Gas grills are also very easy to clean and maintain. (Figure 2-1 shows a popular type of gas grill.)

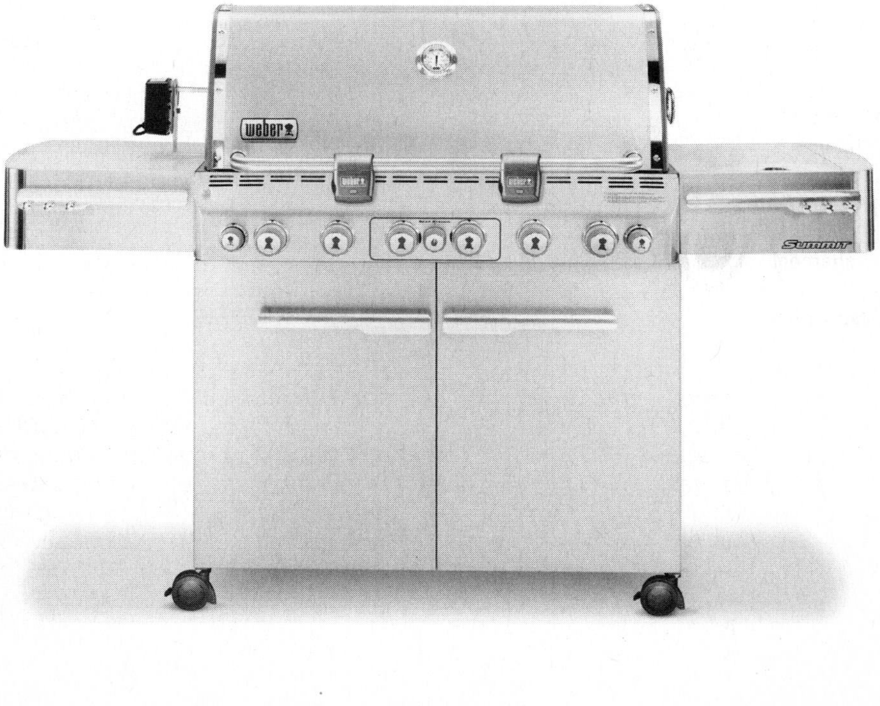

Figure 2-1: Weber's Summit S-670, a gas grill.

A *charcoal grill* is one that's fueled by natural lump charcoal or charcoal briquettes and topped with a grill grid. (See this type of grill in Figure 2-2.) Many people also think that a *kettle grill* — a round, deep, metal kettle that's fueled by charcoal or briquettes and topped with a slatted grid (and sometimes has a gas igniter) — is synonymous with a charcoal grill, but that's not always the case. Charcoal grills come in all shapes and sizes, but they're all identical in their fuel source. They can range from inexpensive ($30 for small, portable models) to expensive (up to $450 for large kettles set into a rolling cart).

Figure 2-2: Weber's One-Touch Gold, a charcoal grill.

A *brazier,* sometimes called a *hibachi,* is really just a portable charcoal-style grill with no frills (see Figure 2-3). This type of grill can be round, square, or rectangular. It has a rudimentary metal grid on which food is placed, and it's fueled by either charcoal or wood. Its portability is its greatest virtue (which makes it great for tailgating), but only if you're cooking for three or four people. That's because the grill grid is usually quite small. You can find these grills for around $20. The term *brazier* also refers to a pot in which foods are cooked with a little liquid, but that's not what we're concerned with in this book.

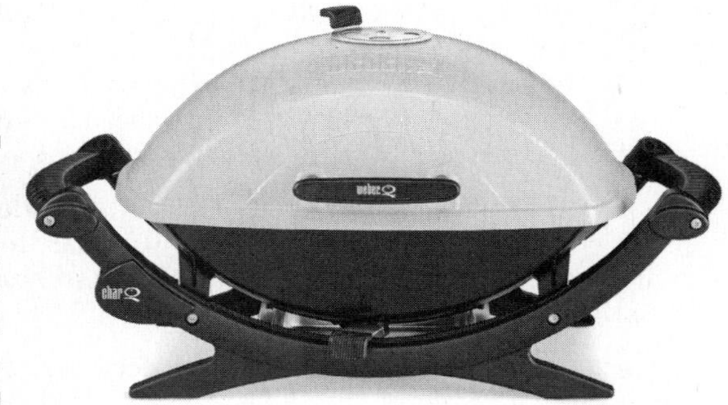

Figure 2-3: Weber's Char Q, a portable charcoal grill.

Other portable grills have come on the market that are remarkably easy to transport and set up in a backyard, a campground, or a tailgate party. They even cook with gas, with push button or electronic ignition, and have excellent BTU-per-hour input of up 12,000.

Grills that don't have covers, such as hibachis and portable picnic grills, are mainly used for grilling small pieces of food quickly and directly over charcoal. Smaller grills like these generally don't have covers because they're for fast grilling, not smoking. Covered grills, on the other hand, give you the option of cover-cooking larger cuts of meat and poultry, such as beef roasts and whole turkeys, over a slow, indirect fire.

An electric grill makes for clean, convenient grilling. You don't need to bother with charcoal briquettes, wood, or ashes, and you don't have to refill propane cylinders. Most electric grills can't provide the smoky charring and flavor that charcoal grills offer, but they're a great answer for apartment dwellers or those who don't want to deal with a large, outdoor grill. Find these at home stores or department stores, usually for $50 to $150.

Comparing the two main types: Charcoal or gas?

Because the two most popular grills are vastly different, buyers are faced with a difficult question: Should I buy charcoal or gas? If you're in the middle of this great grill debate, don't worry. The following list, which compares the major features of those two basic types of grills, can help you make a decision:

- **Cost:** Gas has a much larger initial investment, from $150 up to $5,000 and more! Charcoal grills, on the other hand, fall into the $50 to $450 range.
- **Flavor:** Because taste is so subjective and personal, the debate will continue forever regarding whether charcoal or gas grilling produces

superior flavor. Multitudes of taste tests have demonstrated that most people can't tell the difference between the two. However, we disagree and want to go on record as believing that, despite the many advances in the gas grill industry, a charcoal grill still gives a better — or at least, different — flavor than a gas grill.

- **Temperature capabilities:** Because consumers have demanded grills that can achieve the kind of searing and light char that has in the past been possible only at professional steakhouses, BTUs and heat have been increased dramatically.

  Charcoal grills, for example, can go above 500 degrees, so they cook food faster and sear better. The only caveat with these grills is that you must watch your food closely. A gas grill usually stays below 500 degrees, and so food takes longer to cook. However, some gas models, including those from Weber, now have embedded burners that can reach 900 degrees.

  Charring by gas grill is also possible if you get it as hot as possible and then grill the steaks or lamb on one side for about 4 minutes to achieve searing. Then flip the meat and close the cover, thereby building up intense heat. But be very careful to check the meat after just two or three minutes. Otherwise that nice light char may have become black soot on your steak.

- **Convenience:** Convenience is a major factor for most people. Many folks are often pressed for time these days, particularly during the week. Because grilling has become so popular, 29 percent of Americans nowadays own at least two grills — a gas grill to use during the week and a charcoal grill for the weekends.

- **Ease of lighting the grill:** Gas grills are a snap to light. You simply turn on the gas, push the igniter button, and adjust the control to high. Wait about 10 minutes, and you're ready to cook.

  Many people would argue otherwise, but we say that charcoal grills are *not* difficult to light. The fact is that charcoal grills are extremely easy to light and take only about 30 minutes to reach a medium stage of heat. Using a chimney starter can shave another 15 minutes off that time. For more information on the starter and other simple and foolproof ways to light a charcoal grill, flip to Chapter 3.

- **Ease of maintaining the temperature:** Gas grills have adjustable flame controls, so turning the heat up or down is as simple as turning a knob; they also offer a steady supply of heat. Charcoal grills, on the other hand, are more difficult to manage. They usually come with a damper control that allows you to adjust the amount of oxygen and therefore the amount of heat and fire in the grill, but adjusting the heat to your liking takes more attention than a simple turn of a knob. Also, in order to maintain the heat if you're grilling for more than 45 minutes, you have to replenish the coals, which can be a bit of a pain.

- **Practicality for cold winter months:** Because a gas grill requires so little effort to use, you can grill with it year-round. Building a fire isn't fun when outdoor temperatures drop, so most people are far less inclined to grill out during the off-season with a charcoal grill.
- **Ease of grill maintenance:** Gas grills are easy to clean and maintain because they don't have the sooty build-up or the ash deposits left by a charcoal grill. Charcoal grills, on the other hand, require more scrubbing to remove the soot, burned on fat, and ashes.
- **Cosmetic appeal:** This one's a tie. With people spending more and more money to spruce up their backyards, you have dozens of attractive grills to choose from, whether you're cooking with charcoal or gas. Grills come in all sorts of styles, including high-tech, contemporary, gleaming stainless steel, or wonderful bright-colored porcelain enamel. Choose from bright red, cobalt blue, or teal. Even painted gas grills come in colors like hunter green or burgundy. Handsome carts or cabinets in stainless steel or wood finishes add to the sturdiness and beauty that will enhance your patio or deck.

There's also no question that the larger, more expensive gas grills have become sexy toys for those who like to really show off their grilling skills. When you buy one of these monsters, you pay for finish, cooking area, rotisserie attachments, wood chip boxes, lighted controls, and even color. (See the following section for more on grill features.)

Bringing the inside out: The ultimate grilling experience

As most things in life do, meal preparation is circling back to the past — with some serious style. Nowadays, increasing numbers of homeowners and builders are taking their kitchens back to the great outdoors, making the backyard patio the ultimate dining and gathering place.

Outdoor kitchens are similar to their indoor counterparts, with the addition of the grill of your choosing. They have countertops (made of brick or stone), cabinets, stovetops, refrigerators, sinks (fed with a hose or connected to the home's water supply) — you name it. The difference between the out and the in? Everything needs to be waterproof. If you like, you can add a shelter — just don't put it over the grill area.

You have many versatile grill options for an outdoor kitchen. An outdoor fireplace, for example, can easily be transformed into a place you can cook. A fire pit gives you a place to commune around as well as cook over the open flame with a rotisserie, skewers, or grill. You might even consider adding a brick or stone oven, surrounded by plush outdoor sofas and chairs.

Pre-fabricated grills and grill islands are available from many manufacturers, though you can also order them semi-custom or custom-made. Many Web sites offer tips on designing and setting up your own outdoor kitchen and also refer you to expert resources — HGTV.com, for one, has lots of great advice.

What Do You Have to Offer? Looking at Grill Features

Before you rush out to buy a particular grill based on the advice of a best friend (or even this book), head to a store that carries an assortment of grills from various manufacturers, and spend a few minutes playing with the floor models. Here's list of the grill features you want to pay attention to:

- **Grid size:** Whether you choose a gas or charcoal grill, the size of the grill's cooking surface — the *grid* — is important. Be sure that the food grid is between 350 and 400 square inches so you have the option of grilling several dishes at a time or feeding a party crowd.
- **Heat intensity capability:** BTUs (British thermal units) measure the heat intensity of a gas grill. For the average gas grill chef, 22,000 to 50,000 BTUs is plenty of heat. Don't be misled into believing that the higher the BTU, the better the grill will perform. What's more important is finding out whether the grill burns fuel efficiently; otherwise, you're wasting gas and increasing your fuel costs. Ask your dealer about the fuel-burning efficiency of any grill before buying it.
- **Ease of transport:** Many portable grills have come onto the market. These grills are remarkably easy to transport and set up in a backyard, at a campground, or at a tailgate party. They even cook with gas, with push button or electronic ignition, and have excellent BTU of up 12,000.

SHOPPING TIP

You can spend much more for brand-name grills. Be aware, however, that brand names are usually sturdier, tested over years of production, and may have better warranties than an unknown brand you buy at the local hardware store. The top-of-the-line grills can sell for well over $2,000, in which case you're paying for extras like burnished steel or ceramics, extra drawers, higher BTUs, attached rotisseries, and other things you may not need.

REMEMBER

Buying a grill that suits your style and needs is a little like buying a car, except, unfortunately, you can't take it out for a test drive. So before you buy the grill of your dreams, make sure you assess the quality of it by doing the following:

- Stand before the grill and lift up its hood. Does it seem sturdy and durable or cheap and flimsy?
- If it's a gas grill, do the knobs turn easily? Does it have two burners so you can use the indirect cooking method?

Contacting grill manufacturers for more information

Call the following grilling manufacturers for information on their grills and grilling accessories:

- Barbeques Galore: Web site: www.bbqgalore.com; phone: 800-Grill-Up (800-474-5587)
- Bradley Smoker Inc.: Web site: www.bradleysmoker.com; phone: 800-665-4188
- The Brinkmann Corporation: Web site: www.brinkmann.net; phone: 800-527-0717
- Broilmaster: Web site: www.broilmaster.com; phone: 800-255-0403
- Char-Broil, Division of W.C. Bradley: Web site: www.charbroil.com; phone: 800-241-7548
- Ducane: Web site: www.ducane.com; phone: 800-DUCANES (800-382-2637)
- Fiesta: Web site: www.fiestagasgrills.com; phone: 800-396-3838
- The Holland Company: Web site: www.hollandgrill.com; phone: 800-880-9766
- Masterbuilt: Web site: www.masterbuilt.com; phone: 800-489-1581
- Thermador: Web site: www.thermador.com; phone: 800-735-4328
- Viking Range Corporation: Web site: www.vikingrange.com; phone: 888-VIKING1 (888-845-4641)
- Weber: Web site: www.weber.com; phone: 800-446-1071

Playing with Tools and Toys

In this section, we introduce you to time-saving, flavor-enhancing, safety-heightening accessories that no griller — beginner or guru — should be without. We also alert you to some advanced options that make you a pro in no time.

Kid in a grilling shop: Looking at basic grilling utensils

Step into a hardware store or kitchen gadget shop and you'll see an amazing array of tongs, brushes, and spatulas in a variety of shapes and configurations. In this section, we list the utensils that we recommend. Keep in mind, however, that manufacturers and prices affect the exact sizes, shapes, and features.

SHOPPING TIP

Think of these accessories as investments and purchase the best ones that you can afford. Premium accessories usually have heavy-duty finishes and strong, comfortable handles.

Basting brushes and mops

The most common *basting brush* is brush-shaped, sometimes with an angled brush head, and is useful for all kinds of basting. However, it's most often used for light basting sauces. The most important virtue of such a brush is its length; look for ones at least 16 inches long so you can baste while the food is on the grill.

The bristles on a brush should be fairly pliable and extend at least 3 inches from the end of the handle. You don't need to spend much on a good brush, but don't spend too little either; otherwise it will fall apart quickly. Between $5 and $8 is a good range to look for.

A *basting mop*, sometimes called a *Texas-style barbecue brush,* is just that — a little cotton mop for quickly slathering on thick sauce. When soaked with barbecue sauce, this brush isn't likely to catch on fire, but be attentive anyway.

Cleaning brush

The only tool you need for cleaning your grill grid is a good, stiff wire brush. You can find these at most hardware stores. A stiff brush does a better job than any scraper, but many cleaning brushes have a self-contained scraper on the top that allows you to scrape off the really tough grime that may build up over time.

Oil your grid before grilling to alleviate the elbow grease needed to remove the cooking grease. But here's the easiest way to clean a grill grid: Attack the grid with a cleaning brush right after the meal, while the grid is still warm. It's more difficult to scrape away bits of food after the grill has cooled down.

A small, crumpled-up ball of aluminum foil makes a handy improvisational tool for scrubbing down the grill grid when you can't find your wire grill brush. A nylon or plastic scouring pad, sponge, and a pail of soapy water can also help with a thorough cleaning of the grill, inside and out. Never, ever use a wire brush or oven cleaner to clean the exterior of a grill — it can damage the finish.

Fork and knives

A good knife isn't nearly as important as a good *fork* when you're grilling. And a good fork isn't nearly as important as a *long* fork — 16 inches or more — with a wooden handle and two tines.

When moving around large pieces of meat — such as roasts — with a grill fork, try not to pierce the meat too deeply. By the same token, be careful not to spear the meat too delicately that it falls off and causes flare-ups.

Given the fact that much of what comes off your grill (slabs of meat, ribs, or sausage) needs to be cut, invest in a good, heavy-handled, well-balanced carving knife, curved butcher's knife, or chef's knife.

Knives may seem like the most obvious of utensils, but the availability of more (and sharper) knives makes the choice more appealing than ever. The innovations have come in terms of design and balance. Today's knives let cooks chop, slice, shave, and dice easily, and they keep their keen edge better because of the harder steel that's used. Nevertheless, you still need to invest in a knife stone and steel to keep your knife at its cutting edge. The stone is used to sharpen the knife, and the steel keeps the edge keen and the same width all along the blade.

Asian cleavers are excellent for cutting vegetables, but they take some experience when used with meat. The new ceramic knives we have found are pretty, but they lose their edge quickly and break far more readily than you may imagine. There are also now very beautiful sets of steak knives, based on steakhouse models, which have a thick wooden grip and serrated edges with which to cut through meat on the plate.

Grill cover

A grill cover protects your grill from rain, wind, and heat, which in turn prolongs its life. Made from vinyl and cloth, grill covers come in all shapes and sizes to fit over the top of the grill. Just be sure to purchase one that fits your particular grill and always give the grill time to cool down completely before covering it.

Grilling mitt

We can't stress enough the importance of a good grilling mitt. A dish towel or fireproof pot holder just doesn't give you the protection you need to grill safely. The mitts should be flexible and should allow you to pick pots, pans, skewers, and other items off the grill with ease.

A mitt also should be long enough to reach past your elbow — the longer the better, at least 15 inches — and have a flame-retardant coating. Long-lasting, sturdy mitts start at about $7 and can run as high as $20. If you can afford it, pay a bit extra to get a fully insulated, thick pair with a thumb.

Skewers

Skewers are wonderful grill accessories that allow you to cook and easily turn foods like kebabs and satays. (Check out Chapter 8 for some outstanding kebab and satay recipes.) They should be between 15 and 18 inches long. Skewers that are 6 to 8 inches long, however, are perfect for cocktail party kebabs.

Bamboo skewers are popular and do a good job when you're grilling kebabs. Before using them, soak them in water for a half hour so the ends don't catch fire.

Metal skewers come in many beautiful configurations now, and because they usually have a small handle on the end, they're easy to turn. Be very careful, however, because those handles can heat up every bit as hot as the parts that touch the fire. Always use mitts to handle them!

Spatula

We never get tired of repeating ourselves on the issue of length: Use a spatula that's 15 to 18 inches long from the tip of the handle to the end of the blade. And be sure that the spatula you use has a handle that's made of wood or another insulating material. Also, be sure *not* to use the following for grilling purposes:

- A Teflon or nonstick kitchen spatula that's used to flip pancakes — it may burn or melt.
- An outdoor metal spatula with a metal handle. The handle will transfer heat to your hand.
- A long spatula that's usually used to spread icing on a cake. Such a tool is completely useless at a barbecue because it's too thin and flexible to hold a heavyweight piece of meat, poultry, or fish.

Thermometer and temperature gauge

One of the single biggest challenges faced by inexperienced — and even many experienced — grillers is turning out food that's moist, juicy, and cooked to perfection, both inside and out. A good food *thermometer,* which tells you the temperature inside the food being cooked, can solve this problem for you. Some models even speak to you when something is at the right temperature!

The simplest, quickest, and most dependable way to test the doneness of food on the grill is what professional chefs use — a *cake tester,* which is used to indicate when the center of a cake is done. This tool is nothing more than a metal needle with a plastic handle that you insert into the thick part of the food on the grill for about 5 seconds then remove. You then — carefully! — touch the tester to your chin or lips to get an idea of the temperature. If the food isn't cooked through, the needle will be cool; if it's medium-rare, it will be warm; and if it's quite hot, it's well-done.

You also can use a thermometer to get the exact temperature of a piece of meat. You can find two basic types of thermometers for use on a grill (see Figure 2-4):

- **Stainless steel insert thermometer:** This heat-resistant thermometer that you use for a roast in an oven works effectively on a grill, too. To use this thermometer, insert the stainless steel spike into the meat at the beginning of the cooking process. Throughout cooking, the thermometer registers the temperature on the glass-faced dial. This thermometer is intended only for foods that allow you to place the probe at least 2 to 2$^1/_2$ inches into the grilled food. It isn't intended for use on steaks, chops, chicken breasts, or other thin food.
- **Instant-read thermometer:** This type of thermometer does exactly what it says; that is, you can insert it into the meat at any moment and get — you guessed it — an instant reading! Thus, it's our favorite. You must immediately remove the thermometer, however. Some models display digital numbers, and they come in two forms: a standard digital thermometer with bigger buttons and display, or the tinier version, a pocket thermometer. You don't have to buy an instant-read thermometer that's digital, but if you do, be sure that the numbers are easy for you to read.

A *temperature gauge* tells you the temperature inside the grill itself. Just about all gas and electric grills now have built-in temperature gauges, but kettle and other charcoal-fueled grills usually don't. You may find it worthwhile to buy a temperature gauge to set within the kettle, especially for closed-lid grilling and smoking. You can monitor cooking times much more easily this way.

Figure 2-4: A digital thermometer or a digital pocket thermometer is great to have on hand.

Tongs

Outside on the patio, tongs are essential equipment for turning foods on the grill. Tongs are a better choice than a long fork because you can flip food over without piercing it (which can let out the juices). They also allow you to maneuver most foods better than a spatula does.

Keep length in mind when buying tongs. Never use short, overly flexible ice tongs at the grill. A good pair of grilling tongs should be between 15 and 18 inches long, and they must have a wooden or insulated grip (hot metal burns!).

Torch light

When twilight falls and the shadows creep across the grill, you can't see what you're cooking, and you certainly can't see the degree of doneness of the food. Torch lights come in very handy at this point. *Torch lights* are poles atop which a lamp, fueled with oil or other fuel, is set. They can be stuck in the ground almost anywhere. You also can set them permanently in concrete. They come in all sizes and price ranges, and they always add a lovely flicker to a dinner after dark.

Water bottle

Keep a water bottle equipped with a spray nozzle close at hand to douse occasional flare-ups of flames and to lower the heat on a fire that has become too hot. You can also spritz rotisserie grilled food with water (or other liquid) to retain moisture as the food rotates on the spit. You don't need anything fancy — a spray bottle of any kind will do. But do make sure it shoots out a fine spray of water so you don't extinguish the fire by spraying too much water on the wood or coals.

Work table

Even fancy grills with optional side tables don't provide enough space for your grilling chores. Set up a small table next to your grill for food, platters, and grilling tools.

Surveying tools and toys for the serious griller

As you move into grilling guruhood, you may find yourself searching for more advanced tools than those in the previous section. If so, this section is for you. In the following sections, we describe all those fancy grilling toys that folks use when they fall hard for grilling.

Baskets

We are really big believers in hinged, wire, grilling baskets of every kind. Numerous shapes and sizes are available for every conceivable ingredient. Baskets are a real aid for grilling delicate pieces of fish and shellfish and for small pieces of food that aren't skewered and would otherwise fall through the grid. You can also use baskets to more easily turn onion rings and thinly sliced meat. We think that you can get away with a few basic baskets (see Figure 2-5). Consider the following:

- Boxlike baskets are good for just about any ingredient that's large enough not to fall through the basket.
- A fish-shaped basket is ideal for a whole fish. Easy to turn, this basket keeps the flesh intact without adhering to the skin and produces a beautifully cooked fish. Figure 2-6 shows a fish-shaped basket.
- Other flat baskets are built to hold hamburgers, chicken, sausages, shrimp, and most fish fillets. (Steaks, lamb chops, and barbecued ribs are better when they're turned individually on the grill grid rather than locked into a basket.)

SHOPPING TIP

When purchasing a grilling basket, look for one with a handle that's long enough to extend well beyond the grilling surface. Because the baskets stand on the grill for several minutes at a time, the heat from the grill transfers to the basket handles (even if they're long), so always use a mitt when removing them. Baskets range in size and price. Most are made of steel and are designed not to be flexible. (You don't want to carry a flapping basket of fish or chicken from grill to table.) You can buy them at the hardware store for around $10.

Figure 2-5: Baskets are excellent for turning many pieces of food at one time.

Grill topper

A *grill topper* — sometimes called a perforated grid, fish grid, or delicate foods grid — is a porcelain grid with holes about half the size of a dime. (See Figure 2-7.) Place it on the grill grid (the one that comes with your grill, where you normally place the food) when you want to cook small foods (such as shrimp, scallops, delicate fish, mushrooms, and cut-up vegetables) that would otherwise fall into the fire. A grill topper makes it simple to turn delicate food. Lightly coating the food with oil makes the food even easier to turn.

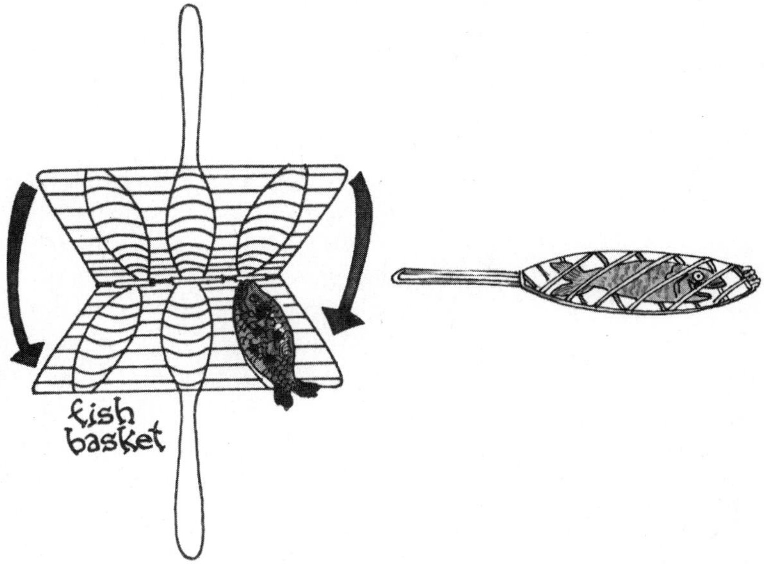

Figure 2-6: Fish-shaped baskets make grilling whole fish a breeze.

Grill toppers come in several different sizes, so consider the size of your total cooking surface before selecting one. After all, you may want room to cook other foods on the regular grid at the same time. Prices range from $15 to $30.

Figure 2-7: A grill topper helps you grill delicate or small foods.

Vegetable holder

The *vegetable holders* that we've seen are little more than bent metal wires that hold potatoes and ears of corn upright on the grill (see Figure 2-8). These gadgets allow vegetables to bake more slowly, without getting scorched. Basically, they allow you to be a bit less attentive than you would be if you placed your vegetables directly on the grid.

Rib rack

A *rib rack,* shown in Figure 2-8, is a lattice of metal rods that are arranged into a "U" shape, into which the ribs and other meats can be placed and kept slightly elevated above the heated grid. A rib rack allows you to cook more food on one grill.

SHOPPING TIP

When purchasing a rib rack, make sure that the metal rods are sturdy and that the rack doesn't wobble on the grill.

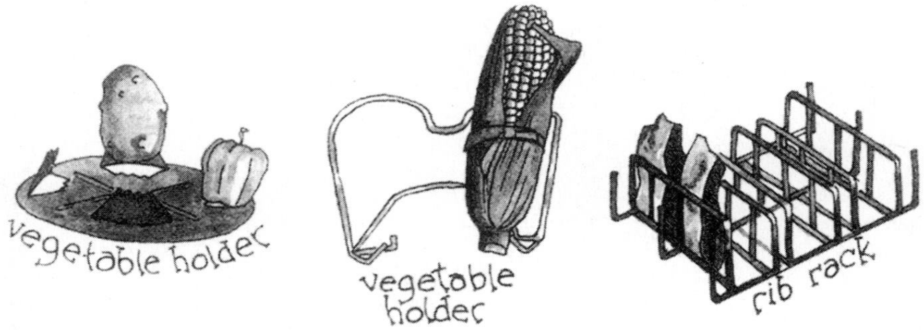

Figure 2-8: Vegetable holders and a rib rack are handy for grilling.

Drip pan and charcoal divider

A *drip pan,* shown in Figure 2-9, is a shallow pan placed under the grid that catches the drippings from the meat that's cooking on the grill. You can buy inexpensive disposable aluminum foil pans at the supermarket, or you can use a shallow metal rectangular baking pan (which is a bit messier to clean up afterwards). You can also make a drip pan out of heavy-duty aluminum foil. Simply fold up the edges of the foil to give it sufficient sturdiness.

ON THE GRILL

In a gas grill, set the pan directly on the lava rock or ceramic briquettes under the meat to be grilled. In a charcoal grill, place the pan on the charcoal grate with coals banked to one side or placed on either side of the pan and the meat directly over it.

When using a drip pan on a charcoal grill, use a *charcoal divider* (shown in Figure 2-10). This metal divider holds the charcoal firmly in place so it doesn't tumble into the drip pan (which is shallow). Even though this gadget isn't an absolute necessity, a charcoal divider — sometimes called a *rail* or *char-basket fuel holder* — is a good investment.

Figure 2-9: A drip pan catches dripping fat that can otherwise fall into the fire.

Figure 2-10: A charcoal divider helps a drip pan do its work.

Smoker box

A *smoker box* (see Figure 2-11) is quite handy and very simple to use. It's nothing more than a lidded, heavy metal box with holes to allow smoke to pour from burning wood chips (and, sometimes, a few aromatic herbs) that you've placed inside. A smoker box is an easy way to add smokiness to your foods.

If you use wood chips with a gas grill, a smoker box is a must, because it keeps the ashes from clogging the burner. If you're using a charcoal grill and want a smoky flavor without buying a smoker box, you can make a smoker pouch. Figure 2-12 shows you how.

Figure 2-11: A smoker box allows aromatic smoke from wood chips to pour out.

How to Make a Smoker Pouch
1. Put the soaked wood chips in the center of a sheet of heavy duty aluminum foil.
2. Pull the short sides of the foil up and over the center of the pile of chips.
3. Fold the edges over 2 times to form a seal.
4. Next, fold up the sides of the pouch, folding twice, to create a seal.
5. Use a knife to poke holes in the top so the smoke can escape.
6. The pouch will make smoke when heated up!

Figure 2-12: A smoker pouch is a cheaper alternative to a smoker box.

Side burner

One accessory we highly recommend for anyone who wants to do more than simple grilling is an attachable side burner. On pricier grills, they're standard, but you can buy one for your existing grill, too. These handy accessories (for gas grills only) allow you to do just about anything on the grill that you can do on a burner in your kitchen — from sautéing to sauce making. They're great for reheating foods, too. They're even pretty simple to hook up. Side burner prices start at about $70.

Motorized rotisserie

We cover the subject of rotisseries in depth in Chapter 10, but we want to mention here that they're a useful accessory that every serious grill cook should consider. Some of the more expensive gas grills have built-in rotisseries, while others allow for rotisseries to be purchased as attachments.

The purpose of a rotisserie is to allow slow, even cooking that's especially good for doing roasts, whole chickens, and even ribs. Rotisseries are handy, too, because you don't have to tend them constantly; just baste the food occasionally with a marinade or sauce.

Ash can

Yes, the grill industry actually sells special cans in which you're supposed to put your spent charcoal ashes, called, fittingly, *ash cans.* An ash can may have come in especially handy in the nineteenth century when people used wood and coal for their hearths and fireplaces. These days, you use them to cart away ash residue after your grill fire is out. This is different from an *ash catcher,* which attaches under the body of a charcoal kettle grill.

Caring for Your Grill

The outer units of most grills carry a lifetime guarantee, but that shouldn't stop you from keeping your grill oiled, clean, and stored properly. These tasks are essential to a long, happy grill life.

Oiling the grids

Keeping your grill grid lightly oiled improves your grilling in two ways:

- Prevents food ingredients from sticking while you're cooking
- Makes grid clean-up easier after each meal

To oil your grill grids, you just wipe a little vegetable oil on them with a soft cloth. Or you can use one of those aerosol vegetable oil sprays. But only spray these on a cold — never a hot — grill.

We would be less than honest if we didn't mention that replacement grids are pretty cheap — about $15 to $20 at any good hardware store. So it's definitely worthwhile to replace the grid at the beginning of spring. That way, you don't have any old dirt, residue, or rust on the grill when you go to use it.

Cleaning the grill inside and out

Grills can last a lifetime if you take good care of them. Here are some pointers:

- **After each use, use a wire brush to clean off the food particles remaining on the grid.** Close the lid of the grill and, if you have a gas grill, turn up the heat for about 10 minutes to burn off any excess food remaining on the grid. Some grillers believe that leaving the grill overnight is a good idea because the residue protects the grill from rust. If you do that, be sure to clean the grill just before using it the next time.
- **Periodically clean the grids with a solution of warm, soapy water.** Use nylon or plastic woven pads to avoid damaging the grid. You can use nonabrasive scouring powder on stubborn stains if you want, but remember that a small amount of grease left on the grids helps preserve

the metal — it will burn off the next time you use the grill. Cast-iron grids should be seasoned after cleaning by applying a light coating of oil.

- **Clean the interior of the grill with the same soapy solution as the grid or use a can of aerosol grill cleaner.** Scour with a scrub brush and then rinse with water and air dry. Never use anything but soapy water on the exterior of the grill because a cleaner may damage the paint or porcelain.
- **Unclog the burners periodically.** Your grill won't work properly if the burners become clogged, so if you see an uneven flame, remove the burner and clean the ports with a wire. You can also force water through the removed burner until you're sure that it's coming through each hole. If the burners rust to the point of showing cracks or breaks, buy new ones.
- **Replace lava rock and ceramic briquettes as needed.** Lava rocks or ceramic briquettes get extremely greasy and contribute to flare-ups. Depending on how often you grill, you should turn them over periodically. Because they're quite inexpensive, replace the lava rock or briquettes at least once every 12 to 18 months (perhaps more often if you're a frequent griller). Doing so ensures better grilled dishes.

Storing your grill

Most people like to grill year-round, regardless of the weather. But, if you decide to pack your grill away for the coldest winter months, you certainly can. Be sure to thoroughly clean your grill before storing it. If you have a gas grill, make sure that the gas lines are completely and tightly closed off and that the gas cylinder is removed.

Many grill manufacturers sell heavy plastic covers specifically to fit their grills; these are a good, inexpensive investment because they keep dust and dirt from getting on or into your grill.

WARNING!

If storing your grill indoors, always remove the propane cylinder and store it outside in a cool, shaded spot. Never, under any circumstances, store a propane cylinder inside your home or garage. It could be deadly.

Chapter 3

To Build a Fire

In This Chapter

- Preparing for the maiden cookout
- Choosing your fuel source
- Selecting a fire starter for your grill
- Keeping your heat under control

Chances are that if your food turns out perfect, your fire was perfect, too. This chapter shares the fine points of getting your fire — whether it's in a gas grill or charcoal grill — to burn the way it should for maximum results. In this chapter, we discuss the various kinds of fuel, fire-starting accessories, and fire-lighting tools for your grill.

Getting Your Grill Ready for Use

"Safety first!" should be the guiding principle whenever you're grilling. You're going to be dealing with a fire hazard unless you take strict precautions from the moment you light the coals or turn on the gas, so please pay attention and read through this chapter carefully before beginning to cook.

WARNING!

Where you place your grill can affect its efficiency and your safety. Placement depends on how much room you have and how massive your grill is. But here are some general rules:

- Unless the grill is electric (which is made for indoor use), use the grill outdoors only! Never grill in your trailer, tent, house, garage, or any enclosed area.
- Place the grill away from anything — and we mean anything — that could possibly be flammable: piles of leaves or dry grass; structures of any kind; gasoline and any machines containing gasoline, especially

automobiles; paint and aerosol cans; newspapers; awnings; children's toys; and trees.

- If you place the grill on a wooden deck, it's a good idea to use a deck protector under the grill. You can find one at most hardware stores.
- Don't place your grill in the path of strong winds, which may tend to stir up the embers and make them fly.
- Stay close to your kitchen for easy access to platters, utensils, and food.
- When grilling at night, place the grill near a light source.

WARNING!

After you've placed your grill in a safe spot, you're ready to get started with your first grill-out. But as you're preparing to light the grill, be sure to follow these hard-and-fast rules about gas grill safety prior to ignition:

- Periodically check the tubes leading from the propane cylinder to the grill. Make sure they're securely attached and free of blockages such as grease, insects, or cobwebs.
- Make sure that hoses aren't cracked, and examine them for holes.
- If you smell gas, don't attempt to light the grill.
- Keep all lighted cigarettes and matches away from the propane cylinder.
- Propane cylinders can, over several years, rust. If you notice any rusting (which may indicate a hole developing in the skin), get rid of it and buy a new one. You can return the cylinders to the place where you bought them to have them refilled or recycled.

REMEMBER

Always thoroughly check out the entire system of a gas grill after a winter's storage.

Fueling a Hunk of Burnin' Fire

For gas grills, choosing a fuel source is easy — that propane cylinder attached to the grill is your only option, unless your grill is built specifically to hook up to the main gas line from your house. Charcoal grill owners, however, have two options for their heating source: natural lump charcoal and charcoal briquettes. I discuss the options in the following sections. I also show you how to enhance your grilling flavor by adding hardwood chips or chunks.

Using propane with your gas grill

Your most important decision as a gas grill owner will be when to replace the propane cylinder. You can tell the cylinder is low with three different methods:

- **Weigh the cylinder.** This is the simplest method. A full cylinder weighs approximately 38 pounds. An empty one weighs about 18 pounds. So if it weighs in at about 28 pounds, your supply is about half empty. Of course, if you're an optimist, it's half full.
- **Use a gauge that measures the level of fuel remaining.** A gas cylinder usually doesn't come with a gauge, but you can purchase one at any hardware store for about $10 to $15. They're portable, and they can easily, without tools, hook up to any cylinder and tell you how much fuel is left in your cylinder. Make sure you look for the label "UL Approved."
- **Use *Accu-Level Tape,* which works sort of like litmus paper.** You stick the cellophane-like tape to the outside of the cylinder. When you pour boiling water over the tape, it shows you the level of propane left in the tank by changing color at the level where the propane has been used up. The tape costs about $3 and is available wherever propane tank supplies are sold.

Going with the old standard: Charcoal briquettes

Charcoal briquettes, shown in Figure 3-1, are made from powdered charcoal that has been compressed, bound with coal dust and starch, and formed into a uniform little brick. Briquettes don't burn as intensely as natural lump charcoal, but they can be much easier to control. They give a hot, even heat, and, because of their uniform size, they give you consistent results. You'll always know you're working with a predictable fuel source!

Figure 3-1: Charcoal briquettes are uniform in shape; not so for natural lump charcoal.

SHOPPING TIP

To find the best briquettes, you have to do some sleuthing among the brands available in your markets. Try buying different brands a few times and keeping track of how they perform. You may notice that some burn more quickly than others, which means that they provide a less consistent heat and you need more of them. You may find store brands that are as efficient as some of the more familiar brands, like Kingsford. It won't take long to discover which ones you like best. And don't forget that the briquettes should be uniform in size — not crumbly — or you lose a good portion in the bag before you even set them in your grill.

You can step up to still more convenience with *fire-starter briquettes,* which are simply briquettes to which charcoal lighter fluid has already been added. You can place a few of these in with your regular briquettes for fast, easy lighting or cook with them exclusively. We don't recommend them as the sole source of heat for longer term grilling, however. That's because they tend to burn more quickly and require frequent replenishment. You should reseal the bag tightly after removing briquettes or the lighter fluid will evaporate, leaving you with plain-old briquettes!

The ultimate in convenience is *light-the-bag briquettes,* which contain just enough fuel for a single fire. There's no fuss or muss, because you simply place the bag in the grill and touch a match to the corner of the bag. Then, as with regular briquettes, wait until they've reached an ashy gray color to start cooking.

Grilling like a pro with natural lump charcoal

Natural lump charcoal, which is shown in Figure 3-1 in the preceding section, results when hardwoods — such as maple, oak, and hickory — are burned at super-high temperatures. The wood breaks down, dries out and, after hours of roasting, comes out ebony and almost weightless. The result is a clean-burning fuel, with a price — natural lump charcoal costs considerably more than the familiar briquettes. You may have to call around to find a reliable vendor as well.

Natural lump charcoal is an excellent fuel source because it lights more quickly than charcoal briquettes and burns much hotter at the start. The temperature is always changing with natural lump charcoal. It starts out very hot, peaks quickly, and then drops rapidly. This intense initial heat results in quick searing, which imparts a bit more flavor to the food. For this reason, professional grillers and barbecue pitmasters prefer it to any other kind of fuel.

However, if you've never cooked with natural lump charcoal, keep these tips in mind:

- A natural charcoal fire sparks and snaps, which may initially scare you, but there's no need for alarm, because these special effects are perfectly normal.

- Because natural lump charcoal burns very fast, your food cooks much faster than with briquettes. You'll find out through trial and error how hot your grill gets using differing amounts of charcoal, so your cooking time will vary. But assume that lump charcoal will take 5 to 10 minutes less time to cook than food on a gas grill. But again, this depends on the temperature *you* maintain in the grill by using more or less charcoal.

Adding hardwood chips or chunks

If you're lucky enough to have access to a natural supply of old hickory, oak, or fruit-tree wood, it will serve as an excellent supplemental fuel or flavoring for outdoor cookery. If you aren't so lucky, you can pick up commercial bags of hardwood for grilling at a nearby hardware store or grilling-supply store.

The appeal of hardwoods as supplements to briquettes is that they add an intensely smoky flavor that enhances the fairly subtle smokiness that comes from charcoal. They make the fire burn more intensely, which is a virtue when you want high heat for searing and quick cooking. They also burn longer, which means you don't have to replenish them as often.

Considering your options

You have two types of hardwood to choose from — chips or chunks — and the one you choose depends on what's available in your area. Chips light and burn more quickly, while chunks retain their heat more consistently.

Flavoring your food with hardwood

Here are some hardwood varieties that we think work particularly well on the grill:

- **Apple** is very good with poultry.
- **Alder** provides a nice delicate flavor when used with seafood.
- **Cherry** is wonderful with game birds.
- **Hickory** is essential for real pork barbecue.
- **Mesquite** has a strong flavor that's great for big red meats like beef and venison.
- **Maple** is fine wood to use for ham and pork.
- **Pecan** works best for poultry and seafood.

One good source for ordering hardwoods is Barbecue Wood Flavors Company, 141 Lyons Road, Ennis, Texas (972-875-8391). Visit `www.bbqwoodflavors.com` for the company's Web site.

Because chips burn very quickly, you want to use them when you're grilling food slowly in a covered grill. Grilled fish's delicate flesh quickly absorbs the smoke from chips, so you don't need a lengthy cooking time to reap the benefits of the wood chips. Chips also are easy to use; they simply require presoaking in water for 15 to 30 minutes to keep them from burning up too quickly.

WARNING!

Wood chips and chunks can ignite into flames on the grill; read your manual for specific information on how to use them safely with your grill.

Including hardwood in a charcoal grill

For charcoal grills, scatter the presoaked wood chips — a handful or two will do — over the charcoal briquettes after the coals turn ashy gray, or just before you're ready to cook. When the chips burn out, or when the smoke stops pouring from the cover vents, you can add another handful as a replacement. Don't overdo it though — the chips may smother the glowing coals.

If you're using wood chunks, you can mix half a dozen or more chunks into a charcoal briquette fire. However, wood chunks take a few minutes longer to burn than charcoal does. To keep the chunks from scorching your food, ignite them a few minutes before the charcoal. Or try igniting them with the charcoal and then spritzing them lightly with water. Another solution is to start the coals and chunks together and, when the charcoal is ashy gray, move the chunks to the edges of the fire so they surround and barely touch the coals. This way, the chunks produce just what you want — a steady supply of smoke without any flame.

ON THE GRILL

For a more intense, smoky flavor, you can build a fire entirely with wood chunks, which don't require presoaking; however, you'll probably have a hard time controlling the fire because the chunks burn so intensely. In addition, your wallet may suffer because the chunks are expensive.

Smoking with hardwood on a gas grill

You can add light, smoky wood flavoring to food when cooking with a gas grill. Both chips and chunks are appropriate. Increasingly, gas grills offer built-in smoking drawers or boxes to hold hardwood. Only a handful of chips is necessary to do the job; use more and the smoky flavor will be too harsh.

If your gas grill doesn't have a built-in smoking drawer or box, you can still get the wood flavor you want if you do one of the following:

- Place presoaked chips in a small foil pan or wrap them in heavy-duty aluminum foil. Poke holes in the foil to allow the smoke to escape, and place the pan or packet directly on lava rocks or ceramic briquettes (see

Chapter 2 for further instructions on making these smoker pouches). The heat of the grill will cause the wood to smolder and smoke. After the grill has cooled, simply remove the pan or packets and discard. (Douse the chips with water before throwing them out if they're still smoldering.)

- Purchase a small steel or cast-iron container, called a *smoker box* (see Chapter 2), to hold the presoaked chips. You place it directly on the heat source.

Arranging the Coal to Suit Your Fancy

When getting your grill ready for showtime, you have two things to consider if you're using charcoal: how much to use and how to arrange it. Many people use far too much natural lump charcoal or far too many briquettes in their grill. The number of briquettes needed depends on the size of fire you wish to create, which is in turn dependent on how much food you're cooking.

When arranging the coals, you need to decide whether you're grilling directly or indirectly (Chapter 1 covers those fundamentals so you can decide which method you'll use or whether you'll use both). Use these general guidelines to arrange these coals after you decide what type of grilling you'll do:

- **If you're grilling directly,** a single layer of coals should extend 1 to 2 inches beyond the food being cooked. Pour the briquettes into the grill and spread them out to determine how many you need; 30 briquettes will grill about a pound of meat. Count on an average of 2½ pounds of charcoal for grilling meat directly over the coals. After you figure out how much you need, stack the coals in a pyramid in the center before lighting. When most of the coals begin to burn, spread them out in an even layer. To keep the fire and temperature going, you may need to replenish the coals as they burn down.
- **If you're grilling indirectly,** start with about 25 briquettes (give or take, depending on the size of your grill — 25 works well for a 22½-inch kettle grill) on either side of the grill. Add eight briquettes to each side every 45 minutes.
- **If you're grilling both directly and indirectly (for foods that need longer, slower cooking),** simply set up the coal for an indirect fire, place the meat directly over the coals initially to brown and crisp the skin, and then move the meat over to the side of the grill that doesn't have coals. Moving the coals allows you to finish cooking the food more slowly and thoroughly. ***Note:*** You may or may not be using a drip pan (see Chapter 2); a drip pan is useful when you're grilling especially fatty meats like roast or duck.

Let There Be Flames: Igniting Your Grill

If you're using a gas grill, you're in luck — one major advantage of these grills is that they're so easy to light. Today nearly all of them come with an automatic ignition. Check the manual that came with your grill before trying to light it but, after that, follow these steps:

1. **Open the cover of the grill — and keep it open while lighting.**
2. **Fully open the valve on the gas cylinder.**
3. **Turn the burner control(s) to high.**
4. **Immediately push in the ignition button to light the grill.**
5. **If the grill doesn't light instantly, push the ignition button again.**
6. **If the grill still doesn't light, turn off all burner controls and close the valve on the cylinder. Wait 5 minutes for any gas fumes to dissipate, and then repeat Steps 1 through 5.**

After the flame lights, set the controls to high for preheating (which should last about 10 to 15 minutes). Always be sure that the flame is burning before closing the cover.

Many contemporary gas grills have a built-in temperature gauge that tells you when they're hot enough to cook on. Some indicate actual temperatures — 350 degrees is medium and 500 degrees is hot — while others are marked "low," "medium," and "high," which corresponds to the directions in most of our grilling recipes.

If you're using a charcoal grill, you may come across a bunch of gadgets for creating a flame with which to ignite a fire, and quite honestly, we believe that just about all of them beat a match. The following sections show the alternatives to burning your fingers with a stubby match.

Your very best bet: An electric charcoal igniter

An *electric charcoal igniter* is a metal coil, usually made of stainless steel, that's placed underneath the charcoal briquettes and heated up to a red-hot, glowing point that transfers heat to the immediate area. (See Figure 3-2.) The great thing about electric igniters is that you don't use any sort of fire-starting aid, like kindling or lighter fluid, with them. Left in place for a maximum of 8 minutes, the igniter starts coals glowing, and those coals rapidly ignite the coals that surround them. This method is a safe, easy way to start a grill. Such gadgets cost about $10.

Here's how to use the coil for best results:

1. **Plug the electric charcoal igniter into an electrical outlet and place the coil on the charcoal grate of the kettle grill.**
2. **Pile charcoal on top of the coil and wait about 8 minutes.**

   You'll see a little smoke rising from the kettle, and several of the coals atop the coil will be glowing brightly. If you leave the coil in much longer than 8 minutes, the coil itself may be damaged from the heat it has generated.
3. **Unplug the coil, carefully remove it from the grill, and store it safely to cool.**

   WARNING!

   Be very careful when removing the coil, which can stay hot for several minutes. Unplug it first, remove it from the grill, and set it away from the grill on a nonflammable surface to cool.
4. **Using long-handled tongs, shuffle the coals around to make them level, and let them sit.**

   Within 20 to 30 minutes, you'll have perfect ashy gray charcoal ready for grilling.

Figure 3-2: An electric charcoal igniter.

The runner-up: A chimney starter

An electric igniter is great (see previous section), but another way to light a charcoal fire is with the amazing chimney starter, shown in Figure 3-3, which is really, really cool — and cheap (one usually costs around $10). A *chimney starter* is nothing more than a wide-mouthed tin pipe that has a handle and a grate in the bottom. Using chimney starters can be a bit tricky, but if you don't have access to an electrical outlet, they're a good alternative to the electric starter. Once you get the hang of using them, they're a cinch.

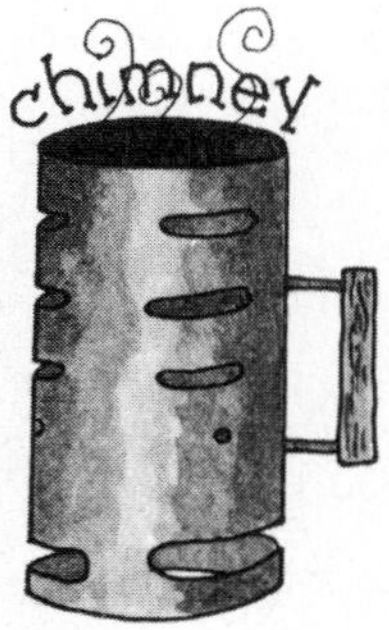

Figure 3-3: Ignite coals quickly with a chimney starter.

When you use a chimney to heat charcoal, you must use some sort of unwaxed paper (such as newspaper) as kindling to get the fire started. Follow these steps to use your chimney starter:

1. **Stuff a crumpled-up sheet of newspaper in the bottom of the chimney.**
2. **Add charcoal briquettes to the chimney.**
3. **Place the chimney on the lower grating of the grill and light the newspaper at the bottom using a butane lighter (see the upcoming section for more on the butane lighter).**

   By forcing intense heat up through the shaft, the burning newspaper ignites the charcoal, which starts to burn brightly within a few minutes.
4. **Release the burning charcoal from the chimney into the charcoal in the kettle either by squeezing the handle or by picking up the chimney and dumping the contents into the grill.**

When lighting your chimney and releasing the burning charcoal from it, be safe and wear a mitt! Check out Chapter 2 for more on mitts.

Old-school style: A butane lighter

If you want to start your fire the old-fashioned way, use a butane lighter. Because they ignite a small flame at the flick of a switch, you can use them to light paper, fire-starter briquettes, or gas grills. Good butane lighters have safety locks, regulators for the flame, and even little viewing windows so you can see how much butane is left. They're either disposable (cheaper) or refillable and cost about $10. There are no cons to using a butane lighter. It's just like a match only handier.

Fire starting doesn't have to be a struggle if you own a charcoal grill and are stuck using the old method of lighting with a lighter. Just choose a good fire-starting aid from the following list:

- **Kindling:** *Kindling* is any material that's highly and quickly combustible and creates a fast flame that will burn long enough to ignite a fuel such as charcoal briquettes. We recommend one of the following materials:
  - **Wood:** Make sure that the wood you use for kindling is very, very dry and brittle. Any moisture or "greenness" will result in a slow start, a poor burn, and bitter smoke. Old twigs and cut-up branches are best, and you should snap them to expose the more flammable inner core of the wood.
  - **Newspapers:** Newspapers make excellent kindling, but be aware that you may need several wads. And be aware that burnt newspaper can fly all over the place, which is both messy and dangerous. If you do use newspaper, roll it loosely into thin, branchlike cylinders, leaving plenty of air between the wrappings — air is oxygen, and oxygen is necessary for a good fire.

  To light a fire with kindling, place the kindling on the bottom of the grill and then place a single, uneven layer of charcoal on top. Light the kindling and allow the charcoal to begin to burn.
- **Lighter fluid:** Lighter fluid provides an instantaneous flammable substance to your kindling. Simply arrange the kindling and coals (see preceding bullet), and then squirt $^1/_4$ to $^1/_3$ cup of lighter fluid on top of the coals. Wait a minute to let the fluid soak into the briquettes and then light the kindling. You can place a match on top of the coals or hold a butane lighter to the kindling.

  Lighter fluid has two main disadvantages. Because it's liquid fuel, it's more dangerously flammable and spreadable than paper or wood. It also has the potential of lending a slight chemical taste to your food. But we've found that if you use it correctly, it doesn't affect your food's taste. Simply make sure you wait 20 to 30 minutes after starting the fire to place the food over the coals; by then, the fumes will have burned off.

Never use gasoline or kerosene as a lighter fluid because both can cause explosions. And if you think the fire is a bit sluggish and needs more lighter fluid, never squirt it into burning coals, because the fire can flare up or travel back up the stream of fluid to the can and cause a disaster. Rather, take a few new briquettes, place them in a clean can (such as a coffee can), and add enough lighter fluid to soak them. Then with long-handled tongs, carefully place the soaked briquettes among the other briquettes.

- **Miscellaneous fire starters:** The grill industry has come up with a lot of useful items for fire starting: compressed sticks of wood compound or sawdust that's soaked or treated with a safe, combustible fuel; wax by itself; wax in wood; and various chemical mixtures. You merely place these around the edges of your briquettes or natural lump charcoal and light the fire starters. They will burn quickly and ignite the charcoal.

  We have found that, despite industry claims, using chemical mixtures to light your grill may impart a chemical taste to your food, so we generally don't recommend them. But any form of kindling, including those compressed sawdust sticks, provide an easy way to get things started.

Controlling and Maintaining the Heat

The general rule for knowing when your coals are ready for grilling is to make sure that 80 percent or more of the coals are ashy gray (at night, they glow red with no flame). If you have less than that, the coals aren't ready, and if all of them are glowing red hot, the fire is probably too hot. A fire that's too hot will scorch your food and rob it of all its flavor.

After you notice that most of the charcoal looks ashy gray, add more charcoal as needed. This additional charcoal brings the temperature back to the same level you had in order to achieve consistent cooking times.

While you're grilling, monitor the temperature of the coals. As you cook your food and turn it over, you'll easily see if the coals are dying down or burning out. Use the following simple technique to gauge the temperature: Place the palm of your hand just above the grid. If you can hold your hand in that position for two seconds (counting "one thousand one, one thousand two"), the coals are hot; a three-second hold tells you the coals are medium-hot; four seconds is medium; and five is low. Unless you're cooking for hours at a time, you'll probably only have to replenish your coals once or twice.

Here are a few steps you can take to adjust the temperature of your fire. If your fire is too hot,

- Spread the coals out a bit more, which makes the fire less intense, if you're grilling over direct heat.
- Lower the grill's grid if it's adjustable.
- Partially close the vents in the grill, which allows less oxygen and damps down the fire. If you close the vents entirely, you'll get more smoke and therefore a smokier flavor. It will also build up the heat initially, but without oxygen the coals will die down in temperature after a while.
- Move the food to the outside edges of the grill so it isn't directly over the coals.

If your fire is on the weak side,

- Push the coals closer together as they burn down (using long-handled tongs) to intensify the heat.
- Raise the grill's grid if it's adjustable.
- Open the grill's vents to allow more oxygen in so the fire can grow.
- Add 12 to 15 briquettes to the outer edges of the fire after about the first 35 minutes (if you grill more than 45 minutes) to maintain a proper temperature.

WARNING!

In the event of a severe flare-up, spritz the flames with a water bottle. Be careful, though — spraying with water tends to blow ash around and make a mess. To control a grease fire, we suggest baking soda. You may also want to keep a fire extinguisher, garden hose, or bucket of sand nearby.

Part II

Adding Spice to Your Life

The 5th Wave By Rich Tennant

"Jekyll, old man – I think the spices for your barbecue may be a bit too strong."

In this part . . .

When you grill, much of the food's flavorful juices are lost into the fire — that's why we suggest enhancing the flavor of your food (before it sizzles on the grill grid) with marinades, rubs, flavored oils, and basting sauces. In this part, we give you ideas and recipes for marinating, seasoning, and basting grilled meat, poultry, fish, and vegetables. We also offer you shopping advice for stocking your refrigerator and pantry with convenient store-bought products for spur of the moment cooking — the way most of us really cook today. Last but not least, we offer several recipes for finishing sauces, condiments, and more.

Chapter 4

Peeking Inside the Grilling Guru's Pantry

In This Chapter

- Getting a little help from canned and bottled pantry friends
- Exploring the many condiments you can choose from
- Sorting out all those oils and vinegars
- Adding sweeteners and wines to your marinades
- Stocking up on herbs and spices
- Flavoring your grilled foods with fruits and vegetables

Grilling in its simplest form requires nothing more than a hot fire and a piece of meat. But if you want to take up grilling in all its diversity, you should stock your pantry with a few specific savory foods and condiments to complement the meats you choose.

In this chapter, we share our recommended list of items for your grilling pantry (and fridge) — bottled sauces, condiments, oils, vinegars, herbs, and spices — and we end with a brief description of fresh vegetables and fruits that can serve as strong seasoning agents in marinades, rubs, and barbecue sauces.

Adopting Some Kitchen Helpers: Bottled and Canned Goods

In a perfect world, every barbecue sauce and marinade would be made from scratch with the freshest of ingredients. But in this time-pressed world, we rely heavily on good commercial products. Having even a few of the following items on hand in your pantry or refrigerator allows you to whip up an assortment of barbecue sauces, dressings, and marinades in a hurry:

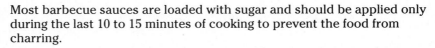

- **Bottled barbecue sauce:** Every year you can find new sauces flavored with hickory, mesquite, Jamaican jerk seasonings, habañero peppers, peaches and pineapple, bourbon, rum, and every kind of imaginable hot chile pepper. Barbecue sauces aren't only meant for ribs or chicken, however; you can also use them to baste salmon, shrimp kebabs, pork, and lamb chops.

  Most barbecue sauces are loaded with sugar and should be applied only during the last 10 to 15 minutes of cooking to prevent the food from charring.

- **Bottled marinades, dressings, and other basting and finishing sauces:** These ingredients provide the grilling cook tremendous variety and convenience. Bottled vinaigrette can substitute as a last-minute marinade for poultry, vegetables, or pork. Check out the many new Asian products, including sauces for satay, kebabs, poultry, and ribs. Especially tasty are the Thai-style products.
- **Canned favorites:** Corn kernels, beans, chickpeas, and artichoke hearts are a few canned items to have on hand for making last-minute salads and salsas.
- **Capers:** These are pickled flower buds of the Middle Eastern caper bush. The smallest capers are called *nonpareil.* They add a distinctive saltiness to dishes. To cut down on the saltiness, always rinse and drain capers before using them in marinades, sauces, and dressings.
- **Hoisin sauce:** A favorite of Chinese cuisine, hoisin sauce is made from soybeans, garlic, hot pepper, and spices. Depending on the brand, its texture can range from runny and thin to very thick. You can use hoisin sauce in marinades and basting sauces for grilled poultry, pork, or lamb. (See Chapter 5 for a delicious Hoisin Marinade and Basting Sauce.)

  We like Ka-Me Hoisin Sauce because it has wonderful flavor and a smooth consistency (without the addition of MSG — monosodium glutamate — or a thickening food starch).

- **Mayonnaise:** No kitchen pantry is complete without a jar of mayonnaise. But for the most part, think of mayonnaise as an incomplete dressing. We like to add a range of ingredients to mayonnaise, such as sun-dried tomatoes, basil, mustard, horseradish, rosemary, Tabasco sauce, or grated lemon peel, to create a whole assortment of dressings, sauces, and spreads.

  Substitute reduced-fat mayonnaise, if you wish, whenever the real thing is called for, or combine them equally to reduce calories and retain flavor.

- **Olives:** Olives add a luscious saltiness to many dishes. Sprinkle them into quick, fresh tomato sauces for grilled fish (Chapter 15) or burgers (Chapter 7). Stir them into mayonnaise-based sauces or salsas (Chapter 6). Add them to pizzas, quesadillas, or grilled sandwiches (all in Chapter 17).
- **Peanut butter:** You can use peanut butter to duplicate some of the sauces and dishes of Pacific Rim cuisine. For example, see Chapter 8 for Satay with Peanut Dipping Sauce or Chapter 6 for Creamy Asian Peanut Sauce.
- **Soy sauce:** A vital ingredient in so many flavorful marinades, basting sauces, barbecue sauces, and dressings, soy sauce adds distinctive flavor, brown color, and saltiness.

  Light soy sauce is sodium-reduced and therefore less salty. You can substitute this anytime for soy sauce when less salt is preferred.
- **Tahini paste:** Made from sesame seeds, tahini is a staple ingredient in Middle Eastern cooking and is used in dips and sauces, or as a sandwich spread.
- **Thai fish sauce:** Throughout Asia, cooks use bottled fish sauce, which is made from fermented fish. It's extremely pungent — it smells and tastes quite strong. But when added in very small amounts (a tablespoon or so) it provides an aromatic and slightly sweet-salty undertone to Asian dishes as part of a marinade. Because of its strength, however, you wouldn't want to simply pour it over food straight off the grill.
- **Worcestershire sauce:** This sauce is a combination of vinegar, molasses, water, sugar, anchovies, and other savory ingredients.

  Add Worcestershire sauce according to your taste to marinades, dressings, basting sauces, or hamburger patties. Or try splashing it over finished grilled foods, such as steaks, lamb chops, poultry, or roasted potatoes.

SHOPPING TIP

Before purchasing a product for the first time, read the ingredient label to get a general idea of its flavor. Try to avoid products in which the primary ingredient is sugar, salt, or fat. Otherwise that's all you'll taste. Purchase and taste test a few different brands of sauces, condiments, and other bottled goods to determine which ones you like best.

Condiment-ry, My Dear Watson

A *condiment* is any small side dish or accompaniment to food that adds flavor, texture, and contrasting color. Condiments can be vinegary (like ketchup), sweet (like preserved watermelon rind), hot and spicy (like salsa), sour (like dill pickles), or salty (like sun-dried tomatoes). The following list describes a few of our favorite condiments, which are available in any major supermarket:

- **Chutneys:** These sweet, tart, and spicy combinations of cooked fruits or vegetables make delectable accompaniments to grilled foods. Keep bottles of store-bought mango or tomato chutney on hand as a last-minute topping for grilled burgers, steaks, poultry, lamb, pork, sea bass, mackerel, and bluefish. Or, look through Chapter 6 for a number of simple, homemade chutney recipes.
- **Horseradish:** A delicious condiment for grilled fish, horseradish also adds zing to dressings, dips, and sauces made with ketchup, sour cream, or mayonnaise.
- **Ketchup:** Ketchup is the ultimate yin and yang of condiments. It's a blend of tangy vinegar, pureed tomatoes, and sweeteners like sugar or corn syrup. Before being knocked off its throne by the now more popular salsa, ketchup was America's favorite condiment. Dress it up by adding chopped scallions, minced ginger, or horseradish. Or use ketchup as an ingredient in marinades, basting sauces, and salsas.
- **Mustards:** There are really two types of prepared mustards available: those that are creamy smooth and those that contain coarse seeds. Either type may be flavored with herbs and spices, red or white wine, Champagne, honey, sugar, chilies, or peppercorns. Here are a few types of mustards you can experiment with:
    - **Classic yellow mustard:** With its mild taste and creamy texture, yellow mustard is the American choice — perfect for a grilled hot dog.
    - **Dijon mustard:** This French classic, made with brown mustard seeds and flavored with white wine and other seasonings, is an extremely useful ingredient for the time-pressed grilling cook.

      Vary It! Combine Dijon mustard with melted butter and Worcestershire sauce as a quick sauce for steaks and burgers. Blend with honey as a basting sauce for turkey or ham steaks. Add to creamy-based salad dressings or to marinades and barbecue sauces.
    - **Honey mustard:** This condiment combines two highly compatible ingredients. Buy the condiment bottled or make your own by combining equal amounts of honey and mustard (or mixing them according to taste).

      Vary It! Use honey mustard as a basting sauce when grilling sausage, ribs, ham steaks, chicken, turkey, duck, or lamb.

- **Whole-grain mustard:** Made with whole mustard seeds, whole-grain mustard has a pleasant crunchy texture and can be flavored with any number of ingredients, such as chilies, wine, mixed herbs, honey, or vinegar.

  Vary It! Whole-grain mustard is a good addition to marinades for beef or pork.

- **Salsa:** Even though salsas are usually tomato-based, the salsa product line is growing to include salsas with roasted corn, red pepper, black olives, and other ingredients. Store varieties range from mild to hot.

  Vary It! Use salsa as a quick condiment for hot dogs, grilled burgers, steaks, chicken, or fish. Try it as a spread for quesadillas, fajitas, or other sandwich wraps. Add it to vegetable salads made with chopped tomatoes, corn, or canned beans. Use it to add flavor and heat to creamy macaroni salads.

- **Sun-dried tomatoes:** Sold either oil-packed or dried, sun-dried tomatoes are somewhat chewy and intensely flavored. You can use them to flavor salads, dressings, and spreads. See Chapter 16 for Macaroni Salad with Sun-Dried Tomato Mayonnaise.

- **Tabasco sauce:** An all-purpose spicy seasoning and condiment made from hot Capsicum peppers, vinegar, and salt, Tabasco sauce adds heat and a pleasant sharpness to marinades, dressings, and finished grilled foods.

Flavoring Foods with Oil

Oils range in taste from the nearly neutral flavor of ever-so-subtle peanut oil to bold and buttery olive oil to nutty, almost bitter-tasting, dark sesame oil. Avoid exposing oils to light and air, because they both cause the oils to deteriorate more rapidly. Instead, always store oils in a cool, dark place. Keep oil containers tightly sealed after opening and use within several months to one year. Throw out any oils that develop a musty or rancid smell.

Here are a few oils you can try:

- **Olive oil:** Use olive oil in dressings, marinades, and basting and finishing sauces. Olive oil is indispensable to the grilling chef — it infuses marinades, dressings, sauces, and salsas with its rich, fruity flavor. Try olive oil drizzled over grilled breads, grilled vegetables, roasted red peppers, and all kinds of grilled chicken or fish. (See the nearby sidebar "Solving the olive oil shopping conundrum" for details on finding a quality olive oil.)

Don't be misled by olive oil labeled as *light.* This is a refined oil with little color and flavor, but it has the same number of calories — 120 — as a tablespoon of any other kind of oil.

- **Nut oils:** Extracted from roasted walnuts, almonds, hazelnuts, and other nuts, these oils are very expensive and rich in flavor. They're delicious in salad dressings and some salsas, especially when the recipe uses the same nut as an ingredient. However, these oils are highly perishable and must be refrigerated.
- **Sesame oil:** Made from sesame seeds, sesame oil has a rich, distinctive flavor. Use it sparingly to accent marinades made with Asian ingredients like soy sauce, ginger, and garlic.

Peanut, corn, safflower, soy, and other mild vegetable oils can be mixed with equal amounts of olive oil to enrich their flavors.

The shelf life of oil depends on its variety and how it's stored. For instance, olive oil can be kept for up to a year if tightly capped and stored in a cool, dark place. But nut oils last only a few months, so purchase them in small quantities.

Flavored oils, seasoned with an assortment of ingredients such as lemon slices, whole peppercorns, dried herbs, garlic, and chilies, are now sold in fancy kitchenware stores and in the gourmet food section of many major supermarkets. They're terrific drizzled over grilled breads, grilled pizzas, grilled vegetables, or grilled steaks, fish, chicken, or lamb.

Solving the olive oil shopping conundrum

When shopping for a quality olive oil, look on the front of the bottle for a sign of its grade, or quality. The purest, most expensive olive oils are marked *extra-virgin* and have the richest aroma and strongest flavors. Other, less expensive grades of olive oil include *virgin olive oil* and *olive oil.*

Be aware, however, that labels don't always tell the whole truth. Consider this: If a label reads "Packaged in Italy" (or Greece or Spain), all this means is that the oils could have come from *anywhere* and were only put into the can or bottle in the country on the label. If the label reads "Made in Italy," the contents are from Italy but from no specific region. The best (and most expensive) olive oils have a much more regional focus, as in, "Produced in Tuscany" or "Produced in Umbria."

You may want to stock your pantry with one bottle of the expensive grade and one bottle of the less expensive grade. Save the more pricey extra-virgin oils to drizzle onto fresh salads, salsas, grilled breads, or grilled vegetables and fish. Use the virgin olive oil when a larger amount is required for marinades, or for barbecue sauces in which the oil's distinctive flavor is more likely to be masked by the other strongly flavored ingredients.

WARNING!

Don't try to make your own flavored oils at home unless you're prepared to use them immediately. Homemade flavored oils can spoil in just a few hours, and they may even develop botulism, which can be deadly.

Adding Tartness with a Splash of Vinegar

Vinegars tenderize cuts of meat as they marinate, but they also add a pleasant tartness to sauces, dressings, and marinades. Vinegars are almost always paired with oils to balance their harshness. We're partial to balsamic vinegar, which is slightly sweet, less harsh, and more complex in flavor than other vinegars.

If, by accident, you add too much vinegar to a dressing or marinade, you can tone down the acidic effect by adding a pinch of salt, more oil, or by whisking in a bit of sugar or other sweetener, such as honey, to taste.

Here are some types of vinegar to keep in your pantry:

- **Apple cider vinegar:** Good for almost all recipes where vinegar is an ingredient, apple cider vinegar is especially good with marinades and dressings that contain a fruit or citrus juice or that have an element of sweetness.
- **Balsamic vinegar:** Bold, rich, and slightly sweet, real balsamic vinegar is outrageously expensive and made only in the area near Modena, Italy. Most of the bottles sold in the supermarkets are imitations. But being a "fake" doesn't mean it's bad; it's just less aged. Balsamic vinegar is delicious in marinades, dressings, and finishing sauces. Try splashing it to taste on grilled lamb, chicken, or pork.
- **Red wine vinegar:** Use this bold and pleasantly pungent vinegar in marinades for beef, pork, or poultry.
- **Rice vinegar:** Slightly milder than other vinegars, rice vinegar works well with sherry or sake in marinades.
- **White wine vinegar:** This type of vinegar can be fruity or very dry. It's delicious in relishes and chutneys, because it counterbalances sweet flavorings.

Sweeten the Pot: Using Sweeteners in Sauces and Marinades

When preparing a sauce or a condiment, you may want it to be boldly sweet, or you may want just a hint of sweet taste. Much like salt, sweet ingredients, when used in moderation, can help blend all the other flavors within a recipe. Try experimenting with the following sweeteners:

- **Fruit jams and preserves:** Jams and preserves enhance grilled foods when used as ingredients in glazes and finishing sauces.

  Vary It! Turn a pork chop or a rack of ribs into something sublime by coating it with a warm glaze of apricot jam, minced ginger, and lemon juice. A spit-roasted duck needs only a slather of black cherry or black currant jam to make it perfect. A broiled lamb chop pairs nicely with a good-quality mint jelly and some freshly ground black pepper.

- **Honey:** Honey can add anywhere from a slight to an overwhelming element of sweetness to marinades and basting sauces, and it mixes particularly well with Asian ingredients like soy sauce, ginger, hoisin sauce, garlic, and sesame oil.

  Like other sweeteners, honey can cause grilled food to char and burn. To lessen the chances of burning, grill the food indirectly or scrape all the marinade off the food before placing it on the grill. For the best effect, apply basting sauces containing honey only during the final minutes of grilling.

- **Light and dark brown sugar:** Brown sugar is white sugar combined with molasses to give it color and moisture. The lighter the color, the less intense (or molasses-like) the flavor.

- **Molasses:** A common ingredient in barbecue sauces, molasses adds sweetness and color to marinades and barbecue and basting sauces.

Wine and Dine Me: Marinating and Basting with Wines

Like vinegars, all wines are tenderizing agents, but their chief function in marinades or sauces is to add bold flavor. White wines are subtle, while the bolder and richer the red wine, the more distinct flavor it will add to a dish.

The following are some of the most common wines used for marinating and basting:

- **Dry red and white wine:** These acid-based wines are tenderizing agents, but more importantly, they add a complexity of flavor to marinades and basting sauces. Add herbs and spices to taste and always have an oil component in a red or white wine marinade to take off some of the acidic edge.

For marinades or sauces, you don't need to spend more than about $8 on a good bottle of red or white wine — and at that price, whatever wine remains in the bottle is good enough for serving with the meal.

- **Marsala:** Marsala, a *fortified* wine (which means that another alcohol, such as brandy, has been added to the wine to raise its alcohol content), is good in marinades for poultry and game birds. This wine adds a tinge of sweetness.
- **Sake:** A Japanese beer made from fermented rice, sake is excellent in marinades. You can use it as a substitute for dry vermouth or pale dry sherry. After it's opened, it can be stored in the refrigerator for 3 to 4 weeks.
- **Sherry:** Sherry, like Marsala, is a fortified wine. Depending on its sweetness, sherry is labeled dry, medium dry, or sweet. Sherry can be used in marinades and basting sauces.

Walking through a Griller's Herb Garden

For most grilled recipes, we prefer fresh herbs and spices — they have more flavor than their dried counterparts. One exception to this rule applies to rubs, which are mixtures of dried, ground spices (and sometimes dried herbs) that are made into compact, dense, and flavorful coatings that easily adhere to the food's surface. Most varieties of fresh herbs are available year-round in supermarkets and Middle Eastern and Asian specialty stores, and many can be grown in a pot on the windowsill or outdoors in mild climate.

Fresh herbs should be washed and dried thoroughly and then stored in damp paper towels in the crisper drawer of the refrigerator, where they will stay fresh for up to five days. To keep them longer, treat them like freshly cut flowers and place the herbs in a glass of water in the refrigerator. Dried herbs and spices should be stored in a cool place, away from direct sunlight and heat. In other words, the top of your stove is not a good place for a spice rack!

Avoid buying dried or preground herbs and spices in large quantities (even if they're discounted in price). There's no fixed rule about how long dried herbs and spices should be stored, but dried herbs seem to lose their original potency after about a year. Ground spices have a longer shelf life. If you doubt the freshness of a dried herb or spice, just smell it. It should smell fresh and aromatic.

The amount of herbs and spices that are blended in a sauce, marinade, rub, salsa, or dressing is usually a matter of personal taste. Experiment with different combinations, adding them to taste, usually at the end of cooking, when they will best retain their color and flavor. When substituting dried herbs for fresh herbs, use about 1/3 the amount of fresh herbs called for in the recipe.

Table, sea, or kosher: Choosing a salt to cook with

Most of the regular or fine-grained salt that finds its way to the supermarket and eventually to your table is rock salt mined from salt deposits. *Sea salt,* prized by chefs for its more complex taste, is made by evaporating sea water, so it contains minerals from the sea. Many chefs and savvy home cooks prefer the seasoning effect of coarse-grained *kosher salt.* With its oversized crystals, kosher salt clings to foods better than fine-grained salt.

Take a look at some of the most essential herbs and spices for grilling:

- **Allspice:** Spice berries from the evergreen pimento tree are combined with tastes of cinnamon, nutmeg, and cloves — hence the name. An important ingredient in Jamaican jerk seasonings and Caribbean sauces, allspice adds an almost sweet element. Use it in barbecue sauce, rubs, and marinades.
- **Basil:** Fresh basil has a slightly sweet, pungent flavor (some say it reminds them of licorice) that goes with garlic, mint, lemon peel, lemon juice, tomatoes, grilled fish, lamb, or poultry. Basil, which is the main ingredient in Pesto Sauce (Chapter 15), is easy to grow outdoors in temperate climates. To maximize flavor, add basil at the end of cooking, or consider sprinkling chopped, fresh basil leaves generously over grilled foods.

  Dried basil has little flavor and is a poor substitute for fresh. Instead, freeze fresh, washed basil in a freezer bag, using it as needed when fresh basil isn't available.
- **Cayenne or red pepper:** This hot, powdered, red-colored mixture of several types of chile peppers is usually sold ground. Use it in small amounts in marinades, rubs, and sauces.
- **Chili powder:** This is a fiery mixture of dried chilies, cumin, oregano, garlic, coriander, and cloves. You'll see this spice sold ground.

  Vary It! Use chili powder as a multipurpose seasoning when you want to add heat as well as flavor. It's especially popular in Tex-Mex-style kebabs, marinades, and sauces. Chili powder mixes especially well in rubs for chicken or beef with cumin, oregano, ground chile peppers, cayenne or red pepper, and salt.
- **Fresh cilantro:** Also called *Chinese parsley* and fresh *coriander,* this herb is cherished by Chinese, Southeast Asian, Mexican, and Latin American cultures and cooks. Its parsley-look-alike leaves have a distinctive taste and smell.

Vary It! Use cilantro in marinades for fish, chicken, or beef. Cilantro mixes well with ginger, citrus juices and peels, mint, hot chilies, and garlic. To make a delicious dipping sauce for chunks of French bread, skewered chicken, or fish, mix together extra-virgin olive oil, finely chopped cilantro leaves, salt, and freshly ground black pepper.

- **Cinnamon:** A sweet and aromatic spice harvested from the bark of a tropical tree, cinnamon is commonly sold ground or as whole dry sticks. Cinnamon is a popular ingredient in Caribbean sauces and rubs where its sweetness contrasts with the heat of chilies and other spicy ingredients.

  Vary It! Add cinnamon to poultry rubs and barbecue sauces or sprinkle it on grilled fruits.

- **Cumin:** This aromatic, nutty-flavored spice is sold as whole dried seeds or in ground form. Cumin is essential to Middle Eastern cooking and Southwestern cooking in the United States. Ground cumin is one of the main ingredients in curry powder and some chili powders. Cumin is terrific with grilled fish, lamb, pork, or beef, and in rubs, marinades, and barbecue sauces.

- **Curry powder:** This pungent spice blends more than a dozen different herbs and spices, often including cinnamon, cloves, cardamom, chilies, mace, nutmeg, turmeric, red and black pepper, and ground sesame seeds. Use curry when you want a Middle Eastern or Indian accent. You can also use it as the main ingredient in chicken, lamb, or pork rubs.

- **Five spice powder:** This aromatic seasoning powder, used throughout China and Vietnam, usually combines the following ground ingredients: star anise (a star-shaped spice filled with small seeds), Szechwan peppercorns, cinnamon, cloves, fennel seed, and sometimes ginger or cardamom. Cardamom is a mellow spice that's frequently used to make curries, spiced cakes, and garam masala — the most important spice blend of north Indian cooking.

  Five spice powder, available in Asian markets and many supermarket spice sections, may become one of your favorite grilling ingredients. Use it as a seasoning rub for chicken, pork, lamb, or fish, or try adding it to marinades made with other Asian ingredients like soy sauce, sesame oil, or garlic.

- **Fresh gingerroot:** Found in the produce section of the supermarket, fresh gingerroot is peeled and then sliced, minced, or grated before it's added to marinades, dressings, and basting sauces. It mixes well with garlic, soy sauce, sesame oil, hot peppers, and other Asian seasonings. Fresh gingerroot also contains an enzyme that breaks down and softens animal gelatin, so it can be an effective tenderizing agent when used in meat marinades.

To store fresh gingerroot in the refrigerator, wrap it in a paper towel and then place it in a plastic bag punctured with a few holes (to let in some air). It will stay fresh for up to 3 weeks.

- **Ground ginger:** Sold in the spice section, ground ginger blends well with spices common to Indian cuisine, such as cumin, curry, turmeric, and coriander, or with Caribbean cooking spices, like allspice, nutmeg, and cinnamon. You may substitute ground ginger for fresh gingerroot when you have no choice; however, ground ginger is much spicier than fresh.

  Because it's so spicy, use ground ginger cautiously when substituting for fresh, and be sure to taste after each addition. For a flavorful steak rub, mix together to taste powdered ginger, fresh minced garlic, black pepper, and salt. Cover and refrigerate meat for several hours before grilling.

- **Jamaican jerk seasoning:** If you love spicy foods, run to the store to buy yourself a bottle of this seasoning. Why make it yourself when several superior products are now available in major supermarkets? Jerk is especially good on pork but also works with chicken and fish. Rub it into chops and tenderloins before grilling.

- **Mint:** A fresh, sweet, pungent herb, mint is sold in fresh bunches or crumbled dry and is easily grown outdoors in mild climates. The two most common varieties are peppermint and spearmint.

  Vary It! Mint is terrific with fresh vegetables, and in rice, fruit salsas, and fruit salads. (See Chapter 16 for a refreshing Yogurt Cucumber Salad with mint.) It combines especially well with basil or lemon peel in salads or dressings. Sprinkle chopped, fresh mint on grilled chicken, fish, pork, or lamb or add it to salsas or flavored butters.

- **Oregano:** Oregano has intense flavor and is best if fresh, but it can be purchased crumbled dry as well. Use this herb in marinades and dressings for grilled fish, lamb, beef, or chicken.

- **Paprika:** Lush red in color, paprika varieties range from faintly sweet and spicy to intensely hot, and they're usually sold ground. The Hungarian variety is considered the best. Excellent in rubs for poultry, pork, or beef, paprika also mixes well with cayenne pepper.

- **Parsley:** Sold year-round, parsley is available in fresh bunches or crumbled dry. The most common fresh varieties are curly parsley and the stronger-flavored Italian flat-leaf. Parsley is an all-purpose herb that can be added liberally to marinades, dressings, sauces, or compound butters.

  Vary It! *Gremolata,* a parsley and garlic topping classically served on *osso buco* — a hearty, Italian dish of braised veal shanks, white wine, tomatoes, garlic, anchovies, grated lemon peel, and other ingredients — makes a terrific lowfat garnish for grilled foods. To make gremolata, mix together 1 large clove peeled and finely minced garlic, the grated peel of one large lemon, 1/4 cup chopped parsley, and salt and pepper to taste. Sprinkle over grilled fish, chicken, pork, or beef.

- **Peppercorns:** Like salt, pepper is a universally prized seasoning ingredient. It's used in recipes for foods that range in flavor from savory to sweet. Peppercorns of all types, whether black, green, or white, come from the *Piper nigrum* vine. Peppercorns can be combined to create peppery coatings for grilled meats or poultry. You can buy bottles of mixed peppercorns in the spice section of major supermarkets.

  Freshly crushed pepper is far more aromatic and potent than precrushed pepper in a can. Always use a pepper mill to crush black peppercorns into freshly ground pepper. You can use a couple of other ways to easily crush whole peppercorns before adding them to rubs, sauces, or marinades. For instance, gather them in the middle of a cutting board and press them with the bottom of a heavy skillet. Or wrap them in heavy-duty aluminum foil and pound the package with a meat mallet or a rolling pin until they're crushed to a desired size.

- **Rosemary:** Any serious grilling cook knows that rosemary is a very important herb. Fresh rosemary sprigs have just the right intensity of flavor for rubs and marinades.

  Vary It! Rosemary is perfect for grilled pork, poultry, fish, lamb, potatoes, tomatoes, summer squash, and eggplant. Grill kebabs, fish steaks, or fish fillets on top of fresh, oiled rosemary sprigs. Or strip all the needles and use the stems as flavorful wooden skewers for small pieces of lamb, chicken, or fish. Dried rosemary is also an excellent rub ingredient. Mix it to taste with ground thyme, crushed peppercorns, dried oregano, garlic salt, or other seasonings, and then press onto chicken, steaks, lamb, or fish before grilling. Blend chopped, fresh rosemary leaves and lemon juice into butter for a rich herb butter.

- **Saffron:** Saffron — the world's most expensive spice — is pungent and aromatic; however, a little goes a long way to add flavor and a golden color to mayonnaise dressings or creamy sauces for grilled fish or chicken.

  Saffron is sold as a powder or as whole yellow, orange, or red threads. The threads are better quality. Soak them briefly in a little hot water before adding them (along with the soaking water) to the dish.

- **Thyme:** Fresh or dried, thyme is a terrific herb for accenting tomato and wine-based sauces and marinades for beef, pork, or poultry. Thyme mixes well with basil, sage, rosemary, parsley, marjoram, and garlic. Sprinkle chopped, fresh thyme over grilled vegetables such as potatoes, eggplant, tomatoes, summer squash, mushrooms, or onions.

Spice is just a phone call away

Check out your supermarket spice section for an array of special spice mixes — from mixed peppercorn blends to jerk seasoning — made by McCormick, Paul Prudhomme, Zatarain's, and other companies. You can also mail-order rubs directly from the following companies:

- Vanns (Web: www.vannsspices.com; phone: 800-583-1693)
- Penzeys, Ltd (Web: www.penzeys.com; phone: 800-741-7787)
- Mo Hotta Mo Betta (Web: www.mohotta.com; phone: 800-462-3220)

Penzeys publishes a catalog that reads more like a cookbook, with pictures, tips, recipes, and descriptions of over 250 herbs, spices, and seasoning blends. The Mo Hotta Mo Betta catalog is a must-have for any fan of hot pepper sauces, salsas, rubs, barbecue sauces, and spicy condiments.

Adding Zest with Fruits and Veggies

A griller's pantry or refrigerator should include a range of fresh fruits and vegetables that can be used as seasoning ingredients to add spice, heat, pungency, and other intense flavors to foods. We recommend that you stock the following:

- **Chilies:** Sorting through chilies in the supermarket can be confusing. They're sold fresh, dried, crushed, flaked, and ground. The pungency of a chile can range from almost sweet to excruciatingly hot. Fresh chilies commonly found in Mexican dishes include *jalapeño* (hot), *habañero* (very hot), and *poblano* (mild). See Figure 4-1 for a look at the types of chilies you can buy. Remember that chilies infuse a dish with additional flavor as well as with spiciness.

  Handle all chilies, but especially fresh chilies, with care. To prepare a fresh chile, remove the seeds and ribs — the hottest parts — to reduce the intensity of the pepper by about 90 percent, and then finely chop the chilies into marinades and sauces. Wash your hands and avoid touching your eyes after handling. In fact, you may want to wear rubber gloves when handling chilies!

  Some of the more common dried chilies available in supermarkets today are the ancho, pasilla, and chipotle. The chipotle chile is a smoke-dried jalapeño with a wonderful, hot, smoky flavor. (Check out Chapter 15 for a Grilled Swordfish Steak with Chipotle Salsa recipe.)

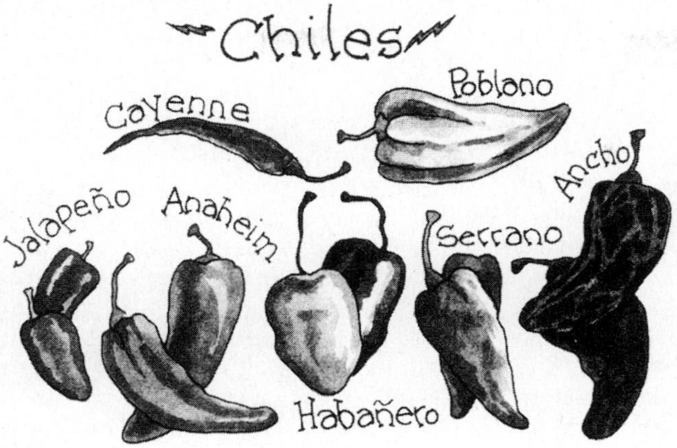

Figure 4-1: Some common varieties of chilies that add spice and flavor.

Cayenne and paprika are chilies that have been ground to a fine powder and range in heat from very hot to mild. Ground chilies, mixed with cumin, garlic, and other spices, are often made into blends of chili powder.

Vary It! For a delicious, quick spice rub, sprinkle your favorite chili powder (homemade or store-bought) onto fish, chicken, or pork, and then coat the meat with a little oil before grilling. (Chapter 5 has more on rubs.)

- **Citrus juice from lemons, limes, and oranges:** These juices are mildly acidic and add a fresh, bold flavor to marinades, dressings, and basting sauces. To some degree, citrus juice is a tenderizing agent in marinades.

  Vary It! Garnish platters of grilled fish, chicken, or lamb with lime or lemon slices, or try grilling delicate fish fillets on slices of lemons, oranges, or limes. (Chapter 15 is filled with fish ideas.) Lemon juice is a delicious marinade ingredient for grilled lamb, veal, chicken, or pork. Orange juice adds natural sweetness to marinades, and it combines especially well with hoisin sauce and soy sauce. Flip to Chapter 5 for a Hoisin Marinade that you can use on pork ribs, lamb, or chicken.

- **Citrus peel from lemons, limes, and oranges:** Grated citrus peel, also called *zest,* contains natural oils that can add intense flavor to grilled meat, fish, poultry, and vegetables. Grated citrus peel doesn't have the slightly harsh acidic quality of the juice; instead, like salt, citrus peel helps punctuate the natural flavor of a food.

  Vary It! Add grated peel generously to dressings, marinades, basting sauces, and rubs. Add peels to white wine vinegar with fresh herbs to make citrus-flavored vinegars. Be sure to grate only the outer, colored portion of the peel because the *pith,* or the white layer underneath the peel, imparts bitterness.

Throw whole peels directly into the coals to create flavorful smoke when grilling pork, fish, or lamb.

- **Garlic:** The potential of garlic for the grilling cook is unlimited — we can't praise garlic enough. Raw garlic cloves are indispensable to all types of marinades. Minced or pressed garlic adds depth and dimension to basting and finishing sauces, dips, salsas, condiments, and side dishes. There's a reason that garlic is a recognizable ingredient in so many ethnic cuisines and dishes — it combines, without objection, with other strong ethnic seasoning like fresh ginger, soy sauce, chile peppers, hot spices, curries, onions, olive oil, and fresh herbs. When foil-wrapped and roasted, garlic loses some of its sharpness and mellows to almost a nutty taste. (See Chapter 16 for tips on roasting garlic.)

  Vary It! When a marinade, dip, or salsa seems to taste flat and lack flavor, try adding a little minced garlic.

- **Red and yellow onions, scallions, and shallots:** In addition to being marvelous choices for grilling on their very own (see Chapter 16), all of these vegetables add flavor to marinades and sauces. You should always stock these items in your pantry.

  - Red onions add color as well as an element of sweetness to salsas and condiments.
  - Yellow onions, in good supply all year-round, are the workhorses of the griller's pantry. Dice and add them to marinades, salsas, chutneys, and relishes.
  - Scallions, which have long green leaves and small white bulbs, are especially welcomed in Asian-style sauces and marinades. (Use both the green and white parts.)
  - Shallots, with their faint purple interior and papery bronze skin, aren't some high-minded ingredient of the rich and famous. Shallots are readily available in all supermarkets and noteworthy because of their distinctive nutty flavor.

Chapter 5

Infusing Foods with Flavor: Marinades, Oils, and Rubs

In This Chapter

- Marinating for taste and tenderness
- Coating foods with flavored oils
- Applying tasty rubs for crispy crust

Recipes in This Chapter

- Hoisin Marinade and Basting Sauce
- Spicy Soy and Cilantro Marinade
- Spicy Cinnamon and Soy Marinade
- Five Spice and Soy Sauce Marinade
- Provençal Marinade
- Moroccan Marinade
- Lime and Cumin Marinade
- Cuban-Style Mojo Marinade
- Greek Marinade
- Gingery Grilled Vegetable Marinade
- Hot and Sweet Spice Rub
- Cajun-Style Steak Rub
- Peppery Dried Herb Rub
- Peppery Parsley Rub for Tender Steaks
- Five-Spice Asian Rub
- Coriander and Fennel Rub
- Middle Eastern Rub

You may say that marinades, oils, and rubs are to grilling what sauces are to French cooking: They layer on flavor to transform ordinary poultry, fish, meat, and vegetables into something divine and memorable. Except, unlike a fancy finishing sauce, marinades, oils, and rubs work their magic before the food is actually cooked.

You can't overestimate the importance of marinating food that's destined for the grill. Marinades change food in two very important ways: by softening or slightly tenderizing meat and by adding flavor. A tender, succulent rib-eye steak may need nothing but a dusting of salt and pepper before it's grilled, but a top blade or shoulder steak will greatly benefit from a little soaking to soften its tougher tissues. Tender cubes of sirloin can be cut and skewered with vegetables and fruits for kebabs, but marinating those cubes first in a seasoned liquid gives you an endless number of flavoring options. Indeed, adding flavor is the main benefit of marinating.

Oils and rubs are the little cousins of marinades — they add moisture and flavor but don't have acidic ingredients such as lemon juice, vinegar, or wine, which slightly tenderize food. Oils can be combined with chopped herbs, grated citrus peel, minced garlic, salt, pepper, and other seasonings to make a thick paste that you apply to cuts of meat, fish, or poultry. They're best used with seafood, which needs protection from the high heat that oil provides. Rubs can be any tasty blend of spices and seasonings. They can be used on most any foods — less on subtle flavors like fish and more on foods with lustier flavors like venison or duckling. In this chapter, I provide you with a number of recipes for marinades, oils, and rubs to help you infuse your food with flavor. I also tell you what foods work best with which recipes.

The March of the Marinades

You're standing in your kitchen looking at a thick and juicy piece of steak that you hope to grill to a perfect medium-rare. And you're thinking that, in addition to a dusting of salt and pepper, you could add more pizzazz by plunging the meat into a spicy marinade. Good idea. But now comes the hard part: deciding what ingredients to use. This section helps you make that decision as well as guides you in using marinades most effectively for the most flavorful finish.

Choosing your marinade ingredients

The typical marinade is a combination of an oil, an acid, herbs, and spices. The fat that lubricates and moisturizes the food is usually a vegetable oil. The acid component may be a vinegar, lemon juice or other citric acid, yogurt, or wine. Although these acids don't actually tenderize the food, they can soften the surface tissues of tougher cuts.

Marinades come in endless flavors — spicy, sweet, savory, tangy, herby, oily, acidic, salty, and so on. We give you plenty of marinades in this chapter and throughout the book, but there's no reason to use only our recipes. What you put into the marinade is a matter of personal taste — if you feel like experimenting on your own, use the marinade combinations that follow as guidelines, adjusting specific ingredient amounts to mix a potion that works for you.

Similarly, many of the marinade recipes in this book are interchangeable. For example, the marinade for Caribbean Pork Chops (Chapter 12) also works with ribs, turkey, or chicken. The Best-Ever Fajitas marinade (Chapter 17) is also good with other cuts of beef, chicken, or cubes of skewered fish. If you like a marinade's flavor, steal it from one recipe and use it with other foods.

When breaking away from a recipe to blend your own marinade, always consider the food that's being soaked. Ask yourself these questions:

- **Is it lean, like a chicken breast or white fish?** As a rule, the leaner the food, the better it does in a marinade with a fairly high concentration of oil.
- **Is it high in fat, like the well-marbled red meat of a rib-eye steak?** Richer foods hold their own against more robust acidic ingredients, such as red wine vinegar or wine.

Also think about how ingredients work best together. Consider the following combinations and ingredient tips:

- Soy sauce is compatible with the flavors of ginger, sesame oil, scallions, and garlic. Spicy Asian-flavored marinades for fish, pork, beef, or chicken often combine dark soy sauce, rice vinegar, garlic, sugar, chilies, fresh ginger, peanut oil, scallions, and cilantro leaves.
- White or red wines mix well with olive oil, chopped garlic, onions or shallots, and fresh herbs, such as tarragon, thyme, rosemary, or bay leaf. Red wine marinades are good with beef, game, and dark-meat poultry. White wine marinades go well with pork, poultry, fish, and shellfish. (Turn to Chapter 10 for Rotisserie-Grilled Chicken, which is made with a white wine, lemon-herb marinade; or refer to Chapter 11 to see a recipe for Grilled Tenderloin Au Poivre with Herb Butter Sauce, which uses a red wine marinade.)
- Fresh or dried chilies, chili powder, cayenne pepper, crushed red pepper, and Tabasco sauce can punch up the flavor in a marinade and leave your mouth with an appealing hot and spicy aftertaste.
- Honey, molasses, brown sugar, and granulated sugar add sweetness to your grilled foods. Compose a tasty marinade for all kinds of poultry by mixing together corn oil, ketchup or molasses, dry sherry, Worcestershire sauce, soy sauce, crushed garlic, chopped onions, Tabasco sauce, salt, and pepper (all to your taste).
- Peanut oil is very mild, while sesame oil is bold and best if used in limited amounts in a marinade.
- Grated lemon, lime, or orange peel is rich in aromatic citrus oil and can be used quite liberally in marinades.
- Whole, minced, and pressed garlic seems to improve nearly every savory marinade.
- Dijon-style mustard added to a marinade of dry white wine, olive oil, fresh lemon juice, lemon peel, and chopped fresh herbs like parsley, rosemary, basil, or thyme is delicious for poultry or fish.

- Yogurt is a mild acid that blends nicely with cumin, turmeric, curry, cayenne pepper, ginger, paprika, chopped onion, and garlic to coat and flavor kebabs of lamb, chicken, or fish. (See Chapter 8 for the Chicken Tikka marinade, which also works with pork or lamb.)
- Contrary to what's written in many other cookbooks, adding salt to a marinade doesn't compel food to release its natural juices, nor does it cause food to toughen or dry out. Water or liquid flows toward the most dense or concentrated cells in a natural effort to dilute them. The cell walls of the food sitting in the marinade take in mostly liquid and very little salt. So, if you wish, add the salt.

Preparing to marinate

When you're about ready to marinate, select a container that's the proper size and shape. You want the food to fit snugly and be immersed in the liquid. As a general rule, you need about 1 to 2 cups of marinade for every $1^1/_2$ to 2 pounds of food. You want enough marinade to completely surround the food. You can use a mixing bowl for your marinade, but make sure it's glass, ceramic, or plastic, because acidic ingredients and alcohol can react with aluminum and iron pans, giving the meat and liquid a metallic flavor and a gray color.

We think a large, resealable plastic bag works best. Just mix the marinade right in the bag, toss in the food, seal the bag, and chill, turning occasionally. (Check out Figure 5-1.) When using a plastic bag, you don't need as much marinade as you would to cover food in a bowl in which you have to keep turning the food to coat evenly. Foods marinated in a bag also take up less room in your refrigerator.

Using a Plastic Bag to Marinate Food
Place food in a plastic bag.
Pour marinade into the bag.
Press all of the air out of the bag.
fold over
Seal shut, making sure the food is surrounded by the marinade, folding over if necessary.

Figure 5-1: How to successfully marinate food in a plastic bag.

Deciding how long to marinate your food

Most foods, except for delicate fish, vegetables, and certain cuts of tender meat, benefit from several hours of marinating time, and many foods like to stand in the liquid overnight. Turn over the food in the marinade (or flip over the plastic bag) a few times during marinating to moisten all the food surfaces. With beef, lamb, and other red meats, it takes more time for the marinade flavors to penetrate the flesh of the food, so hours or even overnight is best.

Ignore the advice of cookbooks and recipes that instruct you to marinate meat, fish, or poultry at room temperature for 2 to 3 hours before grilling. You can safely marinate meat, fish, or poultry at room temperature for only about 30 minutes; after that, you risk the danger of contamination from airborne bacteria. Be on the safe side and keep foods well chilled in the refrigerator. Grilling chilled meats takes a little longer, but you avoid the possibility of contaminating your food.

Using marinades for basting and finishing

Very often the same marinade that's used to soak the uncooked food can be reheated and poured over the grilled food to serve as a delicious finishing sauce. You can also use leftover marinade as a basting sauce.

However, if any kind of raw fish, meat, or poultry was first soaked in the marinade, it must be heated to boiling and allowed to simmer for 15 minutes to destroy any possible bacteria from the raw food.

Marinades that contain sugar can give a nice caramelized coating to grilled food, but they can also burn very quickly. Indirect cooking is better in these cases. If you're basting, do it just 5 to 10 minutes before the food is cooked through.

Hoisin Marinade and Basting Sauce

Hoisin sauce, which you can find in any major supermarket, is a convenient, versatile product that can add sparkle to many grilled foods — especially ribs, chicken, lamb, and shrimp. It's a mixture of sugar, vinegar, soybeans, chile peppers, and garlic. The sugar content is relatively high, so for best results, use the indirect grilling method (see Chapter 1) to prevent the food from charring.

Preparation time: *15 minutes*

Marinating time: *30 minutes to overnight, depending on the food*

Yield: *About 1 cup*

½ cup fresh orange juice

⅓ cup hoisin sauce

2 tablespoons soy sauce

2 tablespoons peeled and minced fresh ginger

2 teaspoons honey

1 teaspoon sesame oil

Pepper to taste

¼ cup finely chopped scallions (white and green parts)

In a small mixing bowl or measuring cup, whisk together the orange juice, hoisin sauce, soy sauce, ginger, honey, sesame oil, and pepper; stir in the scallions. Use as a marinade and basting sauce for about 2 pounds of pork, lamb, chicken, or shrimp. Marinate meat or poultry for several hours or overnight; marinate shrimp for 30 minutes or less. Grill food indirectly or monitor carefully if grilling over a direct fire, to prevent charring. To use as a finishing sauce, bring any remaining marinade to a boil for 15 minutes in a small saucepan and drizzle over grilled food.

Vary It! *For a simple hoisin barbecue sauce, combine equal parts hoisin sauce, ketchup, and water. Use with chicken, ribs, or shrimp, basting the last 10 to 15 minutes of grilling.*

Spicy Soy and Cilantro Marinade

This marinade is delicious with any cut of beef and also works with chicken, fish, or pork. Any leftover marinade can be boiled for a finishing sauce or tossed into cooked noodles with just enough additional peanut oil and soy sauce to coat. You can use any kind of hot chile pepper, such as jalapeño, serrano, or habañero, but beware — habañero is about as hot as peppers get! Using a red pepper rather than a green one adds a nice contrasting note of color to the finished dish. Cilantro gives a nice vegetal edge and mellows the hotness of the chilies.

Preparation time: *15 minutes*

Marinating time: *30 minutes to overnight, depending on the food*

Yield: *About 1 1/3 cups*

1/2 cup dark soy sauce

1/4 cup plus 2 tablespoons rice vinegar

1/4 cup peanut oil

1/4 cup chopped cilantro (coriander) leaves

4 cloves garlic, peeled and chopped

3 scallions, trimmed and chopped (white and green parts)

1 tablespoon plus 1 teaspoon peeled, grated fresh ginger

2 teaspoons sugar

1 to 2 chile peppers, seeded and finely minced

Combine all the ingredients in a small mixing bowl or measuring cup and pour over 1 1/2 to 2 pounds of meat, chicken, or fish. For best results, marinate fish for 30 minutes to 1 hour and other foods for 6 hours or overnight. Turn the food occasionally during marinating.

Spicy Cinnamon and Soy Marinade

Cinnamon adds an Asian or Middle Eastern spiciness to this marinade while the soy buoys it with a saltiness and slight bitterness to give it a delightful balance. You can see this marinade in the color photo section of this book. There you can also see a grilled piece of marinated chicken on a roll.

Preparation time: *5 minutes*

Marinating time: *4 to 6 hours*

Yield: *1 cup*

2 tablespoons soy sauce

2 tablespoons hoisin sauce

1/2 teaspoon ground cinnamon

1/4 teaspoon ground anise powder

1 teaspoon crushed pepper flakes

Juice of 1 lemon

3 cloves garlic, peeled and minced

1 teaspoon salt

6 tablespoons corn or peanut oil

1 scallion, thinly sliced

In a small bowl, combine all the above ingredients and stir to blend. Use as a marinade for 2 to 3 pounds of chicken, pork, or lamb.

Five Spice and Soy Sauce Marinade

Chinese five spice powder is a form of anise, which gives food a terrific licorice-like scent and flavor. The soy sauce adds salt and the true flavor of the Orient.

Preparation time: *15 minutes*

Marinating time: *4 to 12 hours*

Yield: *1/2 cup*

3 cloves garlic, peeled and minced

2 tablespoons soy sauce

1 teaspoon five spice powder

1 teaspoon crushed pepper flakes

1 tablespoon fish sauce

6 tablespoons corn or peanut oil

1 scallion, chopped

In a small bowl, combine all the ingredients and stir to blend. Use as a marinade for 2 to 3 pounds of chicken, pork, or lamb.

Provençal Marinade

This marinade gives your food the aroma and flavor of Southern France, especially the floral notes of the spices along the Riviera. If possible, obtain fresh herbs for this recipe. And if you can find an olive oil made in France, your dish will be even closer to the real McCoy.

Preparation time: *5 minutes*

Marinating time: *30 minutes*

Yield: *1 cup*

3 cloves garlic, peeled and crushed

3 bay leaves, preferably fresh

1/2 teaspoon thyme leaves, fresh or dried

1/2 teaspoon chopped savory, fresh or dried

1/2 teaspoon crushed red pepper flakes

1/2 teaspoon freshly ground black peppercorns

1 teaspoon salt

1/4 cup white wine

6 tablespoons olive oil

In a small bowl, combine all the ingredients and stir to blend. Use as a marinade for 2 to 3 pounds of chicken, pork, lamb, or beef. Or try as a basting sauce at the end of the cooking time.

Moroccan Marinade

The wonderfully savory (and slightly pungent) spices of North Africa make this one of the most delicious of marinades. Don't worry about them overpowering the dish though; they become milder as the food is cooked.

Preparation time: *8 minutes*

Marinating time: *2 to 3 hours*

Yield: *3/4 cup*

1 small onion, minced
1 teaspoon ground cinnamon
1 teaspoon ground cumin
1/2 teaspoon ground ginger
1/2 teaspoon red pepper flakes
1 teaspoon sugar
1/2 teaspoon freshly ground black peppercorns
1 teaspoon salt
Juice of 1 lemon
6 tablespoons corn or peanut oil

In a small bowl, combine all the ingredients and stir to blend. Use as a marinade for 2 to 3 pounds of chicken, beef, pork, or lamb.

Lime and Cumin Marinade

The heat of this terrific marinade is tamed by the zing of the lime juice, giving it a taste of the tropics. Take a look at the color photo section of this book to see the marinade and a few pieces of marinated and grilled chicken on a stick.

Preparation time: *15 minutes*

Marinating time: *4 to 12 hours*

Yield: *1/2 cup*

Grated zest from 1 lime
Juice of 2 limes
3 cloves garlic, peeled and crushed
1 tablespoon paprika
1 teaspoon ground cumin
1 teaspoon crushed red pepper flakes
1 teaspoon salt
6 tablespoons corn or peanut oil

In a small bowl, combine all the ingredients and stir to blend. Use as a marinade for 2 to 3 pounds of chicken, pork, or lamb.

Cuban-Style Mojo Marinade

Cuban cooks love to add the tangy-sweet flavor of orange and lime juices to many of their foods. They also like cilantro, but if you don't like the flavor it brings, feel free to omit it (or you can strain it out after marinating). In the color photo section of this book, we show this marinade along with some marinated and grilled flank steaks.

Preparation time: *15 minutes*

Marinating time: *2 to 4 hours or overnight*

Yield: *1/2 cup*

Juice of 2 limes

Juice of 1 orange

1 tablespoon fresh oregano, chopped, or 1/2 teaspoon dried

6 cloves garlic, peeled and well crushed

1/2 teaspoon coarsely ground black pepper

1 teaspoon salt

6 tablespoons corn or peanut oil

1/3 cup cilantro (coriander) leaves, chopped

In a small bowl, combine all the ingredients and stir to blend. Use as a marinade for 2 to 3 pounds of flank or skirt steak.

Greek Marinade

Fresh Mediterranean oregano is more subtle than most and is a great choice for this marinade, but any dried oregano is fine to use if you can't get fresh flowers of the Mediterranean variety. Greek cuisine uses sauces and marinades with these simple ingredients on numerous dishes just to add a single herbal note along with the sweet pungency of the onion and the mollifying effect of the oil and lemon.

Preparation time: *5 minutes*

Marinating time: *4 hours*

Yield: *1/2 cup*

1 small onion, minced

Juice of 1 lemon

2 teaspoons oregano, fresh or dried

1 teaspoon freshly ground black pepper

1 teaspoon salt

6 tablespoons olive oil

In a small bowl, combine all the ingredients and stir to blend. Use as a marinade for 2 to 3 pounds of chicken, lamb, or pork.

Gingery Grilled Vegetable Marinade

This vegetable marinade combines soy sauce, ginger, and sesame oil with the zing of Tabasco sauce. It's especially delicious with tomatoes, onions, summer squash (zucchini or yellow squash), and mushrooms. However, it clashes with the bitterness of eggplant, so choose vegetables with an element of sweetness, and you won't go wrong. Plum or Roma tomatoes work especially well.

Preparation time: *25 minutes*

Marinating time: *30 minutes to 1 hour*

Yield: *1 cup*

1/2 cup white wine vinegar

1/3 cup light soy sauce

6 tablespoons olive oil

2 tablespoons sesame oil

2 tablespoons fresh ginger, peeled and minced

1 tablespoon brown sugar, packed

2 large cloves garlic, peeled and minced

2 teaspoons Tabasco sauce

Salt and pepper to taste

6 to 7 cups sliced vegetables

1 In a medium mixing bowl or glass measuring cup, make the marinade by combining all the ingredients except the vegetables.

2 Place the sliced vegetables in a 1-gallon, resealable plastic bag or other large container; pour the marinade over the vegetables in the bag or container.

3 Press the air out of the bag and seal tightly, or cover the container. Refrigerate for 30 minutes to 1 hour, turning the bag over once or occasionally tossing the vegetables in the container. Marinate vegetables in the bag for 30 minutes. The marinade may be used as a basting sauce too.

4 Grill over a medium-hot fire. Grilling time will depend on the thickness of the vegetables. (See Chapter 17 for more information on grilling vegetables.)

Go-With: *Arrange these attractive veggies on a large platter, surrounding grilled fish, meat, poultry, or pork. Or try tossing them into hot, steamy pasta or a green salad. Leftovers can be diced up into a tasty relish for hot dogs, hamburgers, and grilled steaks.*

Flavoring with Oils: The Slick Solution

Sometimes all you need to boost the flavor of tender cuts of meat, boneless poultry, or delicate fish is a light brushing of oil, to which you have added chopped herbs, a little garlic, or a few spices. Oils have a way of insulating the foods from being burned and keeping them moist. Never pour oil on food, though, because it may flare up. Instead, always use a brush. After you've created your flavorful oil, refrigerate it for 1 to 2 hours (or even less, if you don't have the time).

Be sure to discard all unused oil. In a short time, the fresh ingredients you add to the oil become a breeding ground for harmful bacteria, so toss it out as soon as you've finished coating the food.

Use any of the following oils to generously brush $1\frac{1}{2}$ to 2 pounds of steak, chicken, fish, or pork. Brush both sides before grilling.

- **Lemon-Rosemary Oil:** You infuse this oil with rosemary and other seasonings by pureeing all the ingredients in a blender. Blend until smooth the following ingredients: 6 tablespoons olive oil, $\frac{1}{4}$ cup minced rosemary leaves, 3 cloves peeled and crushed garlic, 2 teaspoons lemon juice, and 2 teaspoons grated lemon peel. Because you must make this oil with fresh rosemary, you may decide to plant a rosemary pot in a sunny outdoor spot, or even indoors on a kitchen windowsill.

  Go-With: Brush this oil on about 2 pounds of sirloin steaks, or tender beef kebabs; on fish fillets or fish steaks; on boneless chicken breasts; or on sea scallop kebabs. Grill over a medium to medium-hot fire.

- **Ginger-Soy Oil:** Whisk together $\frac{1}{4}$ cup peanut or vegetable oil, 2 tablespoons soy sauce, 1 tablespoon sesame oil, 1 tablespoon peeled and grated ginger (or $\frac{1}{2}$ teaspoon ground ginger), 1 clove peeled and crushed garlic, and salt and pepper to taste.

  Go-With: This oil is delicious brushed on $1\frac{1}{2}$ to 2 pounds of tender beef cuts, chicken or turkey parts, or fish.

- **Mustard-Worcestershire Oil:** Spoon $\frac{1}{4}$ cup Dijon-style mustard in a small mixing bowl. Add $\frac{1}{2}$ cup olive oil in a slow, steady stream, beating constantly with a fork or wire whisk to blend the mustard into the oil until the sauce is smooth and creamy. Whisk in 2 teaspoons Worcestershire sauce (or more or less to taste). Season to taste with salt and pepper.

  Go-With: Brush this sharp, mustard-flavored oil on pieces of chicken, fish, pork, or tender cuts of lamb or beef before grilling.

Rub-a-Dub-Dub: Coating Foods with Dry Rubs

Rubs are usually a dry combination of herbs and spices, although sometimes a little oil is added to moisten the mixture. You simply massage rubs onto the surface of the food and end up with a wonderful crispy crust. Cooking with rubs is beneficial because:

- **Rubs can be added at the last minute.** It's best to give a rub at least 30 minutes (preferably several hours or overnight) to penetrate and flavor meat, but if you don't have the luxury of time, you can still get good results — unlike with marinades, which sometimes need hours to penetrate the meat.
- **Rubs usually contain little or no oil and therefore little fat.** Flare-ups on the grill are eliminated and your waist line will thank you.
- **Rubs stick to the surface of foods better than marinades.** They form a tasty crusty exterior that complements the food's interior flavors.

Small tender pieces of fish or shellfish will benefit from about 30 minutes of standing time after applying a rub. A whole, spice-rubbed turkey or chicken should be plastic-wrapped to hold the rub tightly against its skin and then refrigerated overnight.

The amount of rub used to cover the surface of a piece of meat is entirely a matter of taste, but our rule calls for about 1 tablespoon for every pound of food. To help the rub cling to the food's surface, apply it to food that's either completely dry or coated with a little oil. When seasoning poultry, spread the rub evenly over the surface and also under the skin as much as possible, being careful not to tear it.

Rub mixtures often call for crushed whole spices. You can best accomplish this task with a mortar and pestle; but if you don't have this kitchen tool, place the spices in a plastic bag and pound them with a rolling pin or a meat mallet until finely crushed. You also may use a food processor or even a coffee grinder. However, make sure the residue and oils from the ground coffee are completely removed from the grinder or they will flavor the rub ingredients.

Rubs that are completely dry, without any oil or liquid ingredient, can be stored indefinitely in airtight containers in a cool, dry place.

Hot and Sweet Spice Rub

This rub gives an interesting sweet and spicy flavor to all kinds of meat, especially lamb.

Preparation time: *5 minutes*

Marinating time: *30 minutes to 1 hour*

Yield: *2 tablespoons*

2 teaspoons hot chili powder, like cayenne

1 teaspoon paprika

1 teaspoon brown sugar, firmly packed

$^1/_2$ teaspoon flour

$^1/_2$ teaspoon garlic salt

$^1/_4$ teaspoon ground cinnamon

$^1/_4$ teaspoon ground allspice

Pinch of pepper

Kosher or table salt (optional)

Combine all the ingredients and use as a rub for 2 to 2$^1/_2$ pounds of beef, poultry, or pork. Coat the food lightly with oil before applying the rub. Sprinkle the grilled food lightly with additional kosher or table salt before serving (if desired).

Cajun-Style Steak Rub

This is an all-purpose rub for tender steak cuts that need no marinating. Try it on sirloin, T-bone, porterhouse, tenderloin, and ribeye. It's also excellent on venison. (See Chapter 11 for more on beef cuts.)

Preparation time: *5 minutes*

Marinating time: *20 to 30 minutes*

Yield: *Enough for about 2 pounds of meat*

1 tablespoon olive oil

3 cloves garlic, peeled and minced (about 1 tablespoon)

1$^1/_2$ teaspoons chili powder

$^3/_4$ teaspoon ground cumin

$^3/_4$ teaspoon dried thyme leaves

$^3/_4$ teaspoon dried oregano leaves

$^1/_4$ teaspoon cayenne pepper

$^1/_4$ teaspoon black pepper

$^1/_4$ teaspoon salt

Combine all the ingredients in a small bowl. Using your fingers, generously rub the mixture on both sides of the steaks; cover with plastic wrap and let stand for 20 to 30 minutes as the grill preheats. Grill over medium heat until done as desired. Season with additional salt after grilling (if desired).

Peppery Dried Herb Rub

One of the charms of rub recipes is that they're flexible — they can be altered to satisfy your individual taste. For example, you can increase the spiciness in this rub by adding ground white pepper or additional cayenne pepper. For a touch of sweetness, you can add a little dark brown sugar. If you don't like thyme, eliminate it and substitute another herb, like dried marjoram. Or use freshly grated orange peel instead of lemon peel. It works well with any kind of meat, especially pork.

Preparation time: *10 minutes*

Marinating time: *30 minutes*

Yield: *About 3 tablespoons, or enough for about 1½ to 2 pounds of meat*

1 tablespoon paprika

2 teaspoons grated lemon peel (from about 1 lemon)

1 teaspoon garlic powder

1 teaspoon cayenne pepper

½ teaspoon ground thyme

½ teaspoon dried oregano leaves

¾ teaspoon salt, or to taste

¼ teaspoon freshly ground black pepper

Vegetable or olive oil

Combine all the ingredients except the vegetable or olive oil in a small bowl. Brush the meat generously with the vegetable or olive oil on all sides, and then rub the spice mixture onto the meat with your fingers. Cover the meat with plastic wrap or place it in a resealable bag and refrigerate 30 minutes or more before grilling.

Peppery Parsley Rub for Tender Steaks

In this recipe, 1 tablespoon of crushed black peppercorns gives a subtle peppery flavor. To kick up the heat, add an extra 1/2 to 1 tablespoon of peppercorns.

Preparation time: *15 minutes*

Marinating time: *30 minutes*

Yield: *1/3 cup*

6 tablespoons finely chopped Italian parsley

4 large cloves garlic, peeled and minced (about 4 teaspoons)

1 tablespoon (or more, if desired) whole black peppercorns, crushed

2 tablespoons olive oil

2 teaspoons dried basil

2 teaspoons grated lemon peel

1/4 teaspoon salt, or to taste

1 In a small mixing bowl, combine the parsley, garlic, crushed peppercorns, olive oil, dried basil, and lemon peel.

2 Rub the mixture generously on both sides of the steaks. Wrap the steaks in plastic and refrigerate for 30 minutes or until ready to grill.

Five Spice Asian Rub

Five spice powder is an aromatic mixture of equal parts cinnamon, cloves, fennel seed, star anise, and sometimes ginger or crushed Szechwan peppercorns. Commercial blends of five spice powder are available in Asian markets and many supermarket spice sections.

One batch of this recipe is enough rub for about a pound of steak. You can double or triple the ingredients to cover more food. It's also an excellent rub for pork and poultry.

Preparation time: *10 minutes*

Marinating time: *30 minutes to 2 hours*

Yield: *1/3 cup*

2 teaspoons five spice powder

2 cloves garlic, peeled and minced

2 teaspoons vegetable oil

1/4 teaspoon salt

Pepper to taste

In a small mixing bowl, combine the five spice powder, garlic, oil, and salt and pepper. Using your fingers, generously rub the spice mixture on both sides of the food and then place the rubbed food on a large shallow plate. Cover and refrigerate for 30 minutes to 2 hours.

Coriander and Fennel Rub

This is an ideal Mediterranean-style rub. It has only a few flavors and subtle ones at that, which makes it great for poultry and seafood, especially shrimp. See this rub and a rubbed and grilled pork tenderloin in the color photo section of this book.

Preparation time: *5 minutes*

Marinating time: *1 hour or overnight*

Yield: *1 1/2 tablespoons*

1 tablespoon ground coriander seeds

3/4 teaspoon ground fennel seeds

1/4 teaspoon hot ground chili powder

1/2 teaspoon dried thyme

1 1/2 teaspoon salt

Combine all the ingredients and use as a rub for 2 to 2 1/2 pounds of beef, poultry, or pork. Coat the food lightly with oil before applying. Let rest in refrigerator for at least 1 hour or even overnight.

Middle Eastern Rub

The aromas that this rub will produce on the grill will cause major salivating by your guests (or family). It has many levels of spice flavors that meld beautifully together and give a lot of taste to red meat and chicken. The flavors are probably too much for seafood. The turmeric gives the meat a lovely golden-orange color. Be careful to keep the heat somewhat low or grill indirectly, because these spices can easily burn.

Preparation time: *5 minutes*

Marinating time: *1 hour or overnight*

Yield: *2 tablespoons*

1 tablespoon ground coriander seeds

1 teaspoon turmeric

1 teaspoon ground ginger

½ teaspoon ground cinnamon

1 teaspoon freshly ground black pepper

1½ teaspoon salt

Combine all ingredients and use as a rub for 2 to 2½ pounds of beef, poultry, or pork. Coat the food lightly with oil before applying the rub. After rubbing, let the food rest in refrigerator for at least 1 hour or even overnight.

Chapter 6

The Saucy Side of Grilling

In This Chapter

- Serving up savory sauces
- Concocting classic condiments
- Creating compound butters

Recipes in This Chapter

- Roasted Garlic and Red Pepper Puree
- Mushroom-Butter Sauce
- Ginger Cream
- Mustard and Rosemary Grilled Chicken Sauce
- Tarragon Sauce
- Creamy Asian Peanut Sauce
- Raita
- Creamy Horseradish Sauce
- Tahini Dressing
- Teriyaki Sauce
- Fresh Tomato Salsa
- Roasted Sweet Pepper Salsa
- Black Bean and Red Pepper Salsa
- Sun-Dried Tomato and Basil Mayonnaise
- Tomato Chutney
- Summer Squash Chutney
- Cherry and Pear Chutney
- Tapenade
- Guacamole
- Barbecued Onions
- Compound Butter

Every grilling chef needs an arsenal of recipes for sauces and condiments, such as salsas, chutneys, and compound butters. All these concoctions elevate a humble steak, grilled chicken, pork chop, or hamburger into something sublime. You can prepare many of these recipes ahead of time and store them in the refrigerator, thereby allowing you to focus your full attention on the grill. All of them complement the unique flavors of grilled foods while adding taste, color, and pizzazz.

Adding Flavor with Warm Sauces

When you grill, the wonderful cooking juices that ordinarily end up in the pan (with top-of-stove or oven roasting techniques) are lost into the fire. To compensate for this sad fact, grilling gurus — like yourself — keep a file of quick and easy sauces that add a last-minute finish to that sizzling steak, chop, piece of chicken, or fish fillet. In this section, we give you a few of our favorite recipes for warm sauces you can serve with all kinds of grilled foods. These recipes only make a few servings of sauce, so if you're feeding a crowd, be sure to double or even triple the recipe.

Roasted Garlic and Red Pepper Puree

Pureed vegetable sauces made from blends of tomatoes, cucumbers, greens like watercress or arugula, and a binding ingredient like yogurt, sour cream, olive oil, or mayonnaise are wonderful accompaniments to fresh grilled fish fillets. They're easy to assemble in the blender and often give plain-looking fish a lovely ribbon of color.

Preparation time: *10 minutes*

Grilling time: *15 to 20 minutes*

Yield: *About 1 cup (approximately 8 servings at 2 tablespoons per serving)*

2 large sweet red peppers

1 head of garlic with skin

1 tablespoon butter

¼ cup light cream or half-and-half

Salt and pepper to taste

1 Prepare a hot fire in a gas or charcoal grill.

2 Place the peppers and head of garlic directly on an oiled grill.

3 Grill the garlic cloves for 8 to 10 minutes or until their papery skin is lightly browned and the flesh is soft, turning once. Remove from the grid. Cool slightly and press the cloves out of their skin. Set 4 to 5 cloves aside.

4 Grill the peppers for a total of 15 to 20 minutes, turning every 5 to 10 minutes, until their skin is completely blackened all over. Immediately place the peppers in a brown paper bag and let them stand for 10 minutes to steam off their skin.

5 When the peppers are cool enough to handle, use a paring knife to peel, core, and remove the seeds (see Figure 6-1). (If the skin doesn't slip off easily, grill the pepper for a few minutes more.) Cut the peppers into large pieces and place in a blender container with the roasted and peeled garlic cloves; puree until smooth. (For a terrific low-calorie sauce with plenty of flavor, stop at this point. Serve the sauce over grilled fish or chicken.)

6 In a small skillet, melt the butter over medium-low heat. Add the pureed pepper mixture and the light cream or half-and-half. Cook, stirring constantly, 1 minute or just until warmed through. Remove from heat and season to taste with salt and pepper. Spoon over grilled fish fillets or fish steaks.

Per serving: *Calories 36 (From Fat 21); Fat 2g (Saturated 1g); Cholesterol 7mg; Sodium 77mg; Carbohydrate 4g (Dietary Fiber 1g); Protein 1g.*

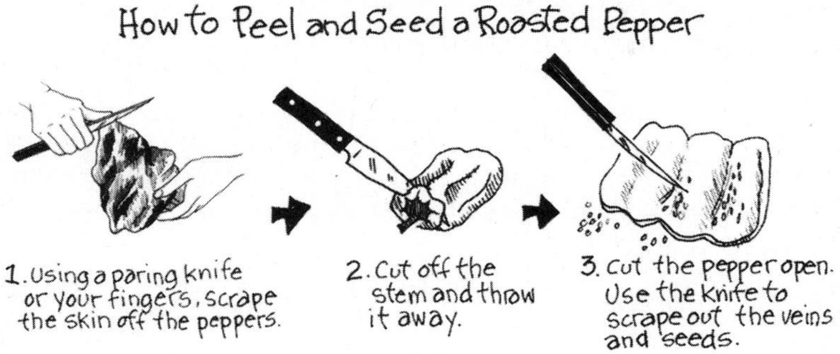
How to Peel and Seed a Roasted Pepper
1. Using a paring knife or your fingers, scrape the skin off the peppers.
2. Cut off the stem and throw it away.
3. Cut the pepper open. Use the knife to scrape out the veins and seeds.

Figure 6-1: How to peel and seed a roasted pepper.

Mushroom-Butter Sauce

This classic butter sauce is a delicious accompaniment to beef or other savory meats or vegetables. Of course, it's great on pasta, too! The shallots give it a nice little kick.

Preparation time: *5 minutes*

Cook time: *20 minutes*

Yield: *2½ cups (approximately 20 servings at 2 tablespoons per serving)*

2 tablespoons butter

1 tablespoon vegetable oil

3 tablespoons peeled and finely chopped shallots

1½ cups chicken broth

⅓ cup finely chopped mushrooms (button, shitake, or a combination)

1 tablespoon finely chopped fresh parsley

1 In a small saucepan or skillet, melt the butter and oil over medium heat. Add the shallots and cook for 2 minutes or until they're softened and lightly browned.

2 Add the chicken broth and boil the mixture gently for 10 minutes, stirring occasionally. Add the mushrooms and cook for another 3 to 5 minutes or until the mixture is reduced by half and has thickened slightly. Remove the mixture from the heat and sprinkle with the parsley. This sauce can be prepared ahead and held in the refrigerator for several hours or days. Reheat in a small saucepan or skillet, over low heat, just before serving.

Per serving: *Calories 26 (From Fat 24); Fat 3g (Saturated 1g); Cholesterol 4mg; Sodium 94mg; Carbohydrate 0g (Dietary Fiber 0g); Protein 0g.*

Ginger Cream

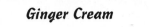

Ginger Cream is a delicious finishing sauce for grilled swordfish, salmon fillets, or shrimp. It has a light pungency and sweetness from the mix of ginger and tomato, and the cream adds a lovely texture that goes especially well with seafood of every kind. If it's more convenient for you, make this sauce in advance, refrigerate, and gently reheat in the top of a double boiler.

Preparation time: *5 minutes*

Cooking time: *10 minutes*

Yield: *About 1¼ cups (approximately 10 servings at 2 tablespoons per serving)*

½ cup dry white wine

½ cup chicken broth

2 tablespoons peeled and minced shallots

2 teaspoons peeled and grated fresh ginger, or ¾ teaspoon ground ginger

⅓ cup seeded and finely chopped tomato

1 cup heavy cream

½ teaspoon grated lemon peel

Salt and pepper to taste

1 In a medium saucepan, combine the wine, chicken broth, shallots, and ginger. Bring to a boil over medium-high heat; boil, uncovered, for several minutes until reduced to about half its volume.

2 Add the tomato and cream; return to a gentle boil over medium heat and cook until thickened and reduced to about 1¼ cups, stirring and occasionally scraping the bottom of the pan with a wooden spoon. Remove from heat and stir in the lemon peel; adjust seasoning with salt and pepper.

Vary It! *For a mustard-flavored sauce, omit the ginger and add 1 to 2 teaspoons of Dijon-style mustard. For a saffron-flavored sauce, omit the ginger and stir in 4 to 5 threads of saffron with the tomatoes and cream.*

Per serving: *Calories 90 (From Fat 81); Fat 9g (Saturated 6g); Cholesterol 33mg; Sodium 118mg; Carbohydrate 2g (Dietary Fiber 0g); Protein 1g.*

Mustard and Rosemary Grilled Chicken Sauce

This basting sauce works well with any grilled chicken — especially if the chicken has been brined. (See Chapter 14 for brining details.) However, if you choose not to brine, be sure to sprinkle the chicken pieces with salt before grilling. This sauce is also good with quail and turkey.

Preparation time: *10 minutes*

Cook time: *2 minutes*

Yield: *About ½ cup (approximately 4 servings at 2 tablespoons per serving)*

¼ cup butter

2 medium cloves garlic, peeled and minced

¼ cup Dijon-style mustard

3 tablespoons chopped fresh rosemary leaves, or 1 tablespoon crumbled dried rosemary

Pepper to taste

1 Warm the butter in a small saucepan over low heat and, before the butter is completely melted, add the garlic; cook for about 30 seconds, being careful not to let either the butter or the garlic brown. Remove from the heat immediately; stir in the mustard, rosemary, and pepper.

2 Divide the sauce in half, reserving about ¼ cup to serve with the grilled chicken. Brush the other half generously on the chicken during the last 4 to 5 minutes of grilling.

Per serving: *Calories 124 (From Fat 115); Fat 13g (Saturated 7g); Cholesterol 31mg; Sodium 381mg; Carbohydrate 3g (Dietary Fiber 1g); Protein 1g.*

Tarragon Sauce

This sauce, the essence of summer itself, is delicious with chicken, veal, fish, and vegetables. It can be made in advance, but the tarragon should be thoroughly rinsed, dried, and chopped just before serving because it loses its aroma quickly. We recommend using *only* fresh tarragon, because that spice's aroma and flavor are altered in the drying process.

Preparation time: *15 minutes*

Yield: *About ½ cup (approximately 4 servings at 2 tablespoons per serving)*

2 tablespoons minced shallots

2 tablespoons sherry vinegar

¼ teaspoon salt

1 tablespoon Dijon-style mustard

½ cup olive oil

2 tablespoons mayonnaise

2 tablespoons thinly sliced chives

1½ tablespoons chopped fresh tarragon

Freshly ground pepper

In a medium-size bowl, combine the shallots, vinegar, and salt and let stand for 5 minutes. Add the mustard and whisk to blend. Slowly add the olive oil, whisking continually to produce a creamy consistency. Then add the mayonnaise and whisk to incorporate. Add the pepper, tarragon, and chives. This sauce can be made hours ahead, but add the tarragon just before it is to be served. Serve at room temperature.

Per serving: *Calories 199 (From Fat 197); Fat 22g (Saturated 3g); Cholesterol 3mg; Sodium 187mg; Carbohydrate 1g (Dietary Fiber 0g); Protein 0g.*

Creamy Asian Peanut Sauce

This sauce recipe, flavored with peanut butter, is especially good drizzled over grilled pork chops. Use it to baste pork or chicken kebabs, or use it as a rich and elegant finishing sauce for grilled pork tenderloin. You can also use it as a sauce for a side dish of noodles (Chinese egg noodles, Japanese noodles, or linguine are best). You can refrigerate this sauce for several days, up to a week, and it can be heated or served at room temperature.

Preparation time: *20 minutes*

Yield: *About 1 cup (approximately 8 servings at 2 tablespoons per serving)*

2 tablespoons soy sauce
2 tablespoons dry sherry
2 tablespoons creamy peanut butter
1 tablespoon fresh ginger, peeled and grated
2 teaspoons sugar
2 teaspoons honey
2 cloves garlic, peeled and minced
¼ teaspoon crushed red pepper flakes
¼ cup peanut or vegetable oil
4 scallions, both white and green parts, chopped
Pepper to taste

In a small bowl or measuring cup, whisk together the soy sauce, sherry, peanut butter, ginger, sugar, honey, garlic, and red pepper flakes. Slowly add the oil in a steady stream, whisking as you pour, until the sauce is smooth and creamy. Stir in the scallions and black pepper.

Vary It! *If you want to serve this sauce over noodles, prepare the pasta and reserve 2 tablespoons of the boiling water before draining. Drain the noodles and transfer them back to the pasta pot; add the sauce and, only if necessary, add 1 to 2 tablespoons of the reserved noodle liquid. Add only enough liquid to help bind the sauce to the noodles, but not so much that the sauce becomes thin and watery.*

Per serving: *Calories 102 (From Fat 82); Fat 9g (Saturated 1g); Cholesterol 0mg; Sodium 250mg; Carbohydrate 4g (Dietary Fiber 1g); Protein 2g.*

Chillin' Out: Working with Cold Sauces

Cold sauces are in many ways traditional to various ethnic foods, but there really is a reason they're served cold: In hot weather and hot climates like the Mediterranean, India, and Southeast Asia, they have a cooling effect on the palate while adding flavor to the hot grilled food.

Raita

No Middle Eastern, Indian, or Pakistani appetizer or main course would be complete without a cooling yogurt-based sauce. The cucumber adds a pleasing vegetal flavor while the mint gives it piquancy. Use it as a dipping sauce or drizzle it over fish, poultry, or meats, especially kebabs.

Preparation: *45 minutes*

Chilling time: *1 hour*

Yield: *About 2 cups (approximately 16 servings at 2 tablespoons per serving)*

2 small cucumbers, peeled, seeded, and grated

2 teaspoons salt

1½ cups plain yogurt, preferably Greek style

½ teaspoon ground cumin

½ seeded and minced jalapeño pepper or to taste

1 tablespoon chopped fresh mint leaves

1½ tablespoons chopped fresh cilantro (coriander) leaves

¼ teaspoon freshly ground black pepper

¼ teaspoon salt

1. In a colander, add cucumbers and sprinkle with 2 teaspoons salt. Mix and let sit and drain for 30 minutes. After draining, place cucumbers on paper towels and pat dry.
2. Meanwhile, roast the ground cumin by placing it in a small fry pan and keeping it over medium-low heat until it starts to smell roasted, about 6 minutes. Remove the pan from the heat immediately.
3. In a medium bowl, toss the drained cucumber, yogurt, roasted cumin, jalapeño, mint, cilantro, black pepper, and salt. Refrigerate for 1 hour.

Per serving: *Calories 17 (From Fat 7); Fat 1g (Saturated 0g); Cholesterol 3mg; Sodium 340mg; Carbohydrate 2g (Dietary Fiber 0g); Protein 1g.*

Creamy Horseradish Sauce

This sauce, which combines sour cream, horseradish, fresh lemon juice, and ripe chopped tomatoes, is terrific with grilled sausage, fish steaks, shellfish, burgers, or poultry.

Preparation time: *10 minutes*

Yield: *About ⅔ cup (approximately 5 servings at 2 tablespoons per serving)*

½ cup sour cream

¼ cup chopped ripe tomatoes

2 tablespoons bottled horseradish, drained

1 tablespoon mayonnaise

2 teaspoons fresh lemon juice

Pepper to taste

Combine all the ingredients in a small bowl; cover and chill until ready to serve.

Per serving: *Calories 67 (From Fat 60); Fat 7g (Saturated 3g); Cholesterol 11mg; Sodium 0mg; Carbohydrate 2g (Dietary Fiber 0g); Protein 1g.*

Tahini Dressing

Tahini, a paste made from sesame seeds, is an important ingredient in Middle Eastern cuisine. This recipe combines tahini with lemon juice and honey into a semi-sweet, nutty dressing that you can drizzle over grilled chicken, turkey, lamb, beef, or vegetables. Or you can use it as a dressing for sandwich wraps made with flour tortillas, grilled chicken, chopped tomatoes, and shredded lettuce. If you want a more tart lemon taste, use only 2 teaspoons of honey rather than 1 tablespoon.

Preparation time: *10 minutes*

Yield: *About ½ cup (approximately 4 servings at 2 tablespoons per serving)*

¼ cup tahini

1 tablespoon fresh lemon juice

1 tablespoon honey

1 teaspoon olive oil

3 to 4 tablespoons water

½ teaspoon grated lemon peel

Salt and pepper

In a blender, combine the tahini, lemon juice, honey, oil, and as much water as necessary to make a smooth, thick dressing. Transfer to a small bowl; stir in the grated lemon peel and season with salt and pepper. This dressing can be covered and stored in the refrigerator for up to 2 weeks.

Per serving: *Calories 116 (From Fat 82); Fat 9g (Saturated 1g); Cholesterol 0mg; Sodium 151mg; Carbohydrate 8g (Dietary Fiber 1g); Protein 3g.*

Teriyaki Sauce

Teriyaki sauce is by tradition used on beef by Japanese cooks, but it's just as good on pork, chicken, and seafood. You can use it either as a finishing sauce (as in this recipe), or you can use it more traditionally — as a sauce reduced to a sweet glaze. You can make it thicker simply by cooking it down in a saucepan for a few minutes. It caramelizes quickly, so keep stirring until you get the consistency you desire.

Preparation: *2 minutes*

Cooking: *3 minutes*

Yield: *1 cup (approximately 8 servings at 2 tablespoons per serving)*

⅓ cup soy sauce

⅓ cup mirin rice wine or sweet sake

⅓ cup sake

1 tablespoon sugar

1 small clove garlic, crushed (optional)

In a saucepan, combine the soy sauce, mirin, sake, sugar, and garlic (if desired). Bring the mixture to a boil and simmer for 3 minutes until syrupy. Let the mixture cool, remove the garlic, if used, and refrigerate until ready to use. The sauce will keep for several days, even weeks in the refrigerator.

Per serving: *Calories 55 (From Fat 0); Fat 0g (Saturated 0g); Cholesterol 0mg; Sodium 607mg; Carbohydrate 3g (Dietary Fiber 0g); Protein 1g.*

Complementing Foods with Condiments

Bottled ketchup, mustard, relish, and tomato salsa are the most popular condiments on any griller's table, and we think that using only those standbys is a mistake. So this section takes you to a new level of grilling greatness with recipes for homemade salsas, flavored mayonnaise dressings, savory pastes, and easy chutneys. Before you run screaming from the room, clutching the ketchup bottle to your chest, why not try a couple?

Salsas

Salsa is the Mexican word for sauce and can denote a combination of cold or hot ingredients. We use salsa in this book as a condiment or as a savory mixture of chopped, fresh, cold ingredients. Fresh salsas take little time to prepare, are a lot more flavorful and viscous than the jarred variety, and are colorful companions to grilled dishes of every kind. And, of course, they're great dips for tortilla chips!

Fresh Tomato Salsa

Fortunately for us, juicy, ripe tomatoes come to market just when the grilling season really kicks into gear.

Preparation time: *15 minutes*

Yield: *About 2 cups (approximately 8 servings at ¼ cup per serving)*

2 large ripe tomatoes, seeded and diced

1 small onion, peeled and diced

1 clove garlic, peeled and minced

3 tablespoons chopped fresh cilantro (coriander) or parsley

½ to 1 jalapeño pepper, seeded and chopped

1½ tablespoons olive oil

Juice of half a lime

Salt and pepper to taste

Tabasco sauce to taste

In a small mixing bowl, combine all the ingredients. Cover and let stand at room temperature for at least 15 minutes before serving. It will keep in the refrigerator for 3 to 5 days.

Go-With: *You must try this salsa with our Best-Ever Fajitas recipe in Chapter 17. It's also good with plain, grilled fish (Chapter 15) or chicken (Chapter 14).*

Vary It! *For salsa with a twist, substitute 2 tablespoons tequila for the lime juice in the original recipe.*

Per serving: *Calories 35 (From Fat 24); Fat 3g (Saturated 0g); Cholesterol 0mg; Sodium 77mg; Carbohydrate 3g (Dietary Fiber 1g); Protein 1g.*

Roasted Sweet Pepper Salsa

Make up a batch of this roasted pepper salsa on the weekend so you can serve it as a side dish for grilled meats, fish, and poultry the rest of the week.

Preparation time: *15 minutes*

Marinating time: *1 hour*

Grilling time: *20 to 25 minutes*

Yield: *About 2 cups (approximately 4 servings at ½ cup per serving)*

2 red bell peppers

1 green bell pepper

1 yellow bell pepper

¼ cup extra-virgin olive oil

1 tablespoon balsamic vinegar

1 to 2 tablespoons capers, rinsed and drained

1 tablespoon chopped fresh Italian parsley

1 large clove garlic, peeled and minced

Salt and pepper to taste

1 Prepare a medium-hot fire in a covered charcoal or gas grill.

2 Place the peppers on a lightly oiled grid. Grill, covered, for 20 to 25 minutes or until blackened all over, giving them a quarter turn every 6 to 8 minutes or when the side facing the heat blackens. Place the peppers in a paper bag; close the bag and let stand for 10 minutes to steam and loosen the skins.

3 Using a paring knife, core and seed the peppers (see Figure 6-1); slice into thin strips about 2 inches long and ½-inch wide and place in a medium mixing bowl.

4 In a small mixing bowl, whisk together the olive oil and vinegar. Stir in the capers, parsley, garlic, and salt and pepper. Pour the dressing over the roasted peppers. Cover and refrigerate for at least 1 hour to mellow the flavors. (The peppers are best if made a day ahead.) Serve with everything from burgers to grilled fish.

Vary It! *You can substitute 2 to 3 tablespoons chopped, oil-packed sun-dried tomatoes for the capers. You also can add 2 tablespoons pignoli, or pine nuts, that have been toasted in a dry skillet until lightly browned.*

Per serving: *Calories 168 (From Fat 125); Fat 14g (Saturated 2g); Cholesterol 0mg; Sodium 214mg; Carbohydrate 11g (Dietary Fiber 3g); Protein 2g.*

Black Bean and Red Pepper Salsa

This salsa is such a pretty mix of colors. It's the best kind of recipe to make — easy and terrific. The black beans give it extra texture and the red pepper gives it a kick!

Preparation time: *35 minutes*

Yield: *About 2½ cups (approximately 10 servings at ¼ cup per serving)*

1 15-ounce can black beans, rinsed and well drained

½ cup diced red bell pepper

⅓ cup peeled and chopped red onion

½ to 1 small jalapeño pepper, seeded and finely diced

2 tablespoons chopped fresh cilantro (coriander) or parsley

Juice of 1 lime (about 1½ tablespoons)

2 tablespoons olive oil

1 large clove garlic, peeled and minced

Pinch of sugar

Salt and pepper to taste

In a medium, nonreactive mixing bowl, combine all the ingredients. Cover and chill until ready to use. Serve with grilled fish, poultry, beef, or pork. It will keep in the refrigerator for 4 to 5 days.

Per serving: *Calories 56 (From Fat 26); Fat 3g (Saturated 0g); Cholesterol 0mg; Sodium 168mg; Carbohydrate 6g (Dietary Fiber 2g); Protein 2g.*

Mayonnaise

Mayonnaise can be flavored with any number of ingredients and transformed into a simple finishing sauce for grilled fish. Try adding these ingredients to suit your taste:

- Grated lemon peel
- Dijon-style mustard
- Balsamic vinegar
- Chopped fresh herbs, such as tarragon or dill
- Grated fresh ginger
- Horseradish
- Plain yogurt
- Pureed roasted garlic

Sun-Dried Tomato and Basil Mayonnaise

This recipe has more uses than we can list. It's great in macaroni or grilled chicken salads, as a garnish for grilled chicken or fish, or as a spread for sandwiches stuffed with grilled vegetables.

Preparation time: *10 minutes*

Yield: *About ½ cup (approximately 8 servings at 1 tablespoon per serving)*

½ cup mayonnaise

2 tablespoons oil-packed sun-dried tomatoes, drained and coarsely chopped

1 tablespoon chopped fresh basil leaves

1 teaspoon fresh lemon juice

Pepper to taste

Combine all the ingredients in a blender or food processor. Puree until smooth, stopping as necessary to scrape down the sides of the container.

Per serving: *Calories 103 (From Fat 101); Fat 11g (Saturated 2g); Cholesterol 8mg; Sodium 83mg; Carbohydrate 1g (Dietary Fiber 0g); Protein 0g.*

Chutneys

Chutney is a condiment of Indian origin containing fruits or vegetables, vinegar, sugar, and spices. It's also called "Indian pickle." In that vast country are thousands of recipes both wet and dry for these savory-sweet-sour condiments. In the 19th century chutneys were bottled and exported to Great Britain, where they became popular with curry dishes, as they are everywhere now. They're usually served at room temperature, and the best, of course, are homemade, like ours. They go well with highly spiced grilled items because the sourness and sweetness cut the heat.

Tomato Chutney

This recipe treats tomatoes like the fruits that they are — sweetening them with brown sugar to make a chutney that's great with grilled foods. This chutney goes especially well with grilled beef, poultry, or pork.

Preparation time: *15 minutes*

Cooking time: *20 minutes*

Yield: *About 2 cups (approximately 16 servings at 2 tablespoons per serving)*

2 tablespoons olive oil

1 onion, peeled and chopped

½ cup light brown sugar, packed

3 tablespoons apple cider vinegar

½ to 1 large jalapeño pepper, seeded and chopped

3 cups seeded and chopped tomatoes

½ teaspoon fresh ginger, peeled and grated

1 In a medium sauté pan or skillet, heat the oil over medium heat; add the onion and cook for 7 minutes or until lightly browned and very soft, stirring occasionally.

2 Add the brown sugar, vinegar, and jalapeño pepper; cook for 4 to 5 minutes, stirring occasionally until the mixture is dark brown and syrupy.

3 Stir in the tomatoes, raise the heat to medium-high, and boil gently for 5 more minutes or until the liquid is reduced and the mixture has thickened. Remove from heat and stir in the ginger, adding more to taste (if desired). Serve warm, or cover and chill.

Vary It! *You can remove the tomato skins before making the chutney. To do so, plunge the whole tomatoes into boiling water for about 15 seconds or until the skins begin to split. Then chill in a bowl of ice water before slipping off the skins.*

Per serving: *Calories 104 (From Fat 33); Fat 4g (Saturated 1g); Cholesterol 0mg; Sodium 12mg; Carbohydrate 19g (Dietary Fiber 1g); Protein 1g.*

Summer Squash Chutney

Summer squash is combined with sweet orange juice, tart lemon juice, honey, and red onion for this chutney. We suggest serving this chutney with grilled chicken, pork, lamb, or beef.

Preparation time: *15 minutes*

Cooking time: *20 minutes*

Chilling time: *1 to 2 hours*

Yield: *About 2½ cups (approximately 10 servings at ¼ cup per serving)*

1 tablespoon extra-virgin olive oil

½ cup peeled and chopped red onion

2 small yellow squash (about 1 pound total), diced

2 small zucchini (about 1 pound total), diced

2 teaspoons fresh ginger, peeled and grated

½ cup fresh orange juice

2 teaspoons fresh lemon juice

2 teaspoons honey

1 teaspoon grated orange peel

Salt and pepper to taste

1 In a heavy, medium saucepan, heat the olive oil over medium heat; add the red onion and cook for about 2 minutes, stirring often until the onion is soft and wilted. Add the squash, zucchini, and ginger; cook, stirring just to coat the vegetables in the oil.

2 Add the orange and lemon juices; raise the heat to high and bring the mixture to a boil. Reduce heat to low and simmer partially covered for 20 to 25 minutes or until the vegetables are soft. (If the liquid has evaporated, cover completely during the last 5 minutes of cooking or add a little more orange juice to moisten.)

3 Remove from heat and stir in the honey and orange peel. Adjust seasoning with salt and pepper. Cover and chill for a few hours before serving.

Per serving: *Calories 22 (From Fat 7); Fat 1g (Saturated 0g); Cholesterol 0mg; Sodium 30mg; Carbohydrate 4g (Dietary Fiber 1g); Protein 1g.*

Cherry and Pear Chutney

Here's a perfect combo of sweet and sour flavors, which is ideal for hot, spicy dishes, especially Indian and southeast Asian dishes. You can serve this chutney with just about anything, including grilled chicken, pork, lamb, or fish.

Preparation: *35 minutes*

Cooking time: *25 to 30 minutes*

Chilling time: *30 minutes*

Yield: *3½ cups (approximately 16 servings at ¼ cup per serving)*

6 ounces dried cherries

½ cup sugar

1 cup water

Thinly sliced zest from 1 lemon

2-inch piece of ginger, peeled and thinly julienned

¼ teaspoon crushed red pepper flakes

Juice of 2 lemons

3 Bosc pears, peeled, cored, and cut into ½-inch cubes

1 small red bell pepper, cut into ¼-inch pieces

¾ teaspoons salt

¼ cup cider vinegar

In a large saucepan, add the cherries, sugar, and water. Bring to a boil and gently simmer for 2 minutes. Add the lemon zest, ginger, pepper flakes, lemon juice, pears, red bell pepper, and salt. Bring to a boil, and then reduce heat, cover, and gently simmer for 10 to 12 minutes or until the pears are tender. Add the vinegar to the pears and simmer for 2 minutes. Let cool and refrigerate for 30 minutes. You can use the chutney immediately, but the flavors blend better if made 1 to 2 days in advance.

Per serving: *Calories 77 (From Fat 2); Fat 0g (Saturated 0g); Cholesterol 0mg; Sodium 125mg; Carbohydrate 22g (Dietary Fiber 1g); Protein 1g.*

Other condiments

Not all condiments fall under the categories in the preceding sections, but we don't want to leave these delicious accents out. Use the condiments in this section however you like — on their own with chips, crackers, or pita bread to dip or scoop them, on top of a burger, or on the side of the grilled food of your choosing.

Tapenade

This oh-so-rich, classic French paste is from the Riviera where the olives are wonderful and the anchovies are canned or bottled in oil. Tapenade makes a great condiment for grilled steaks or fish, served either right on top or on the side. It's especially wonderful served as an appetizer on grilled slices of hard-crusted Italian or French bread.

Preparation time: *15 minutes*

Yield: *About $\frac{2}{3}$ cup (approximately 10 servings at 1 tablespoon per serving)*

1 cup pitted black olives

3 canned anchovy fillets, blotted dry with paper towels

2 cloves garlic, peeled and minced

2 teaspoons capers, rinsed and drained

$1\frac{1}{2}$ teaspoons fresh lemon juice

2 tablespoons olive oil

Pepper to taste

2 tablespoons finely chopped fresh basil, red onion, or tomato, for garnish

In a blender or food processor, combine the olives, anchovies, garlic, capers, lemon juice, oil, and pepper. Process into a coarse puree. (If using a blender, stop as necessary to scrape down the sides.) Transfer to a nonreactive container. Serve at room temperature or cover and refrigerate. Garnish with basil, red onion, or tomato before serving. Use within one week.

Per serving: *Calories 60 (From Fat 52); Fat 6g (Saturated 1g); Cholesterol 1mg; Sodium 249mg; Carbohydrate 1g (Dietary Fiber 0g); Protein 1g.*

Guacamole

Here's our version of the Mexican classic: nice and spicy and very creamy. Just make sure your avocado is properly ripe — the Haas variety is the best. They should be black in color and soft to the touch.

Preparation time: *15 minutes*

Yield: *2 cups (approximately 4 servings at ½ cup per serving)*

2 ripe avocados, peeled and pitted

Juice of 1 lime

1 garlic clove, peeled and minced

½ teaspoon ground cumin

2 teaspoons seeded and minced jalapeño pepper, or to taste

2 scallions, thinly sliced

4 tablespoons chopped cilantro (coriander) leaves

2 tablespoons sour cream

¾ teaspoons salt

¼ teaspoons freshly ground peppercorns

1 Roast the ground cumin by placing it in a small fry pan and keeping it over medium-low heat until it starts to smell roasted, about 6 minutes. Remove the pan from the heat immediately.

2 In a bowl, roughly mash the avocados with a fork to make a coarse puree. Add the lime juice, garlic, roasted cumin, jalapeño, scallions, cilantro, sour cream, salt, and pepper. Mix to blend. Serve immediately or chill for an hour. Guacamole doesn't last long in the refrigerator and may turn brown fairly quickly. However, placing the avocado pits in the guacamole prevents it from turning brown so quickly.

Go-With: *Guacamole is delicious as a garnish or condiment for any kind of tender grilled steak (Chapter 11) and also goes well with Best-Ever Fajitas (Chapter 17).*

Vary It! *You can add all sorts of ingredients to the Guacamole to change its flavor in a heartbeat. Experiment by adding any of the following ingredients to taste: bottled salsa, chopped black olives, onions (rather than scallions), chopped sun-dried tomatoes or chopped fresh tomatoes, or seeded and chopped chile peppers.*

Per serving: *Calories 145 (From Fat 114); Fat 13g (Saturated 3g); Cholesterol 0mg; Sodium 0mg; Carbohydrate 9g (Dietary Fiber 8g); Protein 3g.*

Barbecued Onions

Slow cooking onions in a little oil and butter and then adding a favorite barbecue sauce turns them into a slightly caramelized topping that's perfect for grilled burgers, hot dogs, sausage, or steaks. If you want to make your own barbecue sauce, check out Chapter 9 for the Country-Style Barbecue Sauce recipe.

Preparation time: *10 minutes*

Cooking time: *20 minutes*

Yield: *About 1⅓ cups (approximately 4 servings at ⅓ cup per serving)*

4 large yellow onions

3 tablespoons butter

1 tablespoon vegetable oil

1 tablespoon light brown sugar, packed

½ cup bottled or homemade barbecue sauce

1 Peel the onions; cut each onion in half vertically through the core, lay the halves flat, and slice thinly into half rounds.

2 In a large heavy-bottomed skillet, heat the butter and oil over medium-low heat. Add the onion slices and brown sugar; stir well, coating the onions in the oil and sugar. Cook for 15 to 20 minutes or until the onions are very soft and browned, stirring often and occasionally scraping the bottom of the pan.

3 Stir in the barbecue sauce; continue cooking for 2 to 3 minutes more, stirring often until the onions are very tender and the sauce is warmed through.

Per serving: *Calories 186 (From Fat 115); Fat 13g (Saturated 6g); Cholesterol 23mg; Sodium 261mg; Carbohydrate 17g (Dietary Fiber 2g); Protein 2g.*

Dressing Up Your Meal Using Compound Butters

Compound butter is butter that's dressed up with a few herbs, spices, or other intense seasonings. A small pat on a sizzling steak can increase the pleasure of a beefy meal. Compound butters are great with all sorts of foods, including grilled meats, fish, poultry, and many vegetables, and they're more appropriate than a heavy sauce in warm weather. Place a pat of butter on top of a thick steak, boneless grilled chicken breasts, or grilled fish; or toss grilled vegetables with butter to taste.

Compound Butter

Prepare compound butters according to the steps in Figure 6-2. Following this basic compound butter recipe is a list of tasty variations.

Preparation time: *15 minutes*

Yield: *4 servings at 1 tablespoon per serving*

1 stick of softened, unsalted butter

Herbs and spices to taste

1 Use a food processor, blender, or sharp chef's knife to grind up or finely mince the seasonings.

2 Using a rubber spatula, wooden spoon, or your hands and a small bowl, soften the butter until it's malleable but not too soft.

3 Work in the seasonings with a fork or with your hands.

4 Spoon the mixture onto a sheet of waxed paper and use the paper to shape the butter mixture into a cylinder or log that has a diameter of about 2 inches.

5 Wrap well and refrigerate or freeze until ready to use. The butter keeps frozen for 1 to 2 months. When ready to use, simply slice off into butter pats that are 1- to 1½-inches thick.

Per serving: *Calories 101 (From Fat 100); Fat 11g (Saturated 7g); Cholesterol 31mg; Sodium 2mg; Carbohydrate 0g (Dietary Fiber 0g); Protein 0g.*

In place of "herbs and spices to taste" in the Compound Butter recipe, substitute the following:

- **Lemon and Fresh Herb Butter:** Use 2 tablespoons finely chopped herbs (such as dill, basil, tarragon, thyme, marjoram, parsley, or sage), 1 teaspoon fresh lemon juice, 1 clove garlic (peeled and minced), and salt and pepper to taste. This butter works well with fish, pork, chicken, beef, and roasted vegetables.
- **Spicy Chili Butter:** Sprinkle in 1½ teaspoons chili powder, ¼ teaspoon paprika, 8 drops Tabasco sauce, and salt and pepper to taste. This butter is delicious with grilled corn, chicken, or fish or as a spread for grilled breads.
- **Toasted Cashew and Brandy Butter:** Add ¼ cup toasted and chopped cashews, 1 tablespoon brandy or cognac, and salt and pepper to taste. Pair with grilled steaks or chicken.

- **Ginger and Scallion Butter:** Use 3 tablespoons finely chopped scallions, 2 teaspoons peeled and grated fresh ginger (or ¾ teaspoon ground ginger), a pinch of garlic salt, and salt and pepper to taste. Try this butter with fish, pork, and grilled vegetables.
- **Roasted Garlic Butter:** Roast about 20 cloves (flip to Chapter 16 to find out how to roast garlic on the grill) and slip them out of their skin. (Save and use any remaining cloves for adding to mashed potatoes or for spreading on grilled slices of Italian bread.) Mash the cloves coarsely before blending into butter with salt and pepper to taste. The garlic can also be foil-wrapped and roasted in a 350-degree oven for 45 minutes to 1 hour.

Steps for Making Compound Butters
Put the butter in a bowl and let it get soft... but DON'T MELT IT!
Use a fork to blend in your seasonings!
Turn butter out, onto a piece of waxed paper and roll into a uniform cylinder.
Refrigerate or freeze and cut off pats as you need them.

Figure 6-2: Compounding your butter options.

Part III
For the Fanatics of the Classics

The 5th Wave By Rich Tennant

"Burgers ready in 6 hours!"

In this part . . .

In this part, you start grilling from the ground up by first tackling the basics: hamburgers, hot dogs, and sausages. Then, you master assorted kebabs, barbecued ribs, and rotisserie cooking (which you'll be pleased to discover is the easiest and most carefree way to grill).

Chapter 7

Bun-Lovin' Burgers, Sausages, and Hot Dogs

In This Chapter

- Preparing, grilling, and topping your burger
- Grilling and topping franks and sausages

Recipes in This Chapter

- Turkey Burger
- Gorgonzola Hamburgers with Balsamic Onion Relish
- Lamb Burger
- Grilled Kielbasa with Creamy Mustard Sauce
- Grilled Italian Links with Caraway Sauerkraut

Believe it or not, you can serve a great burger, hot dog, or sausage with as much finesse as you might serve duck or lobster. For, even though these may seem like the easiest, slap-'em-on-the-grill kind of dishes, they can be made well or poorly. In this chapter, however, we give you the basics of serving the kind of burgers, hot dogs, and sausages that make your guests think that you've gone to great lengths or know some long-hidden secrets!

Everyone Loves a Burger

Ground meat patties have been a staple of world cookery for thousands of years. They may come in different sizes and shapes, but the ground meat patty is always a way of taking less-than-prime meat, tenderizing it, and then cooking it quickly for instant gratification. It took some genius — a person still unknown to gastronomic history — to come up with the idea of tossing a meat patty on a soft bun and then heaping ketchup and other condiments on it to make a complete meal in itself. Well, a burger is almost a complete meal — as long as you have french fries on the side and top it with lettuce and tomato.

A hamburger that has been carefully shaped and plumped to a proper thickness, grilled to a perfect medium-rare, with a slightly charred exterior, set on top of a toasted bun, and served with homemade condiments is a grand, glorious, and simple food.

Choosing your burger meat

A grilled burger is probably the easiest and most commonly grilled food in America, but most of us are often disappointed with the results for two reasons: Either the burger patty is too thick to begin with and cooks to a frazzle on the edges, while remaining too pink or even raw in the middle, or the patty meat is too lean and dries out.

Although your choice of burger meat is a matter of personal preference, we believe that the juiciest hamburgers are made with ground beef that's about 80 to 85 percent meat and 15 to 20 percent fat. You can find this ratio in chuck — the best all-around cut for a perfect, juicy hamburger.

Creating the mixture of ingredients

Ground meat (and nowadays, soy, ground veggies, and other vegetarian options) offer plenty of opportunity for burger variety. In this section, we've included a burger recipe that we especially like, but we certainly don't want to leave you, hands tied, with our favorite recipe as the only option we give you. To make a run-of-the-mill burger, simply add ¼ teaspoon of salt and ¼ teaspoon of pepper to 1½ pounds of ground chuck, mixing the seasonings into the meat with your hands.

Vary It! Use the following hamburger variations to spark your own burger creations. Each of these seasoning combinations works for 1½ pounds of raw ground meat:

- **Italian Burger:** Add the following ingredients to the ground meat mixture: 1 egg yolk; ¼ cup grated onion; 1 large clove garlic, peeled and minced; 2 tablespoons chopped fresh basil or 2 teaspoons dried crushed basil; ½ teaspoon dried oregano; and salt and pepper to taste. Place grated Parmesan cheese on top of each burger (if desired) about 2 minutes before the burger is done, and then grill, covered, until the cheese melts.
- **Mexican Burger:** Add the following ingredients to the ground meat mixture: ¼ cup finely chopped onion, ½ to 1 teaspoon seeded and chopped jalapeño pepper, ¾ teaspoon ground cumin, and salt and pepper to taste. (Refer to Chapter 4 for the scoop on how to handle chilies.) Serve on toasted buns or in warmed tortillas with a prepared tomato salsa or taco sauce and slices of ripe avocado.
- **Middle Eastern Burger:** Add the following ingredients to the ground meat mixture: 2 tablespoons finely chopped onion, 2 tablespoons finely chopped raisins, ½ teaspoon cinnamon, ½ teaspoon paprika, and salt and pepper to taste. Serve in warmed pita pockets with Tabbouleh. (Flip to Chapter 16 for a Tabbouleh recipe.)

- **Asian Spiced Burger:** Add the following ingredients to the ground meat mixture: ¼ cup finely chopped scallions; 3 tablespoons teriyaki sauce; 1 large clove garlic, peeled and minced; and salt and pepper to taste.
- **Veggie-Stuffed Burger:** Add the following ingredients to the ground meat mixture: ⅓ cup finely grated carrot; 2 tablespoons finely chopped onion; 6 tablespoons fine dry bread crumbs; 1 beaten egg; 2 cloves garlic, peeled and minced; 1 teaspoon dried crushed marjoram or basil; and salt and pepper to taste. Serve on toasted sesame seed buns with slices of ripe tomato and alfalfa sprouts.

And if these suggestions aren't enough, search your pantry or refrigerator for any of the following ingredients and add them to the raw meat however you see fit: Tabasco sauce, Worcestershire sauce, ketchup, pickle juice, dry sherry, wheat germ, onion soup mix, cayenne pepper, ground ginger, cilantro (coriander), cumin, garlic salt, chopped canned or fresh mushrooms, chopped parsley, tarragon, thyme, sage, other fresh herbs, ground walnuts or pecans, Dijon-style mustard, horseradish, lemon juice, and grated lemon peel.

Preparing your patties for the grill

For the perfect burger, heed the following bits of advice when prepping patties for the grill:

- Be careful not to overmix the patty ingredients; otherwise, you'll toughen the meat. Mix the meat just so it holds together — not so much that it gets pasty.
- When forming your burger patties, try to mold the meat into a uniform, fairly flat patty, no thicker than ¾ inch. A thicker patty, mounded high in the center, is less likely to cook evenly — though we have to admit that big, fat burgers don't taste half bad.

- As you grill the burger, be sure not to press the patty with the flat side of a spatula, despite the great temptation to do so. Pressing the patty squeezes out the flavorful juices and can also cause dangerous flare-ups.

Several grilling cookbooks recommend bringing ground meat to room temperature before placing it on the grill. We disagree. Instead, keep ground meat in the refrigerator until just before grilling. This minimizes exposure to airborne bacteria. And always place cooked burgers on a clean plate. Never return them to the plate you used to carry them to the grill because it may be contaminated with bacteria from the uncooked meat.

Turkey Burger

Turkey burgers are a tasty alternative to beef burgers. Seasonings — like those used in this recipe — make a big difference in flavor.

Preparation time: *20 minutes*

Grilling time: *12 minutes*

Yield: *4 servings*

1¼ pounds ground turkey

1 small red pepper, cored, seeded, and finely chopped

2 scallions, thinly sliced

2 tablespoons parsley, finely chopped

2 tablespoons chopped fresh cilantro (coriander)

1 large clove garlic, peeled and minced

½ teaspoon dried thyme

½ teaspoon ground cumin

1 teaspoon Tabasco sauce

Salt and pepper to taste

4 hamburger buns, toasted on the grill

Mayonnaise or Dijon-style mustard (optional)

1. Prepare a medium-hot fire in a charcoal or gas grill.
2. In a medium mixing bowl, combine the ground turkey, red pepper, scallions, parsley, cilantro, garlic, thyme, cumin, Tabasco sauce, and salt and pepper; mix well (without overmixing). Gently shape the turkey mixture into 4 burger patties, each about ¾-inch thick.
3. Place the patties on a well-oiled grill grid. Grill for 10 to 12 minutes or until done, turning once after 5 minutes. The burgers are done when the juices run clear and the center of the patty is cooked to brown with no sign of pink; cut to test.
4. Serve immediately on buns that have been toasted on the edge of grill until lightly browned. Top burgers with the mayonnaise or mustard (if desired).

Remember: *The USDA recommends cooking all ground meat to medium or until the center is no longer pink.*

Per serving: *Calories 371 (From Fat 140); Fat 17g (Saturated 4g); Cholesterol 103mg; Sodium 505mg; Carbohydrate 24g (Dietary Fiber 2g); Protein 32g.*

Gorgonzola Hamburgers with Balsamic Onion Relish

Here's a modern burger that packs as much flavor as is possible between two buns. If you prefer, blue cheese will do almost as well as Gorgonzola. Check out the color photo section to get a look at this delicious burger.

Preparation time: *25 minutes*

Grilling: *8 minutes*

Yield: *4 servings*

2 tablespoons olive oil

1 thinly sliced Spanish onion

Salt and freshly ground pepper to taste

½ teaspoon crushed red pepper

¼ cup balsamic vinegar

1½ pounds ground chuck or sirloin

1 tablespoon peanut oil for brushing patties

4 ounces Gorgonzola cheese, sliced into ½-inch thick pieces

4 hamburger buns

1. Preheat your charcoal or gas grill to high.
2. Meanwhile, to prepare the Balsamic Onion Relish, heat a medium-size sauté pan, and when it's hot add the olive oil. Add the sliced onions, tossing in the olive oil to coat. Reduce the heat to medium-high and season the onions with salt, freshly ground pepper, and crushed red pepper. Sauté the mixture, stirring often to brown evenly until the onions are soft and brown, about 12 minutes. Reduce the heat to low, add the balsamic vinegar, and then stir and cook for 3 minutes. Add salt and pepper to taste and set the pan aside, leaving the relish in place.
3. Divide the ground chuck or sirloin into 4 equal parts, and then shape the meat into round patties that are 4 inches across and of even thickness in the center and the sides. Lightly brush the peanut oil on both sides of the patties. Generously season both sides of each patty to taste with salt and freshly ground pepper.
4. Place the hamburger patties on an oiled grill and grill for 3 to 4 minutes until nicely browned. With a spatula, turn the patties and grill for another 2 minutes. Then place one slice of Gorgonzola cheese on each patty, put the cover on the grill, and grill the patties for another 1 to 2 minutes to melt the cheese.
5. Place the pan of relish back on the heat and warm for 1 minute.
6. Place the hamburger patties on the buns and divide the onion relish among the 4 hamburgers. Serve immediately.

Remember: *The USDA recommends cooking all ground meat to medium or until the center is no longer pink.*

Per serving: *Calories 527 (From Fat 251); Fat 28g (Saturated 11g); Cholesterol 115mg; Sodium 980mg; Carbohydrate 28g (Dietary Fiber 3g); Protein 39g.*

Lamb Burger

Ground lamb patties can be seasoned simply with a sprinkling of salt and pepper for a child's finicky palate. But why not use favorite spice combinations from world-class cuisines to alter the taste of ground lamb?

Preparation time: *20 minutes*

Grilling time: *12 minutes*

Yield: *4 servings*

1¼ pounds lean ground lamb

1 tablespoon grated red or yellow onion

2 tablespoons dark raisins, chopped (optional)

2 tablespoons chopped fresh parsley or cilantro (coriander)

¾ teaspoon ground cumin

¼ teaspoon cinnamon

¼ teaspoon paprika

¼ teaspoon salt, or to taste

Pepper to taste

4 pita breads, each about 5 inches in diameter

Chutney (optional)

Chopped tomatoes and cucumbers (optional)

1 Prepare a medium-hot fire in a charcoal or gas grill.

2 In a large mixing bowl, combine the ground lamb, onion, raisins (if desired), parsley or cilantro, cumin, cinnamon, paprika, and salt and pepper. Mix well (without overmixing). Shape the meat into 4 oblong patties, each 3 to 4 inches long and ¾- to 1-inch thick. Wrap the pitas in heavy-duty aluminum foil and set aside.

3 Place the lamb patties on a lightly oiled grill grid. Cook the patties for 6 to 8 minutes per side for medium, or to desired doneness; cut into the center of each patty to check doneness. About 3 minutes before the patties finish cooking, place foil-wrapped pitas at the edge of the grid; heat until warmed through, turning once.

4 To serve, place each patty in a bread pocket; allow each diner to top with chutney, chopped tomatoes, or cucumbers (if desired) or other condiments of choice.

Remember: *The USDA recommends cooking all ground meat to medium or until the center is no longer pink.*

Per serving: *Calories 361 (From Fat 94); Fat 11g (Saturated 4g); Cholesterol 85mg; Sodium 545mg; Carbohydrate 34g (Dietary Fiber 2g); Protein 31g.*

When grilling burgers (or anything else for that matter), brush the grill grid with vegetable oil or nonstick cooking spray to prevent food from sticking to the grid. However, to avoid dangerous flare-ups, brush the grid *before* preheating the grill or igniting the charcoal.

Keep in mind that all grilling temperatures are only estimates. Variables — such as the intensity of your grill's heat, weather conditions, and the thickness of the meat — all affect the exact time it takes to cook your burger. To avoid overcooking (or undercooking), test the interior color of your burger. Do this by making a small incision with a thin knife in the center of the patty 1 or 2 minutes before you're done grilling. Or you may use an instant reading thermometer to find out the temperature. At 150 degrees your burger will be medium.

The perfect grilled side dish for hamburgers is — hands down — corn on the cob. Check out Chapter 16 for all sorts of interesting ways to grill vegetables, including corn on the cob. There you'll also find other side dish ideas.

Topping your burger

Some burger fans insist on eating their burgers with no extras; not even a pickle hides under their burger bun. But the rest of us pride ourselves on piling on the toppings. In addition to down-home, old-fashioned ketchup, here are some of our favorite toppings:

- **Avocado:** Slice ripe avocado or mash it into a spread with a little lemon juice and Tabasco sauce.
- **Cheese:** Try Cheddar, Swiss, Muenster, Gruyère, or fontina — any cheese that melts into a thin, velvety layer. Place the slice on the meat a minute or two before the burger is ready and cook. Be sure to cover the grill after adding cheese. Doing so helps to melt the cheese.
- **Crisp strips of bacon:** You can add bacon with or without the lettuce and tomato.
- **Fruit chutney:** Try adding a generous dollop of tomato, peach, or mango chutney. It's a nice counterpoint to grilled meat. (Flip to Chapter 6 for more information on chutney.)
- **Pesto sauce:** Buy it or make your own. (Refer to Chapter 15 for a recipe.) For a smoky flavor, spread pesto sauce on the buns before toasting them on the grill.
- **Pickles:** Choose from dill or sweet pickle slices.
- **Raw or grilled onion slices:** Yellow onions are great, but so are milder red onions.
- **Salsa:** Try making your own (see Chapter 6) or use any of the better bottled brands, such as Newman's Own Salsa.
- **Sautéed or grilled mushrooms:** Portobello mushrooms, with their meat-like texture and woodsy taste are terrific sliced, brushed with oil, and grilled. Turn to Chapter 16 for a complete recipe.

- **Tomato slices:** Raw tomato slices are great, but if you want an extra-special treat, you can brush the slices with your favorite bottled vinaigrette and heat them on the grill for about 2 minutes per side or until they're very lightly browned.

Vary It! To make some simple sauces for adorning burgers when guests come for a patio dinner (or just to treat yourself), jump to Chapter 6, where you find recipes for all sorts of spreads and sauces.

Simple Sausages and Fancy Franks

Sausage-making is a food art practiced around the world. Sold fresh (uncooked), cooked, smoked, and cured, sausages are made with a variety of meats and seasonings and are shaped into links that vary in thickness and length. (See Figure 7-1 for a look at various types of sausages.)

FAT BUSTER

With few exceptions, sausages are made with a fair amount of fat, but some lower-fat varieties are starting to pop up in grocery stores.

Here are just a few of the many varieties of sausage available for grilling:

- **Bockwurst:** Usually sold fresh, but you may also find it cooked. Bockwurst, which is a German favorite, is made from veal and pork and is usually seasoned mildly with parsley and chives.
- **Bratwurst:** A German pork or veal sausage, generally sold fresh, but also available precooked and smoked. This sausage is moderately spicy and seasoned with ginger, nutmeg, coriander, and caraway.
- **Chorizo:** A Mexican fresh pork sausage or a Spanish smoked pork sausage. Both varieties tend to be hot and spicy and flavored with garlic, chili powder, and other hot spices.
- **Frankfurter:** A precooked, smoked sausage, mildly seasoned, and better known as a *hot dog* or *frank.* Hot dogs or franks can be made from beef, pork, turkey, chicken, or veal and are usually packed into a casing. Sizes range from the tiny, delicate *cocktail frank* to the impressive *foot-long.* Kosher franks are all-beef and often heavily flavored with garlic. According to U.S. law, franks labeled "all-beef" must be made without fillers such as cereals or soybean products.
- **Italian:** Fresh pork sausage, which is sold hot (with hot peppers, fennel, and garlic) or sweet (minus the hot peppers).
- **Knockwurst (also known as knackwurst):** Fully cooked and smoked sausage made of beef, pork, and/or veal. Flavored with lots of garlic, this German sausage is mild, not spicy.

- **Polish kielbasa:** A fully cooked and smoked sausage that's usually made of pork but sometimes also made of veal and beef. Flavorings include onion and garlic, so it can be quite spicy.
- **Salami and cervelat:** Both of these are uncooked sausages that are safe to eat without further cooking because they have been preserved by curing. Salami, which includes the popular pepperoni, is air-dried (which makes it firm-textured), is usually heavily seasoned with spices and garlic, and is great for slicing thinly over a pizza destined for the grill. Cervelat sausages, such as mortadella, are preserved by curing, drying, and smoking.

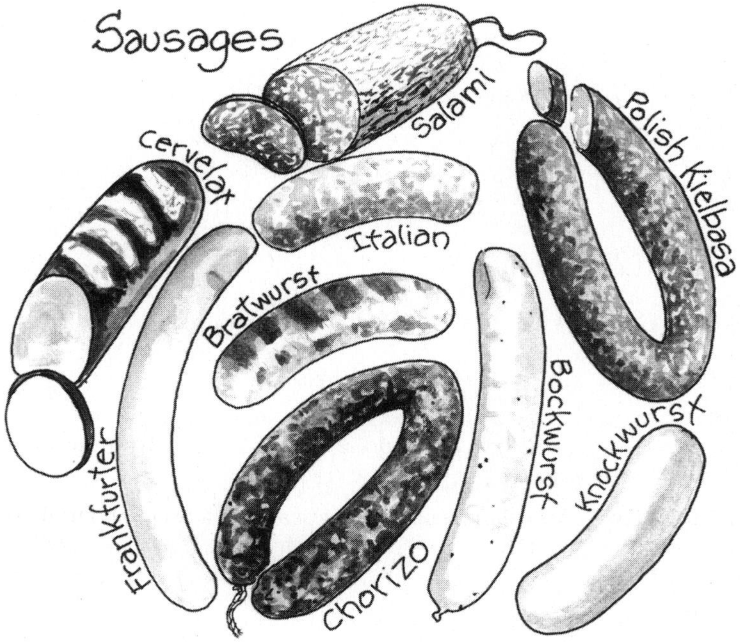

Figure 7-1: Various types of sausages.

WARNING! Even though many sausages are cured and/or cooked, they can't be held indefinitely in warm weather. It's always best to preserve their flavor and quality by placing them in the coldest part of your refrigerator — 36 to 40 degrees is the ideal temperature range.

REMEMBER Freezing sausages isn't a good idea, because the sausages lose flavor, but if you must freeze them, place them in vaporproof plastic bags and then thaw them overnight in the refrigerator when you're ready to eat them. The flavor really starts to decline after about 2 months of freezing, so don't leave them in the freezer any longer than that.

Knowing how long to cook 'em

There's no trick to grilling franks and sausages; the cooking time is basically all you need to know. Here are some tips to keep in mind:

- Uncooked sausage needs to be precooked before grilling to release some of the natural fat, which can cause dangerous flare-ups on the grill.

  To precook, prick each sausage several times, and then simmer in water (flavored, if you wish, with wine, beer, or apple juice) for 5 to 10 minutes or until the sausages are fully cooked with no trace of pink in the center. Then you can grill over medium heat until the meat is browned and crisp on all sides, turning often.
- Cooked sausages need only a few minutes of grilling to acquire that lovely, smoky taste and the bubbly skin that makes them irresistible on a summer afternoon. A hot dog will take about 3 minutes; a thicker bratwurst about 5.
- Remember to keep turning sausages — whether they're precooked or fresh — because they can burn quickly. The best method for turning sausages is to use a square or rectangular grill basket that holds a dozen or more sausages so they can all be turned at once (see Chapter 2 for details).
- Grill frankfurters for about 8 minutes or until browned on all sides, turning frequently.

A lesson in hot dog history

No one knows for sure when the first frankfurter appeared in America, but the best bet is that it was first served under that name in St. Louis in the 1880s by a German immigrant named Antoine Feuchtwanger, whose principal contribution was the soft roll.

The fame of the frank really took off in 1901 after Harry Magely, director of catering at New York City's Polo Grounds (where the New York Giants used to play), exhorted customers to "Get your red hots!" and served the frankfurters on a heated roll with various condiments.

The term "hot dog" was coined by Hearst Newspaper sports cartoonist Tad Dorgan, who often caricatured German figures as dachshunds and, as of 1906, as talking sausages.

So widespread was the name "hot dog" that, to calm patrons' fears, Nathan's Famous Hot Dog Stand in Coney Island, Brooklyn, New York, put up a sign explaining that its sausages did not contain any dog meat.

Loading up on toppings

Good as they are unadorned, frankfurters and sausages are even better with a topping or two. Mustard and ketchup are the world's favorite toppings, but for a little more pizzazz, the next time you fire up the grill and slap down franks for a crowd, offer an assortment of hot dog toppings — some homemade and others straight out of a can or bottle.

For example, let your guests pick and choose from among plates of coleslaw, baked beans, canned and warmed chili, relishes, pickles, grated Cheddar cheese, flavored mustards and chutneys, guacamole, roasted red and green peppers, grilled and raw onion slices, sauerkraut, spicy salsas, and barbecue sauces. (See Chapter 16 for side dish ideas.)

Grilled Kielbasa with Creamy Mustard Sauce

Make Grilled Kielbasa with Creamy Mustard Sauce when you need dinner on the table in just a few minutes or when you're tailgating in the stadium parking lot of your favorite team. (Flip to Chapter 21 for more outdoor barbecue tips.)

Preparation time: *30 minutes*

Grilling time: *10 minutes*

Yield: *4 servings*

¼ cup sour cream

3 tablespoons Dijon-style mustard

2 tablespoons prepared horseradish, drained

Pepper to taste

Tabasco sauce (optional)

1 to 1¼ pounds fully cooked sausage (such as kielbasa or knackwurst)

1 Prepare a medium fire in a charcoal or gas grill.

2 Meanwhile, prepare the Creamy Mustard Sauce by combining the sour cream, mustard, horseradish, pepper, and Tabasco sauce (if desired) in a small bowl. Cover and refrigerate.

3 Slice the sausages, if necessary, into 4 pieces of equal length. Cover and arrange the sausages on a lightly oiled grill grid. Grill, turning 2 or 3 times, until well browned on all sides and warmed through, about 10 minutes.

4 Divide the sausages among 4 individual plates and top each link with a generous dollop of Creamy Mustard Sauce.

Go-With: *Try serving the kielbasa sandwich-style, between wedges of crusty Italian bread. Orange-Ginger Coleslaw (Chapter 16) makes a good side dish.*

Per serving: *Calories 400 (From Fat 314); Fat 35g (Saturated 13g); Cholesterol 82mg; Sodium 1,535mg; Carbohydrate 5g (Dietary Fiber 0g); Protein 16g.*

Grilled Italian Links with Caraway Sauerkraut

In this recipe, the sausages are *parboiled* (gently boiled) in beer before grilling. You can also cook them in equal parts apple juice and water, or in a fruity white wine, such as Riesling.

Preparation time: *20 minutes*

Grilling time: *12 minutes*

Yield: *4 servings*

8 sweet Italian sausages, cut into 3- to 4-inch links (about 1½ pounds total)

1 cup beer

½ cup water

2 14-ounce cans sauerkraut, drained

3 tablespoons cider vinegar

1 teaspoon caraway seeds

Dijon-style mustard (optional)

1 Prepare a medium-hot fire in a gas or charcoal grill.

2 Meanwhile, prick each sausage 2 times. Place the sausages in a skillet or sauté pan large enough to hold them in one layer. Add the beer and water; cover and bring to a boil over high heat. Reduce the heat to medium-low and simmer the sausages for about 5 minutes. Remove the sausages, reserving the liquid in the skillet.

3 Add the sauerkraut, vinegar, and caraway seeds to the liquid in the skillet; stir to mix well. Simmer, uncovered, for about 5 minutes or until nearly all the liquid has evaporated. (The sauerkraut should be moist.) Remove the skillet from the heat, cover to keep warm, and set aside.

4 Place the sausages directly over the heat on an oiled grill grid. Grill for 5 to 6 minutes per side or until nicely browned, turning once. Sausage meat is cooked when it's no longer pink in the center. Cut each sausage in the center to determine doneness.

5 Serve with the Caraway Sauerkraut and Dijon-style mustard (if desired).

Per serving: *Calories 313 (From Fat 203); Fat 23g (Saturated 8g); Cholesterol 68mg; Sodium 1,737mg; Carbohydrate 9g (Dietary Fiber 4g); Protein 19g.*

Chapter 8

Swordplay: Grilling Kebabs and Satay

In This Chapter

- Getting the lowdown on skewers
- Assembling your kebabs
- Grilling all varieties of kebabs
- Discovering satay

Recipes in This Chapter

- Artichoke, Mushroom, and Cherry Tomato Kebabs
- Western Beef Kebabs with Red Peppers and Onions
- Teriyaki Steak Kebabs
- Apple and Tarragon Pork Kebabs
- Pork Kebabs with Nectarines and Red Onions
- Lamb and Eggplant Kebabs with Tarragon Marinade
- Lemony Fresh Lamb Kebabs
- Chicken Tikka
- Mixed Grill Seafood Kebabs with Fresh Lemon Sauce
- Sweet-and-Sour Shrimp Kebabs with Scallions
- Satay with Peanut Dipping Sauce

Kebabs (and their Middle Eastern cousin, satay) are some of the simplest and most popular foods to grill — you simply thread morsels of pork, beef, chicken, or other foods onto a skewer before grilling over an open fire. Kebabs and satays are popular grilled dishes for all of the following reasons:

- They require limited preparation and grill time.
- The thin strips of beef, pork, fish, or poultry quickly absorb the flavors of a marinade or spice rub.
- You can use cheaper cuts of meat such as top round, chicken thighs, and lamb shoulder because they're eaten in small bites and don't need to be as tender as, say, a sirloin steak or breast of chicken.
- You can grill a meal that's almost complete on just one skewer. (In other words, no dishes!)
- The plate presentation can be quite dramatic when assorted colorful foods are strung along the same skewer.
- They're fun to eat and make especially good party appetizers.

In this chapter, you discover the kinds of skewers that work well with different foods and how to prepare different foods that are great as kebabs. I even suggest some side dishes that you can prepare alongside your kebabs and satay.

Ladies and Gentlemen — Choose Your Skewers!

Kebabs can't exist without skewers, so before you can grill a kebab dinner, you need to choose your skewers. Skewers come in many forms and sizes, from the bamboo (or wooden) skewers used in Southeast Asia to the long, swordlike metal skewers that flamed dramatically at restaurants in the 1970s. Some skewers are even quite decorative.

When buying skewers for your own use, you can choose between metal and wood, both of which have advantages and disadvantages. Table 8-1 shows some general guidelines that can help you make a decision on which type you need.

Table 8-1 Comparing Wooden and Metal Skewers

	Wooden Skewers	*Metal Skewers*
Size	Shorter, ranging from 6 to 9 inches long; best for scallops, chicken morsels	Longer, ranging from 10 to 18 inches long, so you can pack them with food
Shape	Usually like round toothpicks but sturdier	Either flat, which makes sliding the food off easier, or square, which keeps slippery food on more firmly; some metal skewers have a sliding block at one end to allow you to push the food down and off the blade
Price	Often sold and packaged by the dozens or hundreds, so they're significantly cheaper	More expensive upfront, but you can use them for years
Appearance	Plain, yet functional	Decorative metal skewers can look quite dramatic on a platter
Preparation for grilling	Must be soaked in water for at least 30 minutes before using to avoid burning; even after you soak the skewers, the ends may burn, so be careful when you transfer them to a plate; wrapping the tips in aluminum foil makes picking them up easier but always use a mitt	No prep before grilling

Check out Chapter 2 for more information on the different types of skewers available.

Mastering the Skill of Grilling Kebabs

Grilling kebabs is so easy. Anyone can do it. If you're a beginner and need some guidance, here are some pointers:

- Pack pieces of meat tightly on the skewer if you want the meat cooked rare or medium-rare. If you want it medium to well, pack the cubes or strips more loosely, with a little space between each piece, allowing more heat to circulate.
- Cut the cubes of food into pieces that are uniform in size to ensure that they all finish cooking in the same length of time.
- Turn hot dogs or sausages into simple kebabs by threading them end-to-end on a skewer. They're best if cut into 1-inch bite-size pieces.
- Take care with foods that are either soft or curved, such as cherry tomatoes and shrimp, because they have a tendency to slip around as the skewer is turned. Try piercing these items with two parallel skewers, rather than one, to hold them in place (see Figure 8-1). Or use square rather than round metal skewers.
- Splash balsamic vinegar, flavored vinegar, or fresh lemon juice over your grilled pork or lamb kebabs for a fat-free flavoring.
- For great-looking appetizers, cut your ingredients into 1-inch cubes or chunks and thread them onto 6-inch skewers.

Use caution when turning your kebabs; always wear an insulated mitt (described in Chapter 2). The skewer handles get hot enough to sear the tips of your fingers.

You can always turn up the heat on your gas or charcoal grill by using the grill cover. For example, if the fish and vegetable kebabs don't seem to be cooking fast enough, cover with the grill hood during the final 2 to 3 minutes. If your grill doesn't have a cover, use a large overturned pot or an aluminum drip pan.

Putting Veggies on a Stick: The Fun Way to Eat Them

If you're a parent or you have ever tried feeding vegetables to a child, you know that he's much more likely to eat the healthy food if doing so involves some element of fun. Usually childhood fun involves some sort of handiwork — emphasis on the *hand.* For whatever reason, vegetables often seem to hold the same allure for adults when presented as part of an interactive meal. Enter veggie kebabs, an enticing way to offer and consume this vital part of the human diet.

Because they come in all shapes, sizes, and densities, vegetables can be a bit tricky to skewer. The firmer vegetables are a cinch and stay put nicely on the skewer. Skewer vegetables that aren't so dense and that are round in shape, such as mushrooms or slices of zucchini or yellow squash, laying flat with their widest surface exposed to the heat of the grill. Pierce them from edge to edge, rather than simply straight through their centers. (See Figure 8-1 for examples.)

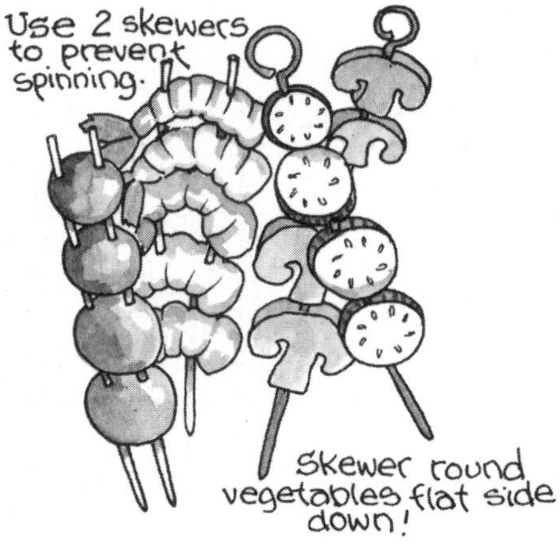

Figure 8-1: Various ways to skewer vegetables and odd-shaped foods like shrimp.

Artichoke, Mushroom, and Cherry Tomato Kebabs

The vegetables in this kebab recipe — cherry tomatoes, bottled artichoke hearts, and mushrooms — grill very quickly and make pretty appetizer kebabs when threaded on short skewers.

Preparation time: *15 minutes*

Marinating time: *30 minutes to 1 hour*

Grilling time: *9 to 10 minutes*

Yield: *6 appetizer servings*

1 6-ounce jar marinated artichoke hearts

12 medium mushrooms

6 cherry tomatoes

3 tablespoons extra-virgin olive oil

Juice of 1 lemon

Grated peel of 1 lemon

1 clove garlic, peeled and minced

Kosher or table salt to taste

Pepper to taste

1 Drain the artichoke hearts, reserving the marinade. Brush the mushrooms clean with a damp paper towel; slice off and discard their stems. Remove any stems from the cherry tomatoes, and then place all the vegetables in a medium mixing bowl or a resealable plastic bag.

2 In a small mixing bowl, combine the remaining ingredients with the reserved artichoke marinade; pour over the vegetables. Cover the bowl or seal the bag, and marinate for 30 minutes to 1 hour. If you plan to use wooden skewers, soak them in cold water while the veggies are marinating to prevent them from burning.

3 Prepare a medium-hot fire in a charcoal or gas grill.

4 Thread 2 mushrooms and 2 artichoke hearts, alternately, on 6 skewers, leaving room to later add a cherry tomato at the top of each skewer. Skewer whole mushrooms lengthwise through the caps so they lie flat on the grill and can brown evenly on both sides. Brush the vegetables generously with the marinade.

5 Place the skewers on a lightly oiled grill grid and grill for about 4 minutes per side, turning once. Brush with the remaining marinade and thread a cherry tomato through the top of each skewer. Grill for 1 to 2 minutes more or until the tomatoes are tender but still intact, turning once.

Go-With: *Serve these colorful skewers with hamburgers, steak, grilled fish, or lamb.*

Vary It! *Add extra-large or jumbo shrimp or 1-inch cubes of green pepper to the marinade with the vegetables. Grill as described but use longer skewers. For a complete meal, remove grilled vegetables from kebabs and toss with steaming pasta, extra-virgin olive oil, chopped fresh parsley, and grated Parmesan cheese. If you don't have time to make the marinade, use your favorite bottled vinaigrette or Italian dressing instead.*

Per serving: *Calories 105 (From Fat 89); Fat 10g (Saturated 2g); Cholesterol 0mg; Sodium 165mg; Carbohydrate 4g (Dietary Fiber 1g); Protein 1g.*

Kebabing for Beef

Most agree that the best beef kebabs are made from tender cuts, such as sirloin, top loin, and tenderloin. However, less expensive beef cuts like top round, chuck, or flank steak also work if you marinate the meat before grilling. (Flip to Chapter 11 for more information on the many beef cuts you can grill. For marinades, oils, and rubs, flip to Chapter 5.)

REMEMBER

Nothing is worse than a charred, dried-out kebab, so timing is critical with beef kebabs. You can honor individual preferences for doneness by cooking kebabs for different lengths of time to get them well-done, medium, or rare. A 1-inch beef cube grills to medium in about 10 minutes over a medium fire. Always check the meat for doneness a few minutes before the end of the estimated cooking time by making a small cut with a sharp knife into the center of a few of the kebab cubes.

Preparing a complete meal with the entree and side dishes all cooked on one grill can be tricky when the cooking times and temperatures differ. On a gas grill, you can adjust the burners, raising or lowering the heat, much as you do on your kitchen range. You don't have this luxury with a charcoal grill, but you can use the edges of the grid for warming and moderate cooking, and the center for foods that need intense heat. Another option is to use your kitchen broiler to grill side dishes. Broiling doesn't produce those wonderful smoky flavors of the grill, but it can help you get the whole meal on the table at once.

Western Beef Kebabs with Red Peppers and Onions

In this recipe, you save the marinade that soaks the raw food and boil it to make a delicious finishing sauce for the grilled food. This particular marinade combines many ingredients common to American Southwestern cooking — lime juice, grated lime peel, garlic, jalapeño peppers, and ground cumin. A touch of butter is added, just as the sauce is reheated, to blend together the various flavors.

Preparation time: *25 minutes*

Marinating time: *6 hours or overnight*

Grilling time: *10 to 12 minutes*

Yield: *4 servings*

1½ to 2 pounds sirloin or other tender beef such as top loin or round tip steak

2 medium red peppers

1 medium onion

½ cup apple juice, divided

6 tablespoons lime juice (from about 3 large limes)

1½ teaspoons grated lime peel

6 tablespoons vegetable oil

3 cloves garlic, peeled and coarsely chopped

1 to 2 large jalapeño peppers, seeded and chopped

¾ teaspoon cumin

1½ teaspoons chili powder

½ teaspoon paprika

Salt and pepper to taste

2 tablespoons butter

1 Working on a cutting board, trim all visible fat from the beef; cut the meat into cubes of about 1½ inches. Place the cubes in a large, resealable plastic bag or in a nonreactive container.

2 On a separate cutting board, core and seed the red peppers and slice them into strips about 1½ inches wide; slice each strip crosswise into 1- to 2-inch pieces. Cut the onion in half lengthwise and remove the skin. Cut each half into thirds; break them apart into slices. Place the peppers and onions in the bag or container with the beef cubes.

3 Combine 6 tablespoons of the apple juice with the lime juice, grated lime peel, oil, garlic, jalapeño peppers, cumin, chili powder, and paprika in a blender container; at high speed, blend the mixture for a few seconds into a coarse puree. Pour the resulting marinade over the beef and vegetables; seal the bag or cover the container, and refrigerate for at least 6 hours or overnight, turning occasionally. Be sure to soak your wooden skewers in water for at least 30 minutes before grilling to prevent them from burning.

4 Prepare a medium-hot fire in a charcoal or gas grill. (Sprinkle coals with a handful of presoaked hickory or mesquite wood chips, if desired.)

5 Remove the beef from the marinade. Reserve any remaining marinade and place it in a small saucepan. Thread 3 to 4 beef cubes, alternating with pieces of pepper and onion, on soaked skewers. Sprinkle kebabs with salt and pepper.

6 Place the skewers on a well-oiled grill grid; grill the kebabs for about 10 minutes for medium-rare or about 12 minutes for medium, turning every 5 to 6 minutes.

7 As the kebabs grill, bring the leftover marinade in the saucepan to a boil for about 1 minute on top of the stove; reduce heat and simmer for 15 minutes. Whisk in 2 tablespoons butter and 2 tablespoons of the remaining apple juice. Spoon the sauce over the grilled kebabs just before serving.

Go-With: *Serve with buttered rice or any of the side dishes in Chapter 16.*

Per serving: *Calories 498 (From Fat 295); Fat 33g (Saturated 7g); Cholesterol 113mg; Sodium 225mg; Carbohydrate 13g (Dietary Fiber 2g); Protein 38g.*

REMEMBER

For best results, follow the marinating times suggested in recipes. But when you're in a hurry, marinate for as much time as you have. The flavor may not be as intense, but the dish should still taste fine.

Teriyaki Steak Kebabs

Grilling succulent oranges (and other citrus fruits) releases the intensely rich and flavorful oils locked in the peel of the fruit. In this recipe, oranges are threaded onto skewers with teriyaki-marinated red onions, peppers, and beef.

Preparation time: *25 minutes*

Marinating time: *6 hours or overnight*

Grilling time: *12 to 14 minutes*

Yield: *4 servings*

½ cup teriyaki sauce

3 tablespoons vegetable oil

2 tablespoons brown sugar, packed

2 cloves garlic, peeled and minced

1 tablespoon peeled and freshly grated ginger

½ teaspoon black pepper

1½ to 2 pounds well-trimmed beef top round steak, cut into 1½-inch cubes

2 medium seedless oranges, quartered

2 medium red onions, each cut into 6 pieces

2 large green bell peppers, seeded and cut into 2-inch chunks

1. In a large bowl or resealable plastic bag, combine the first six ingredients. Add the beef and toss (or shake the bag) to mix. Cover the bowl or seal the bag, pressing out any air; refrigerate the meat for 6 hours or overnight, turning it several times. Drain off and reserve the remaining marinade. Before grilling, bring marinade to a boil for 1 minute, and then simmer for 15 minutes.
2. Prepare a medium fire in a charcoal or gas grill. Be sure to soak your wooden skewers in water for at least 30 minutes before grilling to prevent them from burning.
3. As the grill preheats, alternate pieces of beef, orange, onion, and green pepper on soaked skewers, beginning and ending with the beef. Brush the meat and vegetables with the reserved marinade.
4. Place the kebabs on a well-oiled grill grid. Brush the kebabs once with the remaining marinade during the first 5 minutes of grilling. Grill 12 minutes for medium-rare and 14 minutes for medium, turning about every 5 minutes to prevent charring.

Per serving: *Calories 335 (From Fat 54); Fat 6g (Saturated 2g); Cholesterol 98mg; Sodium 1,457mg; Carbohydrate 29g (Dietary Fiber 4g); Protein 41g.*

Porky Pig on a Stick

Pork kebabs can be cut from almost any part of the pig, including leg, loin, or shoulder, but the best meat for kebabs comes from the tenderloin and boneless loin. The meat should be cut into 1-inch-thick cubes and then marinated before cooking over direct heat. Grill for 10 to 12 minutes total, turning and basting the kebabs frequently to keep them from drying out. The best way to check for preferred doneness is to take one of the kebabs off the skewer and cut into it. For more on cooking times for pork, flip to Chapter 12.

If you apply a basting marinade to kebabs that has come into contact with raw meat, be sure to grill the kebabs for at least 5 to 7 minutes after the application — doing so destroys any bacteria from the raw pork, which may have contaminated the marinade.

Apple and Tarragon Pork Kebabs

The flavor of pork works well with virtually any kind of vegetable and a range of succulent, sweet fruits. In this recipe, apples and apple juice team up with white wine and tarragon to flavor grilled pork kebabs.

Preparation time: *25 minutes*

Marinating time: *4 to 24 hours*

Grilling time: *12 to 14 minutes*

Yield: *4 servings*

¼ cup apple juice

¼ cup dry white wine

1 tablespoon soy sauce

2 cloves garlic, peeled and crushed

2 tablespoons chopped fresh tarragon, or 2 teaspoons dried tarragon

1 tablespoon Dijon-style mustard

Salt and pepper to taste

1¼ to 1½ pounds lean boneless pork loin, cut into 1-inch cubes

2 Granny Smith or Golden Delicious apples, peeled, cored, and cut into 1½-inch cubes

1 Combine all ingredients except the pork and apples in a shallow, nonreactive dish or large, resealable plastic bag.

2 Add the pork, turning to coat in the marinade. Cover the dish or seal the bag, pressing out any air; refrigerate for at least 4 hours, but not more than 24 hours, turning occasionally. Be sure to soak your wooden skewers in water for at least 30 minutes before grilling to prevent them from burning.

3 Prepare a medium-hot fire in a charcoal or gas grill.

4 Remove the pork cubes from the marinade, reserving any remaining marinade.

5 Arrange the pork and apple cubes on the skewers.

6 Place the skewers on a lightly oiled grill grid. Grill the kebabs 6 to 7 minutes, turning and basting them frequently with the reserved marinade. Continue to grill for about 6 to 7 minutes, turning frequently, without basting, until the pork is well browned on all sides and cooked through.

Go-With: *Serve over a bed of Couscous with Apples, Onions, and Raisins (Chapter 16) or with any of the fruit chutneys in Chapter 6.*

Per serving: *Calories 263 (From Fat 91); Fat 10g (Saturated 4g); Cholesterol 80mg; Sodium 529mg; Carbohydrate 13g (Dietary Fiber 1g); Protein 29g.*

Pork Kebabs with Nectarines and Red Onions

Here's a kebab dish that adds both sweetness and a little pungent bite from onions to pork, which is the best meat for any sweet flavorings. Lamb would be fine, too, but we wouldn't serve this with beef. You can see these colorful kebabs in the color photo section of this book.

Preparation time: *25 minutes*

Marinating time: *4 hours to overnight*

Grilling time: *10 to 12 minutes*

Yield: *4 servings*

1½ teaspoons ground fennel

1½ teaspoons ground cumin

3 cloves garlic, minced

Juice of 1½ limes

1½ teaspoons fresh, coarsely ground black peppercorns

1 teaspoons salt

4 tablespoons corn or peanut oil

2 pounds pork loin, cut into 1½- to 2-inch pieces

3 nectarines, not overly ripe, pitted and each cut into 4 sections

2 medium-sized red onions, peeled and each cut into 6 sections (each should retain part of its root to hold the pieces together)

Oil for brushing vegetables

1 In a medium nonreactive mixing bowl or a large, resealable plastic bag, combine the fennel, cumin, garlic, lime juice, black pepper, salt, and corn or peanut oil; add the pork pieces, tossing to coat in the marinade. Cover the bowl or seal the bag, pressing out all the air and refrigerate for 4 hours or overnight. Be sure to soak your wooden skewers in water for at least 30 minutes before grilling to prevent them from burning.

2 Prepare a medium fire in a charcoal or gas grill.

3 Remove the pork from the marinade, discarding any leftover. Thread the pork, nectarines, and red onions alternately on skewers. Brush the nectarines and red onions with oil. Season the meat, nectarines, and red onions with salt. You may want to cook the onions on a separate skewer if you like them softer and more charred, but they will be nice and crisp if cooked with the pork kebabs.

4 Place the kebobs on a lightly oiled grill grid. Grill for 5 to 6 minutes. Turn and cook for another 5 to 6 minutes. Cut a piece of meat to test for doneness. Pork can be slightly pink in the center when done. Don't overcook; pork becomes very dry. Transfer the kebabs to a serving platter and serve.

Per serving: *Calories 310 (From Fat 136); Fat 15g (Saturated 4g); Cholesterol 85mg; Sodium 160mg; Carbohydrate 12g (Dietary Fiber 2g); Protein 31g.*

Lamb Kebabs — the Real Deal

Kebabs originated in the Middle East, where lamb is virtually a staple. The most authentic (and some say, the most tasty) kebabs you can grill up are made with fresh lamb. Lamb kebab cubes grill quickly, in only about 10 minutes. Be sure to hover over the kebabs, checking often for doneness, because they easily overcook and lose their juicy tenderness.

Lamb and Eggplant Kebabs with Tarragon Marinade

As much as lamb is complemented by the sharp tartness of lemon, as in the pre-ceding recipe, it also partners well with sweet ingredients like chutneys, jam glazes, honey, and fruit juices. In this recipe, honey, apple juice, and tarragon are combined to infuse lamb and vegetables with a tinge of sweetness. This marinade is especially tasty with eggplant and summer squash, but we encourage you to use it on any number of other vegetable kebabs.

Preparation time: *30 minutes*

Marinating time: *8 hours or overnight*

Grilling time: *10 to 14 minutes*

Yield: *4 to 6 servings*

1 cup apple juice

⅓ cup cider vinegar

⅓ cup olive oil

⅓ cup chopped scallions (green and white parts)

3 tablespoons honey

2 tablespoons A-1 steak sauce (or your favorite brand)

1½ tablespoons chopped fresh tarragon, or 1½ teaspoons dried tarragon

1 clove garlic, peeled and halved

¾ teaspoon salt, or to taste

¼ teaspoon pepper

1½ to 2 pounds lean boneless lamb, cut into 1¼-inch cubes

¼ cup olive oil (for vegetable marinade)

1 small eggplant (about 1 pound), cut into 1-inch pieces

2 small yellow squash, cut into ½-inch rounds

1 In a medium saucepan, combine the apple juice, vinegar, ⅓ cup olive oil, scallions, honey, steak sauce, tarragon, garlic, and salt and pepper; simmer the mixture for 10 minutes over low heat, uncovered. Cool to room temperature.

2 Place the lamb in a large, resealable plastic bag or a nonreactive mixing bowl; pour 1¼ cups of the marinade over the lamb, reserving the remaining ¼ cup of marinade. Cover the remaining marinade and refrigerate until ready to marinate the vegetables. Seal the bag, pressing out any air, or cover the bowl; refrigerate for 8 hours or overnight, turning the meat occasionally.

3 About 1 hour before you're ready to grill, combine the reserved marinade with the ¼ cup olive oil. Place the vegetables in a large, resealable plastic bag or nonreactive bowl; pour the marinade-oil mixture over the vegetables, tossing to coat. Seal the bag or cover the bowl, and refrigerate for about 30 minutes to 1 hour, turning occasionally. Be sure to soak wooden skewers in water for 30 minutes to prevent them from burning.

4 Prepare a medium fire in a charcoal or gas grill.

5 Remove the lamb and vegetables from their marinades, reserving the lamb marinade. Thread lamb, eggplant, and squash pieces alternately onto long skewers. Thread the pieces of squash and eggplant so they lie flat on the grill. Brush kebabs generously with the reserved lamb marinade and (if desired) sprinkle with additional salt and pepper.

6 Place the skewers on a well-oiled grill grid. Grill for 5 to 7 minutes; brush with marinade, and turn. Grill for about 5 to 7 minutes more for medium-rare or until the lamb is browned on the outside but pink and juicy inside; the vegetables should be lightly browned and crisp-tender. Cut into a kebab to test for doneness.

Per serving: *Calories 628 (From Fat 363); Fat 40g (Saturated 7g); Cholesterol 98mg; Sodium 610mg; Carbohydrate 36g (Dietary Fiber 5g); Protein 33g.*

Lemony Fresh Lamb Kebabs

These lamb kebabs come to life with the flavors of fresh lemon juice, grated lemon peel, minced garlic, and fresh rosemary. They make terrific party appetizers.

Preparation time: *20 minutes*

Marinating time: *6 hours or overnight*

Grilling time: *10 minutes*

Yield: *4 servings*

6 tablespoons olive oil

Grated peel of 1 large lemon (about 2 teaspoons)

Juice of 1 large lemon (about 3 tablespoons)

1 tablespoon finely chopped fresh rosemary, or 1 teaspoon dried, crushed rosemary

2 large cloves garlic, peeled and minced

½ teaspoon salt, or to taste

Pepper to taste

2 pounds lamb (from the leg), cut into 1- to 1¼-inch cubes

8 to 10 long sprigs fresh rosemary (optional)

Oil for brushing rosemary sprigs

Lemon wedges for garnish

1 In a medium nonreactive mixing bowl or large, resealable plastic bag, combine the olive oil, lemon peel, lemon juice, rosemary, garlic, and salt and pepper; add the lamb cubes, tossing to coat in the marinade. Cover the bowl or seal the bag, pressing out any air. Refrigerate for 6 hours or overnight. Be sure to soak wooden skewers in water for 30 minutes to prevent them from burning.

2 Prepare a medium fire in a charcoal or gas grill.

3 Remove the lamb from the marinade, reserving any remaining marinade. Thread the lamb on skewers. Brush the lamb with the reserved marinade.

4 If using rosemary sprigs, brush them generously with oil. Place the sprigs on a lightly oiled grill grid. Set the lamb kebabs on the rosemary sprigs (or directly on the oiled grid, if you're not using the rosemary). Grill the kebabs for about 5 minutes; brush them with more marinade and turn. Grill for about 5 minutes more for medium-rare. Cut the meat to test doneness. The lamb should be pink to rosy in the center of each kebab when done. Transfer immediately to a serving platter and garnish with lemon wedges.

Per serving: *Calories 465 (From Fat 284); Fat 32g (Saturated 7g); Cholesterol 130mg; Sodium 391mg; Carbohydrate 2g (Dietary Fiber 0g); Protein 42g.*

REMEMBER

Threading pieces of food tightly together on skewers increases the overall cooking time. Leave a little space between each piece of food to allow the heat to surround and cook the food evenly and more quickly.

Chicken Flying Full Mast, Half-Mast, All Over the Mast

Tender, plump, boneless chicken breasts are easily cut up into thin strips, chunks, or cubes for threading on skewers. Chicken's mild flavor makes it suitable for any number of sweet or spicy marinades, barbecue sauces, or rubs. Chicken kebabs, depending on their thickness, cook very quickly — usually in about 10 minutes. Chicken wings or legs may take twice as long. A decent-sized chicken kebab should be about 2 inches by 2 inches.

Use soy sauce, ginger, and crushed red pepper together in a marinade; or try garlic, lemon, olive oil, and fresh rosemary. Or you can simply squeeze a little lemon or lime juice over the chicken chunks or strips and then sprinkle them with a commercial jerk seasoning before grilling. Chicken kebabs are great with many of the side dishes in this book (see Chapter 16) as well as just a nice bowl of white, brown, or Chinese rice.

Chicken Tikka

In this Indian recipe, you marinate cubes of chicken in yogurt along with spices common to Indian curries — turmeric, cumin, and cayenne pepper. The turmeric gives these kebabs a yellow glow.

Preparation time: *25 minutes*

Marinating time: *6 hours or overnight*

Grilling time: *10 to 12 minutes*

Yield: *4 servings*

2 pounds boneless, skinless chicken breasts

½ cup plain yogurt

1 medium onion, peeled and quartered

3 large cloves garlic, peeled and crushed

2 tablespoons fresh lemon juice

1 tablespoon peeled and grated fresh ginger

2 teaspoons vegetable oil

1 teaspoon salt, or to taste

½ teaspoon ground cumin

¾ teaspoon cinnamon

½ teaspoon turmeric

¼ teaspoon cayenne pepper

Black pepper to taste

15 to 20 cherry tomatoes

1 Rinse the chicken breasts under cold running water and pat dry with paper towels; trim any loose fat and cut into 1¼-inch cubes. Place the chicken in a large, resealable plastic bag or a medium nonreactive mixing bowl.

2 In a blender container, combine the remaining ingredients, except the cherry tomatoes; puree the mixture until smooth. Pour the marinade over the chicken in the bag or bowl; toss to coat well. Seal the bag, pressing out any air, or cover the bowl, and refrigerate for at least 6 hours or overnight. Be sure to soak wooden skewers in water for 30 minutes to prevent them from burning.

3 Prepare a medium-hot fire in a charcoal or gas grill.

4 As the grill preheats, remove the chicken from the marinade, discarding the remaining marinade, and thread on skewers, 3 to 4 pieces to a skewer.

5 Place the skewers on a well-oiled grill grid; grill the kebabs for 5 to 6 minutes per side or until done and nicely browned, turning once. Using a barbecue mitt to protect your hands from the heat, place a cherry tomato on the top of each skewer after grilling for 5 minutes.

Go-With: *Serve on a bed of white rice and boiled peas; complete the meal with the Yogurt Cucumber Salad in Chapter 16 or with Summer Squash or Tomato Chutney (Chapter 6).*

Vary It! *The yogurt-flavored marinade can also be used with about 2 pounds of skewered beef or lamb cubes or with extra-large shrimp.*

Per serving: *Calories 272 (From Fat 56); Fat 6g (Saturated 2g); Cholesterol 126mg; Sodium 266mg; Carbohydrate 5g (Dietary Fiber 1g); Protein 47g.*

Gone Fishin' and Sea Divin' (For Kebabs)

What seafood is best for kebabs? Any firm-fleshed fish or shellfish that you can easily cut into 1-inch-thick chunks. Some examples include large sea scallops, monkfish, halibut, tuna, salmon, swordfish, and, of course, large to jumbo-sized shrimp.

"Large" and "jumbo" aren't legal terms, so the number of shrimp you receive can vary. Actual *shrimp count* is determined by the number of shrimp in a pound according to the size of the shrimp. So "20 count" means 20 shrimp to the pound. The smaller the number, the larger the shrimp. Shrimp are sold fresh and whole, frozen with their shell, or frozen and shelled. You can skewer any of them through the fleshy part of the tail at its two ends (refer to Figure 8-1, earlier in this chapter, to see how).

Turn and brush fish kebabs frequently with a basting sauce, marinade, or herb butter to keep them from drying out during grilling. One-inch pieces of fish take 6 to 8 minutes to cook through. Shrimp are done as soon as the body meat loses its translucence. Any further cooking will result in tough shrimp.

You may find it necessary to *parboil* (boiling a few minutes to soften) tougher vegetables and fruits before skewering them with tender, quick-cooking fish.

Mixed Grill Seafood Kebabs with Fresh Lemon Sauce

These mixed seafood kebabs are doused twice with the lively flavor of fresh lemons — one time in the marinade and again in the finishing sauce. You can also use limes or oranges if you prefer. The citric acid in such fruits really makes the flavor come alive.

Preparation time: *25 minutes*

Grilling time: *6 to 8 minutes*

Yield: *4 servings*

Fresh Lemon Sauce

Grated peel of 1 lemon

3 tablespoons fresh lemon juice (about 1 large lemon)

1 tablespoon minced fresh parsley, or 1 teaspoon dried parsley

1 tablespoon minced fresh herbs, such as oregano, thyme, rosemary, basil, or dill, or 1 teaspoon dried herbs

2 teaspoons Dijon-style mustard

Salt and white pepper to taste

½ cup virgin olive oil

In a jar with a tight-fitting lid, combine all the ingredients except the olive oil; seal the jar and shake until the ingredients are well blended. Add the olive oil, about ¼ cup at a time, tightly sealing the jar and shaking after each addition.

Mixed Grill Seafood Kebabs

¾ pound firm fish, such as halibut, shark, swordfish, monkfish, salmon, or tuna, cut into 1- to 1¼-inch cubes

¾ pound shellfish, such as peeled, deveined extra-large shrimp, whole sea scallops, or lobster tail meat cut into large chunks

1 large red pepper, seeded and cut into 2-inch pieces

1 medium red onion, peeled and cut into 2-inch pieces

8 fresh herb sprigs, such as thyme, rosemary, oregano, or dill

Oil for brushing herbs

1 Prepare a medium-hot fire in a charcoal or gas grill. Be sure to soak wooden skewers in water for 30 minutes to prevent them from burning.

2 Arrange the seafood, red pepper, and red onion on 8 metal or wooden skewers, alternating different pieces of fish with the vegetables.

3 Pour half (about ⅓ cup) of the Fresh Lemon Sauce into a small bowl; baste the skewered fish and vegetables with the sauce. Reserve the remaining sauce to drizzle over grilled kebabs.

4 Just before grilling the kebabs, brush the herb sprigs with oil and place them directly on a well-oiled grill grid.

5 Place the kebabs on the herbs, one to a sprig. Grill, basting and turning the kebabs every 2 to 3 minutes, for a total of 6 to 8 minutes or until the fish is opaque. (Don't baste during the last 3 minutes of cooking.) Cut the shellfish with a thin-bladed knife to check for doneness; the shellfish should be firm and opaque but still moist throughout.

6 Remove the kebabs from the grill and place on a large serving platter; drizzle with the reserved lemon sauce. Serve over steaming white rice (if desired).

Per serving: *Calories 533 (From Fat 397); Fat 44g (Saturated 7g); Cholesterol 168mg; Sodium 429mg; Carbohydrate 7g (Dietary Fiber 2g); Protein 28g.*

Sweet-and-Sour Shrimp Kebabs with Scallions

These skewered extra-large or jumbo shrimp (16 to 20 per pound) are brushed with a sweet-and-sour glaze. To add a little contrasting color and crunch, wrap a long green scallion around and through each skewered shrimp. Or cut the scallions into 2-inch pieces and alternate them on the skewers with the shrimp.

Remember that tender-fleshed shrimp, like other seafood, quickly absorb smoky flavors from wood chunks and chips. Build your charcoal fire by using a few hardwood chunks — pecan, apple, and mesquite are all good with fish — or toss a handful of presoaked chips onto the fire or into a smoker box before grilling.

Preparation time: *20 minutes*

Marinating time: *30 minutes to 1 hour*

Grilling time: *6 minutes*

Yield: *4 servings*

26 to 28 extra-large shrimp, shelled and deveined (about 1½ pounds)

6 tablespoons soy sauce

3 tablespoons sesame oil

3 tablespoons vegetable oil

3 tablespoons balsamic vinegar

2 tablespoons honey

3 cloves garlic, peeled and minced

1 tablespoon peeled and coarsely chopped fresh ginger

1 to 2 teaspoons seeded, minced fresh hot chile pepper, such as jalapeño or habañero

8 scallions, trimmed (optional)

1. Rinse and drain the shrimp under cold running water.
2. In a medium nonreactive mixing bowl or a large, resealable plastic bag, make the marinade by combining the remaining ingredients, except the scallions; add the shrimp to the marinade, tossing them to coat well. Cover the bowl or seal the bag, pressing out any air; refrigerate for about 30 minutes to 1 hour. Be sure to soak wooden skewers in water for 30 minutes to prevent them from burning.
3. Prepare a medium-hot fire in a charcoal or gas grill.
4. Arrange the shrimp, 3 to 4 to a skewer, on 8 skewers. Pierce a scallion through its white bulb with the tip of a skewer (if desired), and then thread the long green part through and around the shrimp to hold in place. Repeat with remaining scallions and skewers. Brush the scallions and shrimp generously with the marinade, dabbing on bits and pieces of the chopped ginger and chilies.

5 Grill the kebabs on a lightly oiled grill grid about 3 minutes per side or until the shrimp are opaque and pink, brushing with the marinade once before turning.

Per serving: *Calories 367 (From Fat 197); Fat 22g (Saturated 3g); Cholesterol 252mg; Sodium 1,674mg; Carbohydrate 12g (Dietary Fiber 0g); Protein 30g.*

Allowing fish to marinate longer than an hour, particularly when the mixture contains an acid like lemon juice or vinegar, can cause the fish flesh to begin to toughen. One way to strengthen the flavors of the marinade without risking this undesirable firming is to chill the marinade in the refrigerator a few hours *before* adding the fish. When the fish is finally added, the marinade flavors are at their peak.

Please Satay for Dinner

If you travel throughout Malaysia, Singapore, and Indonesia, you can see vendors grilling all kinds of satay (pronounced sah-TAY) along the roadside on small portable hibachis. *Satay* is sort of a kebab, except that the meat (beef, lamb, or pork) or poultry is cut into thin strips, about ½-inch thick, instead of cubes or chunks. The skewers are inserted like a needle, and the strips are threaded from one end to the other in a kind of ripple. After grilling, the strips are served with a thick and scrumptious peanut sauce.

In Asia, cooks usually use wooden skewers, but you can purchase pretty metal skewers with Asian designs on the handles in Asian stores or kitchenware stores.

Whether made with pork, beef, lamb, or chicken, satay-like dishes make great party appetizers. You can also serve a pile of them on a big platter as a hefty main dish and accompanied by spicy side dishes.

Satay with Peanut Dipping Sauce

We use chicken as the meat of choice for this satay recipe, but you can easily substitute other meats such as pork or beef with very good results.

Preparation time: *25 minutes*

Marinating time: *4 hours or overnight*

Grilling time: *8 minutes*

Yield: *4 main servings, or 8 to 10 appetizer servings*

2 whole boneless, skinless chicken breasts (about 2½ pounds)

⅓ cup olive oil

¼ cup lime juice

2 tablespoons grated lime peel

2 tablespoons fresh cilantro (coriander), chopped with stems

2 small scallions, trimmed and chopped

1 teaspoon Tabasco sauce

1 large clove garlic, peeled and minced

1 Lay one chicken breast on a cutting board or other flat surface between 2 pieces of waxed paper. Using a meat mallet (a rolling pin or the bottom of a heavy skillet also works), pound the breast to flatten slightly; cut across the grain into 1-inch-thick strips. Repeat this step with the second breast. Place the strips in a large, resealable plastic bag or a nonreactive mixing bowl.

2 In a small mixing bowl or glass measuring cup, make the marinade by combining the remaining ingredients; pour the marinade over the chicken strips. Seal the bag, pressing out any air, or cover the bowl; marinate in the refrigerator for at least 4 hours or overnight. Be sure to soak wooden skewers in water for 30 minutes to prevent them from burning.

3 Prepare a medium-hot fire in a charcoal or gas grill.

4 Remove the chicken from the marinade and thread on bamboo or metal skewers. Discard the remaining marinade.

5 Place the skewers on a well-oiled grill grid. Grill for about 4 minutes on each side or until done to your preference. Serve with Peanut Dipping Sauce (see following recipe).

Peanut Dipping Sauce

An inspired, spicy peanut sauce, sweetened with just the right amount of creamy unsweetened coconut milk, is the traditional dipping sauce for skewered pieces of pork, chicken, or beef satay.

Preparation time: *15 minutes*

Yield: *About 1¼ cups sauce*

1 tablespoon corn oil

1 clove garlic, peeled and minced

1 teaspoon peeled and minced fresh ginger

⅔ cup canned unsweetened coconut milk

⅓ cup crunchy peanut butter

2 tablespoons soy sauce

1 tablespoon lime juice

1 tablespoon rice vinegar

1 teaspoon Tabasco sauce, or to taste

2 tablespoons chopped fresh cilantro (coriander) leaves

1 In a medium skillet or sauté pan, heat the oil over medium heat; add the garlic and ginger and cook for 1 to 2 minutes, stirring, until the garlic is softened. (Be careful not to let the garlic brown.)

2 Add the coconut milk, peanut butter, soy sauce, lime juice, rice vinegar, and Tabasco sauce to the pan. Stir well to combine. Bring the mixture to a boil, reduce heat, and simmer for 1 to 2 minutes. Transfer the sauce to a small bowl and sprinkle it with cilantro. Serve with grilled chicken strips as a dipping sauce.

Per serving: *Calories 737 (From Fat 320); Fat 36g (Saturated 13g); Cholesterol 241mg; Sodium 788mg; Carbohydrate 7g (Dietary Fiber 2g); Protein 95g.*

Chapter 9

Maybe Messy, Definitely Delicious: Ribs Worth Drooling Over

In This Chapter

- Shopping for various cuts of pork ribs
- Grilling pork ribs to perfection with rubs and sauces
- Barbecuing beef ribs according to the cut

Recipes in This Chapter

- Just-Right Pork Ribs
- Gingery Spice Rub
- Apple-Beef Basting Sauce
- Country-Style Barbecue Sauce
- Donna Myer's Baby Back Ribs with Sweet-Hickory Barbecue Sauce
- Soul Food Pork Ribs
- Southern Soul Barbecue Sauce
- Korean Beef Short Ribs

In this chapter, we take a bit of a breather from grilling, which is loosely defined as cooking relatively tender foods quickly and directly over intense heat. Here, however, we venture into the barbecuing realm. Even though grilling is the complete opposite of barbecuing — the cooking of relatively tough foods, long and slow, with lots of smoke — sometimes these cooking methods overlap. A person with good grilling skills can barbecue without building a smoke pit in the backyard; the old, reliable charcoal kettle grill will do just fine. In this chapter, we give you the techniques that enable you to barbecue ribs like a Kansas City pitmaster.

If ever a single food item seems perfectly matched to a covered charcoal grill, it's ribs. Barbecued ribs are very much a passion for the grilling chef, and succulent, tender, finger-lickin' ribs aren't all that difficult to achieve. We find that most die-hard barbecuers call for pork and not beef ribs. The last recipe in this chapter, however, is a beef rib recipe that really takes us back to the grilling method. With that recipe, you discover how to cook very tender, thinly cut Korean-style beef ribs directly over the heat of the grill in about 10 minutes.

Back, Spare, and Country-Style: Recognizing Pork Rib Varieties

REMEMBER

Pork rib cuts can be a source of confusion if you aren't familiar with them. Three cuts are available at your grocery store, so you should get to know the distinctive characteristics of each type of rib before tossing them on the grill. Here are the varieties you should know:

- **Back ribs:** Also called *baby back ribs,* back ribs are cut from the blade and center section of the loin chops, close to the spine, and include the finger meat between the ribs. This cut is very meaty and tender, and it's small enough to almost qualify as dainty finger food. Plan on a pound of back ribs per person. A slab (or rack) of these ribs weighs about 1½ to 2 pounds and will take about 1½ to 2 hours to cook indirectly on the grill.
- **Spareribs:** These ribs, which are the most popular pork rib choice, come from the underside or belly of the pig, next to the bacon. Even though they're the least meaty portion of the pig, spareribs are packed with tremendous flavor. A full slab (or rack) can weigh from 3 to 5 pounds — plan on a pound of ribs per serving. Set the heat on your grill at medium to medium-low and cook the ribs from 1½ to 2 hours. Use a covered grill, turn the ribs once, and brush them with sauce during the last 15 minutes of cooking (if desired).
- **Country-style ribs:** These ribs are cut from the shoulder or the blade end of the loin and have the most amount of meat in proportion to bone. They come from the top of the backbone instead of the rib cage. Because they're loaded with meat, you may want to braise them in a small amount of water on top of the stove until very tender before grilling them. One pound of country-style ribs serves 3 to 4 people.

The Many Ways to Grill Pork Ribs

Depending on whom you ask, you'll find a conglomeration of assorted techniques, methods, and preferences for cooking pork ribs. Some like the meat falling off the bone and smothered in barbecue sauce. Others like their ribs a little bit chewy and crispy, with just a hint of sauce and a lot of hickory wood flavoring.

Today, rib rubs often replace sweet, tomato-based barbecue sauces that have for so long been a traditional part of southern U.S. barbecue. Dry spice rubs add flavor without completely masking the natural taste of the pork, which overly rich sauces can do if applied throughout the cooking process.

Rubs, which can be mixed from any number of spices or herbs probably already on hand in your kitchen, are usually free of the unwanted calories from oils and other fats that are often loaded into rich barbecue or finishing sauces. Flip to Chapter 5 for more recipes and information on how to prepare and apply rubs.

In terms of technique, we've talked with some cooks who strongly believe in *degreasing* — eliminating excess fat from pork ribs by first roasting them in the oven or parboiling them on the stove before finishing on the grill. Other cooks recommend foil-wrapping the ribs before cooking them over direct heat in a covered grill. The foil is removed when the ribs are tender, and then the basting sauce is applied just a few minutes before they're fully grilled.

Both of these methods produce a pork rib with meat that's moist and tender. And generally, both methods cook the ribs in less time than it takes to grill them. But by not cooking pork ribs on the grill from beginning to end, we think that you lose much of that rich, slow-cooked barbecue flavor that only grilling indirectly and slowly over hot coals can produce. If you want to try out this long, slow, indirect grilling technique for pork ribs, check out the recipe for our Just-Right Pork Ribs later in the chapter.

The following steps sum up the process for successfully barbecuing your slabs of pork ribs:

1. **Build an indirect fire by piling the coals on one side of the grill.**

   This is our preferred method because it gives you plenty of room to place the large rib slabs away from the heat of the fire. However, you also can stack the charcoal in a circular ring around the edges of the grill. (Turn to Chapter 1 for complete instructions.) You can cook the ribs indirectly in a gas grill, but a charcoal fire gives them more flavor.

2. **Cook the ribs slowly for 1½ to 2 hours over medium heat (325 degrees to 350 degrees) and over a drip pan half filled with water.**

   Long, slow cooking makes for moist and tender ribs with a crisp crust. The drip pan of water helps so that the fat falls into the water rather than splattering onto the coals or grill. If your ribs brown too quickly within the first 30 minutes, shut the grill vents.

   You can toss in a large handful of presoaked wood chips each time you add fresh coals to the fire. Or build the fire using a combination of charcoal and hardwood oak or hickory chunks to achieve extra smoky flavor. (Refer to Chapter 3 for more on using wood during grilling.)

3. **If desired, add a sauce to your ribs.**

   Add any basting sauce that has a component of tomato or other sweet ingredient to the ribs during the last 20 minutes of cooking. Adding the sauce late in the process prevents the sauce from burning.

4. **Keep an eye on the ribs and take them off the heat when they're fully cooked.**

   Determining when pork ribs are done is a little tricky, but after 1½ to 2 hours, you can be virtually certain that the ribs are fully cooked. Keep in mind that the meat's color isn't an indication of doneness. Smoke from the coals or from burning wood chips can turn the interior of the meat pink and leave you with the impression that it isn't cooked. If you can move the rib bones back and forth without a lot of resistance after 1½ to 2 hours, the meat is cooked.

When grilling your ribs, remember that some spots on the grill will be hotter than others. You can move rib slabs to hotter or cooler spots to speed up or slow down cooking.

Regional ribs

Not everyone in the U.S. agrees on the best way to cook ribs. Here are some regional differences:

- People in the South overwhelmingly prefer pork to any other meat for ribs.
- You can find tomatoey barbecue in parts of western North Carolina, where the folks call it *Lexington-style* barbecue, after Lexington, North Carolina. Very often, barbecue in this part of the world is chopped pork taken from the bone or pork shoulder, but ribs are very popular too.
- Eastern North Carolinians prefer vinegar-based rib sauces with chile pepper flakes and spices like cinnamon, nutmeg, oregano, and paprika.
- Kansas City, Missouri, rib sauces are famous for their thick, ketchupy consistency.
- In Louisiana, Cajun spices — cayenne pepper, black pepper, garlic powder, Tabasco sauce, and thyme — often reign in rib rubs and sauces.
- In the Pacific Rim states — California, Washington, Oregon, and Hawaii — rib sauces can have a distinct sweetness, usually from fruits like pineapple.
- Ironically, a Midwestern state — Ohio — hosts the annual National Rib Cook-Off in Cincinnati, serving up 350,000 pounds of ribs during one weekend.
- Memphis, Tennessee, hosts the International Barbecue Cooking Contest; the rules state that "any nonpoisonous substances" may be used in the sauces. However, vinegar must be one of those substances.

Just-Right Pork Ribs

To make our pork ribs, we combine three recipes — a spice rub, a basting sauce, and a barbecue sauce. Apply the Gingery Spice Rub — a mixture of ginger, brown sugar, lemon peel, and salt and pepper — to the slab of raw ribs and allow it to stand for about 30 minutes (or about as long as it takes to build an indirect fire in a charcoal grill). After you place the ribs on the grill, brush them about every 20 minutes with the Apple-Beef Basting Sauce to keep them fully moist. Finally, 15 to 20 minutes before they're removed from the grill, you brush them again, but this time you use a rich and delicious Country-Style Barbecue Sauce. This sauce gives the ribs a glossy finish and also doubles as a dipping sauce.

Step 1: Mixin' the Gingery Spice Rub and Rubbin' the Ribs

You can prepare the Gingery Spice Rub up to a week ahead of time, using all the ingredients except the grated fresh lemon peel. You hold off on adding this ingredient because you want to retain the fragrant oil in the peel. Add the grated peel just before smearing the rub onto the ribs. If you have any leftover rub, store it in an air-tight container and use within a few days on other pork cuts, grilled fish, or chicken.

Preparation time: *5 minutes*

Yield: *Enough rub for 3 to 4 pounds of pork ribs*

1 tablespoon brown sugar

2 teaspoons ground ginger

2 teaspoons salt

1 to 2 teaspoons pepper, according to taste

1 teaspoon grated lemon peel (optional)

1 Combine all the ingredients in a small, clean jar or container with a tight-fitting lid. Seal the jar and shake until well mixed.

2 Set the ribs on a flat cookie sheet, and then trim off any loose or large pieces of fat. Cut the slabs into pieces that are 8 to 10 inches wide. (Doing so makes it easier to turn the ribs as they grill.)

3 Sprinkle the ribs with the rub, pressing the seasoning firmly into the meat on both sides. Cover loosely and set in the refrigerator for about 30 minutes (or as long as it takes to prepare the fire in the grill).

Vary It! *For a spicy dry rib rub, add cayenne pepper, seeded and chopped jalapeño pepper, or Tabasco sauce to taste. For a jerk-flavored rub, add cayenne pepper, allspice, and cinnamon to taste.*

Step 2: Fixin' the Apple-Beef Basting Sauce

Thick, sugar-loaded barbecue sauces mopped onto ribs too early can burn and char the surfaces of the meat. To keep pork ribs moist as they slow-cook for a long time on the grill, you can use a simple, low-sugar (or sugar-free) basting sauce made from any number of ingredients. Some grill chefs like a peppery solution of crushed red pepper and water. Others mix a smoky-flavored whiskey like bourbon or Scotch with a little water to taste. In this Apple-Beef Basting Sauce recipe, we use a simple combination of apple juice and beef broth. The apple juice does contain a little natural sugar, but it's not enough to char the meat. (You can also use this sauce to keep pork loins and other large cuts of meat moist as they grill.)

Preparation time: *5 minutes*

Yield: *1 cup (enough for 4 to 5 pounds of pork ribs)*

½ cup apple juice

½ cup beef or chicken broth

In a small glass measuring cup or mixing bowl, combine the apple juice and beef or chicken broth. Use the mixture as a basting sauce to brush on 4 to 5 pounds of pork ribs, about every 20 to 25 minutes as they grill.

Step 3: Grillin' and Saucin' Time

As the ribs grill, you have time to prepare the Country-Style Barbecue Sauce. Or, if you prefer, you can make and refrigerate the sauce up to 3 days prior to grilling. Be sure to reheat it in a small pan on top of the stove before basting the ribs, however.

Preparation time: *35 minutes*

Grilling time: *1½ to 2 hours*

Yield: *4 to 6 servings*

1 3- to 4-pound rack of pork spareribs, seasoned with Gingery Spice Rub (see previous recipe)

Country-Style Barbecue Sauce

2 tablespoons vegetable oil

1 small onion, peeled and finely chopped (about ½ cup)

2 cloves garlic, peeled and minced (about 2 teaspoons)

¾ cup water

⅔ cup ketchup

6 tablespoons cider vinegar

½ cup dark brown sugar, packed

1 tablespoon Worcestershire sauce

1 tablespoon molasses

1 teaspoon ground cumin

Salt and pepper to taste

1 Prepare a fire in a covered grill with 45 to 50 charcoal briquettes. After the briquettes are hot, use long-handled tongs to bank them to one side of the fire grate. On the other side of the fire grate, place a large drip pan half filled with water next to the banked coals. The pan should be large enough to completely sit under the ribs. A grill or oven thermometer should read about 350 degrees over the drip pan in the *covered* grill when the fire is ready. Try to maintain this moderate temperature as the ribs continue to cook.

2 Brush the grill grid with oil and set in place. Place the ribs on the grid, fat side up. (Or place the ribs in a rib rack.) Cover and cook over indirect heat for 1½ to 2 hours, turning and basting the ribs every 20 minutes with the Apple Basting Sauce.

Be sure to adjust the grill vents to maintain an even, moderate heat. If the heat is too hot and the ribs are browning too quickly, close the top vents to lower the temperature of the fire. Add hot briquettes to the fire every 30 to 40 minutes, or as necessary to maintain a steady, moderate heat.

3 Meanwhile, prepare the Country-Style Barbecue Sauce. Heat the oil in a medium saucepan over medium heat. Add the onion and garlic and cook, stirring, until the onion wilts, about 3 to 4 minutes. Add the remaining ingredients. Raise the heat to high and bring to a boil. Reduce the heat and simmer for 20 to 25 minutes or until thickened, stirring often.

4 About 15 minutes before removing the ribs from the grill, apply the barbecue sauce, turning and basting the ribs 2 to 3 times.

5 The ribs are done when you can easily cut through the end rib with a sharp kitchen knife and move the bones back and forth without much resistance. Remove the ribs from the grill and cut into serving-size portions. Bring the remaining sauce to a rapid boil in the saucepan and serve with the ribs.

Per serving: *Calories 849 (From Fat 481); Fat 53g (Saturated 18g); Cholesterol 184mg; Sodium 1,981mg; Carbohydrate 54g (Dietary Fiber 1g); Protein 40g.*

For foods that take longer than 40 minutes to grill, you need to replenish the fuel in your charcoal fire in one of two ways:

- Add 10 to 12 fresh briquettes to the burning coals every 30 minutes.
- Keep a metal pail filled with burning briquettes next to the grill and add a half-dozen (or more, depending on the size of the fire) every 40 minutes.

Go for the gold

Assuming that you're going to be proficient at barbecuing ribs after using our tips, you may want to try out your expertise at one of the dozens of barbecue contests held around the U.S. each year. Check with your local county or state fair to see if one is held in your area. Here are some of the best open competitions along with their phone numbers and addresses for more information:

- **May:** Annual Memphis in May World Championship Barbecue Cooking Contest, Memphis, Tennessee; 901-525-4611.
- **May:** Louisiana State Barbecue Championship, Shreveport, Louisiana; write to 239 Hanging Moss Trail, Shreveport, LA 71106.
- **June:** The Great Lenexa Barbecue Battle, Lenexa, Kentucky; 913-541-8591.
- **July:** Midwest Regional Barbecue Championship, Gladstone, Missouri; 816-436-4523.
- **September:** Blue Springs Blazeoff, Blue Springs, Missouri; 816-228-0137.
- **September:** Ribfest, Chicago, Illinois; write to Ribfest, 435 North Michigan Avenue, Chicago, IL 60611.
- **September:** Super Bowl of Brisket, Abilene, Texas; write to Box 3452, Abilene, TX 79604.
- **September:** World Championship Barbecue Cook-Off, Pecos, Texas; write to Pecos Chamber of Commerce, Box 27, Pecos, TX 79772.
- **October:** International Barbecue Society Tournament of Champions, Grand Prairie, Texas; write to Doug Beich, Traders Village, 2602 Mayfield Road, Grand Prairie, TX 75051.

Donna Myers's Baby Back Ribs with Sweet-Hickory Barbecue Sauce

As a spokesperson for the Barbecue Industry Association for the last 25 years, Donna Myers probably knows more barbecuing and grilling secrets than most seasoned pit-masters. In this recipe, Donna protects baby back ribs from the intense heat of the grill by wrapping them in aluminum foil until nearly cooked. In the final 30 minutes, the ribs are grilled over indirect heat where they develop a nice brown crust without any charring or overbrowning. Donna's rib barbecue sauce is savory-sweet with a hint of liquid hickory smoke seasoning, which you should be able to find at most grocery stores. It's one of our very favorite sauces in the book; it's delicious with any kind of poultry, beef ribs, steaks, or even burgers.

Preparation time: *20 minutes*

Grilling time: *1½ hours*

Yield: *3 to 4 main dish servings or 6 to 8 appetizer servings*

2 full racks baby back pork ribs (about 3 ½ pounds)

4 tablespoons water

2 teaspoons liquid hickory smoke seasoning

1½ cups Sweet-Hickory Barbecue Sauce (see following recipe)

1 In a covered grill, prepare a medium charcoal fire or preheat a gas grill to medium.

2 Cut each rack of ribs in half to make 4 equal-sized pieces, with about 6 to 7 ribs to a piece. Lay 2 of the pieces side-by-side on a long sheet of heavy-duty aluminum foil. Wrap tightly, using a drugstore wrap, but leave one end of the foil packet open. (Figure 9-1 illustrates how to use a drugstore wrap.) Repeat with the 2 remaining rib pieces and a second long sheet of foil.

3 Combine the water and liquid smoke seasoning; spoon half of the liquid smoke-water mixture into each foil packet; seal the ends tightly to prevent leakage.

4 Place both packets flat on the preheated grill grid; cover and cook for a total of 60 minutes, turning the packets over about every 20 minutes. Remove the packets from the grill to a large baking pan and let rest.

5 If you're using a gas grill, raise the heat on one burner to create a medium-hot indirect fire. If you're using a charcoal grill, add more coals to the fire to raise the temperature to medium-hot, and then bank the coals to one side. (See Chapter 1 for information about building an indirect fire.)

6 Remove the foil wrapping from the ribs; place the ribs on a lightly oiled grid, opposite the fire or heat. Cover the grill and cook for about 30 minutes or until the ribs are done, turning and basting both sides with the Sweet-Hickory Barbecue Sauce about every 10 minutes. Heat the remaining sauce just to boiling in a small saucepan and serve with the ribs.

Go-With: *Good with Garlic-Grilled Portobellos or Grilled Tomatoes with Cumin Butter (both in Chapter 16).*

Sweet-Hickory Barbecue Sauce

Preparation time: *About 15 minutes*

Yield: *About 2 cups*

⅓ cup soy sauce

½ cup water

4 scallions, cut into 1-inch pieces

6 large cloves garlic, peeled and crushed

¼ cup chili sauce

¼ cup ketchup

¼ cup corn syrup

¼ cup honey

1 teaspoon liquid hickory smoke seasoning

In a small bowl, whisk together all the sauce ingredients; cover and refrigerate several hours or overnight to meld flavors. The sauce can be stored in the refrigerator for about a week.

Per serving: *Calories 1,078 (From Fat 646); Fat 72g (Saturated 27g); Cholesterol 286mg; Sodium 2,145mg; Carbohydrate 45g (Dietary Fiber 1g); Protein 62g.*

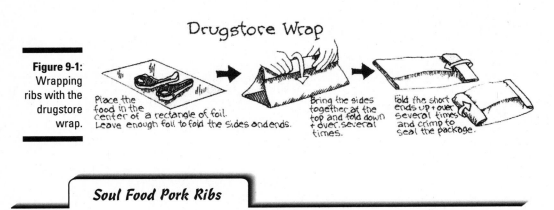

Figure 9-1: Wrapping ribs with the drugstore wrap.

Soul Food Pork Ribs

It's difficult to describe exactly what it is that makes soul food different from other southern food, but we think it's safe to say there's usually a little more sweetness in soul food. When it comes to barbecued ribs, this extra sweetness is certainly the case, and the ribs tend to take more saucing and remain juicier. (See the color photo section to see what these tasty ribs look like when they're finished barbecuing.)

Step 1: Preparing the Mop Sauce

This mop sauce can be prepared at any time — even days — before grilling the ribs because the ingredients used stay fresh for weeks, even months, as long as the mixture is kept tightly closed and refrigerated.

Preparation time: *2 minutes*

Yield: *Enough sauce to mop 3 to 4 pounds of pork spareribs*

1 cup cider vinegar

½ cup water

1 tablespoon salt

¾ teaspoon ground chili pepper

1 Combine all the ingredients in a small bowl, stir to dissolve the salt, and set aside.

2 You may brush the sauce onto the meat at this point and let the meat absorb some of the flavors. Some barbecue cooks like to cook the meat without any sauce, which leads to a smokier flavor in the meat. So if that's how you want to do it, simply add the sauce only in the last hour or so of cooking time.

Step 2: Moppin' and Grillin' the Ribs

You want the temperature of your grill to hover between 300 degrees and 325 degrees to allow these ribs to cook "low and slow." If the ribs appear dry on the outside, you can wrap them in foil with some mop sauce. They'll be happy to slowly cook in the foil for several hours. Then you can remove them from the foil and let them finish cooking over the dryer environment for the last hour.

You want the ribs to become "fall off the bone" tender, but tender ribs can cause a bit of an issue if you aren't prepared. The full racks may come apart as you're trying to flip them over, so at some point they become much easier to manage if you cut them into sections containing two or three ribs per section. We recommend cutting them when you're ready to slather them in barbecue sauce.

Grilling time: *4½ hours*

Yield: *4 to 6 servings*

2 racks of pork spareribs (3 to 4 pounds each)

Mop Sauce (see previous recipe)

Southern Soul Barbecue Sauce (see following recipe)

1 Prepare an indirect fire in a covered grill with about 45 briquettes. After the briquettes are hot, use long-handled tongs to bank the briquettes to one side of the fire grate. On the other side of the fire grate, place a drip pan half filled with water next to the banked coals. The drip pan should be large enough to completely sit under the ribs. A grill or oven thermometer should read about 325 degrees to 350 degrees in the covered grill when the fire is ready. Try to maintain this moderate temperature as the ribs continue to cook.

2 Place the mopped ribs on the hot grill, fat side up. Cover and cook for 4 hours, turning and basting the ribs every 30 minutes with the additional mop sauce. Because one slab of ribs will be closer to the coals than the other, be sure to rotate the ribs every hour.

Throughout the barbecuing, adjust the grill vents to maintain an even, moderate heat. If the heat is too hot and the ribs are browning too fast, close the top vents to lower the temperature of the fire. Add 8 to 10 briquettes to the fire every 40 to 60 minutes, or as necessary to maintain a steady, moderate heat.

3 Meanwhile, prepare the Southern Soul Barbecue Sauce (see the following recipe).

4 Brush on some of the barbecue sauce during the last 30 minutes of barbecuing. You can tell the ribs are fully cooked when the meat is tender and it has shrunken slightly away from the bones. Serve with the remaining hot barbecue sauce on the side.

Vary It! *If you want to add smoke flavor to your ribs, add 1 cup of presoaked drained wood chips to the coals when you begin to barbecue. Then after two hours of barbecuing, add another cup of presoaked, drained wood chips to the coals.*

Southern Soul Barbecue Sauce

Preparation time: *40 minutes*

Yield: *Enough to coat 3 to 4 pounds of pork spareribs*

1½ cups ketchup

½ cup brown sugar

1 large onion, peeled and diced

¼ cup cider vinegar

3 tablespoons Worcestershire sauce

2 cloves garlic, peeled and minced

Juice of 1 orange (about ⅓ cup)

1½ tablespoons chili powder

½ to 1 teaspoon Tabasco to taste

In a medium-size saucepan, combine the ketchup, brown sugar, onion, vinegar, Worcestershire sauce, garlic, orange juice, chili powder, and Tabasco. Stir to blend and bring to a boil. Reduce heat to a low simmer, cover partially, and cook for 30 minutes.

Vary It! *This barbecue sauce is chunkier than the average sauce, so if you prefer a smooth sauce, place the cooled sauce into a blender or food processor and puree.*

Per serving: *Calories 1,407 (From Fat 838); Fat 93g (Saturated 34g); Cholesterol 367mg; Sodium 3,302mg; Carbohydrate 67g (Dietary Fiber 4g); Protein 78g.*

Getting to Know Beef Ribs

Much like pork ribs, beef ribs come in different styles and from different sections of the animal. The most tender beef ribs for grilling come from the rib portion of the steer and are sold as either back ribs (also known as beef spareribs) or beef short ribs.

The National Cattlemen's Beef Association recommends slow grilling beef back ribs over indirect heat to infuse them with lots of smoky flavor. If you purchase short ribs from the chuck portion of the steer and grill them without any precooking, you may be disappointed. Chuck short ribs are too tough for grilling. These ribs are best when they're first braised in the oven or on top of the stove and then finished off on the barbecue grill to give them the smoky flavor you crave.

Beef short ribs are also known as Korean ribs because they're often marinated in a sauce that includes soy sauce, ginger, scallions, sake, and other ingredients common to Asian cuisine. These ribs are cut from the spare rib rack so that each rib piece has three crosswise-cut rib bones. They're juicy and meaty, and best of all, unlike other cuts of beef and pork ribs, beef short ribs grill quickly — in only about 12 minutes. The following recipe is ideal as a party appetizer if you cut each rib into three small pieces after grilling.

SHOPPING TIP

Ask your butcher to cut your beef short ribs into 3-inch lengths, about ⅜- to ½-inch thick, for best results on the grill.

Korean Beef Short Ribs

Korean short ribs are traditionally grilled quickly over medium heat, with frequent applications of a sesame-soy marinade. The result is a rib with a pink, medium-rare interior color and a rich, bronzed exterior. If you prefer your ribs more tender and with the meat falling off the bone, cook them indirectly for a longer period of time.

Preparation time: *25 minutes*

Marinating time: *4 hours to overnight*

Grilling time: *10 to 12 minutes*

Yield: *4 to 6 main dish servings or 10 appetizer servings*

4 green onions, trimmed and finely chopped

½ cup soy sauce

¼ cup sake, dry sherry, or dry vermouth

¼ cup water

¼ cup sesame oil

3 tablespoons dark brown sugar, packed

2 tablespoons sesame seeds

1 tablespoon peeled and grated fresh ginger, or 1 teaspoon ground ginger

3 cloves garlic, peeled and minced

¼ teaspoon cayenne pepper

½ teaspoon crushed red pepper flakes

3 to 4 pounds beef short ribs (also called flanken short ribs), trimmed of excess fat and cut crosswise about ½-inch thick (see Figure 9-2)

1 Combine all ingredients in a large, resealable plastic bag or a large nonreactive container. Seal the bag or cover the dish, and refrigerate for 4 hours or overnight, turning occasionally.

2 Prepare a medium fire in a charcoal or gas grill.

3 Remove the ribs from the marinade, reserving the marinade. Place the ribs on a well-oiled grill grid.

4 Grill for 5 to 6 minutes; baste both sides of the ribs with the reserved marinade. Cover and continue cooking for 5 to 6 minutes on the other side. The ribs should be a rich golden brown on both sides, with a pink interior.

5 Toast sesame seeds in a dry skillet, in a single layer, over medium-low heat until lightly browned. Remove the seeds immediately from the skillet to keep them from overbrowning or burning. Sprinkle over the ribs before serving.

Go-With: *Serve with Stuffed Summer Squash or Grilled New Potato Salad with Fresh Mint (both in Chapter 16).*

Per serving: *Calories 988 (From Fat 762); Fat 85g (Saturated 32g); Cholesterol 154mg; Sodium 1,931mg; Carbohydrate 13g (Dietary Fiber 1g); Protein 41g.*

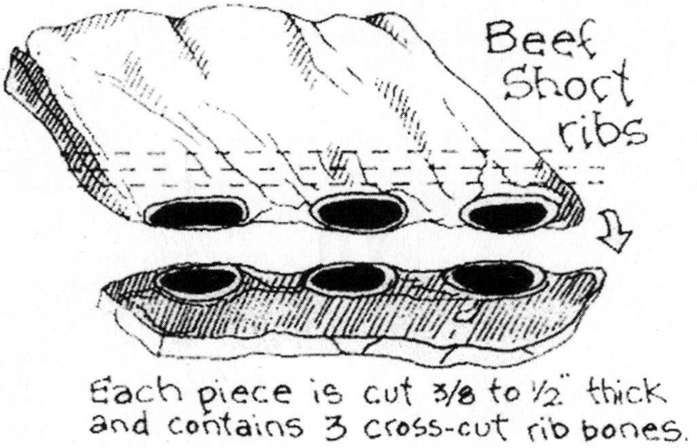

Beef
Short
ribs
Each piece is cut 3/8 to 1/2" thick
and contains 3 cross-cut rib bones.

Figure 9-2: Cutting beef short ribs.

Chapter 10

Pair a Rotisserie with a Grill? Oh Yes, You Can

In This Chapter

- Discovering how to rotisserie cook your food
- Experimenting with recipes for the rotisserie

Recipes in This Chapter

- Rotisserie-Grilled Chicken
- Lemon-Herb Gravy
- Rotisserie Pork Spareribs
- Rotisserie Boneless Pork Loin with Herbes de Provence

The very first grills were some primal form of rotisseries — just a stick that someone turned every once in a while over a fire. Today, electric rotisseries are available as grill accessories and make this once time-consuming chore a leisure-time activity.

In this chapter, you find out about the benefits of rotisserie cooking and how best to use a rotisserie in a covered gas grill. We discuss cooking times — which differ a great deal from tossing food directly on a grill — and give you the low-down on sauces that you can make by reclaiming juices from the rotisserie drip pan.

Grilling Off the Grid: A Primer on Rotisserie Cooking

Although we spend most of this book exalting the pleasures of cooking directly *on* a grill grid, we now state unequivocally that rotisserie cooking a few inches *above* the grid not only offers a few benefits but also imparts wonderful taste and textures to those foods. Rotisserie cooking takes a bit longer than placing the food directly on the grill but really no longer than if you cook it in a kitchen oven.

A rotisserie that turns at a constant, never-varying speed allows the same degree of heat to cook every inch of the food, thereby guaranteeing that a roast or bird will be succulent throughout. Food cooked on a rotisserie holds its moisture better than food cooked in an oven because the surface sears quickly and therefore seals in natural juices.

Rotisserie cooking is also healthier in some ways because you need to add very little extra fat, or none at all, before the food is placed on the *spit* — the rod of the rotisserie that holds the food above the fire — for cooking. The meat self-bastes.

Choosing the best meat for the mill

Rotisserie cookery is best for "round" food, that is, large roasts, whole poultry, and whole fish. The more delicate the flesh, the better results rotisserie grilling provides. Of course, rotisserie cookery isn't ideal for every food. We wouldn't stick a skewer through a whole steak, lamb chop, or beef fillet, and many of our kebab recipes are best placed directly on the grill so they pick up flavor from the burning coals. But if you like moist, juicy roasts and if you have the time to spend, rotisserie cookery is a wonderful process — and, thanks to electric rotisserie units, it's almost foolproof.

The rotisserie seems made for beef roasts because it keeps them juicy inside and nicely crisp on the outside. Beef roasts that are perfect for rotisserie cooking include the boneless beef top sirloin roast, round tip roasts (also called the sirloin tip), boneless rib-eye roasts, and the eye of round roast. Beef roasts practically baste themselves in their own juices as they turn on the spit. Pork is also a favorite for rotisserie cooking. The interior of the meat stays naturally moist while the outside surface develops a nice brown crust.

Keeping some general tips in mind

Rotisserie cooking has its own set of simple rules. Here they are in no particular order:

- **Pay attention to cook times.** As with grilling, many factors, such as wind, air temperature, humidity, and the size and thickness of the food, affect the performance and actual cooking times of your rotisserie. Recipes can only give approximate cooking times, so check the manufacturer's manual for cooking times and guidelines.
- **Keep the pieces of food of more or less equal size.** Cutting food into equal pieces ensures consistency in the cooking time.
- **Watch for floppy limbs and imbalanced spits.** Poultry wings and legs, which may flop around on the rotisserie, should be trussed or tied securely (though not too tightly) to the body with heavy cotton kitchen twine. See Figure 10-1, later in this chapter, for an illustration showing how to truss a bird.

For larger food, such as a roast, make sure that the food is balanced on the skewer before placing it over the grill. Too much weight or an imbalanced weight can cause the machine motor to malfunction and burn out. Weights are often provided on electric rotisseries to help achieve this balance.

- **Always use a drip pan under your rotisserie grilled foods.** Why? A good deal of fat will drip onto the coals — fat that you could use to make a sauce later. By using these drippings to baste the food, you not only keep the food moist but you create more drippings for use in a sauce, just as if you had cooked the food in your kitchen oven.

  If you don't plan to baste or make a sauce, fill the pan half full with water, which adds moisture. Never allow the liquid in the drip pan to evaporate.
- **Use a properly sized drip pan.** Your drip pan should be large enough to accommodate the length and width of the food being cooked, but it shouldn't be so large that it blocks the heat of the grill.
- **Avoid sugary sauces and marinades.** Marinate and baste with any combination of liquids, herbs, and spices, but keep sugared ingredients to a minimum. Don't baste with a sauce that has a high sugar content until the last 15 to 20 minutes of cooking; otherwise the sauce will char.
- **Use a spray bottle to mist and add moisture to rotisserie meats or poultry as they spit-roast.** Fill the bottle with any combination of flavored liquids, such as soy sauce, sherry, apple juice, or beef broth, and your favorite herbs and spices. Mist about every 20 minutes.
- **Keep an eye on your temperature.** If the food browns too quickly, reduce the temperature setting on your rotisserie. The food may take a little longer to cook, but you'll avoid scorching it.
- **Stay safe from the heat.** It's always a good idea to wear a heavy mitt when raising the rotisserie hood.
- **Experiment by adding an extra smoky flavor to the meat.** You can do this by cooking the food until almost done and then reducing the heat of the coals and covering the grill, thereby allowing smoke to build up and permeate the meat.
- **Use a meat thermometer.** If ever there was a good reason to buy a stainless steel insert thermometer (see Chapter 2), a rotisserie is it. You can easily pluck a steak or grill basket off the fire and cut into the food to see if it's cooked the way you like it. Unfortunately, you really can't do that with ease or safety with a turning rotisserie. Even if you shut off the rotisserie and cut into the meat, you'll still create a pocketlike gash in the meat that will get more heat than the rest of the surface and interior when you switch the rotisserie back on.

  So, for rotisserie cooking, the thermometer should be inserted in the deepest part of the food at the beginning of the cooking time. If you think that the thermometer may fall out when the food turns, secure the thermometer with a string.

- **To avoid overcooking the food, check the temperature about 15 to 20 minutes before the final estimated cooking time.** The temperature will rise more rapidly at the end of cooking time than at the beginning. Unlike oven-roasted food, rotisserie-cooked food doesn't increase in temperature and doesn't continue to cook after it's taken off the rotisserie. However, all roasts should rest for 5 to 10 minutes after cooking to allow the juices to settle and to make carving easier.
- **Save your leftovers.** Rotisserie cooks often use large beef, pork, or poultry roasts so they have an abundance of delicious leftovers. Shred or thinly slice leftover meat for hearty sandwiches or add the meat to homemade soups and tossed lettuce or pasta salads. You also may want to mix the leftovers with shredded lettuce and roll the mixture up in soft taco shells.

REMEMBER

For the best results, check your manufacturer's instruction manual for tips, recipes, temperature settings, and cooking times that are specific to your rotisserie and the foods you're cooking.

Heeding meat-specific rotisserie cooking tips

The following list provides a few general tips for rotisserie cooking different cuts of beef, poultry, pork, lamb, and fish. For more specific jargon and shopping tips, refer to the specific meat's chapter in Part IV of this book.

- **Beef roasts:** Coat the exterior of these roasts lightly with olive oil and sprinkle with salt, pepper, and other seasonings, such as garlic powder. Rub the surface with dried herbs and spices to give the exterior a nice brown crust when it's cooked.

  Cooking times and temperatures vary according to the heat intensity of your rotisserie, but a good rule is that the less tender the cut, the more slowly the roast should be cooked. For lean round tip and eye round roasts, set the temperature on medium or medium-low for long, slow cooking. Top sirloin and rib-eye roasts, which are more tender and contain more fat, can be cooked over higher temperatures — from medium to medium-high. For best results, check your grill manual for recommended temperature settings and grilling times. The internal temperature should reach 135 to 140 degrees before the roast is removed from the spit.
- **Pork:** Ribs and boneless pork loins (see recipes for Rotisserie Pork Spareribs and Rotisserie Boneless Pork Loin with Herbes de Provence later in this chapter) are favorite cuts, but rolled shoulders and boned fresh hams are also delicious. Ribs that are rotisserie cooked don't have that soft, "fall off the bone" texture that you get from indirect grilling. Instead, they have a firmer, chewier meat, which some people find more desirable.

Keep the seasoning simple so the rotisserie taste of the meat comes through. Try brushing the surface of the roast or ribs with any of the oils in Chapter 5 or with a good commercially produced flavored oil — such as roasted garlic or herb oil — and then sprinkle with salt and freshly ground black pepper to taste. Cook pork cuts until the internal temperature reaches 145 to 155 degrees.

- **Lamb:** A leg of lamb, with its bone intact, is one of the more difficult meat cuts to balance on a spit. For best results, ask your butcher to remove the bone and to butterfly the leg. Boned and rolled shoulder roasts and racks of lamb can also be spit roasted and are smaller and easier to skewer and cook.

  You can marinate any of these cuts, or you can simply season them with olive oil, garlic, and salt and pepper. Fasten the meat to the spit and cook on medium-high to high heat, or according to the instructions in your grilling manual, until the temperature reaches 135 degrees for rare or 140 or 145 degrees for medium.

- **Turkey:** Turkeys are best if they're first butterflied by your butcher. Whole turkeys have very large bones that tend to prevent even cooking on a spit. The final result can be thigh meat that's undercooked and breast meat that's overcooked and dry.

  Season the butterflied turkey inside and out and tie it back together for rotisserie cooking. You can even add a thin layer of cranberry stuffing or dressing to the inside before you tie the bird. Cook on high and remove the turkey from the spit when the internal temperature reaches 175 degrees. ***Note:*** A stuffed bird takes a bit longer to cook, and the stuffing should be tested with a meat thermometer. Boneless turkey breasts, two at a time, are also great choices for rotisserie cooking.

- **Other poultry:** You can cook a pair of chickens or even four Cornish game hens or squab together on one spit. (See Chapter 14 for more information on Cornish game hens and squab.) Most spit rods can hold about 12 pounds of meat at one time. The length of the rod and barbecue determine the actual number.

  REMEMBER

  Be sure to tie the legs and wings of each bird securely to their bodies before cooking. Doing so prevents the limbs from flopping around as the spit turns. Except for turkey (which I discuss earlier in this section), all poultry should be cooked to an internal temperature of 180 degrees. You also can stuff poultry before rotisserie cooking, but the cooking times will be longer.

- **Fish:** Fish should really be rotisserie cooked in a swinging basket that rocks back and forth over the heat. Fish flesh is so fragile that it can easily fall apart if tied to the spit and rotated over the fire. Rotisserie baskets are becoming increasingly popular; they're available at major department stores that carry a full line of grill equipment, at restaurant supply stores, and through the toll-free numbers of many grill manufacturers. (Check out Chapter 2 for contact information for a list of popular manufacturers.)

Fish fillets are better than whole fish for rotisserie cooking. Whole fish tends to release and splatter oils all over the inside of the grill, causing it to smell fishy for a long time. Brush cod, salmon, or flatfish fillets with a little oil and then dip them lightly into fresh, seasoned bread crumbs to give them a little protective coating. Place them in the basket and cook over medium heat for about 8 to 12 minutes or until the flesh is opaque.

Let the Rotisserie Games Begin!

Rotisserie cooking interjects yet another dimension of fun and games into the grilling story. As a rotisserie chef, you get to attach food to a metal rod or spit and watch with fascination as it rotates over the heat of the grill. (What could be more fun than that?) Except for seasoning and securing the food to the spit, you need to do little else to guarantee success. Just baste a few times and avoid overcooking.

In this section, we give you rotisserie recipes for chicken, ribs, pork, just to get you started. Seafood like shrimp and kebabs are also good for the rotisserie. After you're hooked (or should we say skewered), you'll want to experiment with recipes of your own.

Rotisserie-Grilled Chicken

If you've never used a rotisserie attachment, start with this chicken recipe. The bird produced is juicy, tender, and packed with flavor. You may even decide to forever abandon the technique of roasting poultry in the oven!

Preparation time: *30 minutes*

Marinating time: *3 hours*

Rotisserie time: *1¼ hours*

Yield: *4 servings*

1 3½- to 4-pound chicken

Marinade

1 cup dry white wine

½ cup olive oil

3 cloves garlic, peeled and coarsely chopped

2 teaspoons minced lemon peel (about 1 lemon)

Juice of 1 lemon (about 3 tablespoons)

3 fresh rosemary or thyme sprigs, about 3 to 4 inches long

1 teaspoon salt, or to taste

Pepper to taste

Spice Rub

1 teaspoon ground thyme

½ teaspoon paprika

½ teaspoon salt, or to taste

½ teaspoon grated lemon peel

¼ teaspoon ground ginger

Pepper to taste

1 Remove all excess fat and giblets from the chicken cavity. (Wrap and freeze the giblets for adding to soups or stocks, if desired.) Rinse the chicken in cold water; pat dry with paper towels. Truss the bird to keep its wings and legs from drooping as the spit turns. (See Figure 10-1.)

2 In a medium mixing bowl or a large, resealable plastic bag, make the marinade by combining the white wine, olive oil, garlic, 2 teaspoons lemon peel, lemon juice, rosemary or thyme sprigs, 1 teaspoon salt, and pepper. Add the chicken to the marinade. Cover the bowl with plastic wrap, or press the air out of the bag and seal it shut. The chicken should fit snugly in the bowl or bag, with the marinade covering it as much as possible. Refrigerate for about 3 hours.

3 Preheat a covered grill with a rotisserie attachment to high (or to the temperature recommended by your grill manufacturer for cooking chicken on a rotisserie).

4 While the grill is preheating, in a small bowl, make a spice rub by mixing together the ground thyme, paprika, ½ teaspoon salt, ½ teaspoon lemon peel, ginger, and pepper. Remove the chicken from the marinade; pour the marinade into a drip pan that's only slightly larger than the chicken. Rub the spice mixture all over the chicken, sprinkling some into the cavity as well.

5 Following the rotisserie instructions of your grill manufacturer, arrange the bird on the spit, securing it with the pronged rotisserie forks. (Refer to Figure 10-2.) Set the drip pan with the marinade on the grill grid, directly under the chicken. As the bird cooks, the pan collects juices that flavor the basting sauce.

6 Cook, with the spit turning, in a covered grill for about 1¼ hours or until done, basting 3 times, or about every 20 minutes, with the juices in the drip pan. (For a crispy skin, omit basting during the last 20 minutes.) When the chicken is done, an instant-read thermometer inserted into the chicken between its thigh and breast will register between 180 degrees and 185 degrees.

7 Remove the chicken from the spit onto a serving plate; cover loosely with aluminum foil and let stand for 10 to 15 minutes before carving. Serve with pan juices or, if desired, Lemon-Herb Gravy (see the following recipe).

Go-With: *Suggested side dishes include mashed potatoes or Middle Eastern Rice (Chapter 16).*

Per serving: *Calories 494 (From Fat 279); Fat 31g (Saturated 8g); Cholesterol 156mg; Sodium 587mg; Carbohydrate 1g (Dietary Fiber 0g); Protein 49g.*

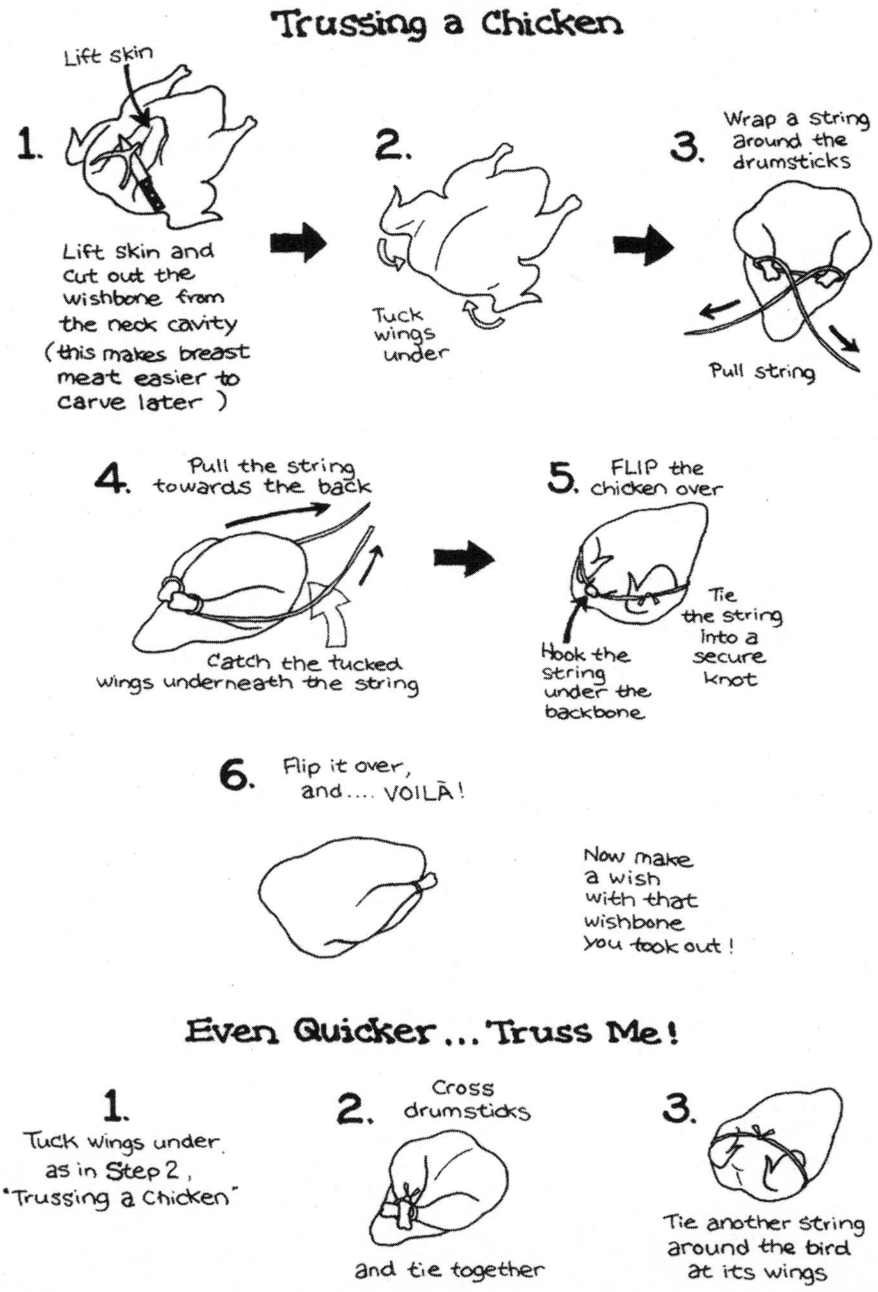

Figure 10-1: Two ways to truss a chicken. The easier, quicker way is just fine for rotisserie cooking.

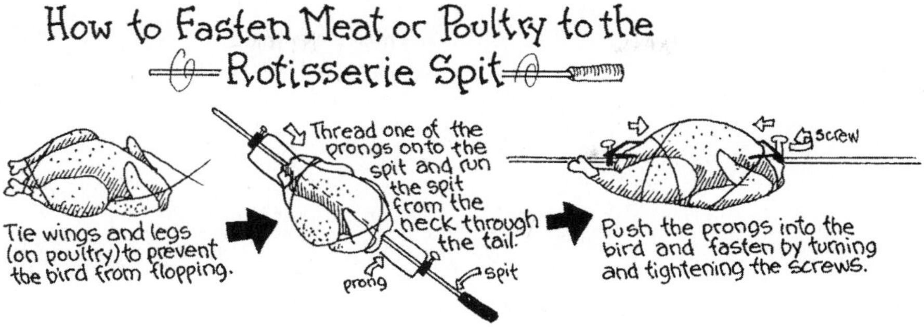

Figure 10-2: The right way to secure and balance a chicken on a rotisserie spit.

Lemon-Herb Gravy

You can make a delicious gravy from the rotisserie chicken pan juices. Strain the juices in the drip pan through a strainer or sieve over a glass measuring cup. Discard the solids left in the strainer. Pour off and discard all but 2½ tablespoons of the fat. (The fat is the darker liquid that rises to the surface of the measuring cup.) Save all the other juices in the measuring cup. At this point, you can spoon some of these juices over the carved chicken. Or you can use these same juices to make this Lemon-Herb Gravy. It's especially wonderful with mashed potatoes.

Preparation time: *15 minutes*

Yield: *¾ cup, approximately six servings at 2 tablespoons per serving*

2½ tablespoons fat from rotisserie chicken pan juices

2½ tablespoons flour

¾ cup pan juices (fat removed)

½ cup chicken broth or water

Juice of 1 lemon

Pepper

Pour the fat into a small saucepan over medium heat. Using a fork or wire whisk, blend the flour into the fat to make a roux, or thickening paste. Gradually whisk in the reserved pan juices, the chicken broth or water, and lemon juice. Keep whisking over medium heat until the gravy comes to a boil; boil 1 minute. Adjust the seasoning with pepper to taste.

Per serving: *Calories 68 (From Fat 56); Fat 6g (Saturated 2g); Cholesterol 6mg; Sodium 208mg; Carbohydrate 3g (Dietary Fiber 0g); Protein 1g.*

When spit roasting poultry, run the spit through the breast, parallel to the backbone and out through the body cavity, centering the rod as much as possible. The spit prongs should be attached through the breast and tail areas to firmly secure the bird. Be sure that the bird is properly balanced on the rod; test the balance by turning the shaft in the palms of both hands. (See Figure 10-3.) If during the course of cooking, the spit prongs become detached from the bird, simply shut off the motor and, using a protective mitt, push the prongs back into the bird and retighten the fastening screws.

Balance Your Bird
The bird should rest as much as possible in the center of the spit. Test the balance by turning the shaft in the palms of both hands. If it flops around on the spit, reposition and try it again!

Figure 10-3: Do the balance test.

Rotisserie Pork Spareribs

Pork spareribs are an excellent choice for rotisserie cooking. Spit cooking naturally bastes the ribs and keeps them from burning, while the fat melts into the drip pan, becoming part of a delicious basting sauce. Apply sweet barbecue sauces only during the last 15 minutes of cooking time to prevent charring. The delicious drip pan juices in the following recipe may be stored frozen in a covered container and added to gravies or stews later.

Preparation time: *20 minutes*

Marinating time: *3 hours or overnight*

Rotisserie time: *1 hour*

Yield: *4 servings*

Chicken alla Mattone (Chapter 14); Lime and Cumin Marinade (Chapter 5), with marinated and grilled chicken on a stick; Frozen Mango Martini (Chapter 18)

Gorgonzola Hamburger with Balsamic Onion Relish (Chapter 7); Spicy Cinnamon and Soy Marinade (Chapter 5), with marinated and grilled chicken on a Ciabatta roll; Caipirinha (Chapter 18)

Seasoned and Breaded Catfish Fillets with Basil Mayonnaise (Chapter 15); Cuban-Style Mojo Marinade (Chapter 5), with marinated and grilled flank steak; Mojito Mojo (Chapter 18)

Coriander and Fennel Rub (Chapter 5); Coriander and Fennel Rubbed Pork Tenderloin (Chapter 12)

Gorgonzola and Fig Sandwiches (Chapter 17); Mango and Cheese Quesadillas (Chapter 17);

Grilled Pound Cake and Fruit with Brandy Sauce; Grilled Figs and Prosciutto (Chapter 18)

1 3- to 4-pound rack of pork spareribs

1 tablespoon lemon juice

1 tablespoon brown sugar

2 teaspoons salt

1 teaspoon pepper

2 teaspoons ground ginger

½ teaspoon garlic powder

1 cup apple juice or cider, or more if necessary

1 cup beef broth, or more if necessary

1 cup bottled or homemade barbecue sauce for basting ribs

1 Sprinkle the ribs on both sides with the lemon juice. In a small bowl, combine the brown sugar, salt, pepper, ginger, and garlic powder. Rub the seasonings all over both sides of the ribs. Cover with plastic wrap and refrigerate for several hours or overnight for best flavor.

2 Preheat a covered grill with a rotisserie attachment to medium-hot. (Grill temperatures and heat settings on gas grills vary from one manufacturer to the next. Check your grill manual for the recommended heat setting and estimated times for rotisserie cooking pork ribs.)

3 Slide one of the metal spit prongs onto the spit rod. Starting midway up and at one end of the rack, stick the spit rod between the first and second rib. (Refer to Figure 10-4.) Skip 2 or 3 ribs and skewer again until the entire rack of ribs is "accordion-pleated." Fasten the second spit prong into place on the rod; slide both prongs into the ribs to help secure the ribs to the rod. The rack should be balanced on the spit to ensure even cooking and to keep the rotisserie motor from straining as it turns. (Refer to Figure 10-3 for more on balancing your food on a spit.)

4 Center on the grill a disposable aluminum drip pan that's just large enough to fit under the ribs. (If the pan is too large, it may obstruct the heat of the grill.) Pour the apple juice and beef broth into the pan. Put the spit in place and baste the ribs with the apple-broth mixture. Cover and cook for 45 minutes to 1 hour, basting every 15 minutes with the drip pan juices, until the ribs are tender when pierced with a thin, sharp knife. (Actual cooking time depends on the heat of the rotisserie.) Be sure to keep the drip pan filled with at least an inch of the apple-broth mixture (or water if you run out) at all times to prevent the ribs from charring.

5 Brush the ribs with your favorite barbecue sauce (or use one of the barbecue sauces in Chapter 9). Cover and rotisserie cook for another 15 minutes or until the meat is fully cooked but still moist. (Unlike ribs cooked indirectly in a covered grill, rotisserie ribs won't result in meat that "wiggles" or falls off the bone. The rotisserie cooked meat will be firmer in texture.)

Go-With: *Serve with Orange-Ginger Coleslaw or Grilled Tomatoes with Cumin Butter (both in Chapter 16).*

Per serving: *Calories 676 (From Fat 426); Fat 47g (Saturated 17g); Cholesterol 184mg; Sodium 2,082mg; Carbohydrate 20g (Dietary Fiber 1g); Protein 40g.*

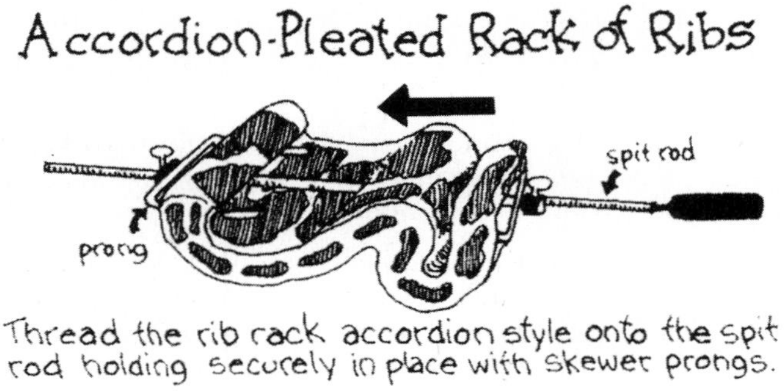
Accordion-Pleated Rack of Ribs
spit rod
prong
Thread the rib rack accordion style onto the spit rod holding securely in place with skewer prongs.

Figure 10-4: Accordion-pleating spare ribs onto a rotisserie spit rod.

ON THE GRILL

If you want to keep ribs or other rotisserie foods warm while taking 15 to 20 minutes to assemble the side dishes for the rest of the meal, leave the food on the spit in the rotisserie with the cover down and the heat off.

Rotisserie Boneless Pork Loin with Herbes de Provence

When it comes to rotisserie cooking, few people are more qualified to give advice than Ed Newman. A chef and restaurateur for more than 30 years, at press time for this book's first edition, Ed ran Solutions, Inc., a Florida-based food consulting company.

In this recipe, Ed calls for seasoning the boneless pork loin with herbes de Provence — a blend of dried herbs commonly used in French cooking. Several herb and spice companies, like McCormick, sell this blend, or you can make your own. You probably already have these dried herbs in your kitchen pantry.

Preparation time: *15 minutes*

Marinating time: *8 hours or overnight*

Rotisserie time: *30 to 35 minutes*

Yield: *4 servings*

2 pounds center-cut boneless pork loin

¼ cup olive oil

2 tablespoons dried herbes de Provence (or a combination of 3 or 4 of the following dried herbs: oregano, thyme, basil, chervil, marjoram, rosemary, summer savory, or sage)

2 tablespoons cracked black peppercorns

1 tablespoon garlic powder

1 tablespoon Dijon-style mustard

¼ teaspoon salt

1 Place the loin in a shallow baking dish. In a small mixing bowl, combine all the remaining ingredients; rub the mixture over the pork. Cover with plastic wrap and refrigerate for at least 8 hours, or overnight.

2 Preheat a covered grill with a rotisserie attachment to hot. (Grill temperatures and heat settings on gas grills vary. Check your grill manual for the recommended heat setting and estimated cooking time for rotisserie cooking pork.)

3 Remove the pork from the dish. Center and secure to the spit rod. Put the spit into place over the grill. Place a disposable aluminum pan under the pork on top of the grill grid. The pan should be half filled with water to catch juices and provide moisture to the roast as it turns. It should be only slightly larger than the pork. (Using a pan that's too large cuts off the grill's heat.)

4 Cook for a total of 30 to 35 minutes. After about 25 minutes, check the internal temperature with an instant-read thermometer inserted into the thickest part of the roast. When the pork is done, the internal temperature will register 155 degrees, and the carved slices will be very moist with a light pink blush.

5 Let the loin rest for 5 to 10 minutes on the rod. Remove the spit rod and carve the roast across the grain into thin slices.

Go-With: *This pork loin is excellent when served with Tomato Chutney (Chapter 6).*

Per serving: *Calories 543 (From Fat 333); Fat 37g (Saturated 11g); Cholesterol 136mg; Sodium 350mg; Carbohydrate 5g (Dietary Fiber 2g); Protein 46g.*

Part IV
Grilling Everything Under the Sun

The 5th Wave By Rich Tennant

"Sid wants to grill everything. He'd grill a camel if he could find a grill lid with humps."

In this part . . .

If you haven't guessed, we're crazy about grilling! We firmly believe that just about everything that you can cook on a stove or in the oven tastes better when cooked outdoors on a grill. In this part, we give you recipes for meats, poultry, and seafood. Each chapter begins with quick hints and tips — like temperature settings and the best cuts of meat — before you set out to sizzle that juicy steak or luscious piece of salmon. And if you think that fresh vegetables taste best when eaten raw, steamed, or boiled, we hope to alter that opinion with an entire chapter on grilling veggies. In that vegetable chapter, we also include some quick side dishes that you can serve alongside your grilled foods. Finally, in this part, we expand your grilling repertoire with recipes and tips for sandwiches, pizzas, and fruits, and we help you wash down a great meal with our very favorite cocktails.

Chapter 11

Beef: It's What Grills Were Made For

In This Chapter

- Choosing grades and cuts of beef
- Marinating and grilling beef
- Grilling roasts to perfection

Recipes in This Chapter

- Grilled Steak 101
- Texas Beef Barbecue
- Chuck Steaks Marinated in Red Wine
- Grilled Steak Salad
- Grilled Tenderloin Au Poivre with Herb Butter Sauce

Beef — thick, juicy, and full of flavor — is the quintessential grilled food. Whether you like your beef rare or well done, rubbed and marinated or plain, in the form of filet mignon or a T-bone, this chapter has tips and tricks for all your beef grilling needs.

REMEMBER

This chapter isn't the only place you can find beef recipes in this book. For tips on grilling the perfect hamburger, turn to Chapter 7. To discover how to grill a variety of beef kebabs, flip to Chapter 8. In Chapter 9, you can find a delicious recipe for Korean-style beef ribs. You can also find a large assortment of rubs, flavored oils, and compound butters — perfect for a variety of beef cuts — in Chapter 5.

All You Need to Know to Grill a Mean Hunk of Beef

Concerns over the high fat and cholesterol in beef, in our opinion, have been overemphasized by zealots who neglect to mention beef's healthful properties. True, a 16-ounce steak with baked potato and sour cream, onion rings, and a piece of cheesecake for dessert is not what you'd call a low-cal dinner, but it's not the beef that accounts for most of those calories.

Beef is an excellent source of protein, iron, zinc, niacin, phosphorus, and B vitamins. And both fat and cholesterol — in moderation — are essential to a human diet. A portion of meat, in today's definition, is a piece the size of a deck of cards — about 4 ounces.

Despite its innate healthfulness, beef, like other animal products, may carry potentially harmful bacteria. So be sure to follow these precautions:

- If the meat has been frozen, don't thaw it at room temperature. Bacteria can build up during the thawing process. Besides, thawing in the refrigerator overnight makes for a better texture in the meat.
- Always store meat of any kind in the refrigerator or freezer after purchase.
- To kill off all bacteria, cook all ground beef hamburgers to 160 degrees (or medium), with no trace of pink remaining in the center of the patty. Bacteria problems are almost always due to meat that's ground in enormous volumes and shipped to a supermarket. Freshly ground meat from a reliable butcher is, however, unlikely to contain bacteria, and so you must decide if you want to cook it to rare or medium-rare. You can cook other beef cuts to lower internal temperatures.
- Never place the cooked or grilled meat on the same platter that held the raw meat.

The relative quality of beef depends on its grade and on the cut you choose. The following sections give you a rundown on the different grades and cuts you'll hear about when talking beef with buddies or your butcher.

Grading beef

Since 1927, the U.S. Department of Agriculture has graded beef through a voluntary program on behalf of the meat packers. For consumers, grade is a gauge for determining eating quality.

The more *marbling* (flecks of fat within the meat) — which, by the way, should be evenly distributed — the more flavorful the steaks. In addition to marbling, meat graders look at characteristics such as age or maturity, color, and meat texture.

The USDA has eight grades for meat, and the particular grade is clearly displayed on the package label. Over the last 20 years, however, the grading of meat has changed to reflect a rise in demand for the higher cuts of beef now served in expensive steakhouses. There are still eight grades, but the top grades tend to have considerably less fat marbling than they used to. As a result, a carcass that may once have been graded as "Top Choice" may now be graded as "Prime," which fetches top dollar for meat sellers.

The following list shows the three grades that are most often found at your supermarket or butcher shop. Rarely would you find any grade below Select sold — although you might find it served to you on an airplane or at a hospital!

- **Prime:** Young beef with the most marbling is given this Prime (highest quality) grade. Most USDA Prime is sold to better-quality restaurants and to specialty butcher shops and grocery stores, especially in major cities. Because only about 2 percent — sometimes less — of meat today is graded as Prime, it's difficult to find and is quite expensive. In the future, with corn supplies increasingly expensive for feed lots, producers don't see much profit in bringing a steer up to Prime marbling, which is, in any case, more genetic than mere bulking up of the animal. Note that most USDA-graded Prime has less of the "beefy" flavor that the grade used to signify a decade ago.

  Be aware that if a restaurant, market label, or ad reads "prime" with a lowercase "p," and doesn't use the name "USDA," you're probably *not* getting true Prime beef.

  You should be aware of the difference between *dry aged* and *wet aged* beef. Although beef in the rest of the world is rarely aged at all, American beef usually is. Aging intensifies flavors by breaking down the enzymes in the muscle's connective tissue and driving out moisture, making for a more tender, tastier, beefier beef. In the process, up to 20 percent of the carcass weight may be lost, which explains why Prime is so expensive. Consider the differences between the two types of aging:

  - **Dry aged beef** is stored in a temperature-and-humidity controlled locker for several weeks — 21 days, 28 days, even 6 weeks. It comes out with a rich, powerful, mineral flavor and aroma — not to everyone's taste, although, as noted above, it's more and more difficult to find Prime beef of this caliber.
  - **Wet aged beef** is sealed in plastic after slaughter and then refrigerated with its own juices, which themselves help break down the muscle tissue. While wet aged beef (both Prime and Choice) can be delicious, it doesn't have the flavor of dry aged beef.

  REMEMBER

  Be wary of claims made about dry aged beef from large supermarkets or restaurant chains. Sometimes they advertize "dry aged" beef but in reality only stick wet aged beef in their own cold locker for a few more days, which does next to nothing to improve flavor or tenderness.

  "Prime rib" of roast beef is not a grade at all, but a cut from meat that's between the primal chuck and short loin. It would be extremely rare to find USDA Prime prime rib.

- **Choice:** Choice is a juicy, tender grade of meat, though not quite as tasty as Prime. Currently about 44 percent of graded meat is Choice. It's the most widely available grade of meat in America, and is still your best bet for a good price.

"Angus," which appears on many steakhouse menus, isn't a grade of beef but a breed of steer, which may be of any grade. "Certified Black Angus" (CAB) is a proprietary name for a company that sells mostly high-grade Top Choice beef and a smaller percentage of Prime.

- **Select:** Select has the least amount of marbling of the three grades and, although it may be less expensive than Prime or Choice, it's usually not as juicy, flavorful, or tender, either. About 27 percent of graded meat is classified as Select. This grade of beef is better for stewing or braising rather than for grilling.

Also, about 27 percent of all meat is ungraded and sometimes referred to as *no roll.*

Prime, choice, and select grades of meat are all suitable for grilling, but a Prime or Choice beef is more tender, juicy, and savory than Select. So, if you have a choice, choose prime or choice grades for grilling.

Naming the cuts of beef

Names of meat cuts can be confusing because there are regional and colloquial differences in the way butchers describe a particular cut. For instance, Midwesterners may refer to a luscious short loin without the fillet and bone as a New York strip, while people in New York call the exact same cut a Kansas City strip. Elsewhere it might be called a shell steak. London broil, often sold as a particular cut of beef, started out as a recipe made with flank steak. Today the term *London broil* is often used to identify beef top round or sirloin, beef chuck shoulder steak, or flank steak.

When shopping for cuts most suitable for grilling, here's what you'll find at your supermarket (see Figure 11-1):

- **Top loin (strip) steak:** The classic beef steak — also known as Kansas City strip, New York strip, and club. The top loin or strip steak is considered by many steak lovers to be the single finest cut because of its rich marbling, perfect texture (which is neither too firm nor too mushy), and its real beefy flavor. Strip steaks are usually sold boneless, but the bone provides an added succulence to the finished product. A 16-ounce strip steak should take about 12 to 15 minutes, turned once, to cook to medium rare.
- **Tenderloin:** This is a long, boneless piece of meat with three sections. The middle is called the *center section;* the larger, thicker end is called the *butt;* and the tapered end is referred to as the *tip.* The whole tenderloin weighs about 4 to 6 pounds, but it can be cut and bought as a smaller roast, as individual steaks, or as tenderloin tips that are good for kebabs. A 16-ounce strip steak should take about 12 to 15 minutes, turned once, to cook to medium rare.

What's so wonderful about wagyu?

Ten years ago you would have had to go to Japan to sample what's called *wagyu beef.* Now it's become all the rage at high-end steakhouses and butchers here in the United States — even though it can get pricey! You could spend $160 a pound at the store, and a 12-ounce steak at a restaurant might set you back $200. For several years, true wagyu (also called Kobe, after the city in Japan where its main producers are) wasn't allowed to be imported into the U.S., but that ban lifted in 2007. Believe it or not, wagyu cattle are treated to massages, a beer diet (high in carbs), and tender loving care. This special treatment helps build up as much intermuscular fat as possible, making the beef that comes from them taste and cut like butter. This imported beef is like no other in the world, and a little goes a long way — four to six ounces per person is more than enough. A wagyu-style beef is now being produced in Australia and the U.S. (mostly Texas). This beef is extremely rich (and expensive), but its flavor really doesn't compare with the Japanese original.

- **Filet mignon:** A term for steaks cut from the small end of the tenderloin. These steaks, which are the most tender beef cut available, cook quickly and are best if cut between 1 and 2 inches thick. A 1-inch-thick filet, grilled directly over medium heat, takes about 13 to 15 minutes for medium-rare to medium.
- **T-bone and porterhouse steaks:** Cut from the short loin section of the animal, these two cuts are basically the same. Each of these steaks has two muscles — the tenderloin and the top loin (also called the *strip*). The distinctive T-bone (a bone down the middle of the steak that's shaped like the letter "T") helps identify each of these steaks. The difference between these cuts is the size of their tenderloin muscles: The porterhouse has a tenderloin muscle about the width of a silver dollar or bigger, while the T-bone's tenderloin muscle is smaller than a silver dollar. The porterhouse is also called a *sweetheart steak,* because it's really two steaks in one and big enough for two servings. A T-bone or porterhouse that's, say, 2 inches thick, will cook in about 20 minutes. However, the timing will depend on the thickness of your cut.
- **Rib-eye:** This boneless cut comes from the rib section. Ask for rib-eye steaks from the small end, which is farthest from the chuck and closest to the more tender loin. The small end also has less fat, which is better for grilling. Cut the steaks about 1-inch thick and grill over medium heat for about 11 to 14 minutes, uncovered. If sold with the bone, these steaks are called *rib steaks.* These cook in less time, about 9 to 12 minutes over medium heat (for a 1-inch-thick steak).
- **Sirloin:** Situated next to the round and actually cut from the loin or hip portion of the animal, most sirloin steaks are sold boneless. They are fairly economical, tender, and versatile — they make great cubes for kebabs or strips for stir-frying. A 1-inch-thick sirloin, grilled over medium heat, takes about 15 to 17 minutes to grill to medium.

- **Flank:** Although considered less tender than the other cuts in this list, the flank steak has wonderful flavor when grilled and needs only a little marinating to soften. Cook only to medium-rare, usually just 5 to 10 minutes, carving across the grain into thin slices. Turn to Chapter 17 for Best-Ever Fajitas made with flank steak.

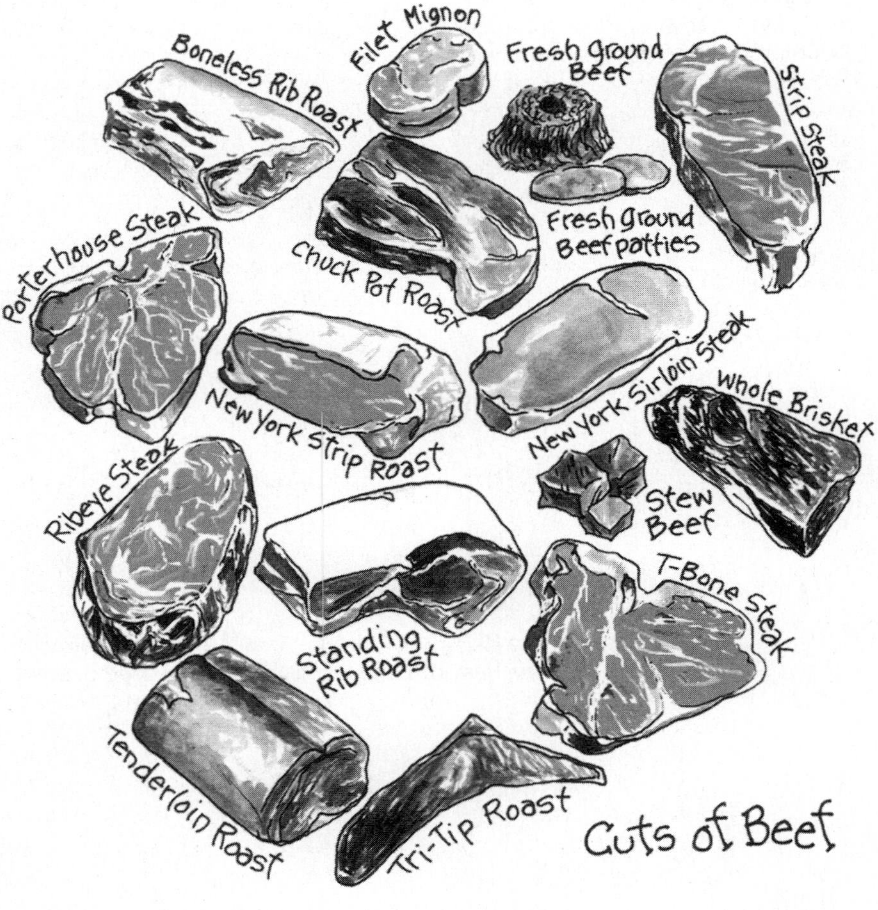

Figure 11-1: The various cuts of beef.

Making the most of lesser cuts

The U.S. market for lesser cuts of beef has never been better, and their availability is high at both specialty butchers — where they waste nothing! — and at ethnic food markets. Italian, Greek, Latino, Chinese, and Polish butchers, in particular, are great sources of many cuts of beef that you won't easily find in your supermarkets.

Here are some of the lesser — or lesser known — cuts of beef that make for great eating:

- **Flat iron steak:** Also known as *top blade,* flat iron steak has a sliver of gristle in its center, which simply needs to be cut out with a sharp knife. Then you're left with two steaks that are great for cutting into kebabs.
- **Hanger steak:** Often misspelled "hangar" steak, the term refers to the way this meat hangs from the carcass. There's only one hanger steak per animal, and it has a tendon that you or your butcher should remove. This is the quintessential piece of beef that French bistro cooks use for steak frites (steak with French fries), because it has plenty of mineral flavor, grills quickly, and has a pleasantly chewy texture.
- **Skirt steak:** You can easily find skirt steaks at your butcher or supermarket these days. This cut of meat, which comes from the diaphragm, is long, somewhat sinewy, and streaked with marbling, making it juicy and rich in flavor. Skirt steak can be a little tough, however, so marinate it first. This is the classic, preferred cut for Mexican fajitas (even though flank is popular too).

Preparing and Grilling Your Steaks

Is the thickness of a good steak merely a matter of personal preference? Not to us. We say that the best thickness for grilling any type of steak is 1 inch. However, the most commonly sold steak in the supermarket is only ¾ inch. A steak that's 1-inch thick allows you more control than a thinner steak. A ¾-inch steak's degree of doneness can change in a heartbeat from medium-rare to medium on a medium-hot grill. So ask your butcher to cut your steaks 1-inch thick. You don't need to score the fat on a steak, but you may want to trim it, leaving the fat ⅛- to ¼-inch thick. A little fat makes the steak moist and juicy. Too much fat causes dangerous flare-ups.

We recommend a medium heat to grill a 1-inch-thick steak. Medium heat (a four-second, hand-held count over the hot coals) gives you a nice brown crust without any serious charring. If you use charcoal, be sure to build an adequate fire — one that extends about 2 inches beyond the edges of the meat — so you don't run out of fuel during the last few minutes of grilling.

Always thoroughly wash and dry your utensils and cutting surfaces after handling any form of beef (and chicken, too!). Also make sure you wash your hands just as thoroughly.

Love them tender: Marinating meats before grilling

Some beef is tender and some is not. Marinating the tougher cuts helps tenderize the meat. Even though we like our tender steaks relatively plain, you can gussy them up with other flavors if you'd like.

Tender beef steaks, such as sirloin, porterhouse, T-bone, rib-eye, and tenderloin, don't require marinating to break down or soften the exterior surface of their tissues. These cuts can be simply rubbed with combinations of seasonings that flavor the exterior of the meat as it grills. Use the rub and flavored oil recipes in Chapter 5, create your own rub from your spice rack, or check out your supermarket spice section for the commercial rubs suitable for beef.

Even though you don't have to marinate the tender beef steaks, they still may benefit from a little dunking — from 15 minutes to 2 hours — to absorb additional flavors. Overmarinating tender beef cuts in liquid with an acid ingredient, such as lemon juice or wine, can turn the surface tissues slightly mushy.

Less-tender and less-expensive cuts — flank, skirt, top round, eye round, and chuck steaks — need a longer marinating time than their tender counterparts. Marinate less-tender cuts in the refrigerator for at least 6 hours, or even overnight. Marinating adds flavor and helps soften the tougher muscle tissues. When marinated and then grilled to medium-rare, these cuts can be quite juicy and delicious.

Within the categories of round and chuck, some cuts are tougher than others. Top blade and chuck eye, which are very tender cuts considering they come from the chuck, don't need to be marinated longer than 6 hours. However, other chuck and top round steaks benefit from long marinating — 6 hours or overnight.

Grilling 'em up!

Usually, you don't need to *sear* a steak — that is, cook it for a few minutes over very high heat until well browned on both sides — as the initial step in the cooking process. However, bigger pieces of meat, like a thick roast or a 2-inch-thick steak may benefit from searing first, followed by cooking slowly over lower heat. For these bigger cuts, sear them, but don't cook long enough to blacken the exterior.

Doneness is a matter of taste, but remember that even the finest prime beef has little taste or texture left if you cook it beyond medium. The National Cattlemen's Beef Association defines the approximate degree of doneness in beef as the following:

- **Very rare:** 130 degrees
- **Rare:** 140 degrees
- **Medium-rare:** 145 degrees
- **Medium:** 160 degrees
- **Well-done:** 170 degrees
- **Very well-done:** 180 degrees

These temperature guidelines are helpful when you're using a meat thermometer to take the guesswork out of cooking large roasts, but for steaks and smaller cuts, doneness is defined by the meat's interior color. Rare meat is bright red and juicy. Medium meat has a light pink center with light brown edges. Well-done meat is brown-gray throughout.

The intensity of the heat of gas and charcoal grills varies. Keep in mind that the cooking times throughout this chapter are only estimates. Check the interior of the meat by making a small cut with a sharp knife a few minutes before the estimated time of doneness, to avoid overcooking. Unfortunately, after a piece of beef is overcooked, you can't reverse the results.

We're squarely in the camp of those who insist that allowing grilled meat to stand a few minutes before carving makes for a better steak. The juices inside stabilize and redistribute throughout the meat, and the meat will cook a bit more.

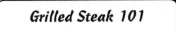

Grilled Steak 101

Compared to the more expensive rib-eye or porterhouse, a sirloin steak gives you lots of flavor for the money. It provides more versatility, too, because it's also perfect for cutting into kebab cubes. (See Chapter 8 for steak kebab recipes.)

This recipe features the flavor of a simply grilled sirloin and relies on only a little garlic, olive oil, and salt and pepper as seasoning. However, if you care to embellish a little, turn to Chapters 5 and 6 for an assortment of flavored oils, seasoned rubs, sauces, and compound butter recipes.

Preparation time: *5 minutes*

Grilling time: *15 minutes for medium-rare*

Yield: *4 servings*

2 tablespoons olive oil

1 clove garlic, peeled and crushed

2 boneless sirloin beef steaks, cut 1-inch thick (about 2 pounds total)

Salt and pepper to taste

1 Prepare a medium fire in a charcoal or gas grill.

2 In a small bowl, combine the olive oil and garlic. Generously rub or brush the flavored oil on both sides of the steaks. Sprinkle the steaks lightly with salt and pepper.

3 Place the steaks on a well-oiled grill grid, directly over medium heat. Grill, uncovered, 14 to 16 minutes for medium-rare to medium doneness, turning every 5 minutes.

4 Remove the steaks from the grill; cover loosely with foil and let the steaks rest for a few minutes before thinly slicing across the grain. Season with salt and additional pepper (if desired) before serving.

Go-With: *Serve with any of the side dishes in Chapter 16; with the Tapenade, Tomato Chutney, or Guacamole that are shown in Chapter 6; or with any of the compound butters in Chapter 6. You can also top with the Pesto Sauce in Chapter 15.*

Vary It! *You can substitute porterhouse steaks, cut 1-inch thick and totaling about 2 pounds, for the sirloin steaks.*

Per serving: *Calories 511 (From Fat 340); Fat 38g (Saturated 13g); Cholesterol 124mg; Sodium 244mg; Carbohydrate 0g (Dietary Fiber 0g); Protein 40g.*

Texas Beef Barbecue

This marinade uses beer, lots of chili powder, cumin, and red pepper flakes to give an inexpensive piece of top round an authentic hometown barbecue flavor — without actually barbecuing.

Preparation time: *10 minutes*

Marinating time: *3 hours or overnight*

Grilling time: *14 minutes for medium-rare*

Yield: *4 servings*

1 cup bottled chili sauce

½ cup beer

⅓ cup vegetable oil

¼ cup finely chopped green onion (white and green parts)

3 tablespoons chili powder

1 teaspoon ground cumin

½ teaspoon dried red pepper flakes

1 boneless beef top round steak, cut 1-inch thick (about 1½ to 2 pounds)

Salt to taste (optional)

1 In a medium bowl, prepare the marinade by combining all the ingredients except the steak.

2 Place the steak in a glass baking dish or a large, resealable plastic bag. Pour the marinade over the steak, turning to coat. Cover the dish or seal the bag, pressing out as much air as possible. Refrigerate 3 hours or overnight.

3 Prepare a medium fire in a charcoal or gas grill.

4 Remove the steak from the marinade, shaking off any excess. Discard the marinade. If desired, sprinkle the steak with salt. Place the steak on a well-oiled grill grid and grill 12 to 14 minutes for medium-rare or about 15 minutes for medium, turning every 5 to 6 minutes.

5 Transfer the steak to a cutting board and let rest for 5 minutes, loosely covered with foil. Thinly slice across the grain.

Go-With: *This steak is absolutely heavenly when served with the Barbecued Onions in Chapter 6.*

Vary It! *You can substitute 1½ to 2 pounds of flank steak for the chuck steak in this recipe.*

Per serving: *Calories 279 (From Fat 96); Fat 11g (Saturated 2g); Cholesterol 98mg; Sodium 567mg; Carbohydrate 6g (Dietary Fiber 1g); Protein 37g.*

Chuck Steaks Marinated in Red Wine

If you're looking for a way to turn inexpensive chuck shoulder steaks into a very tasty grilled dinner, try this recipe. For other steak marinade recipes, which are also good with tougher steaks, flip to Chapter 5.

Preparation time: *15 minutes*

Marinating time: *8 hours or overnight*

Grilling time: *15 minutes for medium-rare*

Yield: *4 servings*

2 boneless beef chuck shoulder steaks, cut about 1-inch thick (about 1½ to 2 pounds)

1 cup dry red wine

½ cup chopped onions

3 tablespoons olive oil

2 tablespoons peeled and grated fresh ginger

1 tablespoon red wine vinegar

2 large cloves garlic, peeled and minced

½ to 1 large jalapeño pepper, seeded and minced (optional)

¼ teaspoon salt, or to taste

Pepper to taste

1 Place the steaks in a large, resealable plastic bag or a shallow nonreactive dish.

2 In a small mixing bowl, prepare the marinade by whisking together the remaining ingredients.

3 Pour the marinade over the steaks in the bag or dish, turning to coat. Cover the dish or close the bag securely, pressing out any air, and then refrigerate for 8 hours or overnight, turning occasionally.

4 Prepare a medium fire in a charcoal or gas grill.

5 Remove the steaks from the marinade, discarding the marinade. If desired, sprinkle with additional salt and pepper to taste. Place the steaks on an oiled grill grid, directly over the heat.

6 Grill, uncovered, 14 to 16 minutes for medium-rare to medium, or until desired doneness, turning every 7 to 8 minutes. (Check for doneness by making a small cut into the center of the meat with a sharp knife. For best results, less-tender steaks should be cooked from medium-rare to medium.) Carve into thin slices across the grain.

Go-With: *Serve with the Garlic-Grilled Portobellos or with any of the other side dishes in Chapter 16.*

Vary It! *Flank and top round cuts also work well with this red-wine marinade. A flank steak about 1½ to 2 pounds will cook to medium-rare or medium in 17 to 21 minutes, depending on thickness. One beef top round steak (1-inch thick) takes 16 to 18 minutes for medium-rare to medium doneness.*

Per serving: *Calories 302 (From Fat 106); Fat 12g (Saturated 4g); Cholesterol 107mg; Sodium 267mg; Carbohydrate 1g (Dietary Fiber 0g); Protein 44g.*

Cook any type of beefsteak according to your personal preference, but remember that overcooking tightens and toughens muscle. The longer a steak is cooked, the less juicy it becomes. Cooking to medium-rare or medium gives you the most tender steaks.

If you intend to use a marinade as a basting or dipping sauce, pour off and reserve a small portion before adding the uncooked meat. Otherwise, any marinade that has previously come in contact with raw meat, fish, or poultry must be brought to a full rolling boil and then simmered for about 15 minutes before it can be used as a finishing sauce.

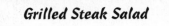

Grilled Steak Salad

In this recipe, grilled sirloin or top round strips are tossed with salad greens, bell pepper, red onion rings, and dressing. Serve with a crusty loaf of French or Italian bread to complete the meal.

Preparation time: *25 minutes*

Marinating time: *3 hours or overnight*

Grilling time: *12 to 14 minutes for medium-rare*

Yield: *4 servings*

½ cup reduced-sodium soy sauce

¼ cup rice wine vinegar

3 tablespoons water

2 tablespoons Asian-style sesame oil

2 cloves garlic, peeled and minced

1 tablespoon peeled and minced fresh ginger

1 teaspoon hot chili oil

1 pound boneless sirloin or top round steak, 1-inch thick

8 cups torn salad greens, such as spinach, watercress, romaine lettuce, or Boston lettuce

1 large red bell pepper, seeded and cut into thin strips

½ red onion, thinly sliced and rings separated

3 tablespoons minced fresh cilantro (optional)

1. In a small bowl or jar, prepare the dressing (which is also the marinade) by combining the first 7 ingredients. Mix or shake well.
2. Place the steak in a shallow glass dish or a large, resealable plastic bag; add ½ cup of the dressing. Turn the meat to coat. Cover the dish or seal the bag, pressing out as much air as possible, and then refrigerate 3 hours or overnight, turning occasionally. Refrigerate the remaining dressing.
3. Prepare a medium fire in a charcoal or gas grill.
4. Drain the meat, reserving the marinade. Place the steak on a lightly oiled grill grid. Grill 12 to 14 minutes for medium-rare, or to desired doneness, turning once and brushing once with the reserved marinade. When the steak is cooked to desired doneness, discard any remaining marinade. Allow the steak to stand 5 minutes, loosely covered with foil on a carving board. Slice thinly across the grain.
5. In a large bowl, mix the salad greens, red pepper, and onion; transfer to a serving platter. Top with the sliced steak. Pour the reserved, refrigerated dressing over the salad, sprinkle with cilantro (if desired), and serve.

Vary It! *You can substitute 2 boneless beef top loin steaks (cut 1-inch thick and about 1 pound total) for the sirloin or top round steak.*

Per serving: *Calories 351 (From Fat 148); Fat 17g (Saturated 4g); Cholesterol 101mg; Sodium 1,315mg; Carbohydrate 10g (Dietary Fiber 4g); Protein 39g.*

Giving Grilled Beef Roast a Chance

Grilled beef roast is a wondrous thing. It takes on a lovely smokiness that you can't get when you cook it in an oven, and if turned carefully on a spit, it reproduces the most primal of all cooking processes. Even though you won't have the wonderful aroma wafting through the house or enjoy the promise of Yorkshire pudding made with the pan drippings, you may never want to cook roast beef in your oven again after you try it on the grill.

The following is a short list of beef roasts that we recommend for grilling:

- **Tenderloin:** This most elegant piece of meat is so perfectly suited to grilling that our mouths water just thinking about it. A tenderloin is also one of the most expensive meats in the supermarket, so you want to grill it perfectly. The first rule when grilling a tenderloin is to remove it from the grill 5 to 10 degrees shy of the final, desired internal temperature. The internal temperature of a roast will increase 5 to 10 degrees after it has been removed from the grill and allowed to rest for 15 minutes under a tent of foil. For rare meat, remove the roast when the temperature is between 130 and 135 degrees; for medium-rare, remove between 135 and 140 degrees; for medium, remove when the internal temperature is between 145 and 150 degrees.

  The second cardinal rule when roasting a tenderloin is to be sure that the roast is evenly thick from end to end to ensure even cooking. A tenderloin has a thin and a thick end. Often the butcher tucks and ties the thin end underneath the roast to make it uniformly thick. However, to ensure even cooking, it's better to have the thin tail end cut off rather than tied. (If we've piqued your interest, check out the recipe for Grilled Tenderloin Au Poivre with Herb Butter Sauce, later in this chapter.)

- **Rib-eye roast:** This is a very tender, boneless roast that readily absorbs the strong, smoky flavors of a live charcoal fire. With the bone in, this cut is called a *prime rib-eye roast.* Cook the boneless roast indirectly in a covered grill, over medium-low heat, for 15 to 20 minutes per pound.

- **Beef round tip roast:** Sometimes called *sirloin tip,* this economical cut comes boneless. It's packed with flavor and really is quite tender if cooked to medium-rare (about 135 degrees). Cook indirectly in a covered grill, over medium-low heat, for about 20 minutes per pound. This roast may also be rotisserie-grilled.

- **Tri-tip roast:** One of California's best kept secrets for years, the tri-tip roast can now be purchased in supermarkets and meat markets coast to coast. This relatively small, thin roast with its distinctive triangular shape weighs a maximum of 2 pounds. It cooks over direct medium heat in approximately 30 minutes. For tri-tip steaks, cut the raw steak across the grain into 1-inch-thick steaks, beginning at the long, flat end of the roast. A 2-pound raw roast slices into 4 to 5 steaks, with some meat remaining for kebabs or stir-frying.

- **Boneless chuck roast:** Perhaps the most economical of meats, the boneless chuck roast comes from the shoulder and weighs about 3 to 4 pounds. Because it isn't a very tender cut, marinate the roast for a long time, about 8 to 24 hours, before grilling. Grill it indirectly, covered, over medium-low coals, for about 25 minutes per pound for rare to medium-rare. Then slice it thinly across the grain.
- **Brisket:** A brisket needs several hours of long, slow, indirect cooking or water-smoking to tenderize its tough muscle tissue. After it's barbecued, the meat is usually sliced across the grain and is smothered in a thick, rich, tomato-based barbecue sauce.

Accompany any of these roasts with baking potatoes (like Idaho potatoes). Put them on the grid about 1 hour before the roast is done. (See Chapter 16 for more information on grilling potatoes.)

Grilled Tenderloin Au Poivre with Herb Butter Sauce

Beef lovers, after trying this recipe, you may never again roast a tenderloin in your oven. The smoke and heat of a covered charcoal grill cook this tender piece of meat beyond compare.

Poivre is French for pepper, and a red wine marinade and cracked peppercorns infuse this beef tenderloin with flavor and just the right touch of stimulating spice. (Turn to Chapter 14 for information on how to crack peppercorns.) For you pepper fans out there, about a tablespoon of pepper produces a roast that's quite peppery; use ½ tablespoon or less if you want only a hint of heat. Grilling the tenderloin directly over medium coals and giving it a quarter turn every 5 minutes cooks it evenly and quickly, without any unpleasant charring. For best results, be sure to use at least a 2-pound tenderloin.

Preparation time: *15 minutes*

Marinating time: *2 hours*

Grilling time: *20 minutes*

Yield: *4 to 6 servings*

½ cup dry red wine

3 tablespoons olive oil

1 tablespoon coarse-grained mustard

2 large cloves garlic, peeled and minced

1 large shallot, peeled and minced, or 2 tablespoons minced onion

1 teaspoon dried oregano or thyme leaves, crumbled

¼ teaspoon salt

½ to 1 tablespoon whole black peppercorns, cracked (optional)

1 beef tenderloin, 2 to 2½ pounds, trimmed

Herb Butter Sauce (optional) (see following recipe)

1 In a small bowl or large glass measuring cup, prepare the marinade by combining the first 7 ingredients. Place the meat in a large, resealable plastic bag or a shallow nonreactive dish. Pour the marinade over the meat, turning to coat. Cover the dish or seal the bag (pressing out all the air). Refrigerate for 2 to 3 hours, turning occasionally to coat the meat in the marinade.

2 Remove the meat from the dish or bag; discard the marinade. Spread the cracked pepper evenly onto all sides of the meat, pressing it into the surface with the palm of your hand. Cover loosely with foil or plastic wrap and allow the meat to warm slightly before grilling. The meat will grill evenly when brought to room temperature, which takes about 35 minutes, depending on the air temperature.

3 Prepare a medium fire in a charcoal grill, using wood chunks (if desired).

4 Place the tenderloin in the center of a well-oiled grid, directly over the heat. Cover and grill for 5 minutes; give the roast a quarter turn and grill for another 5 minutes. Proceed, grilling covered and turning every 5 minutes, until the roast reaches an internal temperature of between 135 degrees and 140 degrees for medium-rare. Check the temperature with an instant-read thermometer after 15 minutes and then each time you turn the roast.

5 Remove the roast from the grill and place on a carving board (preferably one that collects the juices); cover the roast loosely with foil and allow it to stand for 10 to 15 minutes. Carve into ½-inch-thick slices. Serve with Herb Butter Sauce (if desired).

Herb Butter Sauce

In a small pan, melt ¼ cup butter; stir in 1 tablespoon Worcestershire sauce and 2 tablespoons chopped fresh parsley. Pour over tenderloin slices.

Go-With: *Suggested side dishes include Garlic-Grilled Portobellos or any of the other side dishes in Chapter 16.*

Vary It! *If you're lucky to have any leftovers, use them to make tenderloin sandwiches the next day, spreading the slices of bread with chutney or mustard.*

Per serving: *Calories 484 (From Fat 270); Fat 30g (Saturated 13g); Cholesterol 173mg; Sodium 319mg; Carbohydrate 2g (Dietary Fiber 0g); Protein 48g.*

REMEMBER

The internal temperature of a roast rises most rapidly at the end of the estimated cooking time. So check the temperature often toward the end of grilling to avoid overcooking the meat.

For a hunk of tenderloin that's even more flavorful, mix in a few pieces of hardwood hickory chunks with your charcoal. Keep in mind, however, that wood chunks burn hotter than charcoal. Light the chunks before lighting the charcoal to give them more time to burn to a medium stage. If the chunks are still too hot and the charcoal is ready, spritz the chunks with a little water or move them to the outer edges of the coals, where they will add smoke to the food without flaming and burning the meat.

Chapter 12

Pork — The King of Barbecue

In This Chapter

- Selecting cuts of pork
- Choosing rubs, marinades, and brines for pork
- Grilling pork tenderloins and chops successfully

Recipes in This Chapter

- Lemony Tarragon Pork Chops
- Grilled Pork Chops with Rosemary Oil
- Apricot-Glazed Pork Chops
- Caribbean Pork Chops
- Brined and Grilled Loin O' Pork
- Soy-Marinated Pork Tenderloin with Asian-Flavored Vegetables
- Curried Pork Tenderloins
- Coriander and Fennel Rubbed Pork Tenderloin

In this chapter, we help you choose the best cuts of pork for the grill and show you how to season them to your liking. We also make sure that you don't mistreat that beautiful piece of pork and cook it until it's a dried-out, gray wad — in the past, too many people thought this was the correct way to cook it! By the time you finish this chapter, you may be convinced that pork is actually one of the most delicious and delicate meats you can put over a fire.

Hit Me with Your Best Cut

Many people avoid eating pork because they think it's a fatty meat. If they're talking hot dogs and sausages (covered in Chapter 7) or spareribs (in Chapter 9), they're right. But pork taken from the loin and leg isn't particularly fatty. The better-tasting pork, however, is fattier. The fat adds a great deal of flavor, especially for barbecue. Very lean ribs, on the other hand, will wither away on the grill and not provide the kind of taste that fattier ribs will.

The main characteristic to look for in a cut of pork is a firm, finely-grained meat. Check to see that the lean part of the meat has a healthy pink color and that the fat is firm and white, not yellow.

REMEMBER

By the way, the iridescence that you sometimes see on the surface of pork is perfectly natural and in no way affects the flavor or quality of the pork. It's simply a reflection of light off the cut ends of muscle fibers.

Undercooked pork: Don't believe everything you hear

The long-held fear people have about eating "undercooked" pork is based on outdated information that says hogs can possibly carry trichinosis, a parasite that can be transferred to human beings through consumption of tainted meat. Today, however, the standards of pig production are so controlled and so sanitary that the chances of a hog carrying trichinosis are next to zero. In fact, of the less than 50 reported cases per year in the U.S. of trichinosis in humans, almost all were contracted from eating wild game, not pork. To find out how to cook pork properly, see the section in this chapter "And This Little Pork was Done Just Right."

SHOPPING TIP

The meat industry produces a dizzying array of cuts, but only a few — usually the choicest parts — show up at the butcher shop or supermarket. See Figure 12-1 for a survey of the many cuts available. You'll most likely find the following cuts at your local meat market or grocery store:

- **Leg:** The rear leg is one of the most tender and succulent cuts of pork. The meat from this portion of the animal, which can weigh 15 pounds, basically consists of two delicious parts: the *butt* and the *shank.* It's often cut by the butcher into several boneless roasts. A roast from the rear leg may be called a *fresh ham* or a *boneless fresh ham roast.* The butt must be cooked slowly for a long time to achieve tenderness; the shank, which isn't as large or meaty, takes less time.
- **Loin:** The loin is next in line to the leg in terms of tenderness, and it's available either with or without the bone. From the loin you also get the best, meatiest ribs (we cover ribs in detail in Chapter 9). The leg and the loin are delicious prepared in any number of ways — from chops (covered in the section "Chop, chop who's there?") to kebabs (included in Chapter 8) — on the outdoor grill.
- **Shoulder:** The shoulder has two principal cuts:
    - **Boston butt:** This cut weighs up to 6 pounds and is fatty but juicy. You'll find this cut delicious for steaks or cooked whole. It's also the best sausage meat. (We give you the scoop on sausages in Chapter 7.)
    - **Picnic ham:** This cut is farther down the shoulder — toward the leg — and is less tender than the Boston butt. The picnic ham is inexpensive and best cut into steaks or used as chunks for stews.

All three massive pork roasts — the Boston butt, the picnic ham, and the fresh ham (from the rear leg) — can be turned into delicious barbecued dishes. However, the Boston butt, with its high proportion of fat, is prized most by pitmasters because it remains juicy and succulent during the long, slow barbecuing process. To make a pulled pork sandwich, the classic barbecued dish, the Boston butt is cooked for hours and then pulled apart or torn into thin strips, tossed with barbecue sauce, and served on white bread or hamburger buns.

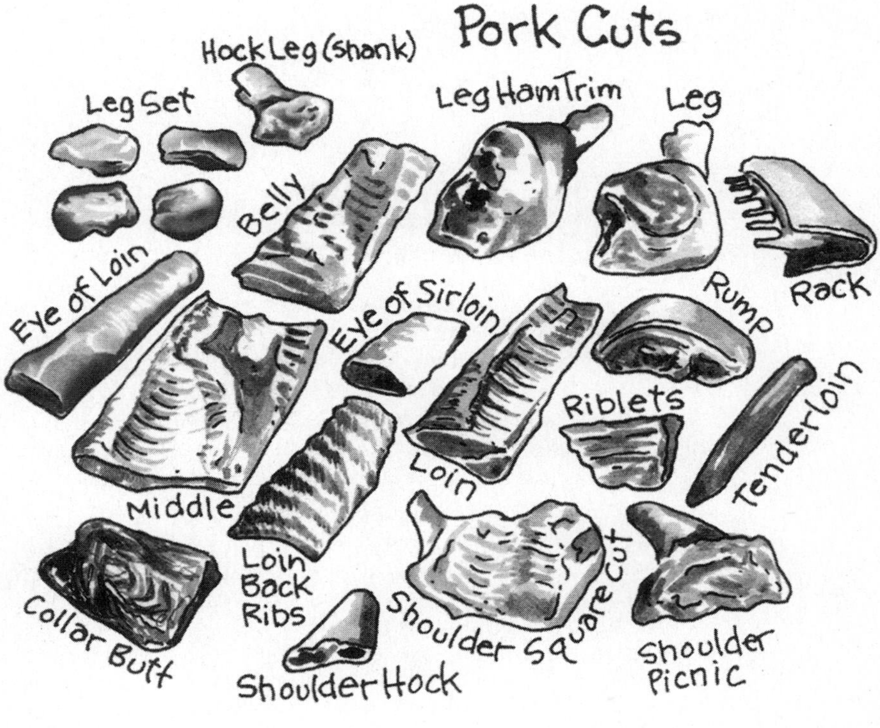

Figure 12-1: Pork has numerous parts and cuts.

Hog wild!

Wild pigs, called *peccaries* or *javelinas,* came to North America across the Bering Straits during the Stone Age, but domesticated pigs only arrived when Spanish explorer Hernando de Soto brought 13 of them to Tampa, Florida, in 1539. All the domesticated pigs in the United States have been bred from this small herd.

Here's the Rub: Flavoring Pork with Herbs and Spices

Grilled foods don't produce the drippings that you get when you cook indoors. When you sauté, pan-fry, roast, or bake foods, the pan drippings (the browned bits left in the cooking pan) provide you with the start of an exquisite sauce to add flavor to your foods. When you grill foods, however, the raw sauce materials drip, splatter, and waste away into the hot coals. That's why the marinades and rubs in this chapter are important for imparting flavor on grilled foods.

Many international spice and seasoning combinations work well with pork. Here are some of our favorites, both in rub and marinade form:

- **French Provençal rubs:** Combine dried, crushed herbs like rosemary, thyme, bay leaves, salt, and black pepper.
- **Asian spice rubs:** Combine anise seeds, cinnamon, ground cloves, ground ginger, and red pepper flakes.
- **West Indian and Jamaican rubs:** Combine cayenne, paprika, and hot peppers with the sweet complementary tastes of allspice, cinnamon, ginger, and dark brown sugar.
- **Greek-style marinade:** Combine olive oil, fresh lemon juice, oregano, garlic, salt, and pepper.

REMEMBER

If you marinate your pork, use a resealable, plastic bag. That way you can discard the bag after the food is marinated, saving you a dish to wash. But more important, the bag allows more of the food to come into direct contact with the marinade. A dish, bowl, or pan has to be exactly the right shape and size for the marinade to cover the food. A bag, however, can be pressed to conform to the exact shape of the food. Be sure to press all the air out of the bag, and close it tightly to prevent leaking.

And This Little Pork Was Done Just Right

Grilling pork can be tricky business, and it takes some practice to get the timing just right. Depending on the thickness of the cut and the amount of fat, muscle, bone, and grain of the meat, the cooking time for pork can vary considerably. Final cooking time also depends on the heat of the fire and the distance the grill grid is placed from the heat.

Our grandmothers used to disregard timing and simply cook pork to an internal temperature of 185 degrees, believing that to cook it less would subject the family to trichinosis. But we now know that trichinae are killed at 135 degrees. So, cooking pork to 155 or 160 degrees is considered safe, and it yields a much juicier piece of meat. Today's pork is leaner than the pork of our grandparents' day, with far less fat, so cooking it to 185 degrees results in a tough, dry chop or roast. So hover over pork as it grills.

One way to check the doneness of a piece of pork is by using a meat thermometer (discussed in Chapter 2). The other way is to cut into the meat (while it's still on the grill) near the bone when you're close to the end of the estimated cooking time. You'll know the meat is cooked when its juices run clear and the meat is no longer pink near the bone. If the meat is boneless, this will take only a little less time — cut into the thickest part of the meat to check for doneness.

If you insist on grilling your pork until it's well done (just because you like it that way!), you may still see some red areas in the meat, especially near the outer edges. Not to worry: In braising, this color comes from naturally occurring nitrites and nitrates (not additives); in grilling, the presence of exhaust gases from your grill may cause this red color. It's all perfectly natural.

In the end, you're trying to produce a fully-cooked, moist and juicy piece of meat that has a slight give in the center so that when you push gently with your finger or the tip of a spatula, the meat springs back. It's an art — the best results come with practice. Consider these tips as you hone your handiwork:

- **If the meat is cooking too fast,** turn it over or move it to a cooler spot on the grill.
- **If the meat is cooking too slowly or if the coals are losing heat too quickly,** cover the grill to increase the heat. (It isn't necessary to sear a chop or other piece of pork like you do a thick roast or lamb.)

So far, even the grilling experts haven't been able to decide whether you should cover the grill when cooking pork. Our advice: Do what makes you happy. We tested pork both with and without the grill cover, and each technique has its rewards and shortcomings. For example, covering the grill eliminates the problem of unevenly cooked meat and produces a smokier flavor than when you leave the grill uncovered — an absolute advantage if you're using wood chips or chunks. However, grilling with a cover also cranks up the grill's heat and can overcook or even burn the meat, especially if they're marinated with sweet ingredients.

After you decide whether you'll use a covered grill, keep the following general guidelines in mind:

- **If you choose to cover the grill,** we recommend using moderate or medium heat and cooking 1-inch chops for about 5 minutes per side. But check them before this estimated time and remove them sooner, if necessary; covering requires close monitoring. Other pork cuts may take more time.
- **If you grill without a cover,** you risk ending up with unevenly cooked meat, especially near the bone where it takes longer to cook. If you grill without the cover, increase the heat to medium-hot and grill for 5 to 6 minutes a side. Other cuts of pork may take more time.

ON THE GRILL: Whether you cover the grill or not, move the meat around on the grill, to cooler or hotter spots, to keep it from burning and to ensure even cooking. If you're grilling with glazes or sauces that contain any sweet ingredients like sugar or honey, brush them onto the meat during the last few minutes of grilling to keep the meat from burning.

Chop, chop, who's there?

Even those who aren't particularly keen on roast pork or ribs are often delighted by the prospect of a nice, thick, juicy pork chop with trimmings like applesauce and sauerkraut. And grilling is one of the tastiest ways to cook pork chops, which are especially delicious marinated, rubbed, or glazed, or simply seasoned with a dusting of salt and pepper.

ON THE GRILL: Pork chops for the grill should be cut about 1-inch thick for best results. This thickness allows the chop to develop a nice exterior crust without drying out. In any recipe that calls for a pork chop, you can use a chop with or without a bone — but we find a lot more flavor in a chop with its bone intact.

ON THE GRILL: Whenever you're grilling a relatively thin piece of meat — such as a chop — with the grill cover down, you lose some control over the grilling process because you can't see whether the food is cooking too fast or not fast enough. Remove the lid of the grill to check on how each chop is cooking before the chop is ready to be turned; make adjustments, if necessary, by moving, the chops to cooler or hotter spots.

Lemony Tarragon Pork Chops

Citrus juices are natural meat tenderizers, and lemon, orange, and lime are especially wonderful with pork. Tart, tantalizing lemon juice is the principal flavor in this recipe. You can use the Lemony Tarragon Marinade to marinate pork chops, pork roasts, or kebabs.

Even a few hours of marinating can make a difference in the flavor of a pork chop. The length of time needed to marinate pork can vary from 15 minutes (for extremely tender pieces of meat) to 24 hours (for tougher pieces). Be sure to marinate in the fridge.

Preparation time: *15 minutes*

Marinating time: *12 to 24 hours*

Grilling time: *10 to 12 minutes*

Yield: *4 servings*

⅔ cup olive oil

½ cup fresh lemon juice

2 tablespoons chopped fresh tarragon or sage, or 2 teaspoons dried

2 teaspoons grated lemon peel (from about 1 lemon)

1 clove garlic, peeled and crushed

¼ teaspoon salt, or to taste

¼ white pepper, or more to taste

Black pepper to taste

4 pork loin chops, each about 1-inch thick (about 2 pounds total)

1 To prepare the marinade, combine all the ingredients except the pork chops in a large, shallow, nonreactive baking dish or a large, resealable plastic bag. Stir until well blended.

2 Trim all but ¼ inch of the fat from the edges of the chops. Add the trimmed chops to the marinade. Cover the dish or seal the bag (after squeezing out all the air) and refrigerate for 12 to 24 hours, turning occasionally.

3 Prepare a medium fire in a covered charcoal or gas grill.

4 Remove chops from the marinade, discarding the remaining marinade. Place chops on a lightly oiled grill grid.

5 Cover and grill the chops with the vents open for about 10 minutes or until done, turning once. Cut near the bone to determine doneness. Chops are done when the meat is browned on the outside, with a slight pink blush in the center, and no longer pink near the bone.

Go-With: *If desired, serve with Black Bean and Red Pepper Salsa (Chapter 6).*

Vary It! *Punch up the flavor of these chops by adding Dijon-style mustard, red pepper flakes, Tabasco sauce, or other fresh herbs like basil, parsley, or rosemary.*

Per serving: *Calories 315 (From Fat 181); Fat 20g (Saturated 5g); Cholesterol 93mg; Sodium 224mg; Carbohydrate 1g (Dietary Fiber 0g); Protein 31g.*

Grilled Pork Chops with Rosemary Oil

In this grilled chop recipe, the marinade is actually a flavored oil, deliciously seasoned with a little honey, balsamic vinegar, red wine vinegar, grated orange peel, and rosemary. Grilling any kind of chop on fresh herb sprigs, as we suggest here, adds another dimension of flavor. However, be sure that the sprigs are lightly oiled before placing them on the grill. (***Note:*** There have been safety concerns about flavored oil turning rancid or developing bacteria, so if you make one, be sure to use it right away and keep it refrigerated after making it until you're ready to use it.)

Preparation time: *15 minutes*

Marinating time: *12 hours or overnight*

Grilling time: *10 minutes*

Yield: *4 servings*

6 tablespoons olive oil

2 tablespoons honey

2 tablespoons red wine vinegar

2 tablespoons balsamic vinegar

1 tablespoon minced fresh rosemary, or 1 teaspoon dried

1 tablespoon grated orange peel (from 1 large navel orange)

2 cloves garlic, peeled and minced

¼ teaspoon salt, or to taste

Pepper to taste

4 pork loin chops, cut 1-inch thick (about 2 pounds total)

4 3- to 4-inch long sprigs fresh rosemary, brushed with oil (optional)

1 Combine the first 9 ingredients in a large, shallow, nonreactive baking dish or resealable plastic bag. Trim all but ¼ inch of fat from the edges of each chop. Place the chops in the dish or bag, turning the chops to coat all sides. Refrigerate for 12 to 24 hours, turning two or three times. (The longer you marinate, the better the flavor.)

2 Prepare a medium fire in a covered charcoal or gas grill.

3 Remove the chops from the marinade, shaking off a bit of the excess; discard the remaining marinade.

4 Place the chops on the oiled grill grid, directly above the heat. Place a rosemary sprig on the top of each chop (if desired). Cover the grill and cook for 5 minutes. Turn the chops so that the rosemary sits under them. Grill the chops, covered, for another 5 minutes or until the meat is browned on the outside with a slight blush of pink in the center and no sign of pink near the bone. Cut to determine doneness. If desired, season with salt and additional pepper before serving.

Per serving: *Calories 538 (From Fat 252); Fat 28g (Saturated 9g); Cholesterol 193mg; Sodium 310mg; Carbohydrate 3g (Dietary Fiber 0g); Protein 65g.*

Apricot-Glazed Pork Chops

In this recipe, apricot jam is mixed with cider vinegar, soy sauce, fresh ginger, garlic, and cayenne pepper for a sweet and spicy glaze.

Thick, sweet glazes that are laced with honey, brown sugar, jam, molasses, and other sweeteners all work well with chops and ribs. But remember that the sugar content means the glaze must be applied only during the last 5 minutes of cooking; otherwise, the glaze may burn and you may taste char instead of chop.

Preparation time: *15 minutes*

Grilling time: *10 minutes*

Yield: *4 servings*

1 cup apricot jam

3 tablespoons cider vinegar

1 tablespoon plus 1 teaspoon soy sauce

2 teaspoons grated fresh ginger

2 cloves garlic, peeled and minced

¼ teaspoon cayenne pepper, or to taste

4 loin pork chops, cut 1-inch thick (about 2 pounds total)

Oil for brushing chops

Salt and pepper to taste

1. Prepare a medium-hot fire in a charcoal or gas grill.
2. Meanwhile, in a small saucepan, combine the jam and the vinegar. Cook, stirring over low heat, until the jam melts. Stir in the soy sauce, ginger, garlic, and cayenne pepper. Remove from the heat and set the glaze aside.
3. Trim all but ¼ inch of fat from each pork chop. Brush the chops lightly with oil; sprinkle with salt and pepper.
4. Place the chops on a well-oiled grill grid. Grill the chops for 3 minutes on each side. Brush both sides generously with the glaze and grill for another 4 to 5 minutes or until done, turning once. Cut to determine doneness. The chops are cooked when the meat has a light pink blush and there's no sign of pink near the bone. If desired, simmer the remaining glaze for 2 to 3 minutes and then drizzle over the grilled chops before serving.

Vary It! *Just about any fruit-flavored sweet chutney, marmalade, or jam (such as plum, apple, pineapple, or orange) works as a quick glaze for pork chops. You can reduce its thickness and sweetness by mixing with a little water or lemon or lime juice.*

Per serving: *Calories 512 (From Fat 158); Fat 158g (Saturated 6g); Cholesterol 102mg; Sodium 452mg; Carbohydrate 54g (Dietary Fiber 1g); Protein 37g.*

Caribbean Pork Chops

In this recipe, pineapple juice gives the meat and bones of these chops a taste and crispness that's reminiscent of slow-cooked pork ribs. Pineapple juice is also a natural tenderizer due to the presence of the enzyme *papain*. Use this marinade for other cuts of pork, adding some cayenne pepper to spice it up, if you wish.

Preparation time: *15 minutes*

Marinating time: *12 to 24 hours*

Grilling time: *10 minutes*

Yield: *4 servings*

1 cup unsweetened pineapple juice

¼ cup honey

¼ cup cider vinegar

1 tablespoon peeled and coarsely chopped fresh ginger

2 cloves garlic, peeled

1 jalapeño pepper, seeded and coarsely chopped

¼ teaspoon ground allspice

4 loin pork chops, cut 1-inch thick (about 2 pounds total)

Salt and black pepper to taste

1 In a blender, blend at high speed all the ingredients, except the pork chops and the salt and pepper, for about 4 seconds, to make a coarse marinade.

2 Trim all but ¼ inch of fat from each chop. Place the chops in a resealable plastic bag or a large, shallow, nonreactive baking dish; pour the marinade over the chops and refrigerate them for 12 to 24 hours, turning two or three times.

3 Prepare a medium-hot fire in a charcoal or gas grill.

4 Remove the chops from the marinade, shaking off most of the excess; discard the remaining marinade. Season the chops lightly with salt and pepper. Place the chops on a well-oiled grill grid and cook them, uncovered, for 5 to 6 minutes per side, turning once. Cut the chops to determine doneness. They're done when the meat has a light pink blush and there's no sign of pink near the bone.

Per serving: *Calories 325 (From Fat 146); Fat 16g (Saturated 6g); Cholesterol 102mg; Sodium 223mg; Carbohydrate 7g (Dietary Fiber 0g); Protein 36g.*

Brine 'n dine

Brine is a solution of water and salt that deeply marinates food. It's an easy way to add flavor and moisture to large pieces of meat. The most famous brined dish — corned beef — is soaked in brine and then rinsed before it's finally boiled with cabbage and other vegetables.

Brined and Grilled Loin O' Pork

In this recipe, a boneless pork loin roast is placed in a brine solution of water, sugar, salt, and seasonings for 2 days before it's cooked indirectly in a covered grill. The result is a deliciously tender and perfectly moist piece of pork. This is a great company dish, and it's one of our favorite recipes.

Preparation time: *25 minutes*

Marinating time: *2 to 3 days*

Grilling time: *50 to 70 minutes*

Yield: *8 servings*

8 cups water

½ cup sugar

⅓ cup kosher salt

3 tablespoons fennel seed

2 bay leaves

2 tablespoons grated orange peel (from about 2 large navel oranges)

3 whole cloves

2 teaspoons black peppercorns

4-pound boneless pork loin roast tied by a butcher

Applesauce (optional)

1 To make the brine, combine all the ingredients, except the pork loin roast and applesauce, in a medium saucepan. Cover and bring to a boil over high heat. Remove from heat and let cool.

2 Place the pork loin in a 2-gallon, heavy-duty plastic bag and then put the bag in a 9-x-13-inch baking pan (or other large rectangular pan). Pour the cooled brine over the roast and seal the bag tightly, pressing out any air. Turn the bag to coat the roast with the brine and refrigerate for 2 days, turning the bag over occasionally.

3 Prepare an indirect, medium-hot fire in a covered grill (use 55 to 60 briquettes for a charcoal fire), with a drip pan that's half-filled with water. If desired, use presoaked wood chips or chunks. To maintain the temperature, be sure to add fresh briquettes to the fire about every 30 minutes. (For more instructions on building an indirect fire, see Chapter 1.)

4 Remove the loin from the brine, discarding the remaining brine; allow the loin to stand at room temperature until the grill is ready. Place the loin on the oiled grill grid directly above the drip pan and opposite the heat.

5 Cover the grill and cook over indirect heat, turning once, for about 15 minutes per pound or until a meat thermometer inserted into the thickest part of the roast reads 155 degrees (about 50 to 70 minutes). The exact grilling time depends on the intensity of the grill's heat and the thickness of the roast. If necessary, be sure to adjust the grill vents to maintain a medium-hot temperature.

6 Remove the roast from the grill, cover it with foil, and let it rest for about 15 minutes. (The internal temperature will rise to 160 degrees.)

7 Cut the roast across the grain into thin, ½-inch slices. Serve with applesauce (if desired).

Go-With: *Serve with Couscous with Apples, Onions, and Raisins (Chapter 16) or Summer Squash Chutney (Chapter 6).*

Per serving: *Calories 577 (From Fat 224); Fat 25g (Saturated 9g); Cholesterol 140mg; Sodium 929mg; Carbohydrate 40g (Dietary Fiber 0g); Protein 46g.*

Tenderloin is the night

A *pork tenderloin* is a boneless, extremely tender piece of meat from the loin of the pig. It weighs only about 1 pound and is often sold in the supermarket meat case wrapped two to a package. Tenderloins can be rubbed or marinated with any number of seasonings and then cooked indirectly or directly. However, the indirect cooking method (see Chapter 1) assures that the meat will be moist, tender, browned, and cooked through (not charred!) in 20 to 30 minutes.

REMEMBER

A pork tenderloin is completely cooked when the interior of the meat reaches a temperature of 160 degrees. However, you should remove the tenderloin from the grill when the thermometer inserted into the thickest part of the roast reaches 155 degrees. Let the tenderloin stand, loosely covered with foil, for 10 minutes before slicing. While the meat rests, the internal temperature will continue to rise, and the juices will settle into the meat, making it easier to carve. Be sure to pour any of the flavorful juices that run out of the roast after it's carved over the slices.

ON THE GRILL

The heat of a gas grill usually isn't as intense as that of a charcoal fire, so for most recipes in this book, we cover those differences by giving you approximate cooking times. However, pork tenderloins may take as much as 15 minutes longer to cook indirectly on gas grills than on charcoal kettle grills. Here's what we advise if you're cooking pork tenderloins on a gas grill:

1. **Preheat the grill with both burners on high.**
2. **After the grill is hot, turn one burner off and set the other to medium-hot.**
3. **Cook the tenderloins, indirectly, for 25 to 40 minutes or until done, turning once or twice.**

   If after 40 minutes the tenderloins aren't cooked, reduce the heat to medium, move them directly over the heat, and continue to cook until done.

When you turn the tenderloins over midway into grilling, also switch their positions by placing the tenderloin farthest from the coals closest to the heat.

Curried Pork Tenderloins

Coating the surface of a pork tenderloin with a mixture of herbs and spices is by far the simplest way to season this cut of meat. Slice the grilled meat about ½-inch thick and arrange the slices on a large platter.

Preparation time: *20 minutes*

Marinating time: *30 minutes to 2 hours*

Grilling time: *20 to 30 minutes*

Yield: *6 to 8 servings*

1 teaspoon light brown sugar, packed
1 teaspoon curry powder
½ teaspoon ground cumin
½ teaspoon ground ginger
½ teaspoon garlic salt
Pinch cayenne pepper, or to taste
Black pepper to taste
1 tablespoon olive oil
2 pork tenderloins, about ¾ to 1 pound each

1. Place the tenderloins in a large shallow baking dish. (If necessary, use kitchen twine to fold and tie the thin end of each tenderloin under the meat to give it uniform thickness and allow it to cook evenly.)
2. Rub each loin with the olive oil. Blend the brown sugar, curry powder, cumin, ginger, garlic salt, cayenne pepper, and black pepper in a small bowl; rub the spice mixture evenly over each pork tenderloin. Wrap the pork with plastic wrap and refrigerate for 30 minutes to 2 hours.
3. Build an indirect, medium-hot fire in a covered charcoal or gas grill. (Use about 50 briquettes if the fire is charcoal.) You don't need to place a drip pan under the pork. (See Chapter 1 for complete instructions on indirect grilling.)
4. Place the tenderloins on an oiled grid, opposite the heat. Cover and grill for 10 minutes. Turn, cover, and grill for 10 to 15 minutes more (maybe longer for a gas grill) or until a meat thermometer inserted into the thickest part of the roast (not the folded part) registers 155 degrees.
5. Let the roast stand for about 10 minutes, covered with foil, before slicing across the grain. The sliced meat should have a hint of pink.

Vary It! *You can tone down or crank up the spice in this tenderloin recipe by adjusting the amount of cayenne and black pepper to suit your taste. Any leftovers can be served the next day as delicious grilled pork sandwiches. Lay the meat between dark bread slices and garnish with a fruit chutney or pickled watermelon rind.*

Go-With: *Serve with Creamy Asian Peanut Sauce, Tomato Chutney, or Summer Squash Chutney (all in Chapter 6), or any of the grilled vegetables in Chapter 16.*

Per serving: *Calories 191 (From Fat 81); Fat 9g (Saturated 3g); Cholesterol 78mg; Sodium 134mg; Carbohydrate 1g (Dietary Fiber 0g); Protein 25g.*

Soy-Marinated Pork Tenderloin with Asian-Flavored Vegetables

In this recipe, you heat the soy marinade and serve it as a finishing sauce for the grilled tenderloin slices and a colorful side dish of steamed carrots, red pepper, zucchini, and broccoli.

Preparation time: *20 minutes*

Marinating time: *6 hours or overnight*

Grilling time: *20 to 30 minutes*

Yield: *6 to 8 servings*

Tenderloins

2 pork tenderloins, about ¾ to 1 pound each

6 tablespoons reduced-sodium soy sauce

1 small onion, peeled and finely chopped

¼ cup light brown sugar, packed

2 tablespoons vegetable oil

2 tablespoons sesame oil

3 tablespoons water

2 cloves garlic, peeled and minced

2 teaspoons ground ginger

½ teaspoon black pepper

⅛ teaspoon cayenne pepper

1 If necessary, use kitchen twine to fold and tie the thin end of each tenderloin under the meat to give it uniform thickness and allow it to cook evenly.

2 Place the remaining ingredients in a large, plastic resealable bag or nonreactive dish; add the tenderloins to the bag or dish. Seal the bag, pressing out as much air as possible, or cover the dish with plastic wrap. Refrigerate for at least 6 hours, or overnight, turning occasionally.

3 Prepare an indirect, medium-hot fire in a covered charcoal or gas grill. (Use about 50 briquettes if the fire is made with charcoal.) You don't need to place a drip pan under the pork. (Turn to Chapter 1 for complete instructions on building an indirect fire.)

4 Remove the tenderloins from the marinade; pour the remaining marinade into a medium saucepan and reserve for making the Asian-flavored vegetables. Place the tenderloins on a lightly oiled grid, on the side opposite the coals or heat. Cover and grill for 10 to 15 minutes; turn, cover and grill for 10 to 15 minutes more or until a meat thermometer inserted into the thickest part of the tenderloin (but not the folded part) registers 155 degrees. The meat should have a hint of pink in the center.

Asian-Flavored Vegetables

3 large carrots, trimmed and scraped

1 small red bell pepper

1 small zucchini or yellow squash, ends trimmed

2 cups broccoli florets

1 tablespoon vegetable oil

¼ cup cold water

1 teaspoon cornstarch

1 While the grill preheats, quarter the carrots and then cut into 2-inch-long pieces. Core and seed the pepper; cut into 2-inch chunks. Cut the zucchini in half lengthwise and then into ½-inch semicircle pieces. Place all cut vegetables in a bowl with the broccoli florets and set aside.

2 While the tenderloins are grilling, bring 1 inch of water and the vegetable oil to a boil in a medium saucepan. Add the carrots, cover, and boil for about 3 minutes. Add the broccoli, and boil, covered, about 3 minutes. Add the red pepper and zucchini and boil, covered, for about 2 minutes more or until all the vegetables are crisp-tender. Drain immediately, cover, and set aside.

3 In a small bowl, combine the ¼ cup cold water with the cornstarch, stirring to blend well. Bring the reserved marinade to a full rolling boil in a medium saucepan over medium-high heat. Add the cornstarch-water mixture and cook for 1 to 2 minutes, stirring constantly, until the sauce is slightly thickened and smooth.

4 Add the boiled vegetables to the saucepan; stir gently to coat in the sauce. Remove from heat as soon as the vegetables are warmed through. Cover to keep warm.

5 Remove the grilled tenderloins to a carving board and let stand 10 minutes, covered with foil. Slice thinly across the grain. Pour any juices that run out from the roast onto the carved slices. Arrange the tenderloin slices surrounded by the vegetables on a large platter. Spoon any remaining sauce over all and serve immediately.

Per serving: *Calories 384 (From Fat 165); Fat 18g (Saturated 5g); Cholesterol 107mg; Sodium 703mg; Carbohydrate 17g (Dietary Fiber 2g); Protein 36g.*

Coriander and Fennel Rubbed Pork Tenderloin

Coriander and fennel add wonderful aromatic flavors to pork without overwhelming its essential taste, which is more delicate than beef or lamb. You can see the finished dish in the color insert.

Preparation time: *5 minutes*

Marinating time: *30 minutes to 2 hours*

Grilling time: *20–25 minutes*

Yield: *6 to 8 servings*

1 tablespoon ground coriander seeds
¾ teaspoon ground fennel seeds
¼ teaspoon ground chili powder
½ teaspoon thyme
1½ teaspoons salt
1 tablespoon olive oil
2½ pounds pork tenderloin

1 Combine the coriander and fennel seeds, chili powder, thyme, and salt in a bowl.

2 Rub the loin of pork with the olive oil, and then rub the dry ingredients over the loin. Wrap the loin with plastic wrap, and then refrigerate for at least 30 minutes and up to 2 hours. However, if you let the pork chill for 2 hours, we suggest you remove the meat from the refrigerator and let it warm up for 5 to 10 minutes before grilling.

3 Build an indirect, medium-hot fire in a covered charcoal or gas grill. (Use about 50 briquettes if the fire is charcoal.) You don't need to place a drip pan under the pork. (See Chapter 1 for complete instructions on indirect grilling.)

4 Unwrap the pork from the plastic wrap and place on the grill opposite the direct heat. Cover and grill for 10 minutes. Turn, cover, and grill for 10 to 15 minutes more (maybe longer for a gas grill) or until meat thermometer inserted into the thickest part of the loin (not the folded part) registers 155 degrees. If you want your pork to be rarer, cook the loin to 140 degrees.

5 Let the roast stand for about 10 minutes, covered with foil, before slicing across the grain. The sliced meat should have at least a hint of pink.

Per serving: *Calories 226 (From Fat 92); Fat 10g (Saturated 3g); Cholesterol 97mg; Sodium 503mg; Carbohydrate 1g (Dietary Fiber 0g); Protein 31g.*

Chapter 13

Savoring the Peppery Meat of the Middle East: Lamb

In This Chapter

- Uncovering everything you need to know about lamb
- Taking a look at lamb chops
- Discovering how to handle lamb shoulder
- Grilling up a leg of lamb
- Preparing a rack of lamb

Recipes in This Chapter

- Grilled Chops with Orange and Rosemary
- Lamb Shoulder Chops with Yogurt and Curry Marinade
- Western Lamb Steaks
- Butterflied Leg of Lamb with Honey-Mustard Dressing
- Rack of Lamb with Hoisin Marinade

Often overlooked as an entrée for grilling, lamb is one of the most succulent meats you can prepare inside or outside the house. In this chapter, you find out which lamb cuts are the best to grill and discover that cooking lamb on the grill is a slightly different process than that used for beef. We feature recipes that represent the best of American barbecue-style lamb — and one Middle Eastern lamb recipe, too.

Lamb and Spice and Everything Nice: What You Need to Know

Lamb is defined as the meat of sheep less than 1 year old, usually slaughtered between 4 and 12 months. If the animal is more than a year old, it's called *mutton. Baby lamb* is milk fed and slaughtered at about 6 weeks old. *Spring lamb* is also milk fed, but it goes to 4 months old. Lamb, which is traditionally served at Easter in many countries, is exceptionally flavorful — and fatty — and is best roasted to medium.

Surveying the cuts

Lamb comes in cutlets, loins, legs, rumps, racks, and several other cuts. It makes terrific ground meat dishes, sensational kebabs, and superb barbecue. After it's trimmed, lamb tastes splendid when prepared with herbs like rosemary and garlic, a gloss of olive oil, a marinade of red wine, or a rub of Eastern spices like cumin, coriander, and cardamom. Figure 13-1 shows the principal cuts of lamb you can find in the American market. Here's the rundown:

- **Breast:** The breast meat is good for braising, but the riblets make for good barbecue. The breast is excellent ground up for burgers as well.
- **Leg:** This cut may be the whole leg, center leg steaks, the boneless leg, the French-style leg, the shank half, or the butterflied leg, all of which do well on the grill. Plus, cubes from the leg make great kebabs (see Chapter 8).
- **Loin:** The loin includes the thick loin chops, loin roast, boneless loin roast, and medallions, all of which are best prepared either under the broiler or on the grill.
- **Rack:** The rack includes various smaller chops, such as rib chops and rack of lamb — which is delicious grilled.
- **Shank:** The shank is best for braising and stewing.
- **Shoulder:** The shoulder includes everything from shoulder chops to boneless shoulder roasts.

All these lamb cuts are now readily available in a supermarket.

SHOPPING TIP

When buying lamb, look for meat that's bright red in color, which indicates freshness. Also make sure it has enough exterior fat — about $^{1}/_{4}$ inch — to ensure succulence.

Looking for lamb by country of origin (yes, it matters!)

The finest lamb in the world is from the U.S. The very best of that is from Colorado, where it's raised by cowboys, many of whom are of Basque origin. American lamb is well fatted, which gives it tremendous flavor, but it's more costly than lamb from around the world.

Even though U.S. lamb is the best, good lamb also is raised in England, Ireland, France, Italy, Greece, and Australia, and much of it can be found fresh in American markets. But through heavy government subsidies, New Zealand has nearly monopolized the export market with its lamb shipments, which are almost always frozen. Of good but not outstanding quality, New Zealand lamb is considerably cheaper than that from other countries.

Figure 13-1: The cuts of lamb.

SHOPPING TIP

When shopping for lamb, remember that the country of origin must, by law, be printed on the package.

Seasoning your lamb

Lamb chops, steaks, and kebabs can be basted or glazed with endless, imaginative sauces and marinades. (You can find out more about lamb kebabs in Chapter 8.) Here are some easy, classic recommendations from the American Lamb Council. Happily, you can assemble most of them from common kitchen and pantry ingredients. Each basting recipe is enough for four ¾-inch-thick leg steaks or chops. Brush the lamb on both sides before grilling over medium-hot heat for 5 to 7 minutes per side or until cooked as desired. For more flavor, marinate the chops for a few hours before grilling.

- **Cracked Pepper:** Combine 2 tablespoons red wine, 1 tablespoon cracked pepper, and 2 tablespoons olive oil.
- **Curry:** Combine ¼ cup plain lowfat yogurt, 1 clove peeled and pressed garlic, and 1 teaspoon curry powder.
- **Honey-Mustard Glaze:** Combine 2 tablespoons each honey and prepared mustard.
- **Lemon Pepper:** Combine 2 tablespoons olive oil, 1 tablespoon finely minced onion, 1 tablespoon red wine vinegar, and 1½ teaspoons lemon pepper.
- **Polynesian:** Combine 3 tablespoons apricot-pineapple jam, ½ teaspoon dry mustard, 1 tablespoon fresh lemon juice, and ¼ teaspoon garlic salt.
- **Southwest:** Combine 2 tablespoons olive oil, 1 clove peeled and pressed garlic, ¼ teaspoon cumin, 1 tablespoon fresh lime juice, and ½ teaspoon dried leaf oregano.
- **Teriyaki:** Combine 2 tablespoons soy sauce, 1 tablespoon honey, 1 clove peeled and pressed garlic, 1 tablespoon dry sherry, 1 teaspoon sesame oil, and 1 teaspoon grated fresh ginger.

WARNING!

We recommend that you keep all meats, fish, and poultry refrigerated until you're ready to grill. However, you'll get a better initial sear, particularly with fatty meats like lamb, if the meat is near room temperature or very nearly so. Our advice is to remove the lamb from the refrigerator as you prepare the fire. By the time the grill is preheated, the meat will be close to room temperature without sustaining any effects from airborne bacteria. Don't let meat, fish, or poultry stand at room temperature longer than 30 minutes.

Grilling your lamb with TLC

Follow this advice when grilling lamb:

- Cook lamb chops over a medium-hot fire for best results.
- The heat of a charcoal grill is much more intense than the heat of a gas grill, resulting in shorter cooking times, especially when you're using an indirect fire. Whatever your grill style, be sure to use a meat thermometer to determine the doneness of lamb roasts. Depending on your desired degree of doneness, follow these guidelines:
    - Grill to between 145 and 150 degrees for medium-rare.
    - Grill to between 150 and 155 degrees for medium.
- The internal temperature increases more rapidly during the final minutes of cooking, so check the meat thermometer often during the final minutes.
- Before carving, let a lamb roast stand for 10 to 15 minutes after removing it from the heat. Doing so helps the meat settle down after all that fire. The juices will be more evenly distributed, and the meat will continue to cook slightly from internal heat. If you're carving the meat and think that it needs a little more cooking, simply place it back on the grid for a few minutes.

WARNING!

Lamb, by its very nature, has a good degree of fat — certainly more than beef — so you have to watch carefully for flare-ups. A good way to avoid flare-ups is to trim unnecessary fat to about ¼ inch of the bone or flesh. However, remember that even grilling trimmed lamb can cause flare-ups. Keep a water bottle handy to douse any flames, and move the chops around to cooler spots from time to time. Covering the grill also extinguishes flare-ups.

REMEMBER

All of our cooking times are just good estimates. Actual cooking times depend on the temperature of the air, the intensity of your grill's heat, the thickness of the cut, and other factors. Make a small incision in the lamb chops with a thin, sharp knife a few minutes before you think they're done to avoid overcooking.

Licking Your (Lamb) Chops

Lamb chops are delicious when cooked on the grill, whether they're the big thick loin chops or the smaller riblets, which take no more than a minute or two on each side to cook. (You can eat the riblets with your fingers. In fact, the Italians call these riblets *scottaditti,* or "finger burners," because you just might torch your digits when grabbing the riblets right off the grill.) A lamb chop needs little seasoning and is delicious when rubbed with a little olive oil, salt, and black pepper before grilling.

SHOPPING TIP

Avoid buying those skinny chops that you see wrapped in plastic in the supermarket refrigerator cases. Rib and loin lamb chops for the grill should be cut at least 1-inch thick; your goal is to keep the center of the chop pink and rosy, and the outside crisp and browned. A thinner chop gives you less control because it turns in a flash from medium to well-done.

Grilled Chops with Orange and Rosemary

In this recipe, we use a touch of garlic and two very compatible seasonings — orange and rosemary — that partner perfectly with these grilled lamb chops.

Preparation time: *15 minutes*

Marinating time: *1 to 4 hours*

Grilling time: *10 to 12 minutes*

Yield: *4 servings*

4 loin lamb chops, cut 1-inch thick

2 tablespoons olive oil

1 large shallot, peeled and minced

2 cloves garlic, peeled and finely minced

1 tablespoon grated orange peel (about 1 large navel orange)

Salt and pepper to taste

4 sprigs fresh rosemary, each about 4 inches long

Olive oil for brushing rosemary sprigs

1 teaspoon balsamic vinegar or to taste

1 If necessary, trim all but about ¼ inch of fat from the edge of each chop.

2 Using a small bowl and a wooden spoon, or a mortar and pestle, lightly mash together the 2 tablespoons olive oil, shallot, garlic, orange peel, and salt and pepper. Brush all surfaces of the chops with the mixture. Place the chops in a shallow baking dish or in a large, resealable plastic bag. Cover the dish or close the bag, and refrigerate the chops for 1 to 4 hours, turning occasionally.

3 Prepare a medium-hot fire in a charcoal or gas grill.

4 Remove the chops from the flavored oil, reserving any extra. Brush the rosemary sprigs generously with olive oil and set them on a lightly oiled grid. Place a chop on each sprig. Grill the chops for 5 to 6 minutes per side for medium-rare, or until desired doneness, brushing each chop with the remaining marinade once before turning.

5 Place the chops on a serving platter; sprinkle about ¼ teaspoon balsamic vinegar over each chop and (if desired) additional salt and pepper.

Per serving: *Calories 275 (From Fat 197); Fat 22g (Saturated 7g); Cholesterol 66mg; Sodium 197mg; Carbohydrate 2g (Dietary Fiber 0g); Protein 17g.*

The Lowdown on Lamb Shoulders

Arm and blade lamb chops from the shoulder aren't the most tender cuts of meat. They contain a fair amount of connective tissue that, when grilled quickly, remains somewhat unattractive and sinewy — so we recommend that only ardent lamb lovers grill shoulder chops. If you do choose to grill shoulder chops, you'll find them loaded with flavor. You also may find that they're considerably cheaper than loin or rib chops.

Ask your butcher to cut shoulder steaks a bit thinner than the rib and loin chops. Thinner cuts allow the marinade to more fully penetrate and soften the sinewy meat.

Lamb Shoulder Chops with Yogurt and Curry Marinade

The key to preparing this recipe successfully is to marinate the chops for several hours or overnight, using a Middle Eastern yogurt and spice mixture, to help soften some of the connective tissue.

Preparation time: *20 minutes*

Marinating time: *6 hours or overnight*

Grilling time: *12 to 14 minutes*

Yield: *4 servings*

4 shoulder lamb chops, cut ¾-inch thick

2 teaspoons peeled and grated fresh ginger

1 large clove garlic, peeled and minced

1 teaspoon ground cumin

¾ teaspoon ground turmeric

¼ teaspoon cayenne pepper

¼ teaspoon salt, or to taste

½ cup plain lowfat yogurt

1 medium onion, peeled and quartered

2 tablespoons finely chopped cilantro (coriander) leaves (optional)

1. If necessary, trim all but ¼ inch of the fat from the edges of the chops; place chops in a shallow baking dish.
2. In a small bowl, combine the ginger, garlic, cumin, turmeric, cayenne pepper, and salt. Spread the spice mixture over both sides of the chops. In a blender, blend the yogurt and onion for a few seconds into a coarse puree; pour the yogurt mixture over the chops in the baking dish, turning to coat. Cover the dish and marinate for 6 hours or overnight.
3. Prepare a medium-hot fire in a charcoal or gas grill.
4. Remove the chops from the marinade, shaking off the excess; discard any remaining marinade. Grill the chops on a lightly oiled grid, 6 to 7 minutes per side for medium-rare, or until desired doneness, turning once.
5. Place the chops on a serving platter; sprinkle with additional salt and pepper and chopped cilantro leaves (if desired).

Go-With: *Serve with Tomato Chutney or Summer Squash Chutney (Chapter 6) or Yogurt Cucumber Salad (Chapter 16).*

Vary It! *This yogurt marinade is also delicious with lamb kebabs, leg steaks, and whole roasts, such as a butterflied leg of lamb. To cover these larger roasts, you need to double the recipe.*

Per serving: *Calories 375 (From Fat 222); Fat 25g (Saturated 11g); Cholesterol 131mg; Sodium 145mg; Carbohydrate 2g (Dietary Fiber 0g); Protein 34g.*

A Leg Up on Lamb

Most Americans who like lamb probably eat it seasonally (at Easter) in the form of a leg roast. The leg roast is a succulent cut with a fine texture that's not unlike prime rib of beef, and it takes to marinades well. It can be cooked medium-rare or medium, but it takes on more of a lamb taste when cooked to well-done.

Grill roasting a leg

You can roast a 5- to 7-pound leg of lamb in a covered grill, with or without a rotisserie unit, with delicious results. Here's how:

1. **Prepare the leg for the grill by first trimming any large pieces of fat.**

   A thin, transparent layer of tissue, called the *fell,* lies between the fat and the meat. Don't remove this layer — it keeps the meat moist as it grills.

2. **With the tip of a sharp knife, make a half dozen or more incisions, or very small pockets, all over the leg.**

   Insert slivers of peeled garlic, as shown in Figure 13-2, into each slit and then rub the leg with olive oil. Sprinkle the leg with pepper, grated lemon peel, and 1 tablespoon of a fresh herb such as rosemary, marjoram, or thyme.

3. **Grill, covered, over a medium, indirect fire, with a drip pan under the meat that's half-filled with water, broth, or apple juice.**

   If you're using charcoal, ignite 50 to 60 briquettes and bank them to one side of the grill after they're ashy gray. Replenish the fire with additional charcoal every 30 to 40 minutes. (See Chapter 1 for more specific directions on building an indirect fire in a gas or charcoal grill.) Grill until an instant-read or oven thermometer registers 140 to 150 degrees for rare to medium-rare or 150 to 155 degrees for medium. If using a regular meat thermometer, insert it into the thickest part of the roast, without touching any bone, before grilling. Approximate grilling time is 15 to 20 minutes per pound, but start checking for doneness 30 minutes before the estimated final cooking time.

   REMEMBER

   The internal temperature of a roast will rise about 5 degrees after it's removed from the grill or oven, causing it to cook a little more. Remove the roast when the thermometer registers about 5 degrees less than the desired final temperature.

4. **Let the roast rest for about 10 to 15 minutes, loosely covered with foil, before carving into thin slices.**

   Be sure to serve any remaining cutting-board juices with the meat.

A roasted or grilled leg of lamb offers meat of varying degrees of doneness. The meat at the thin shank end, which is close to the bone, will be brown and probably well done. The meat at the thicker end is ideally quite pink and medium-rare.

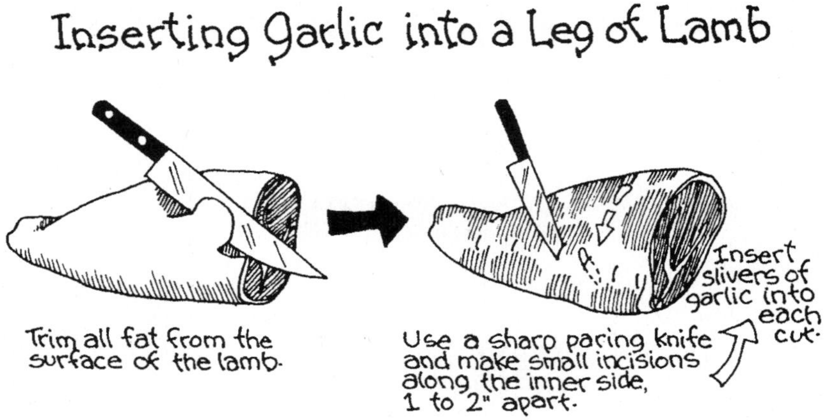
Inserting Garlic into a Leg of Lamb
Trim all fat from the surface of the lamb.
Use a sharp paring knife and make small incisions along the inner side, 1 to 2" apart.
Insert slivers of garlic into each cut.

Figure 13-2: Make cuts into a leg of lamb to hold a sliver of garlic.

Grilling legs, steak-style

Lamb leg steaks can be delicious on the grill, as in the following recipe. They're a good substitute for beef sirloin, and they're best when cooked medium-rare.

Western Lamb Steaks

Ask your butcher to custom-cut lamb steaks from the leg of the lamb for this recipe. Each leg steak will probably weigh a little less than 1 pound, so two steaks are enough to serve four diners. This marinade, or basting sauce, also works with shoulder lamb chops or a butterflied leg. If you're desperate for time, a bottle of your favorite barbecue sauce, especially one with hickory-smoked flavoring, also makes a good sauce for lamb steaks.

Preparation time: *20 minutes*

Marinating time: *4 hours or overnight*

Grilling time: *10 to 14 minutes*

Yield: *4 servings*

2 lamb steaks, center cut from the leg, about ¾- to 1-inch thick

½ cup chili sauce

2 tablespoons cider vinegar

2 tablespoons water

1 small onion, peeled, halved, and thinly sliced

1 large clove garlic, peeled and minced

1 tablespoon Worcestershire sauce

1 teaspoon chili powder

½ teaspoon ground cumin

Generous dashes Tabasco sauce

Salt and pepper to taste

1 If necessary, trim all but about ¼ inch of fat from the edges of the steaks; place steaks in a shallow baking dish or large, resealable plastic bag.

2 In a mixing bowl or glass measuring cup, combine the remaining ingredients, except the salt and pepper; pour the marinade over the lamb steaks, turning the steaks to coat them. Cover the dish or seal the bag, pressing out any air, and refrigerate 4 hours or overnight.

3 Prepare a medium-hot fire in a charcoal or gas grill.

4 Remove the steaks from the marinade, reserving marinade. Sprinkle the steaks with salt and pepper. Place the steaks on a lightly oiled grid. Grill 5 to 7 minutes per side for medium-rare, or until desired doneness, brushing once with marinade before turning.

Go-With: *Try Western Lamb Steaks with the Middle Eastern Rice recipe in Chapter 16.*

Per serving: *Calories 429 (From Fat 190); Fat 21g (Saturated 9g); Cholesterol 151mg; Sodium 1,265mg; Carbohydrate 13g (Dietary Fiber 1g); Protein 45g.*

Butterflying, marinating, and grilling legs: A no-fail method

After you try butterflied and grilled leg of lamb, you'll probably agree that it's one of the best meals you can serve to a crowd of backyard guests. To *butterfly* a leg, you bone it, slit the leg lengthwise, and spread it flat. The boned meat more readily accepts the flavors of its marinade, the grilling time is quick and even, the carving is a cinch, and the taste is delicious. Have your butcher butterfly the leg and trim the fat, or do it yourself by following the instructions in Figure 13-3.

Marinades for butterflied lamb can be as simple as salad dressing. (We know a few excellent home cooks who proudly announce that the best marinade for butterflied leg of lamb is a bottle of Wish-Bone Italian Dressing.) Or you may want to use something a bit fancier, perhaps a multi-ingredient curry marinade. Lamb, with its nearly gamey taste, readily accepts the flavors of yogurt, curry spices, red or white wine, lemon, hot peppers, black pepper, chili powders, balsamic vinegar, assorted herbs, and garlic — the best and simplest lamb seasoning.

Follow your own likes and dislikes into your kitchen lab to assemble a marinade for a butterflied leg of lamb. Ask yourself: "Do I want a hint of orange, lemon, or rosemary? Do I want a slightly sweet taste or something spicier? Do I like the pungency of balsamic or cider vinegar, or the complexity of a fruity red wine?" And then go for it.

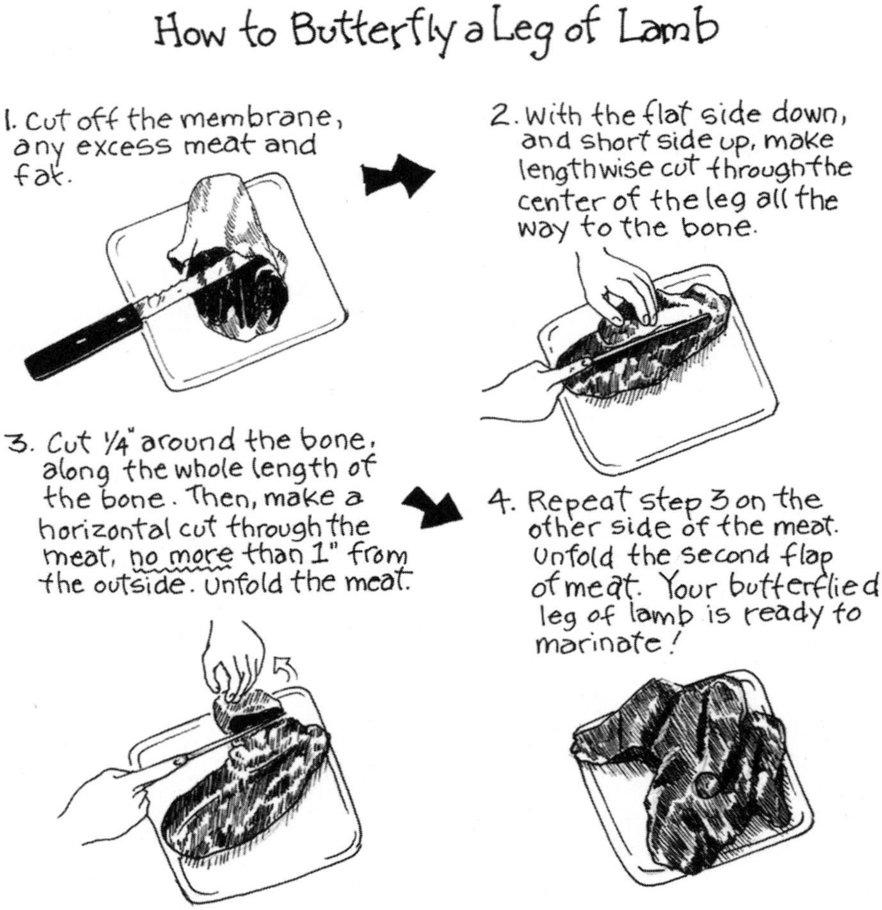
How to Butterfly a Leg of Lamb
1. Cut off the membrane, any excess meat and fat.
2. With the flat side down, and short side up, make lengthwise cut through the center of the leg all the way to the bone.
3. Cut 1/4" around the bone, along the whole length of the bone. Then, make a horizontal cut through the meat, no more than 1" from the outside. Unfold the meat.
4. Repeat step 3 on the other side of the meat. Unfold the second flap of meat. Your butterflied leg of lamb is ready to marinate!

Figure 13-3: When a leg of lamb is butterflied, the bone is removed and the meat lies flat, resembling a butterfly.

Butterflied Leg of Lamb with Honey-Mustard Dressing

The small, boneless leg of lamb used in this recipe is available in most major supermarkets and is perfect for a family of 4 to 6. The leg is often wrapped in a twine bag or netting. Remove the netting and lay the meat flat in the dressing. Be sure to let it marinate for at least 24 hours to completely absorb the vinegar, honey, and mustard flavors.

If you want to feed a crowd of 10 or more, the ingredient amounts can be doubled for a bone-in 6- to 8-pound leg that weighs about 5 pounds butterflied. Or you can use the same marinade with wonderful success on about 2 pounds of lamb for kebabs. A final note: If you really love garlic, use the full 2 cloves; for less garlic flavor, use 1 large clove.

Preparation time: *20 minutes*

Marinating time: *24 hours*

Grilling time: *25 to 30 minutes*

Yield: *4 to 6 servings*

A half or small butterflied leg of lamb (about $2\frac{1}{4}$ to $2\frac{1}{2}$ pounds without the bone)

1 to 2 cloves garlic, peeled and thinly sliced

6 tablespoons extra-virgin olive oil

$\frac{1}{4}$ cup balsamic vinegar

2 tablespoons honey

2 tablespoons Dijon-style mustard

Salt and pepper to taste

Chopped parsley for garnish

1. Trim all fat from the surface of the lamb. Using a sharp paring knife, make small incisions or cuts along the inner side (the side that held the bone), about 1 to 2 inches apart. Insert a sliver of garlic into each small incision.
2. Place the lamb in a large, shallow baking dish or resealable plastic bag.
3. In a small bowl, whisk together the oil, vinegar, honey, and mustard; pour the dressing over the lamb and turn to coat both sides. Cover the dish or seal the bag, pressing out any air, and refrigerate for 24 hours, turning occasionally.
4. Drain the lamb, reserving the dressing. Sprinkle the lamb with salt and pepper on both sides.
5. Prepare a medium fire in a charcoal or gas grill.
6. Place the lamb on a lightly oiled grid. Grill, turning the meat about every 8 to 10 minutes, for a total of 25 to 30 minutes or until the internal temperature in the thickest part of the meat registers 135 degrees to 140 degrees for rare, 145 degrees to 150 degrees for medium-rare, or 150 degrees to 155 degrees for medium. Baste the lamb twice with the reserved marinade during the first 15 to 18 minutes of grilling.
7. Remove the lamb from the grill, place on a carving board, and let it rest, covered loosely with foil, 10 minutes before cutting against the grain into thin slices. Serve the meat with the carving board juices and sprinkle with chopped parsley.

Go-With: *Suggested side dishes include Grand Marnier Grilled Sweet Potatoes, Garlic-Grilled Portobellos, or Grilled Tomatoes with Cumin Butter (all in Chapter 16); Tomato Chutney or Summer Squash Chutney (Chapter 6); and any of the salads in Chapter 16. Make sandwiches with any leftovers, spreading the bread with honey mustard or a little fruit chutney.*

Per serving: *Calories 541(From Fat 292); Fat 32g (Saturated 7g); Cholesterol 150mg; Sodium 453mg; Carbohydrate 12g (Dietary Fiber 0g); Protein 49g.*

Racking Up Lamb for the Grill

Even though some people consider rack of lamb to be a rather dainty dish, we think it's really finger-licking food. You'll want to sink your teeth into the tiny morsels of meat around the back and rib bones and, eschewing fork and knife, pick up the small chops with your fingers. Lamb ribs are a lot like pork ribs — tender, juicy, full of flavor, and great on the grill. A rack of lamb may contain as many as eight ribs, but it's more often cut by the butcher into individual portions of three or four chops per person.

Some cooks prefer to have their racks *French cut* so that the top of the rib bones are stripped entirely of their meat and fat. However, we recommend leaving the rib bone meat alone and intact, shown in Figure 13-4.

How to Trim and Slash a Rack of Lamb For the Grill
Trim all but a paper-thin layer of fat from the rack.
Make about a 1" slash between each chop at the backbone end.
Make about a 1 to 2" slash at the top or narrow rib end between each bone
The rack should remain in one piece. Now apply basting sauces or seasoning into slashes. After grilling. Cut through slashes to separate chops!

Figure 13-4: Preparing a rack of lamb for the grill.

Trim (or have your butcher trim) most of the fat from the back of the ribs, leaving only a paper-thin layer. Slice 2 to 3 inches between each rib down toward the meatier "eye" end. Slash also about 1 inch through the backbone to separate each chop slightly at the bottom of the rack, as shown in Figure 13-4. The rack should remain in one piece, but these slashes allow you to apply basting sauces and seasonings with better results.

Rack of Lamb with Hoisin Marinade

Because orange juice and honey are the principal ingredients in this recipe, the rack of lamb is grilled indirectly to prevent the meat from cooking too fast and charring. Indirect cooking is an excellent method of cooking racks and roasts — even if sweet ingredients aren't present in the recipe. The final result is a moist and juicy piece of meat that needs little attending. In this recipe, the rack is left on the grill for at least 20 minutes before turning. This marinade is terrific with any cut of lamb, from chops to leg, and also works with pork and poultry.

Preparation time: *20 minutes*

Marinating time: *12 to 24 hours*

Grilling time: *45 to 55 minutes*

Yield: *2 servings*

1 8-rib rack of lamb, about 2½ pounds

⅔ cup fresh orange juice

3 tablespoons hoisin sauce

3 tablespoons soy sauce

2 tablespoons olive oil

1 tablespoon plus 1 teaspoon honey

2 large cloves garlic, peeled and minced

2 teaspoons peeled and grated fresh ginger

Salt and pepper to taste

1 Using a sharp knife, cut the rack in half, so that each half has 4 ribs. Make a 1-inch cut between each chop at the backbone end to make carving easier. Make a 2-inch cut between each rib down toward the meaty "eye" end. Trim the fat, leaving a paper-thin layer on the back of each rack (refer to Figure 13-4). (A good butcher can do all of this, if you prefer.)

2 In a small mixing bowl, make the hoisin marinade by combining all the remaining ingredients, except the salt and pepper.

3 Place the lamb racks in a large, resealable plastic bag or a shallow baking dish; pour the marinade over the lamb. Try to work pieces of the ginger and garlic into the slashed areas. Seal the bag (press out all the air in the bag to surround the rack with the marinade) or cover the dish, and refrigerate 12 to 24 hours, turning occasionally.

4 Remove the lamb from the refrigerator and let it stand for about 30 minutes before grilling. Meanwhile, prepare a hot, indirect fire in a charcoal or gas grill, with a drip plan (half filled with water) in place. (For complete directions on how to build an indirect fire, turn to Chapter 1.)

5 Remove the rack of lamb from the marinade. Shake off the excess marinade and reserve any remaining marinade. Season the lamb on both sides with salt and pepper.

6 Place the lamb on the grid, fat side down, over the drip pan on the side without heat. Cover and grill for 45 to 55 minutes, turning every 20 minutes, or until an instant-read thermometer registers 140 degrees to 150 degrees for rare to medium-rare or 150 degrees to 155 degrees for medium. Add hot briquettes to a charcoal fire after 30 to 40 minutes, or when necessary, to maintain heat. If desired, during the last few minutes of grilling, move the lamb to the side of the grid directly above the heat for 3 to 5 minutes per side, to brown the meat more thoroughly.

7 Remove the lamb from the grid and place on a carving platter. Cover the meat loosely with foil and let rest for about 5 minutes. Meanwhile, transfer the reserved marinade to a small saucepan. Bring to a boil and then simmer for about 15 minutes, stirring frequently. Carve the lamb into individual chops; spoon the sauce over the chops and serve.

Go-With: *Rice, noodles, or whole potatoes roasted in a covered grill (see Chapter 16) make excellent accompaniments to this lamb dish.*

Per serving: *Calories 712 (From Fat 356); Fat 40g (Saturated 11g); Cholesterol 167mg; Sodium 2,213mg; Carbohydrate 32g (Dietary Fiber 1g); Protein 54g.*

Chapter 14

Birds of a Feather

In This Chapter

- Grilling different cuts of chicken
- Making turkey year-round
- Discovering the secrets to grilling game birds

Recipes in This Chapter

- Lemon Chicken Breasts
- Jerk-Seasoned Chicken Breasts
- Spicy Chili Chicken Wings
- Orange-Garlic Chicken Wings
- Grilled Chicken Quarters with Barbecue Sauce
- Grilled Lime Chicken with Onion Compote
- Lemon-Cilantro Chicken with Garlic-Ginger Mayonnaise
- Moroccan Chicken Legs and Thighs
- Chicken alla Mattone
- Brined and Grilled Chicken
- Dry Poultry Rub for Brined Chicken
- Grilled Turkey Tenderloins with Honey-Mustard Glaze
- Dale Curry's Hickory-Smoked Whole Turkey
- Rock Cornish Game Hens with Molasses-Rum Marinade
- Whole Game Hens with Asian Flavors

Chicken and other types of fowl offer more than great taste when prepared on the grill. They also provide a healthy, nutritious meal. Almost the whole world loves chicken, and for good reason: It can be used in tons of recipes, it's a fairly inexpensive meat, and as far as we know, there are no religious taboos against it.

If, however, you're getting a little tired of using only chicken in your grilling repertoire, this chapter is for you. We also share delicious turkey recipes — including one for a whole turkey! — and give you tips for grilling up game birds, Rock Cornish game hens, and even poussins (small spring chickens).

Finger-Lickin' Chicken

Chicken's mild flavor is appealing, and its meat adapts extremely well to marinades, rubs, and seasonings. However, you have to be careful when grilling chicken. Hovering pays off. Why?

Especially with its skin on, chicken can be *seared* — browned very quickly — and can then turn charcoal-black just as quickly, without the inside getting cooked at all. You obviously want to avoid this situation. The key to grilling any type of chicken over direct heat is to turn the pieces continually and move them to hotter or cooler spots on the grid when some pieces seem to be cooking faster than others.

More specifically, follow these steps when using direct heat to grill chicken pieces with bone and skin. If you find the meat is cooking too quickly or turning black, immediately remove it to indirect heat and keep turning it to prevent overcooking.

1. **Place thicker, dark-meat pieces, which include the thighs and legs, on the grill first.**

   You do this because they take longer to cook than white-meat pieces. Be sure to place these pieces on the hottest part of your grill grid.

2. **Add the other parts of the bird — the breast and wings — after about 10 minutes, or when the legs and thighs have browned on both sides.**

   Remember that white-meat breasts cook quickly and, if they aren't watched carefully, can dry out.

3. **Throughout the grilling process, continually turn the pieces from side to side, or to hotter or cooler areas of the grid as necessary, making sure that none of them are cooking too fast or turning black.**

   Don't leave your chicken unattended when grilling it directly over the heat. You have to be there, and you have to monitor it. The result of your attention will be a crispy, smoky chicken that's juicy inside and full of the flavor of the grill.

4. **Check your chicken for doneness.**

   If you use an instant-read thermometer to check for doneness, the boneless, skinless breast meat should register 160 degrees, and bone-in breast and thigh meat should reach 170 degrees. To check for doneness without a thermometer, make a small cut into the thickest part of the chicken. The juices should run clear, and the meat should show no trace of pink. Move any fully cooked pieces to the edges of the grid to keep them warm until the remaining pieces finish cooking.

REMEMBER

Covering the grill automatically raises the grill's temperature. To maintain a medium heat, adjust the heat setting on a gas grill or close the vents on a charcoal grill. Closing the cover vents lowers the heat, while opening them adds more oxygen to the fire and increases the heat.

FSIS: The poultry production inspector

American poultry production is carefully monitored by the Food, Safety, and Inspection Service (FSIS) of the Food and Drug Administration. The FSIS monitors more than 4 billion chickens each year for disease. It also has strict regulations as to shopping containers, labeling requirements, and use of trade names. The FSIS inspects the breeding, hatching, and sanitation of the production lots, as well as the chemicals used, but it doesn't oversee any genetic breeding. It also doesn't inspect game birds such as quail, pheasant, and partridge.

Handling chicken with care

Even though American poultry production is carefully monitored and the facilities comply with all government sanitary and safety guidelines, salmonella and other bacteria that can cause sickness in human beings may still be found in chicken. Fortunately, these bacteria are killed off if the chicken is cooked until the internal temperature reaches 160 degrees for boneless, skinless breasts; 170 degrees for bone-in breasts and leg quarters; and 180 degrees for whole birds.

REMEMBER

Here are a few guidelines for safe handling and preparation of chicken in your kitchen:

- Always keep poultry refrigerated until it's ready for cooking — even when in a marinade.
- Always thaw frozen poultry in the refrigerator — never at room temperature. You can usually thaw a chicken in the fridge overnight.
- If any part of the bird has an odd or "off" odor, discard the entire chicken.
- Before cooking chicken, wash it (inside and out if using a whole bird) with cold running water and then pat it dry with paper towels. Discard the paper towels.
- Thoroughly wash your hands, the utensils, and the work surface when you're done handling the raw meat.

Grilling chicken breasts

Chicken breasts offer plenty of interesting grilling options. They can be grilled with or without their skin and bones; seasoned with any number of alluring rubs, sauces, and marinades; and sliced into thin strips or thick cubes for sizzling kebabs. (See Chapter 8 for some kebab recipes.)

Free, free on the range

Free-range chickens aren't penned, so they have the freedom to roam a yard eating both the natural foods that chickens scratch for and the feed provided by the grower. This is a much more expensive process than penning tens of thousands of chickens into a factory space and feeding them in a regimented fashion. But free-range chickens make for a tastier bird. However, they aren't always the most tender bird, because they do roam around actively.

Lemon Chicken Breasts

This recipe's lovely marinade of fresh lemon, olive oil, and herbs keeps the skinless chicken breasts moist and plump on the grill. It's also good for bone-in chicken.

Preparation time: *15 minutes*

Marinating time: *2 to 6 hours*

Grilling time: *10 to 12 minutes*

Yield: *4 to 6 servings*

8 boneless, skinless chicken breast halves (about 2 to 3 pounds)

½ cup extra-virgin olive oil

½ cup fresh lemon juice

Grated peel of 1 lemon (2 to 3 teaspoons)

2 large cloves garlic, peeled and minced

2 tablespoons chopped fresh oregano, or 2 teaspoons dried oregano

1 teaspoon salt, or to taste

½ teaspoon pepper

1 Trim the breasts of any loose fat; rinse them under cold running water and pat dry with paper towels.

2 Place the breasts in a large, resealable plastic bag or a shallow, nonreactive baking dish. In a small mixing bowl or large glass measuring cup, combine the olive oil, lemon juice, lemon peel, garlic, oregano, and salt and pepper; pour the marinade over the breasts in the bag or dish. Cover the dish or seal the bag, pressing out any air; refrigerate for 2 to 6 hours, turning the breasts occasionally to coat in the marinade.

3 Prepare a medium-hot fire in a charcoal or gas grill.

4 Remove the chicken breasts from the marinade; discard the marinade. Place the breasts on a well-oiled grid for 10 to 12 minutes or until done, turning every 4 to 5 minutes. To test for doneness, cut into the breasts; the meat should be white and moist with no sign of pink.

Per serving: *Calories 306 (From Fat 108); Fat 12g (Saturated 2g); Cholesterol 125mg; Sodium 255mg; Carbohydrate 1g (Dietary Fiber 0g); Protein 46g.*

Jerk-Seasoned Chicken Breasts

The smoky heat of the grill, combined with spices common to Jamaican jerk seasoning — cinnamon, allspice, cayenne pepper, thyme, and jalapeño pepper — give these chicken breasts their splendid taste.

Preparation time: *15 minutes*

Marinating time: *6 hours or overnight*

Grilling time: *10 to 12 minutes*

Yield: *4 to 6 servings*

8 boneless, skinless chicken breast halves (about 2 to 3 pounds)

¼ cup vegetable oil

¼ cup orange juice

3 scallions, finely chopped (green and white parts)

4 medium cloves garlic, peeled and finely chopped

2 tablespoons lime juice

2 tablespoons soy sauce

1 small jalapeño pepper, seeded and finely chopped

1 teaspoon brown sugar, packed

½ teaspoon kosher salt, or to taste

½ teaspoon ground allspice

½ teaspoon dried leaf thyme

½ teaspoon cinnamon

¼ teaspoon cayenne pepper

¼ teaspoon nutmeg

1 Trim the breasts of any loose fat; rinse them under cold running water and pat dry with paper towels.

2 In a medium bowl, combine the remaining ingredients, beating with a fork or whisk to incorporate the spices into the oil and orange juice.

3 Place the breasts in a large, resealable plastic bag or shallow, nonreactive dish; pour the marinade over the breasts. Seal the bag, pressing out any air, or cover the dish; refrigerate 6 hours or overnight, turning occasionally to coat the breasts in the marinade.

4 Preheat a medium-hot fire in a charcoal or gas grill.

5 Remove the chicken breasts from the marinade; discard the marinade. Place the chicken breasts on an oiled grill grid. Grill for 10 to 12 minutes or until done, turning every 4 to 5 minutes. To test for doneness, cut into the breasts; the meat should be white and moist, with no sign of pink.

Per serving: *Calories 282 (From Fat 79); Fat 9g (Saturated 2g); Cholesterol 125mg; Sodium 297mg; Carbohydrate 2g (Dietary Fiber 0g); Protein 46g.*

When marinating any food, remember to use a nonreactive container — one made of plastic, glass, ceramic, or other nonmetallic material. Certain metals, such as aluminum, react with acidic ingredients like lemon juice or vinegar, causing the food and marinade to discolor.

Breast meat is juicier and more flavorful if it's grilled with the skin intact. However, the skin contains a lot of fat that can cause dangerous flare-ups. You may want to opt for skinless breasts, or you can pull the skin off before grilling. We start this section with two easy skinless breast recipes that grill in about 10 quick minutes (another advantage of cooking without the skin and bone — it's so fast).

You can grill chicken breasts with the skin intact to add flavor and moisture to the meat, and then reduce calories by removing the skin before serving.

Just wingin' it

Once discarded by many people as not worth eating, the chicken wing has become one of the most popular parts of the bird, thanks, in large part, to a cook in Buffalo, New York.

Back on the night of October 30, 1964, at the Anchor Bar in Buffalo, owner Teressa Bellissimo's sons and their friends came in just before midnight with a roaring appetite. Mrs. Bellissimo had received an oversupply of chicken wings that day, so she popped them in the deep fryer and mixed together a little margarine and hot sauce as well as a blue cheese dressing. The boys gobbled it up, others in the bar loved the idea, and the Buffalo Chicken Wing was born.

Szechwan peppercorns

Though they resemble black peppercorns, Szechwan peppercorns (also known as Chinese pepper) aren't part of the black and white peppercorn family at all. This mildly hot, aromatic spice is actually a berry with a tiny seed. These berries are from a tree that's native to the Szechwan province of China. To release their flavorful oils, heat the berries in a dry, heavy-bottomed skillet just until they give off an aromatic scent, about 1 to 2 minutes. Discard any that blacken. Then crush by using a mortar and pestle or place them on a cutting board and press them with the bottom of a heavy skillet.

Szechwan peppercorns, which are often used in marinades and sauces with other Chinese seasonings, are available in spice sections of Asian markets or other specialty food stores.

Spicy Chili Chicken Wings

In this recipe, the delicate meat of a chicken wing is nestled around flavorful bone and wrapped in succulent skin. Serve these finger-lickin' grilled wings as part of a light dinner or make up a big batch when you need inexpensive party appetizers for a hungry crowd.

Preparation time: *20 minutes*

Marinating time: *2 to 4 hours*

Grilling time: *10 to 15 minutes*

Yield: *4 main dish servings or 8 to 10 appetizer servings*

3 to 3½ pounds chicken wings (about 15 to 18 wings)

3 tablespoons olive oil

3 tablespoons fresh lime juice

4 large cloves garlic, peeled and minced

2 teaspoons ground cumin

2 teaspoons ground coriander

2 teaspoons paprika

1 teaspoon peeled and grated ginger

1 teaspoon salt, or to taste

½ teaspoon hot chili powder or cayenne pepper

½ teaspoon cinnamon

1. Rinse the chicken wings under cold running water and pat dry with paper towels. Cut off the wing tips at the joints and discard the tips. (Or wrap and freeze the tips for later to add flavor to canned or homemade soups and stocks.)
2. Combine all the remaining ingredients in a large, resealable plastic bag or nonreactive mixing bowl, blending them well.
3. Add the chicken wings; toss well to coat the wings in the oil-spice mixture. Seal the bag, pressing out any air, or cover the bowl; refrigerate for 2 to 4 hours.
4. Prepare a medium-hot fire in a charcoal or gas grill.
5. Place the wings on a well-oiled grid. Grill, uncovered, for 10 to 15 minutes or until done, turning with tongs every 2 to 3 minutes to prevent burning and to ensure even cooking. To test for doneness, cut into the thickest part of the wing; the meat should be white, with no trace of pink, and the juices should run clear.

Per serving: *Calories 497 (From Fat 329); Fat 37g (Saturated 9g); Cholesterol 110mg; Sodium 696mg; Carbohydrate 5g (Dietary Fiber 2g); Protein 36g.*

Orange-Garlic Chicken Wings

This dish has a subtle Asian flavor that comes from the soy sauce, the orange peel, and the garlic. It's as simple as any dish you can possibly make on the grill.

Preparation time: *20 minutes*

Marinating time: *6 hours or overnight*

Grilling time: *10 to 15 minutes*

Yield: *4 main dish servings or 8 to 10 appetizer servings*

3 pounds chicken wings (about 15 wings)

¼ cup peanut or corn oil

¼ cup sesame oil

2½ tablespoons grated orange peel

2 tablespoons soy sauce

1½ tablespoons peeled and minced garlic

2 scallions, green and white parts, finely chopped

2 teaspoons peeled and grated ginger

1 tablespoon plus 2 teaspoons Szechwan peppercorns, roasted and crushed (see the sidebar "Szechwan peppercorns")

1 to 2 tablespoons kosher salt, or to taste

1 Rinse the chicken wings under cold running water and pat dry with paper towels. Cut off the wing tips at the joint, discarding tips. (Or wrap and freeze the tips to use later to add flavor to canned or homemade soups and stocks.) Place the wings in a large, resealable plastic bag or a shallow baking dish.

2 In a medium mixing bowl or glass measuring cup, combine the peanut and sesame oils, orange peel, soy sauce, garlic, scallions, ginger, and 2 teaspoons of the peppercorns. Pour the marinade over the chicken wings in the bag or dish, turning to coat all sides. Seal the bag, pressing out any air, or cover the dish, and refrigerate for 6 hours, or overnight, tossing occasionally to coat the wings in the marinade.

3 Prepare a medium-hot fire in a charcoal or gas grill.

4 Remove the wings from the marinade; discard the marinade. Place the chicken wings on a lightly oiled grid. Grill, uncovered, for 10 to 15 minutes or until done, turning every 4 to 5 minutes to ensure even cooking and prevent the wings from charring. To test for doneness, cut into the thickest part of the wing; the meat should be white, with no trace of pink, and the juices should run clear.

5 Place the grilled wings on a large platter. Combine the remaining 1 tablespoon Szechwan peppercorns and the kosher salt; sprinkle the mixture over the wings to taste.

Per serving: *Calories 447 (From Fat 291); Fat 32g (Saturated 8g); Cholesterol 110mg; Sodium 223mg; Carbohydrate 2g (Dietary Fiber 1g); Protein 36g.*

Chowing down on chicken quarters

Choosing chicken quarters simplifies the grilling process because you have fewer pieces to watch and turn. And some grilling chefs believe that quartered pieces retain their moisture and succulence better than individual pieces of chicken. As a bonus, chicken quarters look inviting on the plate. They're especially good as a special occasion or company dish.

Figure 14-1 shows you how to cut a whole chicken into pieces. Obviously, if you're cutting it in quarters, you need only cut it into four pieces: leave the wings attached to the breasts, and leave the drumsticks attached to the thighs.

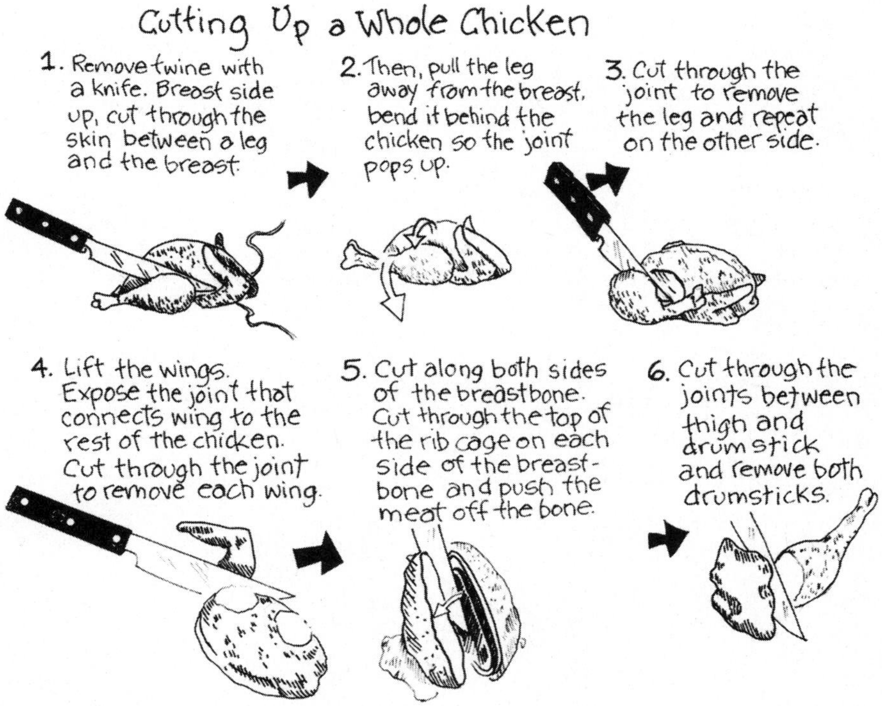
Cutting Up a Whole Chicken
1. Remove twine with a knife. Breast side up, cut through the skin between a leg and the breast.
2. Then, pull the leg away from the breast, bend it behind the chicken so the joint pops up.
3. Cut through the joint to remove the leg and repeat on the other side.
4. Lift the wings. Expose the joint that connects wing to the rest of the chicken. Cut through the joint to remove each wing.
5. Cut along both sides of the breastbone. Cut through the top of the rib cage on each side of the breast-bone and push the meat off the bone.
6. Cut through the joints between thigh and drum stick and remove both drumsticks.

Figure 14-1: How to cut up a whole chicken.

Grilled Chicken Quarters with Barbecue Sauce

This recipe calls for two easy steps — preparing the barbecue sauce and grilling the chicken quarters. We think that you'll like the way sweet, sour, and spicy flavors come together in this barbecue sauce. If you want to crank up the heat, add more Tabasco sauce.

Preparation time: *25 minutes*

Grilling time: *20 to 25 minutes*

Yield: *4 servings*

Barbecue Sauce

1 cup ketchup

½ medium onion, peeled and finely chopped

3 tablespoons fresh lemon juice

3 tablespoons Worcestershire sauce

1 tablespoon olive oil

1 tablespoon molasses

1½ teaspoons cider vinegar

1 teaspoon Dijon-style mustard

1 clove garlic, peeled and minced

¾ teaspoon salt, or to taste

¾ teaspoon Tabasco sauce

¼ teaspoon dried thyme leaves

Combine all the ingredients in a medium saucepan. Bring the mixture to a boil, and then lower the heat and simmer for 10 minutes, stirring occasionally. The sauce can be kept, covered, in the refrigerator up to a week.

Grilled Chicken Quarters

1 whole chicken (about 3 to 3½ pounds), quartered

2 tablespoons olive oil

Salt and pepper to taste

1 Prepare a medium-hot fire in a charcoal or gas grill.

2 As the fire preheats, rinse the chicken under cold running water and pat dry with paper towels. Rub the chicken quarters with the oil, covering all surfaces; sprinkle all over with salt and pepper.

3 Place the chicken parts, skin side down, on a well-oiled grid, directly over the heat, and grill for 15 minutes, turning every 4 to 5 minutes.

4 Baste the quarters thoroughly on both sides with the barbecue sauce. Continue grilling for another 7 to 10 minutes or until the chicken is done, turning every 3 to 4 minutes. Cut into the quarters to test for doneness; when cooked, the juices run clear, and the meat near the bone is no longer pink.

Per serving: *Calories 574 (From Fat 294); Fat 33g (Saturated 8g); Cholesterol 178mg; Sodium 1,589mg; Carbohydrate 25g (Dietary Fiber 1g); Protein 46g.*

Grilled Lime Chicken with Onion Compote

In this recipe, chicken quarters are first soaked in a luscious lime marinade and then they're grilled and smothered with onions that are slightly caramelized from long, slow, top-of-the-stove cooking. The result is divine.

Preparation time: *45 minutes*

Marinating time: *6 hours or overnight*

Grilling time: *20 to 25 minutes*

Yield: *4 servings*

1 3- to 3½-pound chicken, quartered
¼ cup olive oil
¾ cup lime juice
Grated peel of 1½ limes
2 cloves garlic, peeled and minced
½ teaspoon coarsely cracked black pepper
Salt to taste
¼ cup corn oil
3 Spanish onions, or 4 medium yellow onions, peeled, halved, and sliced about ¼-inch thick
½ teaspoon dried thyme leaves
2 bay leaves, crushed
Pepper to taste

1. Rinse the chicken under cold running water and pat dry with paper towels; place the chicken in a large, resealable plastic bag or a shallow, nonreactive baking dish.
2. In a small mixing bowl or large glass measuring cup, combine the olive oil, lime juice, lime peel, garlic, cracked black pepper, and salt. Pour the marinade over the chicken in the bag or dish. Seal the bag, pressing out any air, or cover the dish; refrigerate for 6 hours, or overnight, turning occasionally to coat the chicken in the marinade.
3. Prepare a medium-hot fire in a covered charcoal or gas grill.
4. As the grill preheats, make the onion compote. In a medium skillet, heat the corn oil over medium heat; add the onions and sauté for 15 minutes, turning frequently. Stir in the thyme, bay leaves, and salt and pepper; continue cooking for 10 minutes or longer, until the onions are well browned, turning frequently. When done, remove from heat and set aside.
5. Remove the chicken from the marinade, shaking off some of the excess; reserve the remaining marinade. Season the chicken lightly with salt and pepper and place on a well-oiled grid, skin side down. Cover and cook for 20 to 25 minutes or until the juices run clear and the meat near the bone is no longer pink, turning every 4 minutes.
6. Add the reserved marinade to the onions in the skillet and simmer over medium heat for 15 minutes. When the chicken is done, remove it from the grill onto a serving platter; spoon the onion compote over the chicken and serve immediately.

Per serving: *Calories 1,094 (From Fat 653); Fat 73g (Saturated 16g); Cholesterol 364mg; Sodium 418mg; Carbohydrate 15g (Dietary Fiber 3g); Protein 93g.*

Lemon-Cilantro Chicken with Garlic-Ginger Mayonnaise

The fragrant marinade in this recipe is made with cilantro, fresh ginger, garlic, soy sauce, curry powder, and hot chili powder — all are ingredients common to Pacific Rim cuisine. The mayonnaise garnish, laced with ginger, garlic, and lemon juice, gives it an American twist.

Preparation time: *30 minutes*

Marinating time: *6 hours or overnight*

Grilling time: *20 to 25 minutes*

Yield: *4 servings*

1 3- to 3½-pound chicken, quartered and scored (score by slashing through the skin and into the meat on both sides of each piece, using a sharp knife)

2 tablespoons soy sauce

1 tablespoon corn or vegetable oil

1 tablespoon peeled and grated fresh ginger

Grated peel of 1 lemon

2 scallions, trimmed and finely chopped

6 sprigs cilantro (coriander) leaves and stems, chopped

2 cloves garlic, peeled and minced

¾ teaspoon curry powder

½ teaspoon hot chili powder

Salt and pepper to taste

1 Rinse the chicken under cold running water and pat dry with paper towels; place the chicken in a large, resealable plastic bag or a shallow nonreactive baking dish.

2 In a small mixing bowl or glass measuring cup, combine the remaining ingredients; pour the marinade over the chicken in the bag or dish. Seal the bag, pressing out any air, or cover the dish; refrigerate for 6 hours, or overnight, turning the chicken occasionally to coat in the marinade.

3 Prepare a medium-hot fire in a charcoal or gas grill.

4 Remove the chicken from the marinade, shaking off a bit of the excess. Season the chicken with salt and pepper; place, skin side down, on an oiled grid. Cover and grill for 20 to 25 minutes, turning every 4 minutes, until the juices run clear and the meat is no longer pink near the bone. Serve with Garlic-Ginger Mayonnaise (see the following recipe) and grilled asparagus (Chapter 16).

Garlic-Ginger Mayonnaise

Preparation time: *5 minutes*

Yield: *About ⅔ cup*

⅔ cup mayonnaise

1½ teaspoons peeled and grated fresh ginger

2 cloves garlic, peeled and minced

1 tablespoon fresh lemon juice

Salt and pepper to taste

In a small, nonreactive mixing bowl, combine all the ingredients. Cover and refrigerate until ready to use with Lemon-Cilantro Chicken. You can make this mayonnaise ahead and store it, covered, in the refrigerator for up to 1 week.

Vary It! *Garlic-Ginger Mayonnaise is also delicious with grilled fish (Chapter 15).*

Per serving: *Calories 787 (From Fat 589); Fat 66g (Saturated 12g); Cholesterol 200mg; Sodium 749mg; Carbohydrate 3g (Dietary Fiber 0g); Protein 46g.*

It's thigh time to grill some legs

The legs and thighs of chicken are dark meat with rich flavor. They're delicious when grilled and lend themselves to being eaten with your fingers — always one of our prime considerations when grilling for a party!

Moroccan Chicken Legs and Thighs

Moroccan spices are quite assertive, and the flavors here are heightened by the smokiness of the grill. The marinade in this recipe contains a good amount of honey, so to avoid scorching the skin we use both direct and indirect grilling methods.

Preparation time: *20 minutes*

Marinating time: *6 hours or overnight*

Grilling time: *35 to 40 minutes*

Yield: *4 servings*

4 chicken legs and thighs (about 2½ to 3 pounds total)

¼ cup olive oil

¼ cup honey

¼ cup mixed, chopped fresh mint and parsley

¼ cup plus 2 tablespoons fresh lemon juice

2 teaspoons grated lemon peel

2 large cloves garlic, peeled and minced

2 teaspoons peeled and grated fresh ginger

1 teaspoon ground cumin

¼ teaspoon crushed red pepper flakes

⅛ teaspoon cayenne pepper

Salt and black pepper to taste

1 Rinse the chicken pieces under cold running water and pat dry with paper towels. Unless you purchased the chicken as separate pieces, divide the legs from the thighs by cutting through the thigh-leg joint with a sharp knife. Place the pieces in a large, resealable plastic bag or a large, shallow, nonreactive baking dish.

2 In a small mixing bowl or glass measuring cup, combine the olive oil, honey, mint and parsley, lemon juice, lemon peel, garlic, ginger, cumin, red pepper flakes, cayenne pepper, and salt and black pepper. Pour the marinade over the chicken, turning to coat all sides. Seal the bag, pressing out any air, or cover the dish; refrigerate for 6 hours, or overnight, turning occasionally.

3 Prepare an indirect, medium-hot fire in a covered charcoal or gas grill. (Turn to Chapter 1 for instructions about building an indirect fire.) Place a drip pan under the side of the grill without heat.

4 Remove the chicken from the marinade, reserving the remaining marinade. Place the chicken pieces, skin side down, on a lightly oiled grid, directly over the heat. Grill until well browned on both sides, turning every 2 to 3 minutes. (At this point, you need to hover over the grilling pieces to prevent the skin from burning.) Move the pieces to the side of the grill without heat; baste with the reserved marinade. Cover the grill and cook for 15 minutes. Turn and baste again with any remaining marinade; cover and cook for 15 to 20 minutes more or until done. To test for doneness, cut into the chicken; the juices should run clear, and the meat near the bone should show no sign of pink. Place the chicken on a serving platter and serve with Tomato and Red Onion Salad. (See Chapter 16.)

Per serving: *Calories 615 (From Fat 348); Fat 39g (Saturated 9g); Cholesterol 163mg; Sodium 301mg; Carbohydrate 21g (Dietary Fiber 1g); Protein 46g.*

Dishing up a whole chicken

A whole chicken cooked on the grill is actually a pretty simple dish to make — and it's great to present at the table! Because it's whole, the chicken keeps its juices in well — as long as it's basted frequently and turned so that it doesn't burn or overcook. You should consider moving it to indirect heat if the grill starts to flame up on the skin. Check out Figure 14-1 to see how to cut up a whole chicken.

Chicken alla Mattone

"Alla mattone" is Italian for "under a brick," and you actually do use a brick (covered with aluminum foil) or another heavy weight for this dish. By pressing the chicken down onto the grill, the bird cooks more evenly, gets a nice singe on the skin, and comes out very juicy. It's also about the simplest way to grill a whole chicken! You can see the finished dish in the color photo section of this book.

Preparation time: *15 minutes*

Marinating time: *2 to 6 hours*

Grilling time: *16 to 24 minutes*

Yield: *4 servings*

1 whole chicken, cut in half and backbone removed (refer to Figure 14-1)

Lemon peel from 1 lemon, cut into 1-inch pieces

2 cloves garlic, peeled and thickly sliced

3 to 4 sprigs rosemary, cut into 1-inch pieces

Juice of 2 lemons

2 cloves garlic, peeled and crushed

6 tablespoons olive oil

1 teaspoons salt

½ teaspoon freshly ground black peppercorns

Juice of 1 lemon and 2 tablespoons olive oil to drizzle over grilled chicken (optional)

1 Make slits in various parts of the chicken and insert the lemon peels, the sliced garlic cloves, and half of the rosemary sprigs between the skin and the meat.

2 Place each half of the chicken in its own resealable plastic bag (or in separate nonreactive dishes). In each container, place 1 of the crushed garlic cloves, half of the remaining rosemary, juice of 1 lemon, 3 tablespoons olive oil, ½ teaspoon salt, and ¼ teaspoon freshly ground peppercorns. Mix well and seal the bag, pressing out any air (or cover, if you're using a dish). Place the containers of chicken in the refrigerator, set a foil-wrapped brick or other heavy object on top of each chicken half (to help flatten the chicken before you grill it), and marinate 2 to 6 hours.

3 Prepare a medium-hot grill in a charcoal or gas grill and either wrap two bricks in foil or get a cast-iron skillet handy. Also have some grilling mitts and tongs handy — the grilling gets a bit tricky.

4 Remove the chicken halves from the marinade, reserving any that's remaining and pouring it into a bowl to use as a basting sauce. Place the chicken, skin side down, on a well-oiled grid directly over the hot coals. Lay the bricks or cast-iron skillet over the chicken halves to press them down on the grill.

5 Cook for 3 to 5 minutes or until the skin starts to brown. Check the chicken to be sure it isn't browning too rapidly. Move the pieces to a cooler part of the grill for another 5 to 7 minutes.

6 Remove the bricks from the chicken, baste with some of the marinade, turn the chicken over, and place on the hotter part of the grill. Lay the bricks over the chicken again and cook for 3 to 5 minutes, or until the chicken starts to brown. Move the chicken to a cooler part of the grill and continue to grill for another 5 to 7 minutes until done. To test for doneness, cut into the breast and thigh; the meat should be tender and moist, and the juices should run clear. Remove the meat to a clean platter.

7 Cut the chicken into servings and drizzle with additional lemon juice and olive oil (if desired).

Per serving: *Calories 400 (From Fat 200); Fat 22g (Saturated 6g); Cholesterol 178mg; Sodium 714mg; Carbohydrate 3g (Dietary Fiber 0g); Protein 45g.*

Brined and Grilled Chicken

Brining is an age-old process of preserving food by soaking it in a solution of salt and water (and sometimes, sugar). Brining can also be used to increase the amount of liquid inside food cells in order to make the food juicy, tender, and full of flavor. Think of brining as a long, deep marinade without an acidic ingredient (such as lemon or vinegar). You can enhance the flavor of a salty brine with citrus peel, fresh ginger, cloves, garlic, hot peppers, peppercorns, and most herbs.

After one attempt, you'll see how easy and irresistible it is to brine chicken for the grill. Serve a pretty fruit or vegetable chutney, with contrasting sugar and vinegar flavors, alongside the finished dish. (Try the delicious, quick-cooking chutney recipes in Chapter 6. Or buy a bottle of chutney if you don't have the time to make your own.)

Preparation time: *15 minutes*

Marinating time: *1½ to 2 hours*

Grilling time: *20 to 25 minutes*

Yield: *4 servings*

1 quart water

½ cup kosher salt

½ cup sugar

1 bay leaf, or 1 teaspoon dried sage, thyme, or other herb

½ teaspoon black peppercorns

1 whole chicken (3 to 4 pounds), cut into pieces (refer to Figure 14-1)

Pepper (optional)

1. In a large nonreactive container or a large, resealable plastic bag, combine the water, kosher salt, sugar, bay leaf or other herb, and black peppercorns. Stir the solution for 2 to 3 minutes, until the sugar and salt are nearly dissolved. Add the chicken pieces and submerge into the brine by using a heavy weight (such as a plate), or close the plastic bag, pressing out as much air as possible. Refrigerate for 1½ to 2 hours, stirring the mixture occasionally.
2. Remove the chicken from the brine, rinse well, and dry thoroughly with paper towels. You can leave the bird nearly unseasoned (adding only black pepper, if desired), or you can use the seasonings that we recommend in the following Dry Poultry Rub for Brined Chicken recipe. Be sure not to add extra salt until after grilling; the brine already has plenty of salt.
3. Prepare a medium fire in a covered charcoal or gas grill.
4. Place the chicken pieces, skin side down, on a well-oiled grid. Cover the grill and adjust the temperature or hood vents to maintain medium heat (about 350 degrees). Grill the chicken, covered, for a total of 20 to 25 minutes, turning every 3 to 5 minutes, or as necessary, to keep the pieces from browning too quickly. To test for doneness, cut into the chicken; the juices should run clear, and the meat near the bone should show no sign of pink.

Per serving: *Calories 410 (From Fat 199); Fat 22g (Saturated 6g); Cholesterol 178mg; Sodium 2,893mg; Carbohydrate 5g (Dietary Fiber 0g); Protein 45g.*

Dry Poultry Rub for Brined Chicken

After brining pieces of chicken to make them moist and tender (see the previous recipe), you can rub them with this tasty seasoning blend before grilling. Or turn to Chapters 5 and 6 for additional seasonings and sauces. However, we suggest that you avoid any seasoning or sauce that includes additional salt — the brining process provides plenty.

Preparation time: *5 minutes*

Yield: *Enough for 4 pounds of chicken*

2 teaspoons olive oil

2 cloves garlic, peeled and minced

2 teaspoons ground sage

1 teaspoon paprika

1 teaspoon grated lemon peel

½ teaspoon pepper, or to taste

1. Rub the chicken with the olive oil, covering all surfaces.
2. In a small mixing bowl, combine all the remaining ingredients. Rub chicken pieces generously, applying the spice mixture under the skin and into the cavity as well as on all surfaces.
3. Grill pieces as directed in the Brined and Grilled Chicken recipe.

REMEMBER

Dark meat takes longer to cook than white meat and therefore should be placed on the grill about 5 minutes before the breasts. Or you can start the pieces all at once and move the breasts after they're fully cooked to the cooler edges to keep them warm until the legs and thighs finish cooking.

Being Thankful for the Many Uses of Turkey

Turkey is low in fat, but unlike chicken, it needs a little more love and care to arrive on the plate tender, moist, and perfectly grilled. Turkeys are available in smaller portions (especially as breast meat and as ground turkey, which is featured in Chapter 7), which are extremely versatile at any time of the year, so don't reserve turkey for holidays.

Grilled Turkey Tenderloins with Honey-Mustard Glaze

Tenderloins, from the breast of the turkey, are boneless, skinless, and easily grilled. Many of the marinades and basting sauces that are designed for chicken can be used to flavor turkey tenderloins, but here we chose a Honey-Mustard Glaze. (However, if you need to, feel free to substitute bottled honey-mustard.) Watch the cooking time carefully — turkey tenderloins have little fat and dry out quickly. Try to remove them from the grill just at the point of doneness, when they're still moist and tender.

Preparation time: *25 minutes*

Marinating time: *4 hours or overnight*

Grilling time: *10 to 13 minutes*

Yield: *4 servings*

Honey-Mustard Glaze

½ cup honey

¼ cup plus 1 tablespoon Dijon-style mustard

Pepper to taste

In a small bowl, whisk the honey and mustard until smooth; season the glaze with pepper. Cover and refrigerate until ready to use.

Grilled Turkey Tenderloins

4 boneless turkey tenderloins (about 1¾ to 2 pounds total)

6 tablespoons olive oil

Juice of 1 lemon

2 teaspoons Dijon-style mustard

1 tablespoon chopped fresh rosemary, or 1 teaspoon dried rosemary

Salt and pepper to taste

1 large handful of presoaked hickory or mesquite-flavored wood chips (optional)

1 Rinse the tenderloins under cold running water; pat dry with paper towels.

2 In a small bowl, whisk until smooth the oil, lemon juice, and mustard. Stir in the rosemary and adjust the seasoning with salt and pepper.

3 Place the turkey tenderloins in a shallow, nonreactive baking dish or a large resealable plastic bag. Add the lemon-mustard marinade and turn the tenderloins to coat. Cover the dish or seal the bag, pressing out any air; refrigerate for 4 hours or overnight.

4 Prepare a medium fire in a covered charcoal or gas grill. If desired, throw a large handful of presoaked wood chips onto the coals just before placing the tenderloins on the grill. If using a gas grill, wrap the chips in aluminum foil or place them in a metal smoker box.

5 Remove the tenderloins from the marinade and place them on an oiled grid. Discard the marinade. Grill, covered, for 8 to 10 minutes, or until they're lightly browned on both sides, turning once.

6 Divide the Honey-Mustard Glaze (see the previous recipe) in half. Baste the tenderloins on both sides, using half the glaze; reserve the other half as a finishing sauce. Grill the tenderloins, covered, for another 2 to 3 minutes or until done, turning once. Make a small incision in the center of each tenderloin to determine doneness. The meat is cooked when there's no trace of pink in the center or thickest part.

7 Transfer the tenderloins to a platter and let them stand, covered with aluminum foil, for 5 minutes before slicing across the grain. In a small saucepan, bring the remaining glaze to a boil; drizzle over the tenderloin slices.

Vary It! *This recipe can be varied many ways by simply changing the basting sauce. Instead of the Honey-Mustard Glaze, try using Pesto Sauce (Chapter 15), a bottled barbecue sauce, or a chipotle sauce. Or omit the basting sauce completely and serve with a tomato or black bean salsa (recipes in Chapter 6).*

Per serving: *Calories 407 (From Fat 69); Fat 8g (Saturated 1g); Cholesterol 130mg; Sodium 623mg; Carbohydrate 37g (Dietary Fiber 0g); Protein 48g.*

If wood chips flare up when you toss them onto a fire, spritz them lightly with a spray bottle filled with water. This dampens the flames and increases the smoke.

Dale Curry's Hickory-Smoked Whole Turkey

To find out how to infuse a whole turkey with real smoked hickory flavors, we turned to Dale Curry, food editor of *The Times-Picayune* in New Orleans. Dale was born and raised in Memphis, where eating barbecue is an everyday experience. She says that everybody loves the following smoked turkey recipe.

This recipe shows you a healthy way to cook a turkey. Slow-cooking and smoking over a small fire of only about 30 briquettes allows the turkey meat to stay very moist and succulent without the addition of extra fat or butter-rich basting sauces. It's best to buy a turkey with a pop-up thermometer. Cooking the bird too long results in tough, dry meat. Be sure to check for doneness frequently, about every 15 minutes, toward the end of the cooking time.

Preparation time: *15 minutes*

Grilling time: *4 to 4½ hours*

Yield: *12 servings*

12-pound fresh or frozen and thawed turkey (preferably with a pop-up thermometer)

Creole seasoning (store-bought variety)

About 6 heaping handfuls presoaked hickory wood chips

1 Remove the giblet packages from the turkey cavities; rinse the turkey and pat dry. Sprinkle the bird all over with the Creole seasoning, inside and out. Let the turkey rest at room temperature as you prepare the charcoal fire.

2 Prepare a small charcoal fire, using about 30 briquettes, in a kettle grill with a lid. When the coals are hot, move them to one side of the grill. (See Chapter 1 for complete instructions on building an indirect fire.) Place a drip pan, filled about one-third with water, next to the coals. Sprinkle a large handful of presoaked hickory wood chips over the coals.

3 Place the turkey on a well-oiled grid, directly over the drip pan opposite the coals. Cover the grill. Open the vents directly under the fire and above the turkey to facilitate an even flow of smoke. Open the grill every 40 to 45 minutes, turn the turkey around or from side to side, and add 6 coals and another large handful of presoaked wood chips to the fire. Keep the grill lid closed between these times. Continue to cook the turkey in this fashion until the pop-up thermometer has sprung or until an instant-read thermometer inserted into the thigh registers 180 degrees. A 12-pound turkey will take about 4 to 4½ hours to cook, depending on the heat of the fire, the air temperature, the actual size of the bird, and its distance from the fire. When done, the skin will look quite brown, but the inside meat will be moist and juicy. Remove the turkey from the grill and let it rest at least for 15 minutes before carving.

Per serving: *Calories 529 (From Fat 219); Fat 24g (Saturated 7g); Cholesterol 245mg; Sodium 192mg; Carbohydrate 0g (Dietary Fiber 0g); Protein 72g.*

Creole seasoning is made by many commercial manufacturers, such as Zatarain's, McCormick, Tony Chachere, and Paul Prudhomme, and is commonly found in supermarket spice sections. It's a blend of salt, red and black pepper, garlic, and other spicy seasonings.

Game Birds Make for Healthy Eating

Aside from their wonderful, individual tastes, game birds are extremely healthy foods. They're lower in fat and cholesterol than chicken. A 3.5-ounce portion of domestic quail with skin has about 133 calories and 2.8 grams of fat, compared with 193 calories and 7.6 grams of fat for the same amount of chicken. Because they use their muscles constantly, game birds burn off their fat. The feed of both wild and domestic birds tends to have more minerals and vitamins than poultry feed.

You may think that anything you do with a chicken you can do with a game bird, but that's nowhere near the truth. Because of their unique textures, their differences in flavor, and their relative lack of fat, game birds must be treated differently than a chicken on the grill — the prep and grilling differ a good deal. Due to their lack of fat, wild birds in particular require basting. Farm-raised game birds have slightly more fat (though not as much as chicken), so you usually don't have to baste them. Because game birds cook more quickly, they're wonderful options for a party or for times when you don't want to spend even 30 minutes tending to the grill.

Comparing wild versus farm-raised game birds

There are no two ways about it: Wild game has a flavor you just won't find in farm-raised game. That's not to say that wild game is *gamy,* a term that's acquired the connotation of meaning strong-tasting or bitter. Freshly killed wild game isn't gamy at all — unless, of course, the bird isn't dressed properly or is handled too long.

Not too long ago, wild game birds were a rarity at the market, but today they can easily be ordered from any good butcher with a few days' notice. You can also find many sources for game by mail order and on the Internet.

Freshly killed game properly dressed and hung has absolutely wonderful flavor, much of which comes from the food the birds eat. The variety in each type of bird's food makes different species from different parts of the wild taste remarkably different.

Having said all that, we can't wholly recommend going out and shooting your own wild birds for food unless you are, in fact, an experienced hunter or willing to become one. Aside from needing the knowledge of how to dress and prepare a bird, you need to know whether that bird is healthy, and only a trained inspector or experienced hunter can tell you that. This is why all game birds sold in U.S. markets are produced on farms. The exception is game from Europe (mainly Scotland) that has been inspected immediately after being killed. This game is cleared for export to and sale in the U.S.

Fortunately, farm-raised game birds are now abundant, and although they don't possess the singular flavor of their wild cousins, birds like squab, quail, and pheasant offer superb grilling and dining possibilities. Therefore, although you can order wild birds from reputable dealers at markets or online, we endorse the idea that farm-raised game birds are the safe way to go when it comes to grilling.

Surveying game bird varieties

You can find several varieties of game birds in Figure 14-2; descriptions of each are in the following list:

- **Rock Cornish game hen:** Many people who are squeamish about game birds but bored with chicken take advantage of the fine-flavored Rock Cornish game hen, which, despite its name, doesn't come from a rock or from Cornwall, England. It's actually the result of an American breeding between a Plymouth Rock hen and a Cornish game cock. It weighs only 1 to 2 pounds — quite nice for one or two people. This isn't a wild bird at all, and its popularity in the U.S. means that you almost always find it at the market. Rock Cornish game hens taste great when grilled. (Check out the recipe in this chapter for Rock Cornish Game Hens with Molasses-Rum Marinade.)
- **Grouse:** A very full-flavored red-meat bird with a pronounced taste, grouse is never farm-raised and is difficult to find. The best grouse come in from Scotland in the fall and usually are sold to restaurants. Because this bird feeds on evergreens, it can have a lovely spruce-like undertone. You need one grouse (about 1¼ pounds) per person for a dinner, and be prepared to pick out some of the buckshot from the meat! Grouse is best when roasted on a spit or grilled in halves to medium doneness. If cooked to a gray color, grouse loses its unique flavor.
- **Partridge:** This strong-flavored bird doesn't taste quite as much like liver as grouse does. Partridge is a good plump bird that's best when spit-roasted or grilled in halves. Serve one partridge per person. Partridge is wonderful with braised cabbage or wild rice.

- **Pheasant:** Farm-raised pheasant are becoming more available, and although they don't quite have the flavor of wild pheasant, they make for a delectable alternative to chicken. One bird will satisfy two healthy appetites. Pheasant takes well to light marinades.
- **Poussin:** Poussins — pronounced poo-SAHNS — aren't really game birds. They're small spring chickens that weigh about 1 pound. They have a sweet flavor and tender flesh. With about 25 percent less fat than commercially raised chickens, poussins should be marinated before grilling to ensure a moist bird.

  Poussins are relatively expensive and may not be available in all supermarkets. Check with your grocer — or search the Internet — for sources.
- **Quail:** These tiny birds cook very quickly and have a delicate flavor, so they're best when simply grilled and served with marinades such as soy sauce and ginger. You can stuff them, but their size makes it difficult. A reasonable serving would be two to three quail per person, but one quail with greens can make a terrific appetizer.
- **Squab:** Squab is a nice name for a young pigeon, but we're not talking about those sooty urban rooftop dwellers. We're talking about a nice plump woodlands or farm-raised pigeon, which, like grouse, has a red meatiness and is delicious with lusty red-wine marinades. Wild pigeons are exceedingly difficult to find, but the poultry industry has created a tender, delicious, featherless breed that also goes by the name rock dove. One bird per person is a good portion. Squabs are best when roasted on a spit and braised.

As purveyors of fresh game and other gourmet products, a fast-growing family company, D'Artagnan, is seeing to it that Americans have a steady supply of fresh game birds (both wild and farm-raised) at their local supermarkets and specialty grocery stores. D'Artagnan raises and distributes fresh quail, pheasant, squab, duck, and poussin. If you live in an area without a supermarket that carries fresh game, you can mail-order it direct from D'Artagnan. You can contact the company by calling 1-800-327-8246 or by visiting `www.dartagnan.com`.

Rock Cornish Game Hens with Molasses-Rum Marinade

Cook these lovely hens directly over the heat of the grill, basting frequently with the delicious Molasses-Rum marinade. A few wood chunks — mesquite, maple, pecan, or hickory wood — mixed into the charcoal briquettes can add a subtle layer of pleasant, smoky flavor.

Preparation time: *25 minutes*

Marinating time: *8 hours or overnight*

Grilling time: *25 minutes*

Yield: *2 to 4 servings*

2 Rock Cornish game hens, each about 1¼ to 1½ pounds, split in half (see the sidebar "Splitting hens")

1 tablespoon butter

1½ teaspoons curry powder

¼ cup dark rum

2 tablespoons molasses

⅓ cup fresh orange juice

Juice of 1 large lime (about 2 tablespoons)

½ teaspoon grated lime peel

1 teaspoon kosher salt, or to taste

1 large clove garlic, peeled and crushed

1 teaspoon seeded and chopped jalapeño pepper

1 Rinse the hen halves thoroughly under cold running water; pat dry with paper towels. Place the hen halves in a large, resealable plastic bag or a nonreactive shallow container big enough to hold them snugly in one layer.

2 Melt the butter in a small saucepan, being careful not to let it brown. Stir in the curry powder and cook the mixture for 1 minute, stirring; remove the saucepan from the heat. Carefully add the rum and molasses.

3 Stir in the orange and lime juices, grated lime peel, salt, garlic, and jalapeño pepper; pour the marinade over the hens. Seal the bag, pressing out the air, or cover the container. Refrigerate for 8 hours, or overnight, turning the hens occasionally.

4 Prepare a direct, medium fire in a charcoal or gas grill.

5 Remove the hens from the marinade. Reserve the marinade.

6 Place the hens, skin side down on a well-oiled grill grid, directly over the heat. Cover the grill and cook for a total of 25 minutes, turning and basting with the marinade every 8 minutes during the first 16 minutes. The hens are cooked when an instant-read thermometer registers 180 degrees or the juices run clear.

Per serving: *Calories 818 (From Fat 480); Fat 53g (Saturated 17g); Cholesterol 355mg; Sodium 1,327mg; Carbohydrate 22g (Dietary Fiber 1g); Protein 59g.*

Figure 14-2: Game birds come in many varieties, a handful of which are depicted here.

Splitting hens

Place the hen breast side up and using a pair of poultry shears, cut along the breastbone from the cavity to the neck end. Gently pry open the two sides. Turn the hen over and cut along one side of the backbone, cutting the hen in half. Cut along the other side of the backbone to remove and discard it.

Whole Game Hens with Asian Flavors

In this recipe, the hens are first grilled indirectly for about 1 hour and then shifted directly over the fire for a few minutes to nicely brown and crisp the skin. They are sauced twice — once with a sake-soy marinade and then again with a sweet-and-spicy basting sauce of honey, cloves, lemon juice, and Tabasco.

Preparation time: *25 minutes*

Marinating time: *4 to 6 hours*

Grilling time: *1 hour and 10 minutes*

Yield: *2 to 4 servings*

2 Cornish game hens, each about 1¼ to 1½ pounds

½ cup sake or dry sherry

½ cup plus 2 teaspoons soy sauce, divided

¼ cup honey, divided

½ teaspoon ground ginger

Pepper to taste

2 tablespoons fresh lemon juice

¼ teaspoon ground cloves

Generous dash Tabasco sauce, or to taste

1 Remove the giblets from the cavity of the hens; wrap and freeze the giblets for adding to soups or stocks, if desired. Rinse the hens thoroughly in cold running water; pat dry with paper towels and place in a nonreactive shallow container that's large enough to hold them snugly side by side.

2 In a small bowl or glass measuring cup, combine the following marinade ingredients: sake or dry sherry, ½ cup of the soy sauce, 2 tablespoons of the honey, ginger, and pepper. Pour the marinade over the hens and refrigerate, covered, for 4 to 6 hours.

3 Prepare a hot, indirect fire in a covered charcoal or gas grill, with a drip pan containing about 1 cup of water. (Flip to Chapter 1 for instructions on building an indirect fire.)

4 Remove the hens from the marinade, discarding the marinade.

5 As the grill heats, in a small bowl combine the remaining 2 tablespoons honey and 2 teaspoons soy sauce, the lemon juice, cloves, and the Tabasco sauce to make a basting glaze.

6 Place the hens on the grill grid, over the drip pan, opposite the fire, breast side up; baste the hens with the glaze. Cover the grill and cook for 1 hour, turning the hens over and basting with glaze about every 20 minutes (but not during the last 20 minutes). Be sure to add fresh briquettes about every 30 minutes to maintain the heat in a charcoal grill.

7 Move the hens to the side of the grill directly over the fire; grill, breast side down, covered, for 3 to 5 minutes. Turn the hens breast side up and grill, covered, for 3 to 5 minutes more or until the juices run clear or an instant-read thermometer inserted between the breast and thigh reads 180 degrees. (Watch the hens closely to avoid charring the skin over direct heat. Move them back to indirect heat, if necessary, to finish cooking.)

8 Let the hens rest about 5 minutes before serving. If desired, boil the drip pan juices for 1 to 2 minutes before spooning over the grilled hens.

Per serving: *Calories 758 (From Fat 425); Fat 47g (Saturated 13g); Cholesterol 340mg; Sodium 705mg; Carbohydrate 19g (Dietary Fiber 0g); Protein 59g.*

Chapter 15

She Grills Seafood by the Seashore

In This Chapter

- Choosing the freshest and healthiest seafood
- Grilling steaks, whole fish, and fillets
- Smoking fish
- Grilling mollusks, crabs, and shrimp

Recipes in This Chapter

- Grilled Swordfish Steak with Chipotle Salsa
- Grilled Fish Steaks with Avocado and Citrus Salsa
- Whole Grilled Trout with Thyme and Almond Butter Sauce
- Flatfish Fillets Grilled on Lemon Slices with Mediterranean Skillet Sauce
- Seasoned and Breaded Catfish Fillets with Basil Mayonnaise
- Asian-Style Salmon Fillets with Vegetables
- Smoked Salmon Fillet
- Scallop Kebabs with Pineapple and Bacon
- Grilled Clams and Mussels with Lemon Butter or Fresh Tomato Sauce
- Grilled Soft-Shell Crabs
- Pesto Shrimp in the Shell
- Jimmy Schmidt's Grilled Barbecued Shrimp

Grilling fish is a job that causes many folks to feel like, well, fish out of water. This fear of fish isn't surprising. The flesh of fish is very delicate, so you can overcook it on the grill before you realize what's happening. But don't worry! Here we give you all kinds of tips on how to know when fish is properly cooked and how to avoid drying it out.

Grilling imparts a terrific flavor to the flesh of fish. Beyond that, the health benefits of eating fish are clear: It has a low fat content and omega-3 fatty acids that can lower your cholesterol. Grilling shellfish, on the other hand, may sound like an odd idea, but it really can be deliciously tasty when cooked over an open fire.

In this chapter, we give you a primer on seafood's place in today's ecologically conscious society and introduce you to some delectable — and some less common — ways to prepare it.

REMEMBER: The words fish and seafood aren't interchangeable. Seafood encompasses all edible creatures that live in the sea, including shellfish and swimming fish. So even though all fish is seafood, not all seafood is fish. And there's another little semantics twist: Even if the fish, mussels, or shellfish come from freshwater lakes, rivers, or streams, the term *seafood* still applies.

More Fish at Market, if Fewer Fish in the Sea

Never before have so many species of fish been available at the market. Increasingly, you can now find once-rare species available at your market, including tilapia, orange roughy, branzino, orata, mahi-mahi, ling cod, Arctic char, Dungeness crab, and many species of oysters like Kumomotos and Olympias. Largely this is due to Americans' increased appetite for fish, especially as a healthy alternative to red meat. But we also attribute it to a huge increase in fish farming around the world.

The growth in fish farming is the result of a sharp decrease in the amount of wild fish available, which can be blamed on overfishing, pollution of waters, and even global warming. Many wild fish, like Chilean sea bass, Gulf redfish, and certain species of salmon have gone on and off the endangered species list over the past decade. For those fishes that are caught in the wild, there's a growing interest in what's called *sustainable seafood,* or seafood that isn't currently endangered by overfishing.

Many of the species that aren't overfished are actually among the healthiest species, owing to their being high in beneficial omega-3 fatty acids. These fish include catfish, Pacific halibut, Atlantic mackerel, sardines, shrimp, striped bass, and sturgeon.

WARNING! Be careful when buying fish that's said to be "wild"; if it is indeed wild, it may be a dwindling species, including grouper, monkfish, conch, and bluefin tuna. It may even have levels of mercury poisoning that may be dangerous for human consumption. Your best bet is always to use a reputable fishmonger rather than a supermarket seafood counter.

If you're concerned about seafood and its impact on the environment, visit the Web sites for these organizations: Seafood Choices Alliance (`www.seafoodchoices.com`) and The Monterey Bay Aquarium Seafood Web Watch (`www.mbayaq.org/cr/seafoodwatch.asp`).

Cooking Fresh Fish by the Cut

Fish taken fresh from the sea or rivers has a taste unlike anything else. And anyone disliking fish because it is, well, fishy, just hasn't tasted a truly fresh fish. A fish just out of water, properly dressed and scaled and then grilled, is one of the purest of all culinary pleasures. Anglers take justifiable pride in bringing home fish of this quality.

SHOPPING TIP

The French have a saying about fish: If a fish smells like fish, it's not fresh fish. When shopping for fresh fish, here are some guidelines:

- **Let your nose — not your eye — guide you.** The one foolproof way to tell if a fish is fresh is to put your nose right up to it, especially near the gills. If you get a strong whiff of fishiness, move on.
- **Don't buy fish that's stacked up on top of ice.** When frozen fish is poorly handled, it invariably loses its fresh smell and flavor, emerging from the freezer with a mushy or mealy texture and more than a whiff of fishiness. A good fish seller buries the fish in ice. Another option is to purchase fish that have been flash-frozen — at –60 degrees right onboard gigantic trawlers — which can maintain the freshness of fish much better than catching a fish and letting it sit around on ice for a few days.
- **If you buy or store frozen fish, the best place to thaw it is in the refrigerator.** Let it defrost slowly — 24 hours is best — and when the fish has come to refrigerator temperature, look for a nice plump, shiny appearance. Never, ever refreeze fish.
- **Visit your seafood market frequently and get to know the owner.** Let it be known that you expect good quality and good service. Show that you're serious about getting the best quality, and the owner will deliver the goods.

For some examples of less-traditional fish that grill well, see Figure 15-1.

REMEMBER

Throughout this book, we recommend using a large, resealable plastic bag to marinate food. However, fish is best marinated in a shallow nonreactive (not metal) baking dish. With its very delicate flesh, fish should lie secure and flat in the dish with the marinade swirling around it. Tossing fish into a plastic bag may cause tender fillets to fall apart into small, impossible-to-grill pieces. Exceptions to this rule are, of course, shrimp and scallops.

Fish steaks: The thick and easy cut

If you feel a little uneasy about your ability to grill fish, try thick cuts, especially steaks and kebabs, first. You should have no problem with these cuts.

REMEMBER

If fish steaks are sliced too thin, they will dry out on the grill and then will be more likely to fall apart. So have the fishmonger cut the steaks from 1 to 1½ inches thick for best results. See the section "Being gentle with fillets" later in this chapter for tips on grilling thin fish fillets.

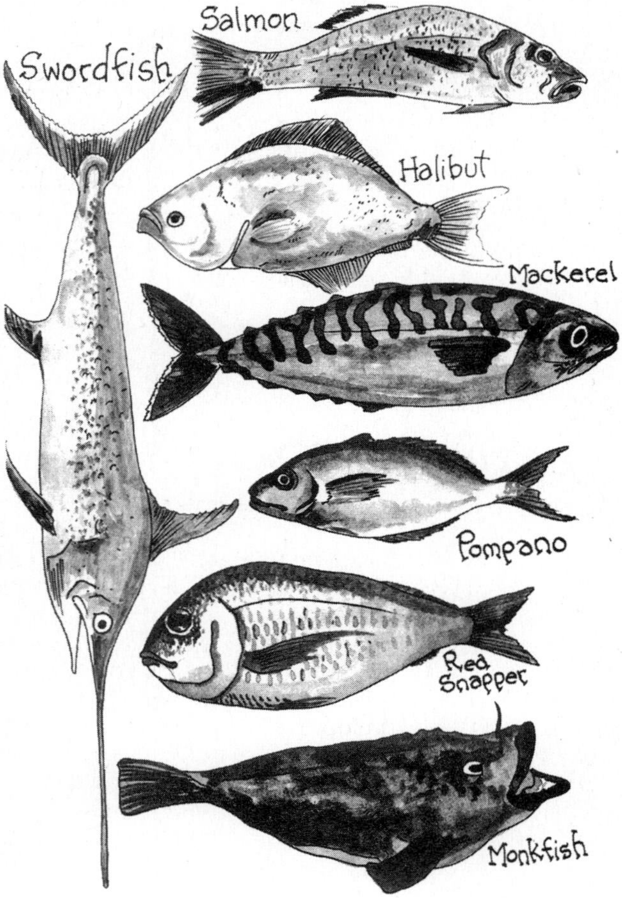

Figure 15-1: These fish varieties are excellent grilling choices.

Timing is still important, but with fish steaks you can at least blink without worrying that your fish is going to overcook. Follow these guidelines to achieve a perfectly grilled fish steak:

- **Grill fish steaks directly over moderately hot coals, turning the steaks only once.** A moderately hot fire gives you plenty of heat to develop a nice brown sear and cook the fish thoroughly, but not so much that the surface blackens or burns.

- **Be mindful of the variables that affect cooking time.** Most 1-inch fish steaks cook in about 8 minutes and continue to cook a little more after they're removed from the grill. However, cooking times vary according to wind, air temperature, and the heat intensity of your grill.
- **Check the interior of the fish for doneness a few minutes before you expect it to be done.** Use a thin-bladed knife to peek between the layers of flesh. Generally, when the flesh is no longer translucent, but rather opaque, and the knife meets no resistance, the fish is cooked.
- **Remove fish steaks a few seconds shy of their fully cooked time, because fish continue to cook after you remove them from the grill.**

Fish steaks need little adornment in the way of seasoning. You can marinate or simply brush them with a little oil and some seasonings before grilling.

Grilled Swordfish Steak with Chipotle Salsa

Chipotles (chee-POHT-lehz) are smoked jalapeño peppers that are sold two ways: canned in adobo (ah-DOH-boh) sauce or dried. Dried chipotles require reconstituting in boiling water for about 40 minutes. Chipotles add bold smoky flavor to food and are a perfect seasoning ingredient for grilled fish, poultry or beef, salsas, salad dressings, mayonnaise, and compound butters. Here, canned chipotles are mixed into a tomato and onion salsa that's served over grilled swordfish. Make the salsa 1 to 2 hours before serving to give the flavors a chance to develop.

Preparation time: *30 minutes*

Marinating time: *15 to 20 minutes*

Grilling time: *8 to 10 minutes*

Yield: *4 servings*

Chipotle Salsa

Yield: *2 cups*

2 cups cored, seeded, and diced plum tomatoes

1 small onion, peeled and diced (about ⅓ cup)

2 chipotle peppers (canned in adobo sauce), undrained and finely minced

2 tablespoons finely chopped fresh cilantro (coriander) leaves

Juice of half a lime (about 2 teaspoons)

½ teaspoon salt, or to taste

½ teaspoon sugar

In a medium bowl, thoroughly mix all the ingredients. Cover and refrigerate for at least 2 hours. Spoon over grilled swordfish steaks.

Grilled Swordfish

1 swordfish steak, about 1 to 1¼ pounds, cut 1-inch thick

Juice of 1 lemon

2 tablespoons olive oil

Salt and pepper to taste

1 Rinse the swordfish steak and pat dry with paper towels. Place the steak in a flat, nonreactive container.

2 In a small mixing bowl, combine the lemon juice, olive oil, and salt and pepper. Pour the mixture over the swordfish; cover and refrigerate for 15 to 20 minutes, turning once.

3 While the swordfish is marinating, prepare a medium-hot fire in a charcoal or gas grill.

4 When the fire is ready, place the swordfish on a well-oiled grill grid. Grill for 4 to 5 minutes per side or until done. To check for doneness, make a small incision in the center of the fish with the tip of a sharp, thin-bladed knife. The fish is cooked when the flesh is opaque and no longer translucent. Remove the fish from the grill and place on a platter. Spoon Chipotle Salsa (see previous recipe) over the top of the steaks before serving.

Per serving: *Calories 218 (From Fat 103); Fat 11g (Saturated 2g); Cholesterol 41mg; Sodium 646mg; Carbohydrate 7g (Dietary Fiber 1g); Protein 22g.*

Grilled Fish Steaks with Avocado and Citrus Salsa

Lime juice, orange sections, cilantro, and avocado give these grilled fish steaks refreshing flavor.

Preparation time: *25 minutes*

Marinating time: *30 minutes*

Grilling time: *8 to 10 minutes*

Yield: *4 servings*

4 salmon, halibut, swordfish, or shark steaks, cut about 1-inch thick, 6 to 8 ounces each

¼ cup torn fresh cilantro (coriander) or basil leaves

¼ cup olive oil

⅓ cup peeled and chopped red onion, divided

2 tablespoons fresh lime or lemon juice

Grated peel of half a lemon or lime (about 1 teaspoon)

Salt and pepper to taste

1 large clove garlic, peeled and minced (about 1 teaspoon) (optional)

1 firm, ripe avocado, peeled, pitted, and finely chopped

1 navel orange, peeled, sectioned, and finely chopped

1 small jalapeño pepper, seeded and finely chopped

1 Prepare a medium-hot fire in a charcoal or gas grill.

2 Rinse fish steaks under cold running water; pat dry with paper towels. Place the steaks in a shallow, nonreactive baking dish, in a single layer.

3 In a blender container, combine the cilantro or basil, olive oil, 1 tablespoon of the red onion, the lime or lemon juice, grated lime or lemon peel, and salt and pepper. Blend for a few seconds until the mixture is a coarse puree.

4 Remove 2½ tablespoons of the mixture and reserve for making the salsa. Add the garlic to the remaining marinade (if desired). Pour the marinade over the fish steaks in the dish, turning to coat well. Cover and refrigerate for about 30 minutes, turning once.

5 Prepare the Avocado and Citrus Salsa by combining the avocado, orange, jalapeño pepper, remaining red onion, and reserved 2½ tablespoons marinade in a medium mixing bowl. Cover the salsa and refrigerate until ready to use.

6 When the fire is ready, remove the fish from the baking dish, discarding the remaining marinade. Place the fish steaks on a well-oiled grill grid, allowing some of the marinade to cling to each steak. Grill for about 8 to 10 minutes, turning once with a wide metal spatula. To check for doneness, make a small incision in the center of the steak with the tip of a thin-bladed knife. The flesh should be opaque, not translucent, when done. Spoon some of the Avocado and Citrus Salsa over each steak before serving.

Per serving: *Calories 429 (From Fat 236); Fat 26g (Saturated 4g); Cholesterol 97mg; Sodium 271mg; Carbohydrate 10g (Dietary Fiber 5g); Protein 39g.*

Making heads and tails of whole fish

We believe that grilling a whole fish — head and tail intact — makes for some of the most delicious eating imaginable. Of course, we exempt from this discussion fish that may weigh several hundred pounds, like tuna, or fish that may take up half a backyard, like swordfish — both of which are sold as steaks. But grilling a beautiful smaller fish like trout, red snapper, bluefish, porgy, sea bass, or pompano (a fish Mark Twain said was as delicious as "the less criminal forms of sin") makes even the simplest recipe a feast.

A whole fish is a good grilling choice because the skin naturally protects the delicate flesh from falling apart as it grills. A whole fish stays juicier and is easier to turn if grilled with the head intact. We aren't unaware, however, that many people don't much care for fish staring back at them while they're eating, so cutting off the head is okay. A whole, beheaded fish will still retain more succulence and flavor than a fillet. And you can always save the fish head to make a good fish stock.

Whole Grilled Trout with Thyme and Almond Butter Sauce

This is one of our favorite recipes in the book, and if you've never before grilled a whole fish, you're in for a pleasant culinary treat. The skin grills to a crisp finish while the flesh stays moist and succulent. Slashing the fish along both of its sides allows the seasonings of olive oil, lemon juice, thyme, and garlic to permeate through the skin and into the tender flesh.

Preparation time: *15 minutes*

Marinating time: *30 minutes to 1 hour*

Grilling time: *10 minutes*

Yield: *2 servings*

1 rainbow trout, about 1¼ to 1½ pounds, cleaned, gutted, and scaled, with head intact

2 tablespoons olive oil

2 teaspoons fresh lemon juice

2 medium cloves garlic, peeled and minced (about 1½ teaspoons)

2 teaspoons minced fresh thyme, or ¾ teaspoon dried thyme

Salt and pepper to taste

3 to 4 fresh thyme sprigs, each about 2 to 3 inches long

Almond Butter Sauce (see following recipe)

1 Rinse the fish under cold running water and pat dry with paper towels. Make 4 or 5 ½-inch slashes (2 inches deep) on each side of the fish, spaced about 2 inches apart. (See Figure 15-2.)

2 In a small mixing bowl, combine the olive oil, lemon juice, garlic, and the minced or dried thyme. Place the fish in a large, shallow, nonreactive dish or container. Rub the marinade into the slashes on both sides of the fish and into its cavity (the hollow area made by cleaning and gutting the fish). Sprinkle salt and pepper on both sides and in the cavity. Place the thyme sprigs into the cavity. Cover and refrigerate for 30 minutes to 1 hour.

3 Prepare a medium-hot fire in a charcoal or gas grill. While you're waiting for the grill to preheat, prepare the Almond Butter Sauce (see the following recipe).

4 Generously oil both sides of a hinged, wire fish basket. Remove the fish from the marinade, discarding any remaining marinade, and then place the fish on one side of the basket with its head closest to the hinged end and its tail at the handle end. (This ensures that the thickest part of the fish is closest to the coals when grilling in a charcoal kettle grill, where the basket will not lay flat.) Close the basket.

5 Place the basket on the grid directly over the heat. Cover and grill for about 4 to 5 minutes or until nicely browned on one side. Turn the basket over; cover and grill for another 4 to 5 minutes or until the fish is done. Insert a thin-bladed knife or an instant-read thermometer into the thickest part of the fish. When done, the flesh near the bone will look opaque, and the thermometer will register 140 degrees.

6 Open the basket; turn the fish onto a warm platter and drizzle the Almond Butter Sauce down the center of the fish. Serve by cutting down through the flesh to the backbone and lifting off sections between the slashes with a metal spatula or large spoon.

Vary It! *To serve four, simply double the recipe and use two fish baskets or one large basket that holds two trout.*

Almond Butter Sauce

It's best to chop and assemble the ingredients for this sauce while your grill preheats, and then finish making it just before the fish is grilled.

Preparation time: *5 minutes*

Yield: *Enough sauce for 1 $1^1/_4$- to $1^1/_2$-pound trout*

2 tablespoons butter

2 teaspoons lemon juice

2 tablespoons slivered almonds, coarsely chopped

Pepper to taste

In a small saucepan, melt the butter with the lemon juice; add the almonds and cook over low heat until the almonds are lightly browned. Season with pepper. Remove from heat immediately to prevent the almonds from overbrowning.

Per serving: *Calories 431 (From Fat 312); Fat 35g (Saturated 11g); Cholesterol 105mg; Sodium 354mg; Carbohydrate 4g (Dietary Fiber 1g); Protein 27g.*

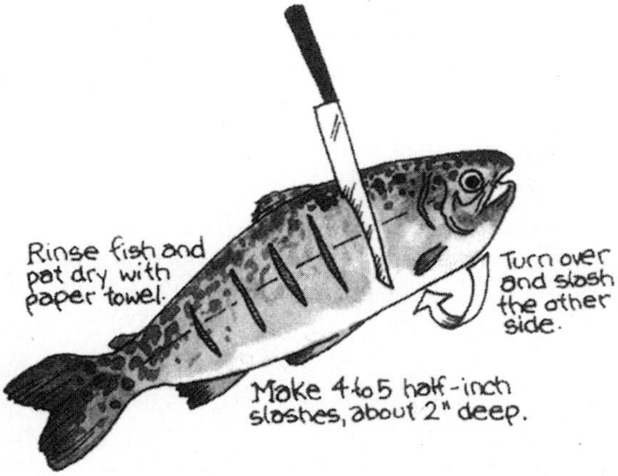
Rinse fish and pat dry with paper towel.
Turn over and slash the other side.
Make 4 to 5 half-inch slashes, about 2" deep.

Figure 15-2: How to correctly slash a fish.

Being gentle with fillets

Delicate whitefish fillets (like those from sole and flounder) aren't the easiest cuts of fish to grill; they need some special care. Grilling is a rough cooking method, so laying thin, skinless fillets directly on a grill grid may cause them to fall apart, as can excessive marinating. Additionally, the biggest mistake people make when cooking fish fillets — on or off the grill — is overcooking them. So follow these tips:

- Grill fillets on a perforated sheet of lightly oiled heavy-duty aluminum foil (simply puncture the foil with fork tines). The foil supports the fillets. However, be aware that you won't get that wonderful grilled, charred flavor — the whole point of outdoor cooking — when you use foil.
- Use a *fish basket* — a basket that's shaped like a fish — which is the most useful basket that we've found. Buy fish baskets made of nonstick or stick-resistant material. Also look for baskets with long handles, which make turning the fish a bit easier. (Chapter 2 shows you what fish baskets look like.) Adjustable baskets conform to the shape and size of the fish, allowing them to hold the fish securely in place. These, too, should be oiled before placing the fish inside.
- Keep your grill grid clean. Fish can easily get stuck on the little particles of cooked food clinging to the rack.
- Coat the fish with a thin layer of oil before placing it on the grid. However, be sure to gently shake off most of an oil-based marinade before placing fish on the grid. Doing so prevents flare-ups.

  If you can't find your basting brush (or you don't want to have to wash it), cut an onion in half and coat the cut side lightly with oil. Stick a fork in the onion and rub the oil-coated side against the grid to oil it.
- Always be sure to oil the grid when it's cold to prevent dangerous flare-ups.
- Don't overmarinate! Fish tissue starts to react to the acid in the marinade and will fall apart. Thirty minutes is plenty of time to add sufficient flavor to most fish.
- After initially placing fish on the grid, resist any immediate attempt to move it around or turn it over. Letting it sear a little makes turning the fish easier.
- Never turn fillets on the grill more than once. In fact, you may not even have to turn the fillets at all. If the fillets are less than 1-inch thick and have their skin on, they will cook through with only small bits of skin clinging to the grid.
- Hover over your grilling fillets like a hen around her chicks. Check the interior for doneness with a thin-bladed knife.

Fillets come dressed or undressed (so to speak). Flatfish varieties, such as flounder, turbot, and sole, are always skinless, as is mahi-mahi. But fillets with their skins on (bass, salmon, and bluefish, for example) offer a natural barrier to the heat, which can prevent overcooking. The skin also holds the delicate flesh together as it grills.

Flatfish Fillets Grilled on Lemon Slices with Mediterranean Skillet Sauce

Want another way besides a basket to protect delicate fish fillets from the harsh heat of the grill? Grill them on lemon slices as we do in this recipe. The thin fillets cook without needing a turn, and the lemons slices make a dramatic, copper-colored plate garnish. If you'd like, use thin slices of red or yellow onion rather than lemons.

Preparation time: *10 minutes*

Marinating time: *30 minutes to 1 hour*

Grilling time: *6 minutes*

Yield: *4 servings*

2 skinless flatfish fillets (cod, haddock, sea bass, or flounder, for example), about 8 to 10 ounces each

2 tablespoons olive oil

¾ teaspoon ground cumin

Salt and pepper to taste

16 lemon slices, thinly sliced about ¼-inch thick (about 3 large lemons)

1 Prepare a medium-hot fire in a covered charcoal or gas grill.

2 Rinse the fillets under cold running water and gently pat them dry with a paper towel. Cut each fillet in half crosswise to make 4 pieces of fish that are about equal in size.

3 In a small bowl, combine the olive oil, cumin, and salt and pepper. Brush both sides of the fillets with the mixture; cover and refrigerate for about 30 minutes to 1 hour.

4 Prepare the Mediterranean Skillet Sauce (see the following recipe) as the fish marinates.

5 When ready to grill your fillets, lay the lemon slices on the oiled grill, using 4 slices to make a square large enough to hold a piece of fish. (Refer to Figure 15-3 to see what we mean.) Repeat with remaining slices to make 4 squares directly over the heat. Remove the fish from the marinade, discarding any that remains, and then set a piece of fish on top of each lemon square.

6 Cover and grill, without turning, for a total of 6 to 8 minutes or until done. To test for doneness, make a small incision with the tip of a sharp knife to peek into the center of each fillet. The flesh in the center should be opaque and moist. Final cooking time will depend on the actual thickness of the fillets.

7 Remove the fish from the grill and place them on individual platters by sliding a wide metal spatula under the lemon slices, picking up the fish at the same time. Gently pull the lemon slices out from under the fish, inverting them on the platter, grilled side up. (They will have a bronzed, slightly caramelized look.) Spoon equal amounts of the Mediterranean Skillet Sauce over each fillet.

Mediterranean Skillet Sauce

Preparation time: *10 minutes*

Yield: *About 1 cup*

1 tablespoon butter

1 tablespoon olive oil

2 cups cored, seeded, and chopped ripe plum tomatoes

1 large clove garlic, peeled and minced

12 pitted black ripe olives, chopped

2 tablespoons rinsed and drained capers

Salt and pepper to taste

1 Combine the butter and olive oil in a medium skillet and cook over medium-high heat until the butter is melted. Add the tomatoes and garlic and cook for 2 to 3 minutes, stirring often. Add the olives and capers, and cook, stirring 1 minute more.

2 Remove from heat and season with salt and pepper. Cover and reserve. Just before serving, reheat, adding a little water or wine to the sauce if necessary. Spoon the sauce over the grilled fillets.

Vary It! *You can substitute green olives or kalamata olives for the black olives, or try adding 1/4 cup chopped, bottled artichoke hearts.*

Per serving: *Calories 201 (From Fat 107); Fat 12g (Saturated 3g); Cholesterol 51mg; Sodium 524mg; Carbohydrate 5g (Dietary Fiber 1g); Protein 19g.*

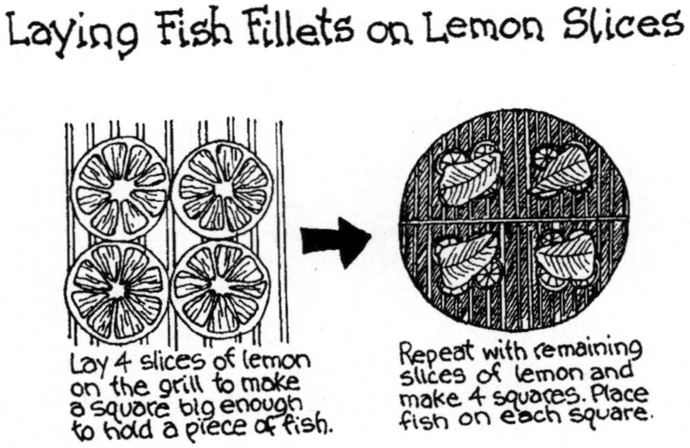
Laying Fish Fillets on Lemon Slices
Lay 4 slices of lemon on the grill to make a square big enough to hold a piece of fish.
Repeat with remaining slices of lemon and make 4 squares. Place fish on each square.

Figure 15-3: Grilling delicate fillets on lemon slices keeps them from falling through the grill grid as they cook.

Seasoned and Breaded Catfish Fillets with Basil Mayonnaise

In this recipe, a bread crumb batter helps to keep the tender catfish fillets from burning on the grill, and the fresh basil and Tabasco sauce mayonnaise makes for a perfect complementary sauce. For a lowfat dish, you can forgo the Basil Mayonnaise and serve these fillets with a simple drizzle of fresh lemon juice. Or use reduced fat mayonnaise — or fat-free yogurt combined with reduced-fat mayonnaise — for fewer calories. You can see this finished dish in the color photo section of this book.

Preparation time: *20 minutes*

Grilling time: *8 to 10 minutes*

Yield: *4 servings*

Basil Mayonnaise (see the following recipe)

1 1/2 pounds catfish fillets

1/3 cup buttermilk

1/4 teaspoon Tabasco sauce, or to taste

1/2 cup fine dry bread crumbs

1 teaspoon grated lemon peel

1 teaspoon dried basil

1/2 teaspoon dried thyme, or 1/2 teaspoon ground cumin

Salt and pepper to taste

4 sprigs of basil (optional)

4 lemon wedges (optional)

1 Prepare Basil Mayonnaise (see the following recipe). Cover and refrigerate until ready to serve.

2 Prepare a medium-hot fire in a charcoal or gas grill.

3 Rinse the fillets under cold running water and pat dry with paper towels. Combine the buttermilk and Tabasco sauce in a shallow dish. Combine the bread crumbs, lemon peel, basil, thyme or cumin, and salt and pepper in a second shallow dish. Dip the catfish first in the buttermilk-Tabasco mixture and then coat both sides lightly in the seasoned bread crumb mixture.

4 Place the fish on a well-oiled grid (directly over the heat) or in an oiled fish basket. Grill for about 4 to 5 minutes per side, turning once, until the fillets are opaque in the center and the crumb coating is lightly browned. To test for doneness, make a small incision with the tip of a sharp knife in the thickest part of each fillet. Catfish fillets vary, from 1/4 to 3/4 inches thick, and so final cooking time depends on the thickness of the fillets.

5 Using a wide spatula, carefully transfer the fillets to individual plates. Top each with a generous dollop of Basil Mayonnaise. Garnish with a sprig of fresh basil and a lemon wedge (if desired).

Basil Mayonnaise

Yield: *About 1/2 cup*

1/2 cup mayonnaise

1/4 cup packed fresh basil leaves

1 teaspoon fresh lemon juice

1/2 teaspoon Tabasco sauce, or to taste

Puree all the ingredients in a blender until smooth, stopping as necessary to scrape down the sides.

Vary It! *For mouthwatering sandwiches, serve these fillets on slices of toasted sourdough or Italian bread with sprigs of tart, crisp watercress or arugula leaves.*

Per serving: *Calories 475 (From Fat 329); Fat 37g (Saturated 7g); Cholesterol 93mg; Sodium 506mg; Carbohydrate 12g (Dietary Fiber 1g); Protein 29g.*

Throughout this book, we generally advise you to avoid using wood chips with foods that grill in less than 30 minutes. The smoke from chips, we feel, is too subtle to really have an effect on quick-grilling foods. However, the exception to this rule is grilling fish. Fish flesh, compared to that of beef, pork, poultry, and lamb, is so tender and delicate that it readily absorbs the gentle flavors of smoking wood chips. So feel free to throw those pre-soaked chips into the fire (or place them in a smoke box if you have a gas grill). They have a very pleasant effect on all kinds of freshwater fish and seafood.

Asian-Style Salmon Fillets with Vegetables

Here's a recipe that tops lovely, center-cut, pink, grilled salmon fillets with thin red peppers, zucchini, and scallions. Center-cut salmon fillets are about 1¼ to 1½ inches thick. Thinner fillets, cut from the tail end of the salmon, can easily overcook and should not be used for this recipe.

Salmon skin grills to a tasty crispness, so purchase fillets with their skin intact. The fresh, thinly sliced vegetables are set on the grill, about 5 minutes before the fish, to steam in an aluminum foil packet.

Preparation time: *30 minutes*

Marinating time: *30 minutes to 1 hour*

Grilling time: *7 to 10 minutes for the salmon and 10 to 15 minutes for the vegetables*

Yield: *4 servings*

4 center-cut salmon fillets, about 6 to 7 ounces each and about 1¼ to 1½ inches thick, with skin intact

2 tablespoons sesame oil

2 tablespoons light soy sauce

1 tablespoon water

1½ teaspoons balsamic vinegar

2 teaspoons peeled and minced fresh ginger

2 teaspoons light brown sugar, packed

1 clove garlic, peeled and minced

⅛ teaspoon crushed red pepper flakes

1 zucchini, cut into strips about ¼- to ½-inch wide and 3 to 4 inches long

1 red pepper, cored, seeded, and cut into ¼- to ½-inch-wide strips

2 scallions, white and green parts, trimmed and sliced into 2-inch-long strips

1½ teaspoon vegetable oil

Salt and pepper to taste

1. Rinse the salmon fillets under cold running water and gently pat dry with paper towels.
2. Remove any pin bones in the fillets. (See Figure 15-4 for tips on how to do this.)
3. In a shallow, nonreactive baking dish, mix the sesame oil, soy sauce, water, vinegar, ginger, brown sugar, garlic, and red pepper flakes. Add the salmon fillets and turn them to coat in the marinade. Cover and refrigerate, skin side up, for about 30 minutes to 1 hour, turning occasionally.
4. Prepare a medium-hot fire in a covered charcoal or gas grill.
5. As the fire preheats, tear off a large piece of heavy-duty aluminum foil (or use two stacked sheets), about 14 inches long. Arrange the zucchini, red pepper strips, and scallions in the center of the foil; season with salt and pepper. Bring the four corners of the foil together to make a packet. Starting at the bottom, crimp together the open edges, leaving a small opening at the top of the packet.
6. Using a metal spatula, lift the salmon fillets from the marinade to a clean plate, shaking off any excess marinade. Pour any remaining marinade into the foil packet over the vegetables. Add the vegetable oil and tightly crimp or close the opening at the top of the packet.
7. Place the packet on the grill grid. Cover and cook for 4 to 5 minutes before placing the salmon on the grill. The vegetables need about 10 to 15 minutes total cooking time. Carefully peek into the packet to check for doneness after about 10 minutes; the vegetables should be crisp-tender. If necessary, set the packet on the edge of the grid to keep it warm until the fish is cooked.
8. Place the salmon fillets skin side up, on the lightly oiled grill grid, over medium heat. Cover and grill for 7 to 10 minutes or until the salmon is done, turning once with a wide metal spatula. Insert a thin-bladed knife into the thickest part of each fillet to check for doneness; the fish is cooked when the pink flesh is almost opaque.
9. Use a wide spatula to remove the fillets to a serving platter. Use tongs or a mitt to carefully remove the foil packet from the grid. Open the packet — watch out for the hot steam. Pour the vegetables and juices over the salmon fillets on the platter and serve immediately.

Per serving: *Calories 325 (From Fat 136); Fat 15g (Saturated 2g); Cholesterol 97mg; Sodium 577mg; Carbohydrate 7g (Dietary Fiber 1g); Protein 39g.*

Remove any pin bones
in the salmon fillets!

Figure 15-4: A pair of tweezers helps to remove tiny pin bones from salmon fillets.

Attempting to guide people about how long to cook their fish is just as difficult as giving advice on how long to cook their steaks or hamburgers. Everybody has a preference for doneness. For example, some people like salmon well done, with no hint of pink in the center. Others like salmon deep pink and almost raw on the inside, with a sizzling, surface sear. So always treat our cooking times as guidelines. Peek into the flesh of the fish to test for doneness a few minutes before the estimated time. Fish, like other food, can be put back on the grid if it's underdone to your liking, but you can't reverse the grilling gears if it's overdone.

Holy Smoked Fish, Batman!

Lightly smoked fish, which can be made at home using an ordinary covered charcoal grill and a steady supply of wood chips, has marvelous flavor that's well worth pursuing. Here are several tips for smoking fish:

- High-fat and dark-fleshed fish are best suited for smoking because they're moist enough to slow-cook and smoke — fish with less fat may dry out on the grill.
- Fish that's ideal for smoking includes mackerel, salmon, tuna, swordfish, and marlin.
- Small fish, like mackerel and trout, can be left whole and should be wet-cured in a solution of water, salt, sugar, and seasonings of your choice.
- You can cut larger fish (such as salmon) into fillets, steaks, or chunks and dry-cure them with equal parts salt and sugar, and your choice of seasonings. Kosher salt and brown sugar flavor the fish nicely. However, white sugar and regular table salt can work as well.
- Whenever possible, leave the skin on the fish — it acts as a protective barrier to the fire. The skin isn't edible, however, so be sure to remove it after you've finished smoking the fish.

Smoked Salmon Fillet

A cloud of steady smoke, made by throwing handfuls of pre-soaked wood chips over your grill coals, permeates the delicate flesh of this dry-cured salmon, infusing it with incomparable flavor. If you love grilled salmon or smoked fish, you'll enjoy making this recipe on your covered charcoal grill.

Preparation time: *15 minutes hands-on, 6 hours or overnight to dry-cure*

Grilling time: *25 to 30 minutes*

Yield: *6 main dish servings or 10 to 12 appetizer servings*

2-pound salmon fillet with skin, about 1 inch at thickest point, rinsed and de-boned

¼ cup coarse kosher salt

¼ cup light brown sugar, packed

1 teaspoon garlic powder

1 teaspoon pepper

Oil for brushing the aluminum foil and the salmon

About 3 to 4 cups hardwood chips, pre-soaked

Lemon slices and watercress sprigs for garnish (optional)

1 Place the fillet completely flat in a nonreactive dish or container. Mix together the salt, sugar, garlic powder, and pepper, and then sprinkle the mixture onto both sides of the fillet. Let the fish sit in the refrigerator for at least 6 hours, or overnight. (The longer, the saltier.)

2 Half an hour before smoking the fish, prepare a small fire in a covered charcoal or gas grill, using about 40 briquettes for a charcoal grill. A drip pan isn't necessary. If using a gas grill, set the temperature to low, about 300 degrees, and prepare an indirect fire as explained in Chapter 1.

3 Cut a piece of aluminum foil about 1 inch longer and wider than the fillet. Perforate the foil with a fork in about 6 or 7 places and oil it lightly. Place the fillet on the foil, skin side down. Brush the top of the fillet lightly with oil.

4 When the coals are hot, bank them to one side of the grill and top with 2 large handfuls of the pre-soaked wood chips. If you're using a gas grill, place the wood chips in a smoker box. Place the fillet on the grid, opposite the coals or heat. Cover the grill, half-closing the top vents, and cook, without turning, for about 25 to 30 minutes or until the flesh is firm and opaque but not dry. (The actual cooking time depends on the thickness of the fish and the intensity of the heat. An instant-read thermometer will register 140 degrees in the thickest part of the fillet when done. Start testing for doneness after 20 minutes.) Be sure to add more wood chips after about 15 minutes and as necessary to keep a steady supply of flavored smoke.

5 Remove the fillet from the grill and let stand 3 to 4 minutes. Carefully invert the fillet onto a large platter and peel off the aluminum foil. (The skin will stick to the foil and should be discarded.) Invert the skinless fillet onto a second platter with the colorful bright flesh facing up. Cover and refrigerate for several hours or until completely chilled. If desired, garnish the platter with watercress and slices of fresh lemons.

Per serving: *Calories 199 (From Fat 51); Fat 6g (Saturated 1g); Cholesterol 86mg; Sodium 1,032mg; Carbohydrate 2g (Dietary Fiber 0g); Protein 33g.*

Mmm, Mollusks! Clams, Mussels, and Scallops

Mollusks (basically, creatures with soft, unsegmented bodies protected by shells) such as clams, mussels, and oysters can be grilled directly on the grill or wrapped first in heavy-duty aluminum foil. The key is to keep the delicious juices in each mollusk from spilling out into the fire. It helps to place them, with their cup side down, facing the fire. Or, better yet, place them in an aluminum pan and then on the grill. The pan catches any juices that may otherwise drip through the grid into the fire.

Grill only those clams, mussels, and oysters with tightly closed shells. Discard any with broken shells or those that don't close when tapped. And never store these live mollusks in water or a plastic bag because they will die and soon become toxic. Instead, place them in a large bowl, uncovered, in the refrigerator and use within 24 hours of purchase.

Use a stiff brush to scrub clean hard-shell clams and oysters under cold running water. Soft-shell clams, like steamers and razor clams, can hold large amounts of sand and grit. Soaking them in salted water with a handful of cornmeal for a few hours eliminates their impurities. Mussels are a little more difficult to clean, however. Rinse them under cold running water and pull off the stiff, beardlike growth attached to each shell.

Be careful not to overcook naturally tender shellfish. Remove oysters from the grill when they open slightly. Clams and mussels will pop wide open when they're done.

Scallop Kebabs with Pineapple and Bacon

Scallops cook very quickly — just 2 to 4 minutes over direct heat — so these kebabs can be grilled as your guests are sitting down. The finished recipe is shown in the color photo section of this book.

Preparation time: *15 minutes*

Marinating time: *30 minutes*

Grilling time: *2 to 4 minutes*

Yield: *3 to 4 servings, at 2 skewers per serving*

1½ pounds large scallops
4 tablespoons olive oil
2 teaspoons paprika
2 tablespoons orange marmalade
1 thinly sliced scallion
2 cloves garlic, peeled and finely chopped
2 tablespoons fresh chopped cilantro (coriander) leaves
Juice of half an orange
Juice of half a lemon
½ teaspoon salt
¼ teaspoon freshly ground pepper
Half of a fresh pineapple
4 thickly cut strips of bacon, each slice cut in half lengthwise

1. Pull off and discard the small muscle attached to the side of the scallop. Rinse the scallops in cold running water and pat dry thoroughly with paper towel. Set aside.
2. Place the cut side of the pineapple on a cutting board and slice off the outer skin. Then slice the pineapple into 1-inch slices. Cut the core from the centers of the slices and discard. Cut each slice into 6 sections.
3. In a resealable plastic bag, combine the oil, paprika, marmalade, scallion, garlic, cilantro, orange juice, lemon juice, and salt and black pepper. Reserve and set aside ¼ cup of the marinade for basting. Add the scallops and pineapple to the remaining marinade in the bag and seal tightly. Let the scallops and pineapple marinate in the refrigerator for 30 minutes. While the scallops are marinating, pre-soak your wooden skewers to prevent them from burning.
4. Prepare a medium fire in a charcoal or gas grill.
5. Remove the scallops and pineapple from the marinade, discarding any leftover marinade. Thread the scallops, pineapple, and bacon onto the pre-soaked skewers. Weave the skewer in and out of the bacon to form a loose ribbon.
6. Place the skewers on an oiled grill grid and grill over direct heat for about 1 to 2 minutes. Brush the kebabs with some of the reserved marinade and turn over and grill for another 1 to 2 minutes or until the scallops are just firm and white.

Per serving: *Calories 856 (From Fat 454); Fat 50g (Saturated 14g); Cholesterol 182mg; Sodium 1276mg; Carbohydrate 28g (Dietary Fiber 2g); Protein 64g.*

Grilled Clams and Mussels with Lemon Butter or Fresh Tomato Sauce

This recipe is the perfect help-yourself party appetizer or light summer meal. Grilled mollusks are also popular with football tailgaters — a little portable grill or hibachi is all you need to get the shells to pop open. Prepare either the Homemade Lemon Butter or the Fresh Tomato Sauce before leaving home, and then reheat whichever sauce you choose in a small saucepan, right next to the shellfish. Don't forget to pack a loaf of crusty French or Italian bread to soak up the wonderful sauce.

Preparation time: *25 minutes*

Grilling time: *2 to 6 minutes*

Yield: *4 main dish servings or 6 to 8 appetizer servings*

36 to 40 hard-shell clams or mussels in the shell (or a combination of clams and mussels), all scrubbed clean

Lemon Butter (if desired; see following recipe)

Fresh Tomato Sauce (if desired; see following recipe)

1 Prepare a hot fire in a charcoal or gas grill.

2 Place mollusks in their unopened shells directly on the grill grid. (Or place them on a large metal baking pan to collect juices as the mollusks open.) Cover the grill and cook 2 to 6 minutes. Remove them as soon as their shells pop wide open; place them in a large bowl or platter. The actual cooking time depends on the size of each mollusk and intensity of the heat.

3 Move the mollusks that don't open after about 5 minutes to a hotter spot. Discard any that do not eventually open. The shells will be roaring hot, so use long-handled tongs or a barbecue mitt to remove them from the grill.

4 Twist off and discard the top shell, being careful not to spill the flavorful mollusk juice. (This is a good task for your guests!) Drizzle Homemade Lemon Butter over the grilled mollusks or serve with the Fresh Tomato Sauce (see the following recipes).

Homemade Lemon Butter

Preparation time: *5 minutes*

Yield: *1/2 cup*

4 tablespoons butter

1 tablespoon olive oil

1 teaspoon Dijon-style mustard

1 tablespoon fresh lemon juice

Tabasco sauce to taste (optional)

Pepper to taste

1 Combine the butter and oil in a small saucepan on top of the stove over low heat (or to one side of the grill). Heat until the butter is melted.

2 Add the mustard and use a wire whisk or fork to incorporate it into the butter and oil.

3 Add the lemon juice, Tabasco sauce (if desired), and the pepper; cook and stir over low heat for 1 minute. Cover to keep the sauce warm, and reheat if necessary.

Vary It! *For the flavors of fresh herbs, add 1/4 cup chopped fresh cilantro (coriander), basil, or Italian parsley to the butter sauce.*

Per serving: *Calories 266 (From Fat 149); Fat 17g (Saturated 8g); Cholesterol 92mg; Sodium 134mg; Carbohydrate 5g (Dietary Fiber 0g); Protein 23g.*

Fresh Tomato Sauce

Preparation time: *20 minutes*

Yield: *1 1/4 cups (approximately four 1/3 cup servings)*

2 tablespoons olive oil

2 tablespoons butter

3 large cloves garlic, peeled and finely minced (about 1 tablespoon)

3 ripe plum tomatoes, seeded and finely chopped (about 1 cup)

1/2 cup bottled clam juice

Juice of half a lemon (about 1 1/2 tablespoons)

1/4 teaspoon red pepper flakes

1/3 cup coarsely chopped fresh basil or Italian parsley

Black pepper to taste

1 Heat the oil and butter in a medium saucepan over medium heat. Add the garlic and cook briefly for 1 minute, or until very lightly browned.

2 Add the tomatoes, clam juice, lemon juice, and red pepper flakes; simmer over medium heat for 4 to 5 minutes, stirring often. Remove from the heat.

3 Just before serving, add the chopped basil or parsley and the pepper. Pour the sauce over grilled mussels and clams that are set into a large serving bowl. Serve immediately with crusty French or Italian bread.

Vary It! *Serve this dish over 3/4 pound of steaming linguine, adding the clams and sauce as soon as the pasta is drained. If the sauce needs additional moisture, add 1/4 to 1/2 cup more bottled clam juice.*

Per serving: *Calories 127 (From Fat 114); Fat 13g (Saturated 5g); Cholesterol 16mg; Sodium 70mg; Carbohydrate 4g (Dietary Fiber 1g); Protein 1g.*

The Softest Swimmer in the Sea: Soft-Shell Crabs

Soft-shell crabs, which are crabs that have lost their hard outer shell, do well on the grill.

SHOPPING TIP

These days, frozen soft-shell crabs are readily available year-round — and they're not bad — but the best fresh soft-shell crabs start to come in mid-May, and the season is over before the end of summer.

Grilled Soft-Shell Crabs

We tested these crabs over a fire made of a combination of hardwood hickory chunks and charcoal. The hickory wood flavor was divine with the crab.

Preparation time: *10 minutes*

Grilling time: *6 minutes*

Yield: *4 servings*

3 tablespoons butter

3 tablespoons olive oil

Juice of half a lemon

Grated peel of half a lemon

3 tablespoons finely chopped fresh basil, or 1 tablespoon dried basil

Salt and pepper to taste

Tabasco sauce to taste (optional)

8 soft-shell crabs, cleaned

1 Prepare a medium-hot fire in a charcoal or gas grill.

2 As the fire is preheating, melt the butter in a small saucepan; add the olive oil, lemon juice, lemon peel, basil, and salt and pepper. If you like a hot, spicy flavor, add Tabasco sauce. Brush the crabs with most of the butter sauce, coating both sides.

3 Place the crabs on a lightly oiled grid, directly over the heat. Turn and brush every 2 to 3 minutes with any remaining basting sauce. Cook for a total of 6 to 8 minutes. The crabs are cooked when they appear bright red and firm to the touch.

Go-With: *Serve with Black Bean and Red Pepper Salsa (Chapter 6) or Grilled Tomatoes with Cumin Butter (Chapter 16).*

Per serving: *Calories 370 (From Fat 186); Fat 21g (Saturated 7g); Cholesterol 205mg; Sodium 795mg; Carbohydrate 1g (Dietary Fiber 0g); Protein 41g.*

Don't Call Me a Shrimp (But Do Feed Me Some!)

Shrimp is a classic grilled dish — especially in kebabs (which you can read about in Chapter 8). In this section, however, we show you a unique way to prepare shrimp: stuffing them with pesto. We also share a famous chef's recipe that's out of this world!

SHOPPING TIP

Try not to buy shrimp that have already been shelled, deveined, and packaged. This shrimp will have lost some of its freshness. Practice deveining it yourself (see Figure 15-5) or have your fish handler devein fresh shrimp the same day you plan to grill it.

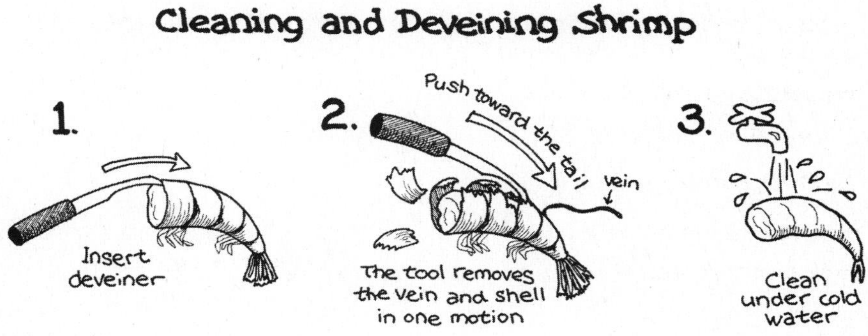
Cleaning and Deveining Shrimp
1.
Insert deveiner
2.
Push toward the tail
vein
The tool removes the vein and shell in one motion
3.
Clean under cold water

Figure 15-5: Getting shrimp ready to grill.

Pesto Shrimp in the Shell

Grilling shrimp in their shells helps to keep the flesh moist and tender. A little pesto sauce stuffed into the shell adds flavor and color. If you have a wire grilling basket, place the pesto-stuffed shrimp in the basket so you can turn them over all at once. Purchase shrimp that are sized about 16 to 20 per pound. These are sold as either extra-large or jumbo.

Even though it's a little messy, this dish makes a terrific party appetizer; just be sure to hand out plenty of napkins. Set the bright-pink grilled shrimp on a large serving platter and garnish with lemon wedges.

Preparation time: *30 minutes (less if you start with cleaned shrimp)*

Marinating time: *1 to 2 hours*

Grilling time: *4 to 5 minutes*

Yield: *8 to 10 appetizer servings*

1½ pounds extra-large to jumbo shrimp (about 24 to 28 shrimp), dark vein removed with shell intact

½ cup Pesto Sauce (see following recipe)

Juice of 1 lemon

Salt and pepper to taste

8 to 10 lemon wedges, for garnish

4 sprigs of fresh basil, for garnish

1 Rinse and drain the deveined shrimp under cold running water.

2 Stuff about ¼ to ½ teaspoon Pesto Sauce (see the following recipe) into the vein cavity and between the shell and flesh of each shrimp. The shell holds the pesto stuffing in place as the shrimp grills.

3 Place the stuffed shrimp in a large, flat dish and drizzle the lemon juice over them; season with salt and pepper. Cover and refrigerate 1 to 2 hours.

4 Prepare a medium-hot fire in a gas or charcoal grill.

5 Place the shrimp in an oiled wire basket, directly over the heat.

6 Grill for 4 to 5 minutes or until the shrimp are pink and opaque, turning frequently. Be careful not to overcook, or they will become dry and rubbery. Before serving, peel and taste a shrimp; serve with additional salt and pepper (if desired) on a large platter garnished with lemon wedges and fresh basil.

Pesto Sauce

Preparation time: *15 minutes*

Yield: *About ½ cup (approximately 8 servings at 1 tablespoon per serving)*

2 cups, loosely packed fresh basil leaves, stems removed (about 2 ounces)

½ cup extra-virgin olive oil

3 tablespoons pine nuts or walnuts

3 large cloves garlic, peeled and chopped

Salt and pepper to taste

¼ cup grated Parmesan cheese

1 Rinse and pat dry the trimmed basil leaves.

2 In the container of a food processor or blender, combine basil leaves, oil, pine nuts or walnuts, garlic, and salt and pepper. Blend to a fine texture but not a smooth puree, stopping once to scrape down the sides of the container.

3 Add the Parmesan cheese and blend for just a few more seconds. Cover and chill until ready to use.

Vary It! *You can also use this pesto on pasta as a sauce or as a condiment for all meats and fish. For a lemony pesto that works well with grilled shrimp and other fish, stir the grated peel of half a lemon into the finished sauce.*

Per serving: *Calories 219 (From Fat 150); Fat 17g (Saturated 3g); Cholesterol 128mg; Sodium 338mg; Carbohydrate 2g (Dietary Fiber 1g); Protein 16g.*

Jimmy Schmidt's Grilled Barbecued Shrimp

Jimmy Schmidt, owner of The Rattlesnake Club in Detroit, Michigan, is considered one of the fathers of New American Cuisine. Chef Schmidt can take a traditional dish and refine it to become something new and exciting, which is what he does with this recipe by adding sweet corn and peppers and the crunchy texture of jícama (pronounced HEE-kah-mah).

Chef Schmidt suggests skewering together the raw shrimp to make them easier to turn on the grid and to keep them from falling through the food grate. Lay 6 to 8 of the cleaned shrimp, side by side on your counter, but with heads and tails facing in opposite directions. Run 2 pre-soaked, wooden skewers parallel to each other, through the shrimp. Repeat with the remaining shrimp, and you're ready to grill.

Preparation time: *25 minutes*

Grilling time: *5 minutes*

Yield: *4 servings*

3/4 cup bottled or homemade barbecue sauce

1/4 cup fresh lime juice

3 tablespoons peeled and grated fresh ginger, divided

Tabasco sauce to taste

1 1/2 pounds jumbo shrimp (16 to 20 shrimp per pound)

1 tablespoon olive oil

Paprika to taste

Salt and pepper to taste

1/2 cup chopped fresh cilantro (coriander) leaves

Roast Corn, Peppers, and Jícama Slaw (see following recipe)

1. Prepare a hot fire in a charcoal or gas grill.
2. In a small bowl, combine the barbecue sauce, lime juice, 2 tablespoons of the ginger, and Tabasco sauce. Set aside.
3. Peel, devein, and rinse the shrimp (refer to Figure 15-5), leaving the tail shells intact.
4. In a medium bowl, toss together the shrimp, olive oil, and remaining 1 tablespoon grated ginger. Season with paprika and salt and pepper.
5. Place the shrimp on a well-oiled grill grid, (skewering, if desired, as described in the introduction to this recipe), directly over the heat. Grill for about 3 minutes; turn and brush with the barbecue-lime sauce. Grill for another 2 to 3 minutes or until the shrimp are pink. (Be careful not to overcook, or the shrimp will become tough and rubbery. If you'd like, remove them from the grill just before they're fully cooked. The stored heat energy in each shrimp will finish cooking it.) Transfer the shrimp to the edges of a large serving platter and brush with more of the barbecue-lime sauce.
6. Mound the slaw (see following recipe) in the center of the platter. Arrange the shrimp around the slaw, slightly overlapping. Sprinkle the cilantro over the shrimp and serve immediately.

Roast Corn, Peppers, and Jícama Slaw

Preparation time: *25 minutes*

Chilling time: *1 hour*

Yield: *4 servings*

2 ears fresh sweet corn, husks on, silk removed

2 red bell peppers, cut into fine julienne

1 jícama root, peeled and cut into fine julienne (about 2 cups)

1/2 cup extra-virgin olive oil

1/2 cup fresh lime juice

1 bunch scallions, green parts only, very finely chopped

1 clove garlic, peeled and finely minced

Salt and black pepper to taste

Red pepper flakes (optional)

1. Prepare a medium-hot fire in a charcoal or gas grill.
2. Place the ears of corn wrapped in their husks, with silk removed, on the grid; cook until well browned on all sides, for 10 to 15 minutes. Remove the corn from the grid and allow to cool.
3. Stand an ear of grilled corn upright on a flat dish and use a knife to scrape or cut the kernels off the cob. Repeat with the second ear. Transfer the kernels to a medium mixing bowl; add the peppers, jícama, olive oil, lime juice, scallions, and garlic; stir until well combined. Season with the salt and black pepper and red pepper flakes (if desired). Cover and refrigerate at least 1 hour before serving.

Vary It! *If you have trouble locating jícama, you can substitute a small green cabbage or head of bok choy.*

Per serving: *Calories 577 (From Fat 302); Fat 34g (Saturated 5g); Cholesterol 252mg; Sodium 939mg; Carbohydrate 41g (Dietary Fiber 13g); Protein 32g.*

Chapter 16

Not for Vegetarians Only: Vegetables and Side Dishes

In This Chapter

- Eating your vegetables — the grilled way!
- Getting tips on grilling a range of veggies
- Dishing out warm and cool sides

Recipes in This Chapter

- Linguine with Goat Cheese and Grilled Asparagus
- Garlic-Grilled Portobellos
- Grilled New Potato Salad with Fresh Mint
- Stuffed Summer Squash
- Grand Marnier Grilled Sweet Potatoes
- Grilled Tomatoes with Cumin Butter
- Couscous with Apples, Onions, and Raisins
- Middle Eastern Rice
- Tomato and Red Onion Salad
- Orange-Ginger Coleslaw
- Tabbouleh
- Macaroni Salad with Sun-Dried Tomato Mayonnaise
- Yogurt Cucumber Salad

Think "grilling" and you won't immediately think of vegetables — but oh, are you missing something if you haven't tried grilling these fresh foods! In this chapter, we show you how to successfully grill vegetables — every time you try. From corn to summer squash, we cover the gamut here.

And since every good dish deserves a side order, we give you some of the tastiest sides to try — from an array of wonderful salads to a terrific Middle Eastern rice dish. If you're bitten by the grill bug, you'll have to face an important fact: You spend most of your energy tending the fire and grilling the main course, so the last thing you want to have to do is give yourself more pressure trying to assemble a bunch of complicated side dishes. So, in this chapter, we promise not to torture you with any 25-step recipes that call for phyllo dough, puff pastry, or any other "I can't handle that" ingredient.

We put our own interesting accent on many of the sides in this chapter. Our macaroni salad, for example, is a happy Mediterranean mixture of sun-dried tomatoes, black olives, basil, and lemon juice in a mayonnaise dressing. And our coleslaw has orange sections, ginger, and spicy jalapeño peppers. We hope you're pleasantly surprised by the unusual flavors that we've added to these old favorites. The best part is that most of them take 30 minutes or less to prepare.

Serving suggestions follow many of the recipes in this chapter. Use them only as guidelines. Compose your own favorite meal combinations by leafing through Parts III and IV to pair these sides with any of our main dishes.

Updating Your Mom's Veggie-Cooking Technique

Maybe if your mother had *grilled* your vegetables when you were a kid, she wouldn't have had to bribe you to clean them off your plate. Grilled vegetables take on the wonderful smoky flavors of the grill while retaining their natural sweetness and crunch. Boiling, on the other hand, robs vegetables of flavor and precious vitamins, while sautéing and deep frying can add unwanted fat and calories.

It's true that delicate veggies need tender loving care while grilling to keep them from charring, but the delicious end results are worth the extra effort.

Here's a list of some vegetables that are particularly well suited for grilling:

- Asparagus
- Corn on the cob
- Eggplant
- Onions
- Potatoes
- Scallions
- Sweet peppers
- Tomatoes
- Zucchini

Simple seasoning (and brief marinating) is best

By far the simplest way to grill vegetables is to give them a brushing of oil — olive, peanut, corn, and safflower oils are all recommended — and a sprinkling of salt and pepper to taste. Other possibilities include:

- Coarse kosher salt sprinkled to taste on any vegetable, before or after grilling, adds great flavor.
- Ground cumin or grated lemon peel is delicious with fresh tomato slices.
- Grated fresh ginger combined with grated lemon peel, garlic seasoned mushrooms, and thin slices of acorn or butternut squash is a quintessential East-West mix that goes well with just about everything.
- Tarragon is terrific with eggplant and summer squash.

- Hot chili powder or Tabasco sauce livens up potato planks or wedges, or small new potatoes.
- Chopped fresh garlic, olive oil, and basil (mixed together) are good with just about any grilled, smoke-infused vegetable.

Many vegetables benefit from a little marinating before grilling. However, unlike meat or poultry, vegetables quickly absorb the flavors of the marinade and require only about 30 minutes to 1 hour of soaking — in fact, any longer may make them soft and mushy. If you don't have time to marinate vegetables, skip this step altogether and simply brush them with a little oil. Then after grilling, toss them in bottled lemon-herb vinaigrette if you like. (See Chapter 5 for loads of marinade recipes.)

Tossing vegetables with oil and seasonings in a large bowl before grilling is easier than brushing pieces individually. But don't try this with onions; they will separate from rounds into rings that are almost impossible to grill. Olive oils or vegetable oils, with their relatively high smoking point, are the preferred choices for brushing on vegetables before grilling.

Many vegetables can be seasoned and wrapped in aluminum foil packets before grilling. They steam in the packet, retaining color, moisture, and flavor. Be sure to pierce a few holes in the top of the packet so the grill's smoke can penetrate and infuse the food with flavor. To make low-calorie vegetable packets, use canned broth, lemon juice, and fresh herbs as seasonings, omitting fats like butter and oil.

Be sure to combine only those vegetables with the same cooking times, however. For example, don't create a packet mixed with snow peas and carrot pieces, unless the carrots are cut into thin julienne strips or parboiled until almost cooked through. Turn the packets occasionally to prevent the food inside from burning, especially if you're grilling the vegetables longer than 15 minutes.

Exercising care while grilling

You can't slough off while grilling vegetables — vigilance is important because vegetables can burn quickly. A slight char is pleasing, but blackened, dried-out vegetables taste horrible.

Here are some quick tips for grilling vegetables:

- **Be sure that your grilling surface is scraped completely clean.** This ensures that vegetables don't take on the flavors of other foods. After scraping, oil the grill grid well to prevent vegetables from sticking.
- **Don't grill vegetables over too intense a fire, or they're sure to burn without cooking through.** Most vegetables contain a fair amount of

sugar, which sizzles beautifully into a light brown crust from the heat of the grill. But if cooked over too intense a heat, this natural sugar causes them to burn. A medium to medium-hot fire is plenty hot.

- **Try a basket for grilling your vegetables.** A hinged wire basket or a grill topper (see Chapter 2) is a terrific grilling gadget to keep veggies, especially onions, from falling through the grid. If you're grilling directly on the grid, cut all vegetables large enough that they don't slip through. Peppers can be halved or quartered before grilling and then sliced into smaller strips after.
- **To determine doneness, use the skewer test.** The vegetable is cooked if it can be easily pierced with a skewer. However, some people prefer a very crisp, almost raw, finish to their vegetables.
- **Keep cooking times in mind as you cook a meal.** When grilling vegetables with other long-cooking foods like chicken or beef, grill the vegetables first and move them to the outer edges of the grid or to a 300-degree oven to keep them warm.

You can save time by *parboiling* (boiling a few minutes to soften) thick, long-cooking vegetables like potatoes, hard-shell squash, and carrots before grilling, but they taste better if you take the time to grill them directly. Cut them into chunks or thin slices to shorten grilling time. Only vegetables with very thick, inedible skins need peeling.

Simply Vegetables

In the following sections, we give you tips for grilling a range of vegetables — from artichokes to tomatoes! We also throw in some surefire recipes along the way.

Artichokes

Whole fresh artichokes should be parboiled for 20 to 25 minutes before grilling over a medium-hot fire. Slice the parboiled artichoke in half lengthwise and, using a spoon, scrape out the inedible, prickly choke. Before grilling, brush the artichoke generously with oil that's flavored with garlic and lemon juice, or marinate it in a lemon and mustard-flavored vinaigrette. Bottled artichoke hearts, packed in oil and already cooked, are easily skewered with other foods before grilling. (Turn to Chapter 8 for Artichoke, Mushroom, and Cherry Tomato Kebabs.)

Asparagus

Grilled asparagus takes on the flavor of charcoal and develops a beautiful brown sheen. To grill, trim off the woody ends and then peel the base to within 3 to 4 inches of the tip. Brush the stalks with oil that's flavored with a little crushed garlic and black pepper. Place the stalks perpendicular to the grill grid over medium-hot coals, turning so they brown on all sides. Pencil-thin stalks will be done in about 5 to 6 minutes, but thicker stalks can take up to 15 minutes. Stalks should be fork-tender before removing. Season the grilled asparagus with freshly ground pepper, kosher salt, and grated lemon peel.

Linguine with Goat Cheese and Grilled Asparagus

This dish tosses together grilled asparagus and tomatoes, linguine, and goat cheese for the perfect summertime appetizer or light dinner. The asparagus and tomatoes can be grilled ahead of time, if you wish, and held at room temperature before the pasta is cooked. Just be sure not to finish cooking the pasta without having the sauce ingredients ready to go. For a version of this dish that's not as rich in calories, omit the shallots and garlic sautéed in the butter and oil.

Preparation time: *25 minutes*

Grilling time: *10 to 15 minutes*

Yield: *4 servings*

1 1/2 pounds fresh asparagus, trimmed

6 large ripe plum tomatoes, cored and halved

Olive oil for brushing vegetables

Salt and pepper to taste

1 pound linguine or fettuccine

1 tablespoon olive oil

1 tablespoon butter

2 shallots, peeled and finely chopped

2 cloves garlic, peeled and minced

6 ounces goat cheese, at room temperature

1/2 cup coarsely chopped fresh basil leaves

1/2 teaspoon red pepper flakes (optional)

1 Prepare a medium-hot fire in a charcoal or gas grill.

2 Brush the asparagus and tomato halves with oil; season with salt and pepper.

3 Place the vegetables on a lightly oiled grid. Grill the asparagus for 10 to 15 minutes, depending on thickness, or until lightly browned on all sides and tender when pierced with the thin blade of a sharp knife, turning once or twice. Grill the tomatoes for 8 to 10 minutes or until lightly browned on both sides, but still intact, turning once. When they're done, remove the vegetables from the grill and place on a cutting board; cut the asparagus into 1 1/2-inch pieces and place in a bowl. Chop the tomatoes coarsely (their skins will slip off easily and can be discarded) and place in the bowl with the asparagus. Be sure to include any tomato juices from the cutting board. Cover the bowl with foil to keep the vegetables warm.

4 When the asparagus and tomatoes are nearly finished grilling, bring 4 to 5 quarts of lightly salted water to a boil in a large covered pot; add the linguine or fettuccine. Stir thoroughly to separate the strands. Boil, uncovered, for 7 to 8 minutes or just until *al dente,* meaning the pasta still has some "bite" and is not overdone.

5 As the pasta cooks, heat the 1 tablespoon olive oil and butter in a small skillet; add the shallots and garlic and cook over medium heat, stirring occasionally, about 2 minutes or until the vegetables are wilted but not browned. (Be careful not to brown the garlic.)

6 Before draining the pasta, use a measuring cup to carefully scoop out and reserve about 1/4 cup of the water. When it's ready, drain the pasta and return to the large pot.

7 Add the grilled vegetables, the goat cheese, the sautéed shallots and garlic mixture, the basil, and the red pepper flakes (if desired). Toss well over medium heat for just 1 or 2 minutes, until warmed through, adding a little of the reserved cooking water if the dish needs more moisture. Adjust seasoning with additional salt and pepper and serve immediately.

Vary It! *Almost any grilled vegetables can substitute for the asparagus in this dish. Try grilled cubes of eggplant, rounds of zucchini or yellow squash, broccoli or cauliflower florets, mushrooms, carrots, artichoke hearts, or bell peppers. If you don't like goat cheese, substitute 3 ounces each of ricotta cheese and grated Parmesan cheese.*

Per serving: *Calories 683 (From Fat 200); Fat 22g (Saturated 12g); Cholesterol 41mg; Sodium 390mg; Carbohydrate 96g (Dietary Fiber 6g); Protein 28g.*

Belgian endive

When you think of endive, you probably think of elegant summer salads and English teas with watercress sandwiches. Think again. Endive is grillin' food. Its bitterness is mellowed when it's roasted over a charcoal fire. Cut endive heads in half lengthwise and marinate them in a good-quality bottled Italian dressing (or make up your own vinaigrette, using lots of lemon juice, olive oil, and garlic). Grill the endive halves, covered, over medium-high heat for 6 to 8 minutes or until tender, turning once and brushing frequently with marinade. Watch carefully so the endive doesn't blacken or char.

Broccoli

Broccoli florets can be grilled, but they need to be blanched or parboiled before grilling. To do so, trim the broccoli, cutting away the thick stalks to within 1 inch of the crown. (You can freeze the trimmed stalks and later add them to soups and stocks.) Cut the crowns into *florets* (small clusters). Place the florets in a covered pot with 1 inch of lightly salted boiling water; boil for about 3 to 5 minutes or until just crisp-tender. Drain and rinse under cold running water. Place the florets in a medium mixing bowl and cover with bottled salad dressing or your vinaigrette of choice. Grill, covered, on a lightly oiled grid or in a hinged wire basket over medium-high heat for about 8 minutes or until lightly browned. Turn and brush frequently with the marinade. Season with salt and pepper, and then serve hot or cold.

Broccoli florets also can be wrapped in heavy-duty aluminum foil with other vegetables that require the same amount of cooking time. For example, try pairing broccoli florets with cauliflower florets, sliced onion, bell pepper chunks, green beans, small cubes of potato, and rounds of zucchini and yellow squash. Add seasonings, butter or oil, and a little liquid such as broth or lemon juice to the foil packet; grill alongside other foods over direct heat. Open the packet carefully to check for doneness.

Brussels sprouts

The robust, cabbagelike flavor of Brussels sprouts stand up to the smoky flavors of the grill. Before grilling, parboil trimmed sprouts for about 7 minutes in lightly salted water. Drain and brush with olive oil or lemon butter and grill on skewers or in a hinged wire basket over medium-high heat for about 12 minutes, turning often and brushing with butter or oil.

Carrots

Grilling carrots brings out their natural sweetness. Cut carrots into 2- to 3-inch pieces, brush with oil, and then grill directly over medium-hot coals for about 20 minutes, until tender, turning as necessary to brown on all sides. You also can first parboil in 1/2 to 1 inch of water for about 10 minutes; drain well and brush lightly with melted butter or oil before grilling for 10 to 15 minutes or until tender.

Toss grilled carrots in a mixture of equal parts melted butter and brown sugar. Season with salt and pepper to taste. If desired, add a little Grand Marnier or other orange liqueur, or try a little powdered ginger and crushed garlic. You also can wrap sliced carrots in heavy-duty foil with butter and seasonings and grill them (without parboiling first) over medium-high heat until crisp-tender.

Corn

Grilled corn on the cob is the classic summer side dish. Some recipes call for soaking the husks first in water for 30 minutes to prevent scorching. However, we find this extra step to be unnecessary.

When you're shopping for corn for the grill, always buy the freshest ears that you can find. As soon as corn is picked, its sugar begins to convert to starch, reducing its sweetness. Look for corn that's sold as fresh-picked or is at least kept cold to slow down the sugar to starch conversion. The green husks should look bright and fresh, and if pierced with a fingernail, the kernels should squirt out a milky-white liquid.

To get started grilling, strip off 5 to 6 of the outer dark green corn husks. Carefully peel back the remaining husks, leaving them attached at the base of the ear, and remove the silky threads. Pull the husks back up and wrap them securely in place, using kitchen twine or a thin strip of husk. Place the ears on an oiled grid, over medium heat, and grill for 10 to 15 minutes, turning every 5 minutes. Peek beyond the husks at the kernels to determine doneness; the kernels should be golden yellow. When the corn is cooked, remove the husks, brush the ears with melted butter (about 1 tablespoon per ear), and season with salt and pepper to taste. Place the corn back on the grid (this time without the husks) and grill for 5 minutes more or until the corn is very lightly charred on all sides.

You can dress up melted butter for corn in endless ways. Add any of the following (to your taste) to melted butter for corn: lemon or lime juice, chili or curry powder, Tabasco sauce, cayenne pepper, soy sauce, minced garlic, finely minced dill, basil or cilantro, dry mustard, or ground ginger. For a butterless, fat-free, corn-eating experience, simply squeeze fresh lemon or lime juice over freshly grilled ears.

If you want your corn on the cob to be served with other grilled foods, you can grill it in stages. Grill the ears in their husks until the kernels are golden yellow and then remove the ears from the grill. About 5 to 10 minutes before the rest of the food is ready, brush each ear with the melted butter and place back on the grid — without the husks — to finish cooking.

Eggplant

Some people say that eggplant is absolutely best when grilled, and boy, do we agree. Eggplant is a firm-textured vegetable that can be cut into large chunks for kebabs, sliced in half lengthwise, or sliced into rounds before grilling. Sautéing eggplant on the top of the stove requires a rich amount of high-calorie oil, but grilled eggplant needs only a thin coating of oil. If the eggplant is large and bitter, try reducing the bitterness by sprinkling the cut rounds with salt and allowing them to drain for about 30 minutes. Before grilling, rinse the slices or wipe off the salt with paper towels. Smaller eggplants and Japanese-style eggplants have little bitterness and don't need this treatment.

To grill, cut the eggplant into 1-inch-thick slices or cubes and brush with a flavored oil. (See Chapter 5 for ideas on flavored oils.) Grill the pieces over a medium-hot fire for 10 to 12 minutes, turning every 4 to 5 minutes until lightly browned on all sides. Toss grilled cubes into steaming pasta or mixed green salads. Or use them, along with sun-dried tomatoes and black olives, as a topping for pizza. Small grilled slices can be wrapped around cubes of feta cheese or mozzarella cheese, secured with a toothpick into a roll, and served as an appetizer.

Garlic

Much of the world is obsessed with the incomparable power of garlic when it comes to enhancing grilled foods. Garlic makes just about every grilled food, except perhaps those with sweet flavors, taste better. A whole head of garlic is a cinch to grill and has dozens of delicious uses. Mix it into mayonnaise-based dressings or rub it onto thin, toasted baguette slices with goat cheese and sun-dried tomatoes for a simple appetizer. Add it to salad dressings or to marinated vegetables or whip it with milk and butter into mashed potatoes.

To grill a whole head of garlic (see Figure 16-1), first remove any outer, loose, papery leaves. Slice across the top of the head, removing about 1/4 inch and exposing the ends of the cloves. Drizzle with a bit of olive oil and then wrap in foil. (If desired, tuck sprigs of fresh herbs such as rosemary or thyme between the cloves.) Grill over medium-high heat for 45 minutes or until the cloves are soft and tender, turning occasionally. Squeeze out the roasted cloves. Individual cloves can also be oiled and grilled on a grill topper over medium heat for 6 to 7 minutes per side or until tender.

How to Trim and Grill garlic
Trim one quarter off the top end of the head of garlic.
Pull off the papery, outside layer.
Wrap in foil and drizzle oil over the top and between the cloves.
After grilling, pull off the cloves and squeeze one end to pop out the insides easily.

Figure 16-1: Get great results with grilled garlic.

Leeks

The leek, which looks like a giant scallion, makes a surprisingly good grilled side dish for a sizzling steak or lamb chop. Remove the green tops of the leeks to about 2 inches from the white base. Discard the tops. Slice the leeks in half lengthwise and rinse thoroughly under cold running water. Gently pry apart the layers to clear out any sand or dirt. Drain well. Brush the leeks with olive oil, flavored perhaps with minced garlic and fresh or dried herbs, and sprinkle with salt and pepper; grill, cut side down, over medium-high heat for 7 to 8 minutes. Brush again with some of the oil mixture, and then turn and grill for another 7 to 8 minutes or until tender and lightly browned.

Mushrooms

All mushrooms, whether cultivated or plucked from the wild, can be grilled. Mushrooms should never be soaked in water to clean them. Wipe off any sand or grit with a damp paper towel, or rinse quickly and pat dry thoroughly. Button or white mushrooms are the most common. Before grilling, slice off their stems so they lay flat — very large mushrooms can be halved or quartered before grilling. Set mushrooms directly on the grid over a medium-hot fire or skewer with pieces of fish, meat, or other vegetables. Baste them with an olive oil dressing before and during grilling. Grill about 5 minutes per side or until lightly browned. Overgrilling makes them dry and tough. Remove mushrooms from the grill when you can pierce their centers with a sharp knife or a skewer.

Garlic-Grilled Portobellos

Portobello mushrooms are huge, dark brown, umbrella-shaped mushrooms with meat-like texture and a woodsy taste that's enriched by the subtle smokiness of the grill. They're sold with or without their thick stems. Here's a simple recipe that bastes them with an olive oil, lemon juice, and garlic mixture. They're also delicious grilled and drizzled with Pesto Sauce. (See Chapter 15 for the pesto recipe.)

Preparation time: *15 minutes*

Marinating time: *15 minutes*

Grilling time: *6 to 8 minutes*

Yield: *4 servings*

4 portobello mushrooms, each about 4 to 5 inches in diameter (about 1 pound)

1/3 cup extra-virgin olive oil

3 tablespoons lemon juice (about 1 large lemon)

2 cloves garlic, peeled and minced

Salt and pepper to taste

2 tablespoons minced fresh parsley

1 Prepare a medium-hot fire in a charcoal or gas grill.

2 Clean the portobellos by brushing off any dirt or grit with a damp paper towel. Remove the stems. (You can save them to later flavor soups or stocks.)

3 In a small bowl, combine the oil, lemon juice, and garlic. Brush the caps on both sides with the flavored oil; sprinkle salt and pepper on both sides and let stand for 15 minutes, stem side up.

4 Place the caps on a well-oiled grid, stem side up; grill for 3 to 4 minutes. Turn the caps over and grill for another 3 to 4 minutes or until you can easily pierce them with a sharp knife. (Careful not to burn or overcook the mushrooms; the center should be tender and moist.)

5 Remove the caps to a platter and cut into thick slices. Garnish with parsley.

Go-With: *Serve with grilled hamburgers, steaks, chicken, or fish, or toss them into salad greens.*

Per serving: *Calories 203 (From Fat 162); Fat 18g (Saturated 2g); Cholesterol 0mg; Sodium 155mg; Carbohydrate 8g (Dietary Fiber 2g); Protein 3g.*

Onions

Something about the taste of grilled onions is so appealing. Whether yellow, white, or red, onions have a natural sweetness that's released when they meet the heat of the grill. Yellow or red onions can be peeled and cut into $^{1}/_{2}$-inch-thick rounds, or they can be quartered or halved. Brush the cut surface with any kind of marinade or dressing and grill over a medium-hot fire. Depending on the thickness, rounds need to cook for 5 to 6 minutes per side. Halves or quarters may take 12 to 15 minutes or more. Invariably, the rounds will separate into rings and fall through the grill grid, so we recommend placing the onions in a grilling basket or on a grill topper. (Chapter 2 has the information about these grilling accessories.) Onion pieces are delicious skewered between pieces of beef, pork, or fish.

REMEMBER

Here are some ways to incorporate grilled onions into your meal:

- Grilled red onions can be served as a side dish or as a colorful hamburger topping. Brush $^{3}/_{4}$-inch-thick rounds with olive oil and grill for 5 to 6 minutes per side, until the onions are tender and lightly browned. Before serving, drizzle with a vinaigrette that's flavored with plenty of chopped fresh herbs.

- Small whole onions can be peeled and skewered or placed directly on the grid after being oiled or marinated. Grill for 15 minutes or until tender when pierced with a skewer. Serve with beef roasts (Chapter 11), rack of lamb (Chapter 13), or pork tenderloins (Chapter 12).
- Whole *shallots* look like baby onions and make a lovely garnish for other grilled foods. First, parboil the peeled shallots in boiling water for 2 to 3 minutes and then brush them with oil or a marinade; skewer and grill over medium heat for 10 to 15 minutes, until just tender.
- Green, leafy *scallions* can be successfully grilled with little fuss or preparation and served with grilled steaks, burgers, and chops. Trim off any roots at the base of the white bulb and remove any limp-looking green leaves. Slice off the tops, leaving 3 to 4 inches of green leaves. Brush with oil (flavored, if you want) and grill over medium-hot coals for 8 to 10 minutes, turning frequently to prevent them from charring; when done, the scallions will be lightly browned and tender through the bulb. Serve them whole or cut them diagonally into bite-size lengths. Scallions can also add flavor and decorative color to skewered kebabs of fish, shrimp, or chicken. (See Chapter 8.)

Parsnips

If you want to grill something different, try parsnips. Just like a carrot, a parsnip retains its sweet nutty flavor when grilled. Look for thick parsnips and scrub them clean (without peeling) under cold running water. Slice lengthwise or cut them into round chunks that can be skewered with other root vegetables. Brush them with oil or butter (flavored, if you want) and grill over medium-hot coals for 15 to 20 minutes, basting with additional oil or butter and turning every 7 minutes. (You can parboil them first to reduce the grilling time.) Check for doneness by piercing the thickest part with the tip of a sharp knife or a wooden skewer. Serve with additional melted butter, chopped fresh herbs, and salt and pepper. Parsnips are delicious with roasts, chops, or steaks. A combination of grilled carrots and parsnips, garnished with chopped parsley, looks lovely on a platter of thin beef or pork slices.

Peppers

We can't heap enough praise on grilled peppers. A roasted pepper is a vegetable transformed to a smoky-flavored, velvet-textured delight. Whether red, green, yellow, or orange, roasted peppers can be used in the following ways. Keep in mind that this list is just for starters:

- For a simple, elegant appetizer, wrap roasted pepper strips around whole balls of fresh mozzarella cheese; secure with a toothpick.
- Serve strips as a salad with a balsamic vinegar dressing, black olives, artichoke hearts, and cubes of mozzarella cheese.
- Toss strips into steaming pasta with creamy goat cheese or with grilled sausages, olive oil, garlic, and herbs.
- Place on any kind of beef, pork, fish, sausage, or vegetable sandwich.
- Slice into omelets with grated fontina or mozzarella cheese.
- Place strips on toasted French bread with oil-packed sun-dried tomatoes, fresh garlic, and chopped basil for a hearty appetizer.
- Chop and combine with diced ripe tomatoes, black olives, and capers as a topping for grilled fish fillets and steaks.
- Puree into a smooth sauce and use as a colorful base for whitefish fillets or steaks.

Potatoes

All kinds of white potatoes are appropriate for cooking on the grill. Scrub them without peeling, and then leave them whole or cut them into rounds, ovals, wedges, or chunks before grilling.

Whole baking potatoes can be ember-roasted with or without a foil wrap. Wash and prick the potato with a fork in several places. Oil the skin and place the potato directly into the hot coals for about 40 minutes or until tender and the skin is completely charred. Pierce each potato with a skewer to check doneness. Cut in half and add butter, salt, and pepper. Don't eat the skin though! To enjoy the skin of an ember-roasted potato, wrap raw, oil-brushed potatoes in heavy-duty or double-thick aluminum foil and nestle in the hot coals. Cook until tender.

Individually foil-wrapped Idaho or other baking potatoes can also be placed directly above a medium-hot fire and cooked, covered, alongside a roast if desired, for 30 to 35 minutes or until tender, turning every 15 minutes. When they're tender, remove the foil, brush the skins lightly with oil, and place the potatoes back on the grill grid for 10 minutes or until the skins are crisp, turning once. The potatoes are done when they can be easily pierced with the thin blade of a sharp knife, a skewer, or the tines of a fork.

Grilled New Potato Salad with Fresh Mint

Small red potatoes, or *new potatoes,* as they are also called, are wonderful when skewered or randomly scattered on the grill to cook until browned and fork-tender. This recipe tosses them, after grilling, in a garlicky olive oil and mint dressing. To see this tasty side dish, check out the color photo section of this book.

Preparation time: *20 minutes*

Grilling time: *15 to 20 minutes*

Yield: *4 to 6 servings*

3 pounds new potatoes

2 tablespoons olive oil for coating the potatoes

1/4 cup olive oil

1/2 cup chopped fresh mint or basil leaves

3 to 4 cloves garlic, peeled and finely minced

Kosher or table salt to taste

Pepper to taste

1 Prepare a medium-hot fire in a charcoal or gas grill.

2 Scrub the new potatoes under cold running water and pat dry with paper towels. Cut the potatoes in half and place in a large mixing bowl. Drizzle olive oil over the potatoes and toss with a spoon to coat on all sides (use more than 2 tablespoons, if necessary).

3 Place the potatoes on a lightly oiled grid or in an oiled, hinged wire basket or grill topper (see Chapter 2); cover and grill for 15 to 20 minutes or until the potatoes are lightly browned on all sides and tender when pierced with the thin blade of a sharp knife. Turn as necessary to prevent the potatoes from charring.

4 Meanwhile, combine the 1/4 cup olive oil, mint or basil, and garlic in a serving bowl. Transfer the grilled potatoes to the serving bowl with the dressing; toss to coat, and season with salt and pepper. Serve immediately or at room temperature.

Go-With: *This potato salad is delicious with pork, lamb, beef, or chicken.*

Per serving: *Calories 402 (From Fat 186); Fat 21g (Saturated 3g); Cholesterol 0mg; Sodium 156mg; Carbohydrate 45g (Dietary Fiber 7g); Protein 9g.*

Squash

Squash can be split into two types:

- **Hard-shelled squash:** Like potatoes, hard-shelled squash can be ember-cooked directly in the coals, with or without a foil wrapping. Be sure to oil the skins well before placing them in the coals, however. Depending on size, they need to grill for 40 to 60 minutes or until fork tender. Butternut, a pear-shaped squash with deep orange flesh, can be cut into rounds or cubes for kebabs. If you're in a hurry, parboil the slices, cubes, or halves with or without the skin; brush them with oil and grill over a medium-hot fire for 15 minutes or until tender.

- **Summer squash:** Summer squash, like zucchini, yellow squash, crooknecks, and pattypans, are great candidates for the grill. They require no peeling and are delicious when marinated, basted with a flavored oil, or even stuffed. Grilled rounds can be tossed into omelets, salads, or steaming pasta or served over couscous. Smaller vegetables are preferable because they have tender skin, few seeds, and fresh (some might even say sweet) flavor.

  Cut zucchini and yellow squash into rounds or cubes for kebabs, or slice lengthwise into 1/2-inch-thick strips. Grill over a medium to medium-hot fire for 10 to 12 minutes or until lightly browned on both sides.

Stuffed Summer Squash

This delicious recipe stuffs summer squash with a mixture of cornbread, red peppers, and thyme. You can use your own cornbread recipe or a commercial mix, or you can buy corn muffins and break them apart into crumbs. If the cornbread is very moist and fresh, be sure to dry it out for 10 minutes in a 325-degree oven before adding it to the other stuffing ingredients. These stuffed squash make lovely side dishes for any grilled meat, fish, or poultry.

Preparation time: *25 minutes*

Grilling time: *20 to 30 minutes*

Yield: *4 servings*

4 medium zucchini or summer squash or a combination of both, each about 8 to 10 ounces

1/4 cup olive oil, divided

1/3 cup peeled and finely chopped red or yellow onion

1/3 cup finely chopped red bell pepper

1 small jalapeño pepper, seeded and chopped (optional)

2 large cloves garlic, peeled and minced

1 cup crumbled, dried cornbread (see instructions at beginning of recipe)

1 1/2 teaspoons chopped fresh marjoram, or 1/2 teaspoon dried marjoram

1 1/2 teaspoons chopped fresh thyme, or 1/2 teaspoon dried thyme

Salt and pepper to taste

1 1/2 tablespoons butter

1 Slice the squash in half lengthwise. Scoop out the pulp with a teaspoon, leaving a shell about 1/4- to 1/3-inch thick. Finely chop the scooped-out squash pulp; set the shells and chopped pulp aside.

2 Prepare a hot, indirect fire in a charcoal or gas grill. (See Chapter 1 for complete directions.)

3 In a small skillet or sauté pan over medium heat, heat 2 tablespoons of the olive oil; add the chopped squash, onion, red pepper, jalapeño pepper (if desired), and garlic. Cook for 5 minutes or until the vegetables are tender, stirring occasionally. Remove from heat and add the cornbread, marjoram, thyme, and salt and pepper; stir to combine.

4 Brush the outsides of the squash shells with the remaining 2 tablespoons oil; sprinkle the inside lightly with salt and place the shells, cut side down, on a lightly oiled grill grid. Grill, uncovered, for 5 minutes or until the shell edges are lightly browned. Remove from the heat.

5 Spoon about 2 tablespoons of the squash mixture into each squash shell, mounding slightly. Dot the stuffing with butter. Place the stuffed squash on the side of the grid opposite the heat; cover the grill and cook for 20 to 25 minutes or until the squash is tender when pierced with the thin blade of a sharp knife. Serve hot or at room temperature.

Vary It! *Add any one of the following to the stuffing mixture:*

- *1/3 cup chopped mushrooms*
- *1/3 cup cooked corn kernels*
- *1/3 cup finely grated Parmesan or Cheddar cheese*
- *1/3 cup finely chopped cooked shrimp or cooked ground sausage*

Per serving: *Calories 280 (From Fat 187); Fat 21g (Saturated 5g); Cholesterol 24mg; Sodium 347mg; Carbohydrate 21g (Dietary Fiber 4g); Protein 5g.*

Sweet potatoes

Delicious, vitamin-A-packed sweet potatoes are superior grilling food. They can be sliced lengthwise into long ovals or wedges, cut crosswise into thin rounds, or cubed and grilled on skewers. You may also place them in a wire grill basket. Brush thin slices or cubes lightly with oil flavored with garlic, salt, and pepper. Grill over medium-hot coals for 15 to 20 minutes until tender. To reduce the grilling time, cook pieces in boiling water until nearly tender, 6 to 8 minutes; then grill an equal amount of time until nicely browned.

Individually wrap whole sweet potatoes in heavy-duty or double-thickness aluminum foil. Pierce the foil several times with a fork and grill for 40 minutes over a medium fire or until soft and tender. Serve with butter, a drizzle of maple syrup or honey, and salt and pepper to taste. Or complement the sweetness of the potato with a squeeze of lemon or lime juice and a pat of butter, forgoing the sweeteners.

Sweet potatoes can also be cooked directly in hot coals rather than over them. Scrub the potatoes clean and oil the skins lightly. Push them down into the coals; cook for 40 minutes or until tender, giving them a quarter turn every 15 minutes. The final result is a potato with completely blackened inedible skin and a fluffy interior. Grilled sweet potatoes are great for a camping trip, and are terrific with pork or turkey dishes.

Grand Marnier Grilled Sweet Potatoes

A splash of Grand Marnier (or other orange liqueur), a little brown sugar, a bit of allspice, and the heat of the grill flavor these wedges of sweet potatoes.

Preparation time: *20 minutes*

Grilling time: *10 to 15 minutes*

Yield: *4 servings*

1½ to 2 pounds sweet potatoes (about 3 medium)

½ cup butter (1 stick)

¼ cup light brown sugar, packed

¼ cup Grand Marnier or other orange liqueur

¾ teaspoon ground allspice

Salt and pepper to taste

1 Prepare a medium-hot fire in a charcoal or gas grill.

2 As the grill preheats, peel the sweet potatoes and cut each into 6 wedges. (To cut them into wedges, slice the potatoes in half lengthwise and then slice each half into thirds.)

3 Place the potatoes in a medium saucepan with lightly salted water to cover. Cover and bring to a boil over high heat. Reduce the heat and simmer for about 5 minutes or until the potatoes are barely tender when pierced with the thin blade of a sharp knife. (Avoid overcooking or they will start to fall apart. You want them to finish cooking on the grill.) Drain immediately in a colander and run cold water over them briefly. Drain again and set aside.

4 In a small saucepan, melt the butter over very low heat; add the brown sugar, Grand Marnier or other liqueur, and allspice. Whisk (or use a fork to stir the mixture) until the sugar is completely dissolved. Immediately remove from the heat and season with salt and pepper. Brush the sauce onto both sides of the sweet potato wedges. Reserve the remaining sauce.

5 Place the wedges on a lightly oiled grid. Grill for 10 to 15 minutes, brushing with the butter mixture and turning to expose each side to the heat of the grill. When done, the potatoes will be fork-tender and lightly charred at their ends and edges. Remove to a serving platter and drizzle with the reserved basting sauce.

Go-With: *Serve these sweet potatoes with pork, chicken, beef, or lamb.*

Per serving: *Calories 370 (From Fat 206); Fat 23g (Saturated 14g); Cholesterol 61mg; Sodium 165mg; Carbohydrate 40g (Dietary Fiber 3g); Protein 2g.*

Tomatoes

Tomatoes, which are plentiful, ripe, and full of flavor in the summer when most of us cook outdoors, are simple to grill. Red, round tomatoes — also known as globe tomatoes — are best when they're cored and sliced in half or into $1/2$-inch-thick rounds. Then simply brush them with oil or butter that's flavored with garlic and chopped herbs. Grill them over a medium-hot fire from 2 to 5 minutes, depending on the thickness, turning once. Overcooking causes the tomatoes to fall apart. Cook only until heated through and very lightly browned. Grilled tomatoes are a fine accompaniment to hamburgers, steaks, and any kind of chop or grilled fish.

Whole cherry and small plum or Roma tomatoes can be skewered and grilled until they're lightly browned and warmed through. Turn them often to keep them from charring. Use square metal skewers to prevent the tomatoes from spinning uncontrollably when being turned. (See Chapter 8 for more tips on skewering.) Combine grilled cherry tomatoes with chopped fresh basil and grated Parmesan or Romano cheese to make a delicious, impromptu sauce for steaming pasta.

REMEMBER

To draw out the most flavor in fresh tomatoes, keep them at room temperature and away from heat and direct sunlight. Refrigerating tomatoes diminishes their taste.

Grilled Tomatoes with Cumin Butter

For an easy, complete meal, combine these grilled tomato slices with burgers, juicy steaks, fish steaks, or kebabs. Change the seasoning any way you wish, substituting other herbs and spices for the cumin. Or simply oil the tomato slices before grilling, and spread with softened goat cheese and chopped fresh basil after grilling.

Preparation time: *10 minutes*

Grilling time: *4 to 6 minutes*

Yield: *4 servings*

$2\frac{1}{2}$ tablespoons butter

1 teaspoon ground cumin

Salt and pepper to taste

2 large, firm ripe tomatoes, sliced about $\frac{3}{4}$-inch thick

1 Melt the butter in a small saucepan; remove from heat and stir in the cumin and salt and pepper.

2 Brush the tomato slices on one side with half of the cumin butter. Place them, brushed side down, on a well-oiled grid (or on a grill topper, which is discussed in Chapter 2) and grill for 2 to 3 minutes or until very lightly browned on one side.

3 Brush the tops of the tomatoes with the remaining cumin butter. Turn and grill for 2 to 3 minutes more or until very lightly browned, but not falling apart. If the tomatoes brown too quickly, move them to the edge of the grill to finish cooking.

Per serving: *Calories 84 (From Fat 68); Fat 8g (Saturated 5g); Cholesterol 19mg; Sodium 156mg; Carbohydrate 5g (Dietary Fiber 1g); Protein 1g.*

Not Grilled, but Still Good: Warm and Cozy Sides

When grilling on chilly early-spring or late-fall days (or for you die-hard grillers who shovel through snow to get to the grill), you may want something more comforting than a cool salad with your meal. So in this section, we include some warmer side-dish recipes that go beautifully with the meat and vegetable dishes in Parts III and IV. Make these on your stovetop or in your oven, and let them cook while you head out to the grill.

Couscous with Apples, Onions, and Raisins

Precooked couscous cooks in about 5 minutes and is a pleasant alternative to rice or noodles. Made from the same semolina wheat as pasta, couscous can be dressed up with a variety of seasonings and vegetables. It's exceptionally tasty when cooked in a beef or chicken stock, such as in this recipe. We give this dish a slightly sweetened slant by adding apple, pecans, raisins, and cinnamon. It makes a lovely bed of grain on which to serve the Apple and Tarragon Pork Kebabs in Chapter 8.

Preparation time: *15 minutes*

Cooking time: *5 minutes*

Yield: *5 to 6 servings*

1 tablespoon butter

1 tablespoon olive oil

1 large onion, peeled and finely chopped (about 1 cup)

1 large firm apple (such as Granny Smith or Golden Delicious), peeled, cored, and diced

$\frac{1}{2}$ teaspoon cinnamon

1 10-ounce package precooked couscous (about $1\frac{1}{2}$ cups)

$2\frac{1}{2}$ cups fresh or canned chicken broth, heated to boiling

$\frac{1}{3}$ cup dark raisins

$\frac{1}{4}$ cup chopped fresh cilantro (coriander) or parsley

$\frac{1}{3}$ cup chopped walnuts or pecans (optional)

Salt and pepper to taste

1 Heat the butter and oil in a medium saucepan over medium-high heat. Add the onion and cook, stirring occasionally, until the onion wilts, about 3 to 4 minutes. Stir in the apple and cinnamon and cook for 1 more minute.

2 Add the couscous, boiling chicken broth, and raisins; stir to combine. Cover tightly, remove from heat, and let stand for 5 minutes. Just before serving, stir in the coriander or parsley and the walnuts or pecans (if desired). Season with salt and pepper.

Go-With: *This couscous dish is especially good with grilled pork (Chapter 12), grilled lamb (Chapter 13), or beef kebabs (Chapter 8).*

Per serving: *Calories 188 (From Fat 65); Fat 7g (Saturated 2g); Cholesterol 9mg; Sodium 623mg; Carbohydrate 29g (Dietary Fiber 3g); Protein 3g.*

Middle Eastern Rice

This top-of-the-stove rice casserole is a mix of pleasing flavors — turmeric, cinnamon, pine nuts, and parsley.

Preparation time: *20 minutes*

Cooking time: *25 minutes*

Yield: *4 to 5 servings*

1 tablespoon butter

1½ tablespoons olive oil, divided

3 tablespoons peeled and chopped onion

1 large clove garlic, peeled and minced

1 cup long-grain white rice

1 teaspoon turmeric

1¾ cup chicken broth (heated just to boiling)

¼ cup dark or golden raisins (optional)

1 lemon slice, seeds removed, about ¼-inch thick

¼ teaspoon salt

¼ cup pine nuts

1 large plum tomato or Roma tomato, chopped

3 tablespoons chopped fresh parsley

¼ teaspoon cinnamon

1 In a sauté pan with a heavy bottom or in a casserole designed for stovetop cooking, melt the butter with 1 tablespoon of the oil over medium-low heat. Add the onion and garlic and cook until the vegetables start to soften, about 3 minutes, stirring occasionally.

2 Add the rice and the turmeric to the pan; cook for about 3 minutes over medium heat, stirring occasionally with a wooden spoon. Add the hot broth, raisins (if desired), lemon slice, and salt. Bring to a boil over high heat, stir with a fork, and then reduce the heat to low. Cover and simmer for about 20 minutes or until the rice is cooked and the liquid is evaporated.

3 While the rice cooks, heat a small skillet or fry pan over medium heat; add the pine nuts and toast for 2 to 3 minutes, shaking the skillet and tossing the nuts with a fork to prevent them from browning too fast. Remove them immediately from the skillet when lightly toasted.

4 When the rice is cooked, stir in the toasted pine nuts, tomato, parsley, cinnamon, and the remaining ½ tablespoon olive oil. (Omit the oil if desired.)

Go-With: *Middle Eastern Rice makes an excellent side dish for just about any grilled lamb main course (Chapter 13). You can also serve with grilled chicken (Chapter 14) or beef (Chapter 11).*

Per serving: *Calories 331 (From Fat 131); Fat 15g (Saturated 4g); Cholesterol 10mg; Sodium 588mg; Carbohydrate 44g (Dietary Fiber 2g); Protein 7g.*

Cool and Refreshing Sides

On hot summer days, nothing goes better with grilled food than cool salads. And the perk about salads and other cool sides is that you can prepare them ahead of time, so they're waiting in the fridge when you're finished grilling.

Tomato and Red Onion Salad

This recipe combines some of our favorite fresh veggies available in the summer-time — ripe tomatoes, red onion, and fresh mint — into a salad that's easily tossed together.

Preparation time: *15 minutes*

Yield: *4 servings*

4 medium, ripe tomatoes, finely chopped (about 2 cups)

1 small red onion, peeled and finely chopped (about 1/2 cup)

1/4 cup mixed, chopped fresh mint and parsley

2 tablespoons olive oil

1 tablespoon plus 1 teaspoon balsamic vinegar

Salt and pepper to taste

Combine all the ingredients in a medium bowl and serve. This salad is best made about 30 minutes to 1 hour before serving, but it can be prepared several hours in advance and refrigerated until serving time.

Go-With: *Serve with grilled chicken, fish, beef, or pork.*

Vary It! *To turn this into a delicious cold rice salad, add 2 cups chilled cooked rice and 2 tablespoons pignoli nuts (if desired). Moisten with additional oil and balsamic vinegar and season with more salt and pepper to taste.*

Per serving: *Calories 110 (From Fat 66); Fat 7g (Saturated 1g); Cholesterol 0mg; Sodium 156mg; Carbohydrate 10g (Dietary Fiber 2g); Protein 2g.*

Orange-Ginger Coleslaw

Everybody has a favorite coleslaw recipe, and this is ours. We toss lots of sliced cabbage with fresh ginger, orange sections, carrot, and green pepper, and then we coat it all in a dressing that's both sweet and sour. This salad actually tastes best if allowed to sit in the refrigerator for a few hours (or even a day) before serving, to blend together the flavors.

Preparation time: *25 minutes*

Chilling time: *2 to 3 hours (or overnight)*

Yield: *6 to 8 servings*

2/3 cup mayonnaise

3 tablespoons fresh orange juice

1 tablespoon finely grated orange peel

2 tablespoons cider vinegar

2 teaspoons peeled and freshly grated ginger (optional)

1 1/2 teaspoons sugar

1 large clove garlic, peeled and minced

1/2 teaspoon salt, or to taste

Pepper to taste

1 small head thinly sliced green cabbage (about 8 cups)

2 navel oranges, peeled, cut into bite-size pieces, and well drained

1 large carrot, scraped and coarsely grated

1 medium green pepper, finely diced

1/3 cup minced onion

1 To make the dressing, in a small bowl or measuring cup, combine the mayonnaise, orange juice, orange peel, vinegar, ginger (if desired), sugar, garlic, and salt and pepper.

2 In a large salad or serving bowl, combine the remaining ingredients; pour the dressing over the salad and toss well. Cover and refrigerate for 2 to 3 hours (or overnight) before serving.

Go-With: *This slaw is delicious with grilled burgers (Chapter 7), chicken (Chapter 14), pork (Chapter 12), or beef dishes (Chapter 11).*

Vary It! *Omit the ginger and add 1 to 2 seeded and chopped jalapeño peppers for a hot, peppery slaw.*

Per serving: *Calories 247 (From Fat 180); Fat 20g (Saturated 3g); Cholesterol 15mg; Sodium 359mg; Carbohydrate 17g (Dietary Fiber 4g); Protein 3g.*

Tabbouleh

Tabbouleh — a salad that's usually made with bulgur wheat, tomatoes, parsley, mint, onions, lemon juice, and olive oil — is especially good with lamb and chicken dishes. You can find bulgur in most major supermarkets and health food stores. To make tabbouleh, soak the bulgur in boiling water until soft and plump. (Read the package for soaking directions; they vary.) If you'd rather open a box than make your own from scratch, we recommend the Near East Food Products brand, which is available in any quality supermarket. This company makes a complete line of convenient, whole-grain side dishes that include tabbouleh, couscous, and rice pilaf.

Preparation time: *30 minutes, including soaking the bulgur wheat*

Yield: *4 servings*

1 cup bulgur wheat

1 large, ripe tomato, diced (about 1 cup)

1/2 cup peeled, seeded, and finely chopped cucumber

1/3 cup chopped scallions

1/3 cup finely chopped fresh mint, or 1 tablespoon plus 1 teaspoon dried mint

1/4 cup chopped parsley

1/4 cup extra-virgin olive oil

3 tablespoons fresh lemon juice

Salt and pepper to taste

1 Put the bulgur wheat in a large bowl; cover with at least 1/2 inch boiling water and let stand for 30 minutes or more, until the wheat is swollen and tender. (Read the package directions, because the soaking time can vary from 30 minutes to 2 hours.)

2 Drain the bulgur in a colander over the sink, pressing out as much liquid as possible. Transfer the bulgur to a mixing bowl. Add the tomato, cucumber, scallions, mint, parsley, olive oil, lemon juice, and salt and pepper. Blend well. Cover and chill before serving.

Vary It! *You can add chopped black olives, capers, or carrots, and a clove of pressed garlic. You also can substitute red onion for the scallions.*

Go-With: *Serve with Lemony Fresh Lamb Kebabs or Chicken Tikka (both in Chapter 8), any of the rib recipes (Chapter 9), a grilled steak (Chapter 11), or a simple hamburger (Chapter 7).*

Per serving: *Calories 261 (From Fat 128); Fat 14g (Saturated 2g); Cholesterol 0mg; Sodium 162mg; Carbohydrate 32g (Dietary Fiber 8g); Protein 5g.*

Macaroni Salad with Sun-Dried Tomato Mayonnaise

This macaroni salad isn't your usual blend of cold pasta coated with mayonnaise. Instead, we jazz it up with two salty-savory ingredients — sun-dried tomatoes and black olives — and add chopped fresh basil and lemon juice to give it a Mediterranean taste.

Preparation time: *20 minutes*

Yield: *4 to 6 servings*

1/2 pound elbow macaroni

3/4 cup mayonnaise

3 tablespoons oil-packed sun-dried tomatoes, drained and finely chopped

2 tablespoons chopped fresh basil leaves

2 teaspoons fresh lemon juice

1/3 cup peeled and diced onion

1 cup chopped celery

1/4 cup chopped pitted ripe olives

Salt and black pepper to taste

1 Cook the macaroni in a large pot of boiling, salted water for 7 to 8 minutes, until tender but still firm. Turn into a colander and rinse under cold water. Drain well.

2 In a large serving bowl, mix together the mayonnaise, sun-dried tomatoes, basil, lemon juice, and onion. Add the cooked macaroni and toss to coat. Gently fold in the celery and olives. Adjust seasoning with salt and pepper. Cover and refrigerate for at least 1 hour before serving.

Go-With: *This salad is delicious with grilled chicken (Chapter 14), beef (Chapter 11), or fish (Chapter 15).*

Per serving: *Calories 547 (From Fat 329); Fat 37g (Saturated 6g); Cholesterol 24mg; Sodium 383mg; Carbohydrate 48g (Dietary Fiber 3g); Protein 9g.*

Yogurt Cucumber Salad

Made with yogurt, chopped cucumbers, and mint, this salad is guaranteed to refresh you on a hot summer day. Salads with yogurt dressings have a natural affinity for lamb and also for dishes with lots of spicy seasoning.

Preparation time: *20 minutes*

Yield: *4 servings*

1 large cucumber, peeled, seeded, and finely chopped (about 2 cups)

1 small red onion, peeled and finely chopped (about 1/2 cup)

1/4 cup plain yogurt

1/4 cup mayonnaise

2 tablespoons chopped fresh mint

2 teaspoons white wine vinegar

1/2 teaspoon sugar

Pinch of salt

Pepper to taste

In a medium mixing bowl, combine all the ingredients well; cover and refrigerate for at least 1 hour, or until serving time.

Go-With: *Serve with grilled chicken (Chapter 14), fish (Chapter 15), or lamb (Chapter 13).*

Per serving: *Calories 128 (From Fat 108); Fat 11g (Saturated 2g); Cholesterol 9mg; Sodium 127mg; Carbohydrate 6g (Dietary Fiber 1g); Protein 2g.*

Chapter 17

Grill to Go: Sandwiches, Pizzas, and Other Finger Foods

In This Chapter

- Getting to know grilled pizza
- Introducing the best toast ever: bruschetta
- Grilling fajitas and quesadillas in style
- Experimenting with grilled sandwiches

Recipes in This Chapter

- Sun-Dried Tomato and Mozzarella Cheese Pizza
- Tomato Bruschetta
- Best-Ever Fajitas
- Mango and Cheese Quesadillas
- Tortilla Towers
- Open-Faced Grilled Eggplant and Goat Cheese Sandwiches
- Gorgonzola and Fig Sandwiches

The idea of grilling sandwiches of any kind is of rather recent origin — which leads us to ask, "What took so long?" In this chapter, you find out how to make crusty pizzas that invite people to join in the cooking process. You also discover how to prepare an easy alternative to pizza, called *bruschetta,* and, finally, how to make quesadillas, fajitas, and open-faced sandwiches — all on the grill.

Giving Pizza the Third Degree

Pizzas fresh off the grill can be a complete meal or a light appetizer. Your kids are sure to love them, and they're a nice change from all those hot dog dinners!

Play dough perfect

On your first try making dough, you may feel like you've got the starring role in an *I Love Lucy* episode. We provide some tips on making pizza dough, but the best advice is to practice. By the second or third try, you'll have the process down cold and be ready to invite the neighbors over for a very impressive pizza party. Here are the tips:

- Be sure to work on a well-floured surface and to flour the rolling pin as well (if you use a pin to shape the dough).
- Shape the pie as evenly and thinly as possible but not so thinly that holes appear in the dough. Some people like a crust that's less than $^1/_4$-inch thick; others prefer it a little thicker. Just remember that when set on the grill, the dough gets firm immediately and also thickens slightly.
- Don't worry about making a perfectly round shape. Free-form shapes are perfectly acceptable. If on the first (or even the 15th!) try your pie comes out looking like the boot of Italy, remember that it's all part of the fun of making pizza.
- Transferring the dough to the grill is the most difficult part. If necessary, slide a long-handled spatula under the dough to gently loosen it from the countertop or work surface. You then can drape the dough over a floured rolling pin and carry it to the grill, supporting any loose, hanging dough with your free hand. Unroll the dough onto the lightly oiled grid and repeat with the second piece. Or shape the dough on a flat, floured cookie sheet; then bring the sheet to the grill and slide the dough onto the grid.
- You aren't working with pie pastry, so you don't have to worry about overworking the dough. If necessary, reshape the dough into a ball and roll it out again.
- Smaller pies are easier to manage. On your first pizza-making attempt, you may want to roll out 3 or 4 individual pies rather than 2 large ones. Small pies make great individual party appetizers.

Can you top this?

Want to have a dinner party without endless fuss and preparation? Invite friends over for grilled pizza. Lay out an assortment of toppings so that guests can design their own individual pies.

Don't worry about using exact measurements. Just don't pile on too much; overloading causes the thin crust to burn before the toppings are hot and cooked through.

As with the beloved hamburger (see Chapter 7), pizza has few topping restrictions; use whatever combinations you like, such as the following:

- Bottled artichoke hearts and grilled eggplant
- Pepperoni slices and mushrooms
- Black olives and capers
- Chopped anchovies or sardines, and roasted red peppers
- Sautéed or grilled peppers and onions

- Chopped cooked and drained spinach, and ground sausage or prosciutto
- Crisp bacon or grilled ham cubes, and bottled artichoke hearts
- Goat cheese and sun-dried tomatoes
- Smoked salmon, chives, and sour cream
- Pesto sauce, bottled salsa, or tomato sauce instead of fresh tomatoes and grated mozzarella cheese
- Grilled eggplant and goat cheese
- Grilled portobello mushrooms and asparagus
- Cooked ground meat, shrimp, scallops, or clams, and chopped fresh tomatoes and basil

Chapter 16 gives you the lowdown on grilling vegetables such as eggplant, onions, peppers, and mushrooms.

Sun-Dried Tomato and Mozzarella Cheese Pizza

This recipe is the real thing — hot and crusty grilled pizza. Even though making pizza dough isn't difficult, it is time-consuming, and we find that very good, ready-to-use, commercial pizza doughs are now sold in the dairy or frozen food section of most supermarkets and in authentic Italian delicatessens. Better yet, many local pizzerias will sell you fresh dough for pennies a pound. If you want to make your own dough, check out *Baking For Dummies* by Emily Nolan (Wiley) for a recipe.

Preparation time: *20 minutes*

Grilling time: *5 minutes*

Yield: *4 to 6 servings*

2 tablespoons plus 2 teaspoons olive oil, divided

2 cups chopped fresh tomatoes

2 large cloves garlic, peeled and minced

1 pound fresh (or frozen and thawed) pizza dough

Olive oil for brushing dough

1 cup shredded mozzarella cheese, packed (about 6 ounces)

1/4 cup chopped oil-packed sun-dried tomatoes, drained

1/4 cup chopped fresh basil

Garlic powder to taste (optional)

Salt and pepper to taste

1 Prepare a medium-low fire in a charcoal or gas grill.

2 In a small saucepan or skillet, heat 2 tablespoons of the olive oil over medium heat. Add the chopped tomatoes and garlic; cook for 1 to 2 minutes or just until the tomatoes are softened, stirring occasionally. Set aside.

3 Working on a well-floured countertop, pastry board, or inverted baking sheet, divide the pizza dough in half. Flatten or use a floured rolling pin to shape each half into free-form rounds, each 9 to 10 inches in diameter and about $\frac{1}{4}$-inch thick. Don't make a lip — the dough should be evenly thick right to the edge of each pie. Generously brush one side of each pizza with oil; place the pizzas, oiled side down, on a lightly oiled grid. (Transferring the dough from the counter to the grid is the toughest part of this recipe. See the "Play dough perfect" section for some help.)

4 Cover and cook until very lightly golden and firm, about 2 to 5 minutes, depending on the heat of the grill. (Don't let the crust get too brown.) Remove from the grill to a large baking sheet. Brush the tops with oil and turn over, grilled side up.

5 Evenly spread the tomato-garlic mixture onto the grilled side of each crust; evenly distribute the mozzarella cheese, sun-dried tomatoes, and basil. Sprinkle each with garlic powder (if desired) and salt and pepper. Drizzle 1 teaspoon olive oil over each pizza.

6 Place the pizzas back on the grill. Cover and grill for 8 to 12 minutes, moving the pizzas to cooler spots if the bottoms get too dark. The pizza is done when the bottom of the crust is lightly browned and the top is hot and bubbly.

Vary It! *You can substitute about $\frac{1}{2}$ cup homemade or bottled pasta or pizza sauce for the sautéed tomatoes and garlic.*

Per serving: *Calories 540 (From Fat 197); Fat 22g (Saturated 8g); Cholesterol 38mg; Sodium 806mg; Carbohydrate 59g (Dietary Fiber 4g); Protein 20g.*

Adding charcoal and hardwood to the mix

For really authentic wood-fired flavor, try grilling the pizzas over a combination of charcoal and hickory or other hardwood chunks. Here's how to prepare the fire by using these fuels together:

1. **Set several large hardwood chunks (don't presoak them) between the charcoal briquettes.**
2. **Ignite the wood chunks and coals together.**
3. **When the coals have burned to a medium-low (or when you can hold your hand above them for 4 to 5 seconds), move the chunks to the outer edges of the coals.**

   If the chunks continue to flame (rather that smolder), spritz them with a little water from a water bottle — not too much that the fire dies out, though.

Refer to Chapter 3 for more on building the perfect grilling fire.

SHOPPING TIP

Oh where, oh where have the hardwood chunks gone?

Finding a source for a variety of hardwood chunks and chips can be anywhere from difficult to downright impossible. Hardware stores and other shops that sell grilling fuels don't always carry hardwood. Fortunately, some producers and packagers of these products now offer mail-order service. Peoples Woods, located in Cumberland, Rhode Island, sells over 25 varieties of hardwood chunks and chips, including flavors like peach, cherry, hickory, oak, sweet birch, and apple. Owner Don Hysko encourages consumers to purchase "fresh-cut" hardwood. It's aged so long that it burns, but not aged so long that it loses its aromatic quality. You can contact Peoples Woods by phone (800-729-5800) or you can visit the company Web site at `www.char-wood.com`. Try searching the Internet for additional hardwood sources.

Bring on the Bruschetta

Bruschetta is a lighter variation of warm garlic bread. In its most basic form, it's a grilled slice of crusty Italian or French bread that's rubbed with fresh garlic and coated with a good-quality olive oil. But that's just the beginning. Italian cooks pile all kinds of toppings onto this tasty morsel, turning bruschetta into more of an open-faced sandwich or hearty snack. Toppings can include chopped fresh tomato and basil, or grilled eggplant and goat cheese, or grilled zucchini and grated Parmesan cheese.

Tomato Bruschetta

Here's a classic recipe for Tomato Bruschetta that requires a minimum of grilling — only the bread slices feel the heat of the grill. You can make the chopped tomato topping ahead of serving time — in fact it's preferable to do so. This recipe makes a terrific appetizer.

Preparation time: *15 minutes*

Grilling time: *4 to 5 minutes*

Marinating time: *30 minutes*

Yield: *6 to 8 appetizer servings*

2 large red ripe tomatoes (about $1\frac{1}{4}$ pounds), cored, seeded, and diced

$\frac{1}{2}$ cup coarsely chopped fresh basil

2 tablespoons peeled and diced red onion (optional)

About $\frac{1}{4}$ cup extra-virgin olive oil, divided

1 clove garlic, peeled and minced

1 teaspoon balsamic or red wine vinegar

Salt and pepper to taste

12 slices crusty French bread, cut diagonally about $\frac{3}{4}$-inch thick

3 cloves garlic, peeled and halved

1 In a small bowl, combine the tomatoes, basil, red onion (if desired), 2 tablespoons of the olive oil, the minced garlic, vinegar, and salt and pepper. Cover and let stand at room temperature for at least 30 minutes but not longer than 2 hours.

2 Prepare a medium fire in a charcoal or gas grill.

3 Place the bread slices on an oiled grid. Grill for 4 to 5 minutes or until the bread is lightly toasted and golden on both sides, turning once.

4 Remove and immediately rub the edges and one side of each slice with a garlic clove half. (Use a half clove for every 2 slices.) Drizzle about $\frac{1}{2}$ teaspoon of olive oil onto the garlic-rubbed side of each slice.

5 Stir the tomato mixture with a large spoon to thoroughly moisten; top each bread slice with about $1\frac{1}{2}$ tablespoons of the tomato mixture. Place on a platter and serve immediately.

Vary It! *Here are some other ways to add flavor to bruschetta: Add chopped black olives or finely chopped prosciutto to the tomato mixture; omit the tomatoes and spread the bread with soft goat cheese or Gorgonzola cheese; or top with pesto or grated Parmesan cheese rather than the tomato mixture. See Chapter 15 for our Pesto Sauce recipe.*

Per serving: *Calories 272 (From Fat 100); Fat 11g (Saturated 2g); Cholesterol 0mg; Sodium 493mg; Carbohydrate 37g (Dietary Fiber 3g); Protein 6g.*

Fixin' Fajitas and Fajita Fixins

Along the Tex-Mex border of the United States, *fajita* (fah-HEE-tah) means "belt" and describes the look of a raw *skirt steak* — the diaphragm muscle of cattle originally used for fajitas.

A skirt steak can weigh from 1 to 2 pounds and is best grilled whole and then sliced into thin juicy strips. Slightly chewy but very tasty, skirt steaks benefit from a long marinating time. You can substitute less expensive flank steak, but, it's thicker and takes a few more minutes to grill.

Even though they aren't difficult to make, fajitas do require a game plan; you need to bring the meat, vegetables, and tortillas to the table all at once and sizzling hot. Mexican restaurants usually present fajitas on cast-iron skillets that retain the food's heat. Home cooks can use their ovens or the edges of the grill to accomplish the same thing. Here are some pointers:

- Grill the vegetables first, and place them in a low oven or move them to the edge of the grill where they will keep warm.
- Foil-wrap and keep the tortillas warm at the edge of the grill until you're ready to assemble the fajitas.
- Prepare the condiments, setting out bowls of sour cream, guacamole, salsa, and chopped cilantro (coriander) on the table, before grilling.
- If you can, have your guests waiting at the table for the meat to arrive hot and sizzling off the grill.

Best-Ever Fajitas

No one knows for sure who created the fajita, but a few stories worth their salt circulate about its origins. Ninfa Laurenza introduced an item similar to fajitas, called tacos al carbon, at her restaurant, Ninfa's, in Houston back in 1973. The creator of the first fajita must marvel today at the ingredients that go into fajitas. We've seen everything from grilled chicken to lobster in fajitas, with only the wheat tortilla as a constant. We still think they're best — and certainly most authentic — when made with skirt steaks, like this recipe.

Preparation time: *25 minutes*

Marinating time: *4 hours or overnight*

Grilling time: *12 to 14 minutes*

Yield: *4 servings*

1¼ to 1½ pounds skirt or flank steak, fat trimmed

1 small onion, peeled and chopped

3 tablespoons vegetable oil

2 tablespoons tequila (optional)

Juice of 2 limes

Grated peel of half a lime (about 1 teaspoon)

1 jalapeño pepper, seeded and diced

2 cloves garlic, peeled and minced

1 teaspoon ground cumin

1 teaspoon paprika

Salt and pepper to taste

2 medium green or red bell peppers

2 medium onions

Vegetable oil for brushing peppers and onions

8 large wheat flour tortillas, each about 8 to 9 inches in diameter

Fresh Tomato Salsa (optional; see Chapter 6)

Sour cream (optional)

Guacamole (optional; see Chapter 6)

1 In a nonreactive dish or a large, resealable plastic bag, combine 1 chopped onion, 3 tablespoons oil, tequila (if desired), lime juice, lime peel, jalapeño pepper, garlic, cumin, paprika, and salt and pepper. Add the steak and turn, coating it in the marinade. Cover the dish or seal the bag, and refrigerate for at least 4 hours or overnight, turning occasionally.

2 Prepare a hot fire in a charcoal or gas grill.

3 Meanwhile, core and seed the green bell peppers and cut each into strips about 1-inch thick. Peel the remaining onion and cut crosswise into $^1/_4$-inch rounds. Brush the vegetables with vegetable oil.

4 Wrap the tortillas in 2 aluminum foil packages of 4 each; set aside.

5 Cook the onions and peppers on a lightly oiled grid. (Better yet, place them in a hinged wire basket or on a grill topper to keep them from falling through the grill grid and to make turning them easier.) Grill, uncovered, for 10 minutes, turning once, until tender and browned. When done, transfer the vegetables to a baking pan, cover with foil, and set on the edge of the grill or in a 300 degree oven to keep warm until ready to serve.

6 Remove the meat from the marinade and drain briefly, reserving the marinade. Place the meat on the center of the grid; grill for 6 to 7 minutes for rare to medium-rare, turning and basting once with the remaining marinade. (Actual cooking time depends on the thickness of the steak and intensity of the heat. Thicker flank steak takes a few minutes longer.) Use a sharp knife to make a small incision in the center of the steak to test doneness. The meat should be browned on the outside and pink and juicy inside. When done, move the steak to a carving board and cover with foil; let rest for a few minutes and then slice thinly across the grain.

7 As the steak grills, place the tortilla foil packages on the edge of the grill for about 5 minutes to warm through, turning once. (Keep warm in foil until ready to serve.)

8 To assemble the fajitas, place a few slices of meat and some of the grilled peppers and onions on each tortilla; top with salsa, sour cream, and guacamole (if desired) before rolling them up.

Per serving: *Calories 509 (From Fat 206); Fat 23g (Saturated 6g); Cholesterol 68mg; Sodium 577mg; Carbohydrate 52g (Dietary Fiber 7g); Protein 35g.*

Let Them Eat Quesadillas

A classic Mexican *quesadilla* (kay-sah-DEE-ah) is a gooey tortilla sandwich filled with a cheese stuffing (*queso* means "cheese" in Spanish) and usually fried in hot oil until crisp and bubbly. Grilling eliminates almost all the calories acquired through pan-frying, with identical results.

Mango and Cheese Quesadillas

This unique twist on the traditional quesadilla yields a wafer-thin, crisp sandwich with a melted cheese filling, the wonderful sweetness of mango, and the zing of jalapeño pepper. You can see these colorful quesadillas in the color photo section of this book.

Preparation time: *20 minutes*

Grilling time: *4 minutes*

Yield: *4 appetizer servings*

4 large wheat tortillas, about 8 to 9 inches in diameter

8 ounces mozzarella, thinly sliced

1 small mango, peeled and sliced in 1/4-inch slices

1/2 to 1 jalapeño pepper, seeded and finely chopped, or 1 to 2 teaspoons jarred chopped hot pepper

1/2 cup cilantro (coriander) or basil, chopped

1/2 teaspoon salt

Oil for brushing quesadillas

1 Prepare a medium fire in a charcoal or gas grill.

2 Brush one side of each tortilla with oil. Place the tortillas on a cookie sheet, oil side down. Distribute half the cheese evenly among the tortillas on only half of each tortilla. Then layer the mango on top of the cheese, followed by the jalapeño pepper and the cilantro or basil. Now add the rest of the cheese. Sprinkle with salt. Fold the unlayered side of the tortilla over the side with the filling to create a half circle.

3 Using a spatula, place the tortillas on the hot grill grid. Cover and grill until the bottoms are lightly browned, about 2 minutes. Using the spatula, carefully flip the tortillas. Cover and grill for about 2 minutes until they're lightly browned and the cheese is melted. Rotate the quesadillas to cooler parts of the grill if they brown too quickly. When they're done, remove them from grill and cut each one into 2 or 3 pie-shaped slices.

Per serving: *Calories 277 (From Fat 126); Fat 14g (Saturated 8g); Cholesterol 44mg; Sodium 675mg; Carbohydrate 30g (Dietary Fiber 3g); Protein 14g.*

Tortilla Towers

If you like quesadillas, you'll love this multilayered version that uses ground meat, barbecue-flavored onions, Monterey Jack cheese, and chopped cilantro. After it's assembled, you grill the pancakelike stack to a crispy finish.

Preparation time: *20 minutes*

Grilling time: *4 to 6 minutes*

Yield: *4 servings*

3/4 pound ground beef

1/2 to 1 jalapeño pepper, seeded and thinly sliced

Salt and pepper to taste

1 tablespoon vegetable oil, plus oil for brushing tortillas

2 medium onions, peeled, cut in half, and thinly sliced

1/2 cup favorite bottled or homemade barbecue sauce

12 6-inch flour tortillas

2 cups grated, loosely packed Monterey Jack cheese

Sour cream (optional)

1/4 cup chopped fresh cilantro (coriander), and extra for garnish

1. Prepare a medium fire in a charcoal or gas grill. In a large heavy skillet or saucepan, cook the meat and jalapeño pepper over high heat until well browned. Use a wooden spoon to break up the ground meat, and stir often. Season with salt and pepper. Use a slotted spoon to transfer the meat mixture to a mixing bowl. Cover the bowl with foil to keep warm.

2. Add 1 tablespoon of oil to the skillet and heat over medium heat. Add the onions; cook, stirring occasionally, until the onions are soft and translucent, 5 to 7 minutes. Add the barbecue sauce and cook for 5 minutes more or until the onions are very tender, stirring and scraping the bottom of the pan often.

3. Brush one side of 4 tortillas with oil and place them, oiled side down, on a large cookie sheet. Spread the barbecued onions evenly over each of the 4 oiled tortillas. Sprinkle 1 cup of the cheese equally over the onions on each tortilla. Sprinkle 1 tablespoon cilantro over the cheese. Cover each of the 4 stacks with another tortilla. Divide and spread the meat mixture over each tortilla. Sprinkle each with the remaining cheese and top the stacks with the remaining 4 tortillas. Brush the tops with oil.

4. Place the layered tortillas on a lightly oiled grid. Cover and grill for 2 to 3 minutes or until the side that's face down on the grill is lightly browned. Using a wide metal spatula, turn each tortilla carefully to avoid spilling out the ingredients, and grill, covered, for another 2 to 3 minutes. Remove the layered tortillas to individual serving plates and cut each into quarters. Serve with a dollop of sour cream (if desired) and a sprinkling of chopped cilantro.

Per serving: *Calories 763 (From Fat 343); Fat 38g (Saturated 17g); Cholesterol 113mg; Sodium 1,216mg; Carbohydrate 62g (Dietary Fiber 4g); Protein 42g.*

Sandwich Face-Off

When you eat a sandwich stuffed with your favorite foods, the experience can range from satisfying to heavenly. Grilling adds another dimension: Both the bread crust and the filling can be infused with smoky, grilled flavors. The sandwich recipes in this section are easy to make on a backyard grill or on a portable hibachi hauled out to the beach.

Several recipes from other chapters can be quickly converted into grilled sandwiches and wraps. For example, use the Cajun-Style Steak Rub (Chapter 5) on thinly cut tender steaks or chicken breasts before grilling, and then sandwich the meat between slices of grilled French or Italian bread. Or turn these dishes into sandwiches:

- Grilled Kielbasa with Creamy Mustard Sauce (Chapter 7) on grilled sourdough or rye bread
- Jerk-Seasoned Chicken Breasts (Chapter 14) on grilled club rolls with shredded lettuce, slices of avocado, and grilled tomato

Open-Faced Grilled Eggplant and Goat Cheese Sandwiches

This healthy-hearty sandwich stacks layers of smoky grilled eggplant, tomatoes, goat cheese, fresh basil, and olives on French bread. Cut into small 3-inch pieces to make lovely appetizers for a summer party.

Preparation time: *20 minutes*

Grilling time: *20 minutes*

Yield: *4 main dish servings or 8 to 10 appetizer servings*

2 small, long eggplants, about 1 pound each

4 medium, ripe tomatoes (about 1 pound total)

1 loaf French bread, about 24 inches long

1/2 cup olive oil, divided

2 large cloves garlic, peeled and pressed or finely minced

Salt and pepper to taste

2 teaspoons balsamic vinegar

4 ounces fresh goat cheese, at room temperature

2 tablespoons chopped fresh basil

Kalamata or other cured black olives (optional)

1 Prepare a medium-hot fire in a charcoal or gas grill.

2 Meanwhile, cut off the eggplant ends. Lay one eggplant on a cutting board and, with a sharp knife, cut off a thin slice lengthwise. Repeat on the opposite side. Discard these slices (they're mostly peel). Slice the remaining eggplant lengthwise into 1/2-inch-thick slices. Repeat with the second eggplant. Core the tomatoes and slice crosswise into 1/2-inch-thick slices. Place the vegetable slices on a large baking sheet. Slice the French bread in half lengthwise and then in half again crosswise, making 4 slices, each about 12 inches long.

3 In a small bowl, combine 6 tablespoons of the olive oil and the garlic. Brush the cut sides of the French bread and both sides of the vegetables with the oil-garlic mixture. Sprinkle the vegetables with salt and pepper.

4 Combine the remaining 2 tablespoons olive oil with the balsamic vinegar; season with salt and pepper and set aside.

5 Place the eggplant on a lightly oiled grid and grill for 6 to 7 minutes per side or until tender and lightly browned; move the eggplant to the edge of the grid to keep it warm. Grill the tomatoes until warmed through, 2 minutes per side. Place the French bread slices on the edges of the grid, cut side down; toast until golden brown, about 2 minutes; transfer, cut side up, to a serving platter or cutting board.

6 Spread the goat cheese on the toasted bread slices, dividing equally. Lay the eggplant and then the tomato on the bread slices, covering the bread completely; drizzle with the oil-vinegar dressing. Garnish with the chopped basil. Cut into main dish or appetizer servings. Serve with kalamata olives (if desired).

Vary It! *Substitute chopped, oil-packed sun-dried tomatoes for the kalamata olives.*

Per serving: *Calories 686 (From Fat 353); Fat 39g (Saturated 10g); Cholesterol 22mg; Sodium 874mg; Carbohydrate 70g (Dietary Fiber 10g); Protein 18g.*

ON THE GRILL

Warming up prebaked breads is a cinch. Here are some ways to do it:

- **Garlic bread:** Slash a loaf of French bread almost through and at 1-inch intervals from end to end. Spread softened butter, flavored with chopped fresh garlic (or garlic salt) and chopped fresh herbs, between the slices. Wrap in aluminum foil and grill for 15 minutes over a medium-hot fire, turning often.
- **Grilled corn or bran muffins:** Slice the muffins in half, spread the cut sides with softened butter, and grill over medium heat until lightly browned.

- **Grilled polenta:** Cut off 1/4- to 1/2-inch thick slices. Oil them lightly on both sides and grill over medium-high heat, uncovered, for 5 minutes per side or until lightly browned and warmed through. Set the slices next to or under a piece of grilled chicken, lamb, or beef. These little grilled polenta rounds can transform a simple dish into something imaginative and elegant.

Gorgonzola and Fig Sandwiches

Gorgonzola is a blue Italian cheese that can be purchased very pungent, fairly mild, or *dolce,* meaning "sweet," which is a balance of both and is much creamier. If you can find *dolce,* by all means use that in this recipe. You should be able to find it at a good Italian grocery. Most domestic Gorgonzola is too salty. If you can't find imported Gorgonzola, a good American blue or French Roquefort will do as well. Check out the color photo section of this book to get a look at the finished sandwiches.

Preparation time: *10 minutes*

Grilling time: *3 to 4 minutes*

Yield: *4 servings*

5 ounces Gorgonzola cheese

8 slices of round Italian loaf bread, cut into 1/2-inch slices

4 to 6 fresh or dried figs, cut into 1/4-inch slices

1 tablespoon balsamic vinegar

Olive oil

1 Prepare a medium fire in a charcoal grill, or heat a gas grill to about 350 degrees.

2 Spread the gorgonzola cheese on four slices of the bread.

3 Pour the balsamic vinegar into a shallow bowl. Dip the fig slices into the balsamic vinegar and distribute them evenly over the gorgonzola bread slices. Cover these slices with the plain bread slices to form a sandwich. Using a pastry brush, coat the sandwiches generously, on both sides, with the olive oil.

4 Using a spatula, place the sandwiches on the heated grid and grill until the bread is lightly browned and the cheese is melted, about 1 1/2 to 2 minutes. Using the spatula, flip the sandwiches and grill for another 1 1/2 to 2 minutes. Serve as a hot appetizer.

Per serving: *Calories 251 (From Fat122); Fat 14g (Saturated 8g); Cholesterol 31mg; Sodium 655mg; Carbohydrate 26g (Dietary Fiber 2g); Protein 10g.*

Chapter 18

Sweets Can Take the Heat, Too (And Cocktails Cool and Refresh)

In This Chapter

- Discovering the thrills of grilling fruit
- Mixing up some great cocktails

Recipes in This Chapter

- Foil-Wrapped Baked Apples
- Grilled Figs and Prosciutto
- Grilled Bananas with Caramel Sauce
- Grilled Pound Cake and Fruit with Brandy Sauce
- Classic Daiquiri
- Mojito Mojo
- Frozen Mango Martini
- Caipirinha
- The Best Bloody Mary Ever

What's a backyard barbecue without some sweetness and — lest we forget — adult drinks to sip throughout the heat of the day? This chapter promises not to leave you — and, in turn, your guests — empty-handed! Read on for tips on grilling fruit, which makes a healthy and delicious complement to savory meats and vegetables as well as a standalone dessert. If you're itching for the alcohol, head straight to the end of the chapter for our favorite, most tantalizing cocktail recipes.

Grilled Fruit? Oh Yeah!

Grilling fruit takes a little more practice than grilling vegetables because the pulpiness of most fruits and the delicacy of their skin can be ruined by a grill that's too hot. Nevertheless, with a little care and imagination, most fruits come off the grill looking very luscious and toothsome — and they're definitely a surprise to most people at an outdoor party!

Don't think of grilled fruit only as a dessert choice, however — they can be dazzling side dishes as well:

- Toss grilled fruit into salads.
- Use grilled fruit as a garnish.

- Combine sweet fruit cubes with savory chunks of vegetable, fish, meat, or poultry on a skewer. For example:
  - Try mixing wedges of oranges with cubes of beef and red onion.
  - Use pineapple wedges with cubes of smoked ham or fresh pork, and bell pepper strips.
  - Combine apple wedges with chicken livers and bacon.
  - Try using plum slices or halves and red onions with cubes of chicken or pork.

Here are some tips for grilling fruit:

- Be sure that the cooking grid is scrubbed completely clean. Leftover pieces of food clinging to the grid can make the delicate-flavored fruits taste like last night's dinner.
- Allow the natural sugar in fruits such as oranges and figs to brown slightly when grilling, to bring out their rich, sweet flavors.
- Brush fruit slices, cubes, or halves with melted butter and brown sugar before grilling over a medium to medium-low fire.
- Brush fruit with the same tangy lemon or balsamic vinegar marinade used for the main dish or salad and serve as a pretty plate garnish with savory grilled foods. Thick orange slices look especially attractive.
- An easy, fat-free basting sauce for any grilled fruit is dry white wine sweetened to taste with honey. For a savory glaze that's nice with pork or poultry, add Dijon-style mustard to taste.
- Half-inch slices or chunks of apples, apricots, bananas, cantaloupe, papaya, peaches, plums, nectarines, pineapple, and pears take about 10 minutes to grill; turn frequently to keep them from burning.

Grilled fruits are enhanced by the bold flavors of brandy, rum, and fruit liqueurs. Impress your guests with this simple dessert: Skewer together assorted fruit chunks (such as slices of plums, nectarines, and peaches) that are brushed with a little melted butter and brown sugar syrup; grill until lightly browned and bring to the table on a warm platter. Pour ¼ cup of warmed brandy, rum, or fruit liqueur over the fruit and ignite the dish. Serve with vanilla or rum raisin ice cream. Ice cream is the best companion to grilled fruits.

Foil-Wrapped Baked Apples

Here's an easy dessert that lets you complete most of the work before you get to the grill. Wrap the cored, nut-and-raisin-stuffed apples in sheets of foil and set them on the back of the grill behind other foods for your meal. If you plan it right, your baked apple dessert will be ready just as you finish the main course.

Be careful not to overcook these apples. Depending on the intensity of your grill's heat, they only need 20 to 25 minutes. Start testing their doneness with a skewer or the tines of a fork after 20 minutes and then every 5 minutes after that. They turn in an instant from cooked through — yet still shaped like an apple — to almost applesauce. Although the more done version is also delicious, it's not nearly as pretty.

Preparation time: *25 minutes*

Grilling time: *20 to 25 minutes*

Yield: *4 servings*

4 tart apples (such as Granny Smith or Macintosh), about 8 ounces each

¼ heaping cup chopped walnuts or pecans

¼ cup light brown sugar, packed

2 heaping tablespoons raisins

1 teaspoon cinnamon

¼ teaspoon ground allspice

2 tablespoons butter

2 tablespoons apple brandy or rum (optional)

Vanilla ice cream or sweetened whipped cream (optional)

1. Prepare a medium fire in a charcoal or gas grill.
2. Core the apples (see Figure 18-1) and place each on a buttered 9-inch square of heavy-duty aluminum foil.
3. In a medium mixing bowl, combine the walnuts or pecans, brown sugar, raisins, cinnamon, and allspice; divide the mixture equally among the apples, packing it into their hollowed centers. Top each apple with a half tablespoon of butter. Fold up the edges of the foil around the apples to make a tight package.
4. Place the foil packages on the grid; grill for 20 to 25 minutes or until the apples are tender when pierced with a fork. (Be careful not to overcook.) Rotate occasionally to different spots on the grid to ensure even cooking.
5. Remove the apples from the grill and foil. If desired, pour ½ tablespoon apple brandy or rum over the top of each and serve with vanilla ice cream or whipped cream sweetened with maple syrup or maple extract and sugar.

Per serving: *Calories 248 (From Fat 100); Fat 11g (Saturated 4g); Cholesterol 15mg; Sodium 8mg; Carbohydrate 40g (Dietary Fiber 5g); Protein 2g.*

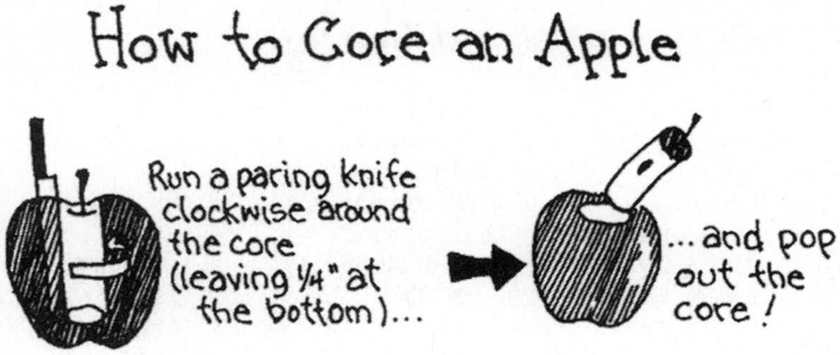
How to Core an Apple
Run a paring knife clockwise around the core (leaving 1/4" at the bottom)...
... and pop out the core!

Figure 18-1: How to easily core an apple.

Grilled Figs and Prosciutto

This dish makes for an impressive appetizer or — without the mustard — an interesting dessert. Thin slices of prosciutto, a salt-cured ham from Italy, are wrapped around fresh figs. The grilled figs caramelize slightly, and the ham loses most of its fat but none of its delicious saltiness. The recipe calls for 4 slices of prosciutto but works with twice that amount for prosciutto lovers. Take a look at the color photo section in this book to see the finished recipe.

Preparation time: *15 minutes*

Grilling time: *5 to 6 minutes*

Yield: *4 servings*

2 tablespoons dry white wine

2 tablespoons honey

1 teaspoon Dijon-style mustard

4 large ripe fresh figs, quartered

4 (or 8, if desired) thin slices prosciutto or other spiced ham

Pepper to taste (optional)

1 Prepare a medium fire in a charcoal or gas grill. If using wooden skewers, soak them in water for 30 minutes to prevent them from burning.

2 In a small saucepan, combine the wine and honey; without allowing the mixture to boil, stir over low heat just until the honey blends with the wine. Remove from heat and stir in the mustard.

3 Thread 4 fig quarters and 1 slice (or 2 slices, if desired) of prosciutto on each of 4 skewers.

4 Brush the figs and prosciutto with the wine-honey basting sauce and sprinkle each with pepper (if desired). Place the skewers on a lightly oiled grid; grill for 5 to 6 minutes, turning often and brushing with the basting sauce. Serve as a light appetizer over mixed salad greens or as a side for grilled duck, turkey, or pork.

Per serving: *Calories 117 (From Fat 19); Fat 2g (Saturated 1g); Cholesterol 13mg; Sodium 306mg; Carbohydrate 21g (Dietary Fiber 2g); Protein 4g.*

Grilled Bananas with Caramel Sauce

A plateful of bananas from the grill is one of our favorite desserts. Because of their natural oils and sweetness, the bananas need surprisingly little or no adornment in the way of fancy sauces or seasonings. In this dessert recipe, we grill bananas right in their skins to shield the soft, sweet, edible fruit from the harsh heat of the grill. After grilling the bananas, drizzle them with a lovely caramel sauce. You also can forgo the rich caramel sauce and serve these bananas unadorned, alongside dishes like satay (Chapter 8) or Jerk-Seasoned Chicken Breasts (Chapter 14).

Preparation time: *20 minutes*

Grilling time: *8 to 10 minutes*

Yield: *4 servings*

1 cup granulated sugar

1/3 cup water

1/2 teaspoon lemon juice

2/3 cup heavy cream

4 medium ripe but firm bananas

1. Prepare a medium fire in a charcoal or gas grill.
2. For the caramel sauce, combine the sugar, water, and lemon juice in a saucepan over medium-low heat. Stir with a wooden spoon for about 3 minutes, until the sugar dissolves.
3. Increase the heat to medium-high and cook, stirring occasionally, until the mixture reaches an amber color, about 3 to 4 minutes. (The mixture boils rather rapidly during these minutes.)
4. If you want a medium-colored caramel sauce, remove the mixture from the heat while it is still light golden; it continues to cook and darken from the heat. For a dark caramel color, remove when the mixture is medium golden-brown. Remove the pan from the heat and gradually pour in the heavy cream, stirring with a wire whisk. (Be careful; the cream bubbles wildly as you pour it into the mixture.)
5. When all the ingredients are incorporated, return the saucepan to medium-low heat and stir for 2 to 3 minutes or until the mixture is velvety. After it cools, the sauce can be reheated in a microwave oven or over low heat on top of the stove.
6. Cut the bananas in half lengthwise without removing the peel; place on a lightly oiled grid, cut side up. Cover and grill for 8 to 10 minutes or until the flesh is warmed and slightly softened; spoon or cut the flesh from the peel.
7. Place the bananas on four individual plates and spoon the hot caramel sauce over the bananas before serving.

Go-With: *The best companion for this dessert is a rich and creamy vanilla ice cream.*

Per serving: *Calories 447 (From Fat 138); Fat 15g (Saturated 9g); Cholesterol 55mg; Sodium 17mg; Carbohydrate 81g (Dietary Fiber 3g); Protein 2g.*

Grilled Pound Cake and Fruit with Brandy Sauce

This dessert, shown in the color photo section of this book, brings together a heavenly combination of foods, sauces, and seasonings — grilled fruit and grilled pound cake, rum, brown sugar, orange peel, and vanilla ice cream. Slice the fruit as if you were preparing it for a pie filling; cut it first in half and then into slices about ½- to 1-inch thick.

Preparation time: *20 minutes*

Marinating time: *30 minutes*

Grilling time: *12 to 14 minutes*

Yield: *4 servings*

2 tablespoons butter

⅓ cup dark rum or fruit-flavored brandy

4 medium nectarines, sliced 1-inch thick

2 large ripe purple plums, sliced ½-inch thick

3 tablespoons brown sugar, packed

Pinch of salt

1 teaspoon grated orange peel

8 slices frozen pound cake, thawed and cut ½-inch thick

1 pint vanilla ice cream or 2 cups sweetened whipped cream

1 In a medium saucepan, melt the butter over very low heat. Add the dark rum or the brandy, the nectarines, and the plums. Sprinkle with the brown sugar and salt; toss to mix well. Cook, covered, over low heat, for 1 minute or just until heated through; remove from heat and sprinkle with the orange peel. Set aside for 30 minutes or longer. (You may prepare the fruit to this point and keep it covered until ready to grill.)

2 Prepare a medium fire in a charcoal or gas grill. Be sure that the grill is thoroughly clean and free of any food particles.

3 Remove the fruit slices from the sauce, reserving the sauce.

4 Grill the fruit slices on a lightly oiled grid, for 7 to 10 minutes or until lightly browned on all sides, turning twice.

5 After the fruit has cooked for 5 minutes, brush both sides of the pound cake slices with the reserved sauce; reserve the remaining sauce. Grill the pound cake for 4 minutes or until it's lightly toasted on both sides, turning once.

6 Transfer the grilled pound cake slices to individual serving plates, two to a plate, and top with grilled fruit slices and a scoop of vanilla ice cream or sweetened whipped cream. Drizzle any remaining brandy sauce over the fruit, cake, and ice cream.

Per serving: *Calories 895 (From Fat 357); Fat 40g (Saturated 22g); Cholesterol 264mg; Sodium 653mg; Carbohydrate 124g (Dietary Fiber 5g); Protein 14g.*

Care for a Cocktail?

When it comes to outdoor cooking and the inevitable parties that surround them, the cocktail hour can become almost as important as the meal itself. What would weekend brunch be without a pitcher of bloody marys? Especially in summer, Latino-influenced cocktails are favored over straight Scotch or bourbon on the rocks, because they usually contain some citrus fruits that are ideal for al fresco parties in warm weather.

In this section, I provide five cocktail recipes that will never go out of style on the patio or anywhere else. If you try all these drinks and want to try some others, check out *Bartending For Dummies* by Ray Foley (Wiley).

Classic Daiquiri

The daiquiri gets its name from the Daiquiri iron mines outside of Santiago, Cuba, where American miners worked after the Spanish-American War. Their chief engineer, Jennings Cox, came up with a cocktail they drank when work was done, using the island's limes, sugar, and rum. Later on, when novelist Ernest Hemingway lived in Havana, and later Key West, he made the drink even more famous by having the bartender make it into one of the first slush drinks ever. This classic drink is shown in the color photo section of this book.

Preparation time: *2 minutes*

Yield: *1 serving*

Juice of 1 freshly squeezed lime (about 3 to 4 tablespoons; not bottled)

1 teaspoon sugar

2 ounces rum (gold rum is best but light rum is fine)

Place lime juice, sugar, and rum into a cocktail shaker and stir to dissolve sugar. Add ice cubes, shake until very cold, strain into a martini glass, and garnish with a slice of lime.

Vary It! *For a frozen daiquiri, follow the previous instructions, except pour the ingredients into a blender with ½ cup of ice and blend at high speed until you have a slushy drink. You can also flavor the beverage with strawberries or bananas.*

Mojito Mojo

The mojito is a cooling, refreshing cocktail with the punch of mint leaves. When mixing this drink, it's important to muddle (push down and twist) the mint at the bottom of the highball glass. Doing so helps to extract the oils and mingle them with the other ingredients. Refer to the color photo section to get a look at this refreshing cocktail.

Preparation time: *2 minutes*

Yield: *1 serving*

Juice of 1 lime (about 1 to 2 tablespoons; reserve the rind)

1 teaspoon sugar

3 sprigs fresh mint

2 ounces light rum

Club soda

In a highball glass, place the lime juice and rind, sugar, and mint and then muddle (push down and twist) for about 20 seconds. Fill the glass with crushed ice, add rum and stir; top off with a dash of club soda. Garnish with a sprig of fresh mint.

Frozen Mango Martini

Martini purists will always drink their favorite cocktail made with nothing but gin and a dash of dry vermouth. But ever since James "007" Bond exchanged the gin for vodka, all bets are off, and you can now choose from plenty of variations. The mango in this recipe goes very nicely with either the gin or vodka martini. You can see this tasty and intensely-colored martini in the color photo section of this book.

Preparation time: *2 minutes*

Yield: *1 serving*

1 ounce Triple Sec

2 ounces vodka or gin

Juice of half a lime

2 ounces mango puree or, if unavailable, mango juice

½ to 1 cup ice

Place all ingredients in a blender with ice and blend until slushy. Pour into martini glasses and garnish with a wedge of mango.

Caipirinha

This very popular Brazilian drink, shown in the color photo section, packs a wallop from the cachaça (pronounced kah-chah-sah) spirits that it's based on. The cachaça spirits are made from sugar cane. It's a good idea to make a pitcher of caipirinha. If you plan to make a pitcher, simply multiply the ingredients by the number of guests you plan to serve.

Preparation time: *2 minutes*

Yield: *1 serving*

1 lime

1 teaspoon sugar

2 ounces cachaça

½ cup crushed ice cubes

Cut the lime into quarters and place in a highball glass with the sugar. Muddle (push down and twist) to release the lime juice and mingle the flavors. Add the cachaça, ice cubes, and stir to mix. Garnish with a lime wedge.

The Best Bloody Mary Ever

The bloody mary actually originated at Harry's New York Bar in Paris during the 1920s when vodka first was brought to the city from Russia. Harry's bartender, Pete Pétiot, brought the cocktail to New York in 1933 to the King Cole Bar at the St. Regis Hotel, where it's still the signature drink. It has become the quintessential brunch drink, usually made in pitchers. The best way to prepare to make a bloody mary is to pour about 2 tablespoons black peppercorns into a bottle of vodka and let sit for two or three weeks, giving the vodka a real bite.

Preparation time: *2 minutes*

Yield: *1 serving*

1½ ounces vodka

2 ounces tomato juice

Juice of half a lemon (about 1½ tablespoons)

2 dashes salt

1 dash black pepper

2 dashes cayenne pepper or Tabasco sauce

3 dashes Worcestershire sauce

½ teaspoon horseradish

Combine all ingredients in a cocktail shaker with ice cubes and shake until very cold. Strain into a highball glass and add a celery stick.

Part V

The Part of Tens

The 5th Wave By Rich Tennant

In this part . . .

In this part, we tell you our ten commandments for grilling success and where to find the best barbecue places in America. If you're happy with all this information, perhaps you'll invite us to come by for some ribs and a glass of wine!

Chapter 19

The Ten Commandments of Grilling

In This Chapter

- Getting some tips before you begin grilling
- Keeping control of fire and food

In this short chapter, we give some general tips that you should always keep in mind for the sake of safety, preparation, and getting the best results. A successful meal takes a lot less time than the process of thinking how to make it come out perfect every time.

Practice Patience with Your Fire

You should never put food on a grill that isn't ready, so be sure to take your time getting the fire going. Be sure that the coals are uniformly ashy gray, and use the handheld test (explained in Chapter 3) to gauge the temperature. And remember that not all foods take well to the same fire or the same temperatures. Check your recipe or your grill manual to find out what temperature you need for each type of food.

Organize Your Grill Space

Set up a small table next to the grill with all your ingredients, utensils, serving platters, and so on. Get your stuff together before you light the grill so that all you have to do is pick up the food, the seasonings, and the plates. Grilling can proceed quickly, and so you have to be ready to serve food when it's at its peak. After all, your burgers won't stop cooking just so you can go grab a clean plate from the kitchen.

Flavor Your Food

Grilling a hamburger, a steak, or some fish on the grill is simple and wonderful all on its own. But to add flavor to the food and seal that flavor in is the mark of a master griller. You can infuse your food with flavor with marinades, oils, and rubs. Marinating, which is a liquid flavor enhancer, adds moisture and is great for almost all foods. Oils are great for keeping delicate foods moist on the grill, and rubs help create a nice crispy crust. In Chapter 5, we provide tons of simple, tasty marinades, oils, and rubs that you can flavor your food with.

Don't Skimp on Fuel

When getting started, be sure to build a fire that won't lose its heat before you finish grilling. This is especially important with a charcoal grill. Even though you can always replenish your coals, it's better to use too many than not enough. Just remember to spread the coals about 2 inches beyond the edges of the food, and if you do replenish the coals, you must wait until they turn ashen gray — usually about 20 minutes — before you get back to your ideal heat.

Police the Fire!

A fire changes constantly and demands your attention at all times. Stay vigilant. At the beginning of the heating process, coals will glow and have a flame above them. When you add food, you'll likely have a small to large flare-up, so it's essential to monitor the cooking closely at that time. If you leave the grill with fire licking the sides of the food, you may come back to a charred meal.

Later on, when the fire has died down, you want to maintain a consistent heat so the food cooks evenly. So replenishing the coals if they start to lose their glow and diminish in size is usually necessary at least once. You may need to replenish more times throughout a long cooking time.

Build a Fire with Different Hot Spots

A fire with different heat areas allows you to shift food around to sear, cook through, and keep warm. If you're using a gas grill, set the burners to different temperatures to provide varying degrees of heat. Or try building an indirect fire in a charcoal grill. Chapter 1 provides tips on grilling indirectly.

Understand the Grilling Variables

Air temperature, wind, grill type, fuel variety, and food temperature (whether or not it has been refrigerated) all affect your grilling times. So you should use recipe cooking times only as rough estimates. As we've noted in many places in this book, a good cooking thermometer is one of the best gadgets you can buy for successful grilling.

REMEMBER

There's no reason you can't grill well into fall and even in winter. (Hey, trappers do it all the time!) Just remember that the heat of the fire is much more variable when the temperature is below, say, 40 degrees and a cold wind is blowing. The wind can also blow the gas burner flames around, so if you have a cover, it's a good idea to use it.

Figure Out When Food Is Done

Unfortunately, overcooked food doesn't have a reverse gear to take it back to rare. And an overdone piece of meat is a crying shame. So be sure to hover over your grill and check the food often. To test for doneness, make a small cut in the center of the food so you can peek inside. Test frequently for doneness a few minutes before the end of the estimated cooking time. Use an instant-read thermometer (see Chapter 2) for thick chops, roasts, and whole poultry.

You should also gauge the searing on the outside of the food. Some folks love a black char and others prefer a light one. However, if you let the fire flare up too much, you may just get a coal-black exterior and a blood-rare interior.

Sprint from the Grill to the Table

Small, thin pieces of food rapidly lose their heat after you take them off the grill. Heated plates are the best way to keep food hot. Aluminum foil is also good to have on hand. But remember that meat has to stand for five minutes or more until the juices settle. So, if you're ready to take the food off the grill, be sure to have your diners ready and waiting at the table for finished platters. Also, be aware that most meats, poultry, and fish will continue to cook inside even after removed from the grill. Meats can sit for 10 minutes before they're at their best temperature and succulence. Chapter 21 provides more tips for cooking for a crowd.

Relax!

Grilling is carefree cooking. Enjoy the live fire, the fresh air, the cool drink at your side, and the friends and family members who gather around to admire your burger-flipping techniques. Just don't get distracted or stray too far from that grill! Within seconds, you can have a disastrous, overcooked, charred mess. And we guarantee you won't be relaxed then.

Chapter 20

Ten of Our Favorite Barbecue Joints

In This Chapter

- Snooping out good barbecue
- Highlighting the best eateries

The key ingredient to a true barbecue joint is long, slow grilling and smoking over hardwood — with no precooking or shortcuts. Marinades, basting sauces, and dry spices can make some difference, but in the end, the talent, skill, and, more often than not, the secret ingredient of the pitmaster make one mess of ribs or beef better than the barbecue from the place down the street.

Choosing a top ten is very tough for us, but here are our picks for the top ten barbecue places in the U.S.A. We've based our selection on regional variety as much as on good taste.

Arthur Bryant's

1727 Brooklyn Avenue, Kansas City, Missouri;
phone: 816-231-1123; Web site: `www.arthurbryantsbbq.com`

Immortalized by author Calvin Trillin as one of the best restaurants in the world, Bryant's is indeed one of the great barbecue legends. Although Mr. Bryant has gone on to that big smokehouse in the sky, his legacy has been maintained, and the lusciousness of his ribs, french fries, and iced beer lives on. The sauce still has a flavor that no one has ever pinned down, but the place is a lot cleaner than it used to be in the old days.

Charlie Vergos' Rendezvous

52 S. Second Street, Memphis, Tennessee;
phone: 901-523-2746; Web site: `www.hogsfly.com`

Although open only for dinner, dinner in Memphis begins at 4:30 p.m., and the Rendezvous is packed by 6 p.m. You'll get some dissenters who think that Charlie has gone commercial, but we find his unique, dry-rubbed, unsauced ribs absolutely addictive. The place, which is right across from the posh Peabody Hotel, has been open since 1948, and you could write a social and business history of the South from the calling cards and newspapers pinned to the wall here. After you've eaten at the Rendezvous, you may also want to order from Charlie's mail-order catalog, which is what his detractors call "going commercial."

Kreuz Market

619 North Colorado (U.S. 183), Lockhart, Texas; phone: 512-398-2361; Web site: `www.kreuzmarket.com`

About halfway between Austin and San Antonio, the little windswept, dusty town of Lockhart is home to one of the most unique beef barbecue places in the country. Kreuz Market has been in this town since 1900, although the market relocated in 1999 to a building that seats 560 people.

Pitmaster Roy Perez has spent more than two decades stoking the huge ovens, cooking the beef brisket until it's smoky and tender, and serving it with nothing more than sauerkraut and white bread — and no sauce! The jalapeño-spiked sausage, the pork chop, and the pork ribs are also good, but this is Texas beef brisket heaven — so much so that *Texas Monthly* gave Kreuz its highest, 5-star rating for great 'cue.

Goode Company Texas Bar-B-Q

5109 Kirby Drive, Houston, Texas; phone: 713-522-2530; Web site: `www.goodecompany.com/goodeRestaurantBBQKirby.aspx`

Curiously enough, Houston isn't teeming with good barbecue places, but Goode Company runs two of the best. The original is set in a no-frills building where you grab a tray, get your food, and head outside into the Houston heat. You take a slug of Lone Star beer, and then tuck into brisket piled high on a po' boy, a leg of smoked turkey, jalapeño-laced pork sausage, a stuffed baked potato, and some jambalaya Texacana. You nurse another beer, wipe your mouth, wash your hands, and then start on the big slab of pecan pie. Finally, you tell yourself you won't eat again until Thursday.

Carson's

612 North Wells Street, Chicago, Illinois;
phone: 312-280-9200; Web site: `www.ribs.com`

Chicagoans are nothing if not fiercely competitive about their sports teams and their barbecue. Carson's, now with four stores, is likely to win more votes for Most Valuable Rib Joint than anywhere else. The River North location is the original and most evocative of Chi-town cool. You start off with some hot, spicy wings, maybe even that Chicago classic Shrimps DeJonghe (baked with sherry, breadcrumbs, and cayenne pepper). Then you dig into a BBQ beef or pork sandwich or a slab of perfectly smoked, luscious baby back ribs. They even do barbecued salmon and chicken (without burning it!), and you can go as upscale as you like here by asking to see the wine list without anyone wincing.

Blue Smoke

116 East 27th Street, New York, New York;
phone: 212-447-7733; Web site: `www.bluesmoke.com`

Only in recent years has New York developed a creditable barbecue scene. (However, we can't forget Sylvia's, a soul food restaurant in Harlem, which has long been known for its wet, well-sauced ribs.) Blue Smoke is the creation of Danny Meyer, a St. Louis native who runs the very upscale restaurants Gramercy Tavern and The Modern. He has put all he has learned about regional American barbecue into this snappy, very popular place (with the Jazz Standard nightclub downstairs). Start off with devilled eggs, and then order the "Rhapsody in 'Cue" — a platter of K.C. ribs, pulled pork, smoked chicken, and sausage.

Lexington Barbecue No. 1

10 Highway 29-70 South, Lexington, North Carolina;
phone: 704-249-9814

You'll hear a lot of argument about which is the best barbecue joint in Lexington, a town that likes to think of itself as the world capital of barbecue. Lexington certainly is the capital of West Carolina-style barbecue. And you won't be disappointed at any of the dozen or more joints in this little town of about a thousand residents. You don't come here for ribs, however. You come for chopped pork on a warm bun, with a vinegary, peppery sauce with a touch of tomato (always made in small batches throughout the day). This sandwich makes Lexington Barbecue No. 1 an essential stop on the 'cue tour.

Sconyers Bar-B-Que

2250 Sconyers Way, Augusta, Georgia;
phone: 706-790-5411; Web site: `www.sconyersbar-b-que.com`

Run by a former mayor of Augusta whose name is honored on his street sign, Sconyers is a maddening place because if you don't happen to be in town from Thursday through Saturday, you ain't gonna eat at Sconyers. The long-time barbecue joint (established in 1956) is closed on Sunday through Wednesday. If you're in town when it's open (and fortunately it opens at 10 a.m. and closes at 10 p.m.) you'll have quintessential, lavishly basted, well-smoked Georgia 'cue — pork hash, T-loin, turkey — with hash-and-rice, potato salad, or cole slaw. Your willpower has no force here.

Sonny Bryan's Smokehouse

2202 Inwood Road, Dallas, Texas;
phone: 214-357-7120; Web site: `www.sonnybryans.com`

The original location (there are newer clones) doesn't look like much, which means it looks just the way you'd imagine a good Texas 'cue stand should. Low-lying, a little scuzzy inside and out, with schoolchildren's desks as tables, Sonny's has been here since 1958 and is a temple of fine barbecue cookery. (Sadly, Sonny is no longer with us.) The ribs are first-rate, but in Texas, the beef brisket is what counts, and Sonny's is fabulous. You line up at the counter, put in your order, and give your initials to the counter help. After a couple minutes, you hear your initials called out, and before you know it, you're in cow heaven.

Ono Hawaiian Foods

726 Kapahulu Avenue, Honolulu, Hawaii;
phone: 808-737-2275; Web site: `www.geocities.com/napavalley/9874`

The Hawaiian word "ono" means "delicious," and while not strictly a BBQ joint, this is one of the best places to try true Hawaiian barbecue. Hawaiian barbecue is known for kahlua pig, which is juicy, very tender, and nice and smoky. Ono Hawaiian Foods is a no-frills place that has been around for four decades under owner Sueko Oh Young, who's now semi-retired at 85 years old. If you visit, we recommend that you try the chicken lau lau steamed in banana leaves, the lomi salmon, and of course, the poi. All of these dishes come on the kahlua pig plate for about $13!

Appendix

Metric Conversion Guide

Note: The recipes in this cookbook were not developed or tested using metric measures. There may be some variation in quality when converting to metric units.

Common Abbreviations

Abbreviation(s)	***What It Stands For***
C, c	cup
g	gram
kg	kilogram
L, l	liter
lb	pound
mL, ml	milliliter
oz	ounce
pt	pint
t, tsp	teaspoon
T, TB, Tbl, Tbsp	tablespoon

Volume

U.S Units	***Canadian Metric***	***Australian Metric***
¼ teaspoon	1 milliliter	1 milliliter
½ teaspoon	2 milliliter	2 milliliter
1 teaspoon	5 milliliter	5 milliliter
1 tablespoon	15 milliliter	20 milliliter
¼ cup	50 milliliter	60 milliliter
⅓ cup	75 milliliter	80 milliliter
½ cup	125 milliliter	125 milliliter

(continued)

Volume *(continued)*

U.S Units	***Canadian Metric***	***Australian Metric***
⅔ cup	150 milliliter	170 milliliter
¾ cup	175 milliliter	190 milliliter
1 cup	250 milliliter	250 milliliter
1 quart	1 liter	1 liter
1½ quarts	1.5 liters	1.5 liters
2 quarts	2 liters	2 liters
2½ quarts	2.5 liters	2.5 liters
3 quarts	3 liters	3 liters
4 quarts	4 liters	4 liters

Weight

U.S. Units	***Canadian Metric***	***Australian Metric***
1 ounce	30 grams	30 grams
2 ounces	55 grams	60 grams
3 ounces	85 grams	90 grams
4 ounces (¼ pound)	115 grams	125 grams
8 ounces (½ pound)	225 grams	225 grams
16 ounces (1 pound)	455 grams	500 grams
1 pound	455 grams	½ kilogram

Measurements

Inches	***Centimeters***
½	1.5
1	2.5
2	5.0
3	7.5
4	10.0
5	12.5

Inches	*Centimeters*
6	15.0
7	17.5
8	20.5
9	23.0
10	25.5
11	28.0
12	30.5
13	33.0

Temperature (Degrees)

Fahrenheit	*Celsius*
32	0
212	100
250	120
275	140
300	150
325	160
350	180
375	190
400	200
425	220
450	230
475	240
500	260

Index

• A •

About.com (Web site), 18
accessories, 28–39
accordion-pleating spare ribs, 176
AccuLevel Tape, 43
alder hardwood, 45
allspice, 66
Almond Butter Sauce recipe, 267
Annual Memphis in May World Championship Barbecue Cooking Contest, 158
apple
  coring, 328
  hardwood, 45
apple cider vinegar, 63
Apple and Tarragon Pork Kebabs recipe, 136
Apricot-Glazed Pork Chops recipe, 207
arranging charcoal, 47
Arthur Bryant's, 341
Artichoke, Mushroom, and Cherry Tomato Kebabs recipe, 130–131
artichokes, 288
ash can, 38–39
ash catcher, 39
Asian spice rubs, 202
Asian Spiced Burger recipe, 117
Asian-Style Salmon Fillets with Vegetables recipe, 272–273
asparagus, 289–290
assessing grill quality, 27
avocado, 121

• B •

baby back ribs, 152
baby lamb, 215
back ribs, 152
bacon strips, 121
balsamic vinegar, 63
barbecue joints, recommended, 341–344
barbecue pit, 13
barbecue sauce, bottled, 58
Barbecue Sauce recipe, 240
Barbecue Wood Flavors Company, 45
Barbecued Onions recipe, 110
barbecuing, 13–14
Barbeques Galore, 28
Bartending For Dummies (Foley), 331
basil, 66, 75, 272, 287
Basil Mayonnaise recipe, 272
baskets, 34
basting
  brush/mop, 29
  defined, 16
  marinades, 77
  sauces, bottled, 58
  wines, 64–65
bay leaf, 75
beef. *See also* burgers; rubs
  Chuck Steaks Marinated in Red Wine recipe, 192–193
  cuts, 184–187
  dry aged, 183
  grading, 182–184
  Grilled Steak 101 recipe, 190
  Grilled Steak Salad recipe, 194
  Grilled Tenderloin Au Poivre with Herb Butter Sauce recipe, 196–197
  grilling, 187, 189
  kebabs, 131–132
  overview, 181–182
  preparing, 187–188
  ribs, 162–164
  roasts, 168, 195–198
  round tip roast, 195
  short ribs, 164
  Texas Beef Barbecue recipe, 191
  wagyu, 185
  wet aged, 183

Belgian endive, 290
Best Bloody Mary Ever recipe, 333
Best-Ever Fajitas recipe, 317–318
Black Bean and Red Pepper Salsa recipe, 103
Blue Smoke, 343
Blue Springs Blazeoff, 158
bockwurst, 122
boneless chuck roast, 196
book
  conventions, 2–3
  icons, 5–6
  organization, 4–5
Boston butt, 200
bottled barbecue sauces, 58
bottled basting sauces, 58
bottled dressings, 58
bottled finishing sauces, 58
bottled goods, 57–59
bottled marinades, 58
Bradley Smoker Inc., 28
bran muffins, 322
bratwurst, 122
brazier, 16, 23
bread
  breakfast, 322–323
  garlic, 322
breast
  chicken, 233–236
  lamb, 216
brine
  defined, 208
  recipes, 209–210, 246
Brined and Grilled Chicken recipe, 246
Brined and Grilled Loin O' Pork recipe, 209–210
The Brinkmann Corporation, 28
briquettes
  ceramic, 16
  charcoal, 16, 43–44
  fire starters, 44
  light-the-bag, 44
brisket, 196
British thermal units (BTUs), 27
broccoli, 290–291
Broilmaster, 28
brown sugar, 75
bruschetta, 315–316
brush, basting/cleaning, 29
Brussels sprouts, 291
BTUs (British thermal units), 27
burgers
  Gorgonzola Hamburgers with Balsamic Onion Relish recipe, 119
  ingredients, 116–117
  Lamb Burger recipe, 120
  meat choices, 116
  overview, 115
  preparing for grill, 117
  toppings, 121–122
  Turkey Burger recipe, 118
butane lighter, 51–52
butter, compound, 110–112
Butterflied Leg of Lamb with Honey-Mustard Dressing recipe, 226–227
butterflying
  defined, 225
  leg of lamb, 225–227

• C •

Caipirinha recipe, 333
Cajun-Style Steak Rub recipe, 86–87
cake tester, 31
canned goods, 57–59
capers, 58
care and maintenance (grill)
  cleaning, 39–40
  oiling grids, 39
  storing, 40
Caribbean Pork Chops recipe, 208
carrots, 291
Carson's, 343
cayenne pepper, 66, 75, 76
ceramic briquettes, 16
cervelat, 123
char-basket fuel holder, 37
Char-Broil, Division of W. C. Bradley, 28
Char Q charcoal grill (Weber), 24
charcoal
  arranging, 47
  direct grilling, 10–11
  gas compared with, 24–26
  indirect grilling, 11
  natural lump, 44–45
  pizzas, 314
  replenishing, 157
  water smoker, 15

charcoal briquettes, 16, 43–44
charcoal chimney starter, 16
charcoal divider, 36–37
charcoal grill
defined, 16, 23
hardwood, 46
Charlie Vergos' Rendezvous, 341–342
cheese, 121
cherry hardwood, 45
Cherry and Pear Chutney recipe, 107
chicken. *See also* rubs
breasts, 233–236
Brined and Grilled Chicken recipe, 246
Chicken Tikka recipe, 142–143
Chicken alla Mattone recipe, 244–245
Dry Poultry Rub for Brined Chicken, 247
free range, 233
FSIS, 232
Grilled Chicken Quarters with Barbecue Sauce recipe, 240
Grilled Lime Chicken with Onion Compote recipe, 241
Jerk-Seasoned Chicken Breasts recipe, 235
kebabs, 141–143
Lemon Chicken Breasts recipe, 234
Lemon-Cilantro Chicken with Garlic-Ginger Mayonnaise recipe, 242–243
Moroccan Chicken Legs and Thighs recipe, 243–244
Orange-Garlic Chicken Wings recipe, 238
overview, 231–232
quartering, 239–243
safe handling and preparation, 233
Spicy Chili Chicken Wings recipe, 237
thighs, 243–244
trussing, 172
whole, 244–247
wings, 236–238
Chicken alla Mattone recipe, 244–245
Chicken Tikka recipe, 142–143
chili powder, 66, 75, 287
chilies, 70–71, 75
chimney starter, 50
Chipotle Salsa recipe, 263
Choice grade (beef), 183–184
chops, pork, 204
chorizo, 122
chuck roast, boneless, 196
Chuck Steaks Marinated in Red Wine recipe, 192–193
chutneys
Cherry and Pear Chutney recipe, 107
fruit, 121
overview, 60, 104
Summer Squash Chutney recipe, 106
Tomato Chutney recipe, 105
cilantro (coriander), 66–67, 75
cinnamon, 67
citrus juice, 71
citrus peel, 71–72, 75
clams, 276, 278–279
Classic Daiquiri recipe, 331
classic yellow mustard, 60
cleaning
brush, 29
grill, 39–40
shrimp, 281
coal grate, 16
cocktails, 331–333
compound butters, 110–111
condiments
Barbecued Onions recipe, 110
Guacamole recipe, 109
overview, 100, 108
Tapenade recipe, 108
types, 59–61
controlling heat, 52–53
conventions in this book, 2–3
cooking time, overview, 18–19
Coriander and Fennel Rub recipe, 89
Coriander and Fennel Rubbed Pork Tenderloin recipe, 214
coring apples, 328
corn, 291–292
corn muffins, 322
corn oil, 75
country of origin (lamb), 216–218
Country-Style Barbecue Sauce recipe, 156
country-style ribs, 152
Couscous with Apples, Onions, and Raisins recipe, 304
covered grills, 11
crabs, soft-shell, 280
cracked pepper marinade, 218
Creamy Asian Peanut Sauce recipe, 97

Creamy Horseradish Sauce recipe, 99
Creole seasoning, 251
Cuban-Style Mojo Marinade recipe, 82
cumin, 67, 76, 286
Curried Pork Tenderloins recipe, 211
curry marinade, 218
curry powder, 67, 76
cuts
  beef, 164, 184–186
  chicken, 239
  fish, 260–274
  lamb, 216
  pork, 199–201
cutting
  beef short ribs, 164
  chickens, 239

• D •

Daiquiri recipe, Classic, 331
Dale Curry's Hickory-Smoked Whole Turkey recipe, 250
D'Artagnan, 253
deboning fish, 274
degreasing, 153
degrees of doneness, 189
delicate foods grid, 34–35
deveining shrimp, 281
Dijon mustard, 60, 75
direct grilling, 9–11, 47
doneness, testing, 339
Donna Myer's Baby Back Ribs with Sweet-Hickory Barbecue Sauce recipe, 158–159
dough, pizza, 311–312
dressings, bottled, 58
drip pan, 16, 36–37
dry aged beef, 183
Dry Poultry Rub for Brined Chicken recipe, 247
dry red/white wine, 64–65
dry smoking, 15
Ducane, 28

• E •

eggplant, 292–293
electric
  charcoal igniter, 48–49
  grill, 16, 24
  water smoker, 15
endive, Belgian, 290
evaluating grill quality, 27

• F •

fajitas
  Best-Ever Fajitas recipe, 317–318
  overview, 316–317
farm-raised game birds, compared with wild game birds, 251–252
features (grill), 27–28
Fiesta, 28
filet mignon, 185
finishing
  marinades, 77
  sauces, bottled, 58
fire
  flare-ups, 17
  hot spots, 339
  safety, 338
fire starters
  briquettes, 44
  defined, 16
  overview, 52
firebox, 17
fish
  cuts, 260–274
  deboning, 274
  fillets, 268–274
  grid, 34–35
  recipes, 263–267
  rotisserie, 169–170
  slashing, 267
  smoked, 274–275
  steaks, 261–265
  whole, 265–267
Five Spice Asian Rub recipe, 88–89
five spice powder, 67

Five Spice and Soy Sauce Marinade recipe, 80
flank steak, 186
flare-ups, 17
flat iron steak, 187
Flatfish Fillets Grilled on Lemon Slices with Mediterranean Skillet Sauce recipe, 269–270
flavored smoke, 14
flavoring
  gas compared with charcoal, 24–25
  with hardwood, 45
  overview, 338
Foil-Wrapped Baked Apples recipe, 327
Foley, Ray (*Bartending For Dummies*), 331
Food, Safety, and Inspection Service (FSIS), 232
forks, 29–30
fortified wine, 65
frankfurter, 122
free-range chickens, 233
freezing sausages, 123
French Provençal rubs, 202
fresh cilantro (coriander), 66–67
fresh gingerroot, 67–68
Fresh Tomato Salsa recipe, 101
Fresh Tomato Sauce recipe, 279
Frozen Mango Martini recipe, 332
fruit chutney
  Chherry and Pear Chutney recipe, 107
fruit, grilled
  Foil-Wrapped Baked Apples recipe, 327
  Grilled Bananas with Caramel Sauce recipe, 329
  Grilled Figs and Prosciutto recipe, 328
  Grilled Pound Cake and Fruit with Brandy Sauce recipe, 330
  overview, 325–326
fruit jams/preserves, 64
fruits, 70–72
FSIS (Food, safety, and Inspection Service), 232
fuel sources
  charcoal briquettes, 43–44
  hardwood chips/chunks, 45–47
  natural lump charcoal, 44–45
  overview, 338
  propane, 42–43

• G •

game birds
  overview, 251
  Rock Cornish Game Hens with Molasses-Rum Marinade recipe, 254
  splitting hens, 255
  varieties, 252–253
  Whole Game Hens with Asian Flavors recipe, 256–257
  wild compared with farm-raised, 251–252
garlic
  bread, 322
  grilling, 293
  leg of lamb, 224
  marinades, 75, 76
  overview, 72
  vegetables, 286, 287
Garlic-Ginger Mayonnaise recipe, 242–243
Garlic-Grilled Portobellos recipe, 294–295
gas grill
  charcoal grill compared with, 24–26
  defined, 17, 22
  indirect grilling, 11–12
  propane, 42–43
  smoking with hardwood in, 46–47
  water smoker, 15
ginger, 68, 75, 76, 286
Ginger Cream recipe, 94
Ginger and Scallion Butter recipe, 112
ginger-soy oil, 84
gingerroot, 67–68
Gingery Grilled Vegetable Marinade recipe, 83
glaze, honey-mustard, 218, 248
glossary of terms, 16–18
Goode Company Texas Bar-B-Q, 342
Gorgonzola and Fig Sandwiches recipe, 323
Gorgonzola Hamburgers with Balsamic Onion Relish recipe, 119
grading beef, 182–184

Grand Marnier Grilled Sweet Potatoes recipe, 301–302
The Great Lenexa Barbecue Battle, 158
Greek Marinade recipe, 82
Greek-style marinade, 202
grid
  defined, 10–11, 17
  oiling, 39, 120–121
  size, 27
grill
  baskets, 17
  cleaning, 39–40
  cover, 30
  features, 27–28
  manufacturers, 28
  preparing, 41–42
  purchasing, 22–28
  storing, 40
  topper, 34–35
  types, 22–26
grill grid. *See* grid
Grilled Bananas and Caramel Sauce recipe, 329
Grilled Chicken Quarters with Barbecue Sauce recipe, 240
Grilled Chops with Orange and Rosemary recipe, 220–221
Grilled Clams and Mussels with Lemon Butter or Fresh Tomato Sauce recipe, 278–279
Grilled Figs and Prosciutto recipe, 328
Grilled Fish Steaks with Avocado and Cilantro Salsa recipe, 264–265
Grilled Italian Links with Caraway Sauerkraut recipe, 126
Grilled Kielbasa with Creamy Mustard Sauce recipe, 125
Grilled Lime Chicken with Onion Compote recipe, 241
Grilled New Potato Salad with Fresh Mint recipe, 298
Grilled Pork Chops with Rosemary Oil recipe, 206
Grilled Pound Cake and Fruit with Brandy Sauce recipe, 330
Grilled Soft-Shell Crabs recipe, 280
Grilled Steak 101 recipe, 190
Grilled Steak Salad recipe, 194
Grilled Swordfish Steak with Chipotle Salsa recipe, 263–264
Grilled Tenderloin Au Poivre with Herb Butter Sauce recipe, 196–197
Grilled Tomatoes with Cumin Butter recipe, 303
Grilled Turkey Tenderloins with Honey-Mustard Glaze recipe, 248–249
grilling
  beef, 187–189
  burgers, 120-121
  chicken breasts, 233–236
  direct, 9–11
  fish steaks, 261-263
  fish fillets, 268-269
  indirect, 11–13
  kebabs, 129
  lamb, 219
  leg of lamb, 225–227
  mitt, 30
  pork, 152–154, 202–204
  sausages and franks, 124
  steaks, 187, 189
  variables, 339
  vegetables, 287-288
ground ginger, 68
grouse, 252
Guacamole recipe, 109
guidelines, 18–19

• H •

habañero pepper, 70
hamburgers
  Gorgonzola Hamburgers with Balsamic Onion Relish recipe, 119
  ingredients, 116–117
  Lamb Burger recipe, 120
  meat choices, 116
  overview, 115
  preparing for grill, 117
  toppings, 121–122
  Turkey Burger recipe, 118
hanger steak, 187
hard-shelled squash, 298–299
hardwood
  flavoring, 45
  including in charcoal grill, 46

pizza, 314–315
smoking in gas grill with, 46–47
hardwood chips/chunks, 45–47
heat
intensity capability, 27
maintaining, 52–53
hens, splitting, 255
Herb Butter Sauce recipe, 197
herbs, 65–69, 75
hibachi, 17, 23
hickory hardwood, 45
Hoisin Marinade and Basting Sauce recipe, 78
hoisin sauce, 58
The Holland Company, 28
Homemade Lemon Butter recipe, 278–279
honey, 64, 75
honey-mustard, 60
honey-mustard glaze, 218, 248
horseradish, 60
hot dogs, 124
hot spots, 339
Hot and Sweet Spice Rub recipe, 86

• I •

icons used in this book, 5–6
igniting
butane lighter, 51–52
chimney starter, 50
electric charcoal igniter, 48–49
overview, 48
indirect grilling
arranging charcoal, 47
overview, 11–13
instant-read thermometer, 32
International Barbecue Society, Tournament of Champions, 158
Italian Burger recipe, 116
Italian sausage, 122

• J •

jalapeño pepper, 70
Jamaican jerk seasoning, 68
Jamaican rubs, 202
jams, fruit, 64
Jerk-Seasoned Chicken Breasts recipe, 235
Jimmy Schmidt's Grilled Barbecued Shrimp recipe, 283–284
Just-Right Pork Ribs recipe, 155–157

• K •

Kansas City strip, 184
kebabs. *See also* satay
Apple and Tarragon Pork Kebabs recipe, 136
Artichoke, Mushroom, and Cherry Tomato Kebabs recipe, 130–131
beef, 131–132
chicken, 141–143
Chicken Tikka recipe, 142–143
grilling, 129
lamb, 138–141
Lamb and Eggplant Kebabs with Tarragon Marinade recipe, 138–139
Lemony Fresh Lamb Kebabs recipe, 140
Mixed Grill Seafood Kebabs with Fresh Lemon Sauce recipe, 144–145
overview, 127
pork, 135–137
Pork Kebabs with Nectarines and Red Onions recipe, 137
seafood, 143–147
skewers, 128
Scallop Kebabs with Pineapple and Bacon recipe, 276-277
Sweet-and-Sour Shrimp Kebabs with Scallions recipe, 146–147
Teriyaki Steak Kebabs recipe, 134–135
vegetables, 129–130
Western Beef Kebabs with Red Peppers and Onions recipe, 132–133
ketchup, 60, 75
kettle grill, 17, 23
kielbasa, Polish, 123
kindling, 51
kitchen, outdoor, 26
knives, 30
knockwurst/knackwurst, 122
Korean Beef Short Ribs recipe, 163
kosher salt, 66, 286
Kreuz Market, 342

• L •

lamb
  Butterflied Leg of Lamb with Honey-Mustard Dressing recipe, 226–227
  country of origin, 216–218
  cuts, 216
  Grilled Chops with Orange and Rosemary recipe, 220–221
  grilling, 219
  kebabs, 138–141
  Lamb Burger recipe, 120
  Lamb Shoulder Chops with Yogurt and Curry Marinade recipe, 222
  mutton, 215
  overview, 215
  Rack of Lamb with Hoisin Marinade recipe, 228–229
  rotisserie, 169
  seasoning, 218
  shoulders, 221–222
  Western Lamb Steaks recipe, 224–225
lamb, baby, 215
Lamb Burger recipe, 120
Lamb and Eggplant Kebabs with Tarragon Marinade recipe, 138–139
Lamb Shoulder Chops with Yogurt and Curry Marinade recipe, 222
lamb, spring, 215
lava rock, 17
leeks, 293–294
leg of lamb
  butterflying, marinating, and grilling, 225–227
  garlic, 224
  grill roasting, 223–224
  grilling steak-style, 224–225
  overview, 216
leg of pork, 200
Lemon-Cilantro Chicken with Garlic-Ginger Mayonnaise recipe, 242–243
Lemon and Fresh Herb Butter recipe, 111
Lemon-Herb Gravy recipe, 173
lemon juice, 71
lemon peel, 71–72, 75, 286
lemon pepper marinade, 218
lemon-rosemary oil, 84
Lemon Sauce recipe, 144
Lemony Chicken Breasts recipe, 234
Lemony Fresh Lamb Kebabs recipe, 140
Lemony Tarragon Pork Chops recipe, 205
Lexington Barbecue No. 1, 343
light-the-bag briquettes, 44
lighter fluid, 51–52
lighting, gas compared with charcoal, 25
Lime and Cumin Marinade recipe, 81
lime juice, 71
lime peel, 71–72, 75
Linguine with Goat Cheese and Grilled Asparagus recipe, 289–290
loin
  lamb, 216
  pork, 200
Louisiana State Barbecue Championship, 158

• M •

Macaroni Salad with Sun-Dried Tomato Mayonnaise recipe, 309
maintaining heat, 52–53
maintenance and care (grill)
  cleaning, 39–40
  oiling grids, 39
  storing, 40
Mango and Cheese Quesadillas recipe, 319
manufacturers (grill), 28
maple hardwood, 45
marinades
  basting, 77
  bottled, 58
  Cuban-Style Mojo Marinade recipe, 82
  defined, 17
  finishing, 77
  Five Spice and Soy Sauce Marinade recipe, 80
  Gingery Grilled Vegetable Marinade recipe, 83
  Greek Marinade recipe, 82
  Hoisin Marinade and Basting Sauce recipe, 78
  ingredients, 74–76
  Lime and Cumin Marinade recipe, 81
  Moroccan Marinade recipe, 81
  overview, 74
  preparation, 76
  Provençal Marinade recipe, 80

safe-handling, 236
Spicy Cinnamon and Soy Marinade recipe, 79
Spicy Soy and Cilantro Marinade recipe, 78–79
sweeteners, 63–64
time, 77
marinating
leg of lamb, 225–227
meat, 188
overview, 19
wines, 64–65
marsala, 65
Masterbuilt, 28
mayonnaise
overview, 58, 103
recipes, 104, 242–243, 272
measurement, metric conversions, 346–347
meat
beef, 131–132, 162–164, 181–198
chicken, 141–143, 172, 231–247
choices for burgers, 116
lamb, 138–141, 169, 215–222, 224–229
marinating, 188
pork, 135–137, 168–169, 199–204, 208, 210–214
rotisserie, 166
thermometer, 167
Mediterranean Skillet Sauce recipe, 270
medium, 189
medium-rare, 189
mesquite hardwood, 45
metal skewers, 128
metric conversions, 345–347
Mexican Burger recipe, 116
Middle Eastern Burger recipe, 116
Middle Eastern Rice recipe, 305
Middle Eastern Rub recipe, 90
Midwest Regional Barbecue Championship, 158
mint, 68
Mixed Grill Seafood Kebabs with Fresh Lemon Sauce recipe, 144–145
Mo Hotta Mo Betta, 70
Mojito Mojo recipe, 332
molasses, 64, 75
mollusks, 276
The Monterey Bay Aquarium Seafood Web Watch (Web site), 260
Mop Sauce recipe, 160
Moroccan Chicken Legs and Thighs recipe, 243–244
Moroccan Marinade recipe, 81
motorized rotisserie, 38
muffins, 322
Mushroom-Butter Sauce recipe, 93
mushrooms, 121, 294–295
mussels, 276, 278–279
mustard
classic yellow, 60
Dijon, 60, 75
honey, 60
overview, 60–61, 75
whole-grain, 61
Mustard and Rosemary Grilled Chicken Sauce recipe, 95
mustard-Worcestershire oil, 84
mutton, 215

• N •

natural lump charcoal, 17, 44–45
newspaper kindling, 51
no roll, 184
nut oils, 62

• O •

oil
corn, 75
ginger-soy, 84
mustard-Worcestershire, 84
nut, 62
olive, 61–62, 75, 287
overview, 19, 61–63
peanut, 75
sesame, 62, 75
types, 84
oiling grill grids, 39, 120–121
olive oil, 61–62, 75, 287
olives, 59
One-Touch Gold charcoal grill (Weber), 23
onions
marinades, 75, 76
overview, 295–296
recipe, 110
red, 72
stocking, 72

Ono Hawaiian Foods, 344
Open-Faced Grilled Eggplant and Goat Cheese Sandwiches recipe, 321–322
Orange-Garlic Chicken Wings recipe, 238
Orange-Ginger Coleslaw recipe, 307
orange juice, 71
orange peel, 71–72, 75
oregano, 68
organization of this book, 4–5
organizing grill space, 337
outdoor kitchen, 26

• P •

pantry helpers
  bottled goods, 57–59
  canned goods, 57–59
  condiments, 59–61
  fruits, 70–72
  herbs, 65–69
  oil, 61–63
  salt, 66
  spices, 70
  sweeteners, 63–64
  vegetables, 70–72
  vinegar, 63
  wines, 64–65
paprika, 68, 76
parboiling, 143, 288
parsley, 68–69, 75
parsnips, 296
partridge, 252
peanut butter, 59
Peanut Dipping Sauce recipe, 149
peanut oil, 75
pecan hardwood, 45
peeling roasted peppers, 93
Penzeys, Ltd., 70
pepper
  cayenne, 66, 75, 76
  habañero, 70
  jalapeño, 70
  overview, 296–297
  peppercorns, 69
  poblano, 70
  red, 66, 75
  roasted, 93
pepper marinade, cracked, 218
Peppery Dried Herb Rub recipe, 87
Peppery Parsley Rub for Tender Steaks recipe, 88
perforated grid, 34–35
pesto sauce, 121, 282
Pesto Shrimp in the Shell recipe, 281–282
pheasant, 253
pickles, 121
Picnic ham, 200
pigs, wild, 201
pizza
  charcoal, 314–315
  dough, 311–312
  hardwood, 314–315
  Sun-Dried Tomato and Mozzarella Cheese Pizza recipe, 313–314
  Tomato Bruschetta recipe, 315–316
  toppings, 312–313
poblano pepper, 70
polenta, 323
Polish kielbasa, 123
Polynesian marinade, 218
pork
  Apricot-Glazed Pork Chops recipe, 207
  brine, 208
  Brined and Grilled Loin O' Pork recipe, 209–210
  Caribbean Pork Chops recipe, 208
  chops, 204
  Coriander and Fennel Rubbed Pork Tenderloin recipe, 214
  Curried Pork Tenderloins recipe, 211
  cuts, 199–201
  Grilled Pork Chops with Rosemary Oil recipe, 206
  grilling, 202–204
  kebabs, 135–137
  Lemony Tarragon Pork Chops recipe, 205
  Pork Kebabs with Nectarines and Red Onions recipe, 137
  rotisserie, 168–169
  rubs, 202
  tenderloin, 210–214
  undercooked, 200
  wild pigs, 201
porterhouse steak, 185
potatoes, 297–298
potatoes (sweet), 300–302
poultry, rotisserie, 169
poussin, 253

preheating, 19
preparing
beef, 187–188
burgers, 117
grill, 41–42
marinades, 76
steaks, 187–188
preserves, fruit, 64
Prime grade (beef), 183
prime rib-eye roast, 195
propane, 42–43
Provençal marinade recipe, 80
purchasing
grills, 22–28
olive oil, 62

• Q •

quail, 253
quartered chickens, 239–243
quesadillas
Mango and Cheese Quesadilla recipe, 319
Tortilla Tower recipe, 320

• R •

rack of lamb, 216, 228–229
Rack of Lamb with Hoisin Marinade recipe, 228–229
rail, 37
Raita recipe, 98
rare, 189
red onions, 72
red pepper, 66, 75
red wine, dry, 64–65, 75
red wine vinegar, 63
replenishing charcoal, 157
rib-eye roast, 195
rib-eye steak, 185
rib rack, 36
Ribfest, 158
ribs. *See also* spare ribs
beef, 162–164
competitions, 158
Donna Myer's Baby Back Ribs with Sweet-Hickory Barbecue Sauce recipe, 158–159
Just-Right Pork Ribs recipe, 155–157
Korean Beef Short Ribs recipe, 163
overview, 151
pork, 152–162
regional, 154
Soul Food Pork Ribs recipe, 160–161
varieties, 152
wrapping, 160
rice vinegar, 63, 75
roast beef, 168, 195–198
Roasted Garlic Butter recipe, 112
Roasted Garlic and Red Pepper Puree recipe, 92
roasted pepper, 93
Roasted Sweet Pepper Salsa recipe, 102
roasting, 17
Rock Cornish game hens
overview, 252
splitting, 255
Rock Cornish Game Hens with Molasses-Rum Marinade recipe, 254
room temperature, 19
rosemary, 69, 75
rotisserie
balancing, 174
beef roasts, 168
best meat, choosing, 166
fish, 169–170
lamb, 169
Lemon-Herb Gravy recipe, 173
motorized, 38
overview, 165–166
pork, 168–169
poultry, 169
roast beef, 168
Rotisserie Boneless Pork Loin with Herbes de Provence recipe, 176–177
Rotisserie-Grilled Chicken recipe, 170–171
Rotisserie Pork Spareribs recipe, 174–175
tips, 166–168
turkey, 169
Rotisserie Boneless Pork Loin with Herbes de Provence recipe, 176–177
Rotisserie-Grilled Chicken recipe, 170–171
Rotisserie Pork Spareribs recipe, 174–175
rotisserie rod, 17
rubs
Cajun-Style Steak Rub recipe, 86–87
Coriander and Fennel Rub recipe, 89
defined, 17

rubs *(continued)*
Dry Poultry Rub for Brined Chicken recipe, 247
Five Spice Asian Rub recipe, 88–89
Hot and Sweet Spice Rub recipe, 86
Middle Eastern Rub recipe, 90
overview, 85, 152–153
Peppery Dried Herb Rub recipe, 87
Peppery Parsley Rub for Tender Steaks recipe, 88
pork, 202

• S •

safe-handling
chicken, 253
marinating, 236
safety, fire, 338
saffron, 69
sake, 65
salami, 123
salsas
Black Bean and Red Pepper Salsa recipe, 103
burger topping, 121
chipotle, 263
Chipotle Salsa recipe, 263
Fresh Tomato Salsa recipe, 101
overview, 61, 101
Roasted Sweet Pepper Salsa recipe, 102
salt, 19, 66, 75, 286
sandwiches
breakfast breads, 322–323
Gorgonzola and Fig Sandwiches recipe, 323
Open-Faced Grilled Eggplant and Goat Cheese Sandwiches recipe, 321–322
overview, 321
satay. *See also* kebabs
defined, 147
Satay with Peanut Dipping Sauce recipe, 148
sauces
bottled basting, 58
pesto, 121
sweeteners, 63–64
sauces, cold
Almond Butter Sauce recipe, 267
Barbecue Sauce recipe, 240
Country-Style Barbecue Sauce recipe, 156
Creamy Horseradish Sauce recipe, 99
Fresh Lemon Sauce recipe, 144
Herb Butter Sauce recipe, 197
overview, 98
Pesto Sauce recipe, 282
Raita recipe, 98
Southern Soul Barbecue Sauce recipe, 162
Sweet-Hickory Barbecue Sauce recipe, 159
Tahini Dressing recipe, 99
Teriyaki Sauce recipe, 100
sauces, warm
Creamy Asian Peanut Sauce recipe, 97
Ginger Cream recipe, 94
Mediterranean Skillet Sauce recipe, 270
Mushroom-Butter Sauce recipe, 93
Mustard and Rosemary Grilled Chicken Sauce recipe, 95
overview, 91
Peanut Dipping Sauce recipe, 149
Roasted Garlic and Red Pepper Puree recipe, 92
Tarragon Sauce recipe, 96
sausages
cooking time, 124
freezing, 123
Grilled Italian Links with Caraway Sauerkraut recipe, 126
Grilled Kielbasa with Creamy Mustard Sauce recipe, 125
hot dogs, 124
overview, 122, 123
toppings, 125
types, 122–123
scallions, 72, 75
Scallop Kebabs with Pineapple and Bacon recipe, 276–277
scallops, 276–277
Sconyers Bar-B-Que, 344
sea salt, 66
seafood
Asian-Style Salmon Fillets with Vegetables recipe, 272–273
availability, 260
clams, 276, 278–279
fillets, 268–274
fish steaks, 261–265

Flatfish Fillets Grilled on Lemon Slices with Mediterranean Skillet Sauce recipe, 269–270
Grilled Clams and Mussels with Lemon Butter or Fresh Tomato Sauce recipe, 278–279
Grilled Fish and Steaks with Avocado and Citrus Salsa recipe, 264–265
Grilled Soft-Shell Crabs recipe, 280
Grilled Swordfish Steak with Chipotle Salsa recipe, 263–264
Jimmy Schmidt's Grilled Barbecued Shrimp recipe, 283–284
kebabs, 143–147
mussels, 276, 278–279
overview, 259
Pesto Shrimp in the Shell recipe, 281–282
Scallop Kebabs with Pineapple and Bacon recipe, 276–277
Seasoned and Breaded Catfish Fillets with Basil Mayonnaise recipe, 271–272
shopping for, 260–263
shrimp, 281–284
smoked fish, 274–275
Smoked Salmon Fillet recipe, 275
soft-shell crabs, 280
whole fish, 265–267
Whole Grilled Trout with Thyme and Almond Butter Sauce recipe, 266–267
Seafood Choices Alliance (Web site), 260
searing
defined, 17, 231
relationship with direct grilling, 10–11
Seasoned and Breaded Catfish Fillets with Basil Mayonnaise recipe, 271–272
seasoning
Creole, 251
lamb, 218
vegetables, 286–287
seeding roasted pepper, 93
Select grade (beef), 184
sesame oil, 62, 75
shallots, 72, 75
shank (lamb), 216
shelf life (oil), 62
sherry, 65, 75
shoulder
lamb, 216
pork, 200
shrimp
cleaning and deveining, 281
count, 143
side burner, 38
sides
Couscous with Apples, Onions, and Raisins recipe, 304
Macaroni Salad with Sun-Dried Tomato Mayonnaise recipe, 309
Middle Eastern Rice recipe, 305
Orange-Ginger Coleslaw recipe, 307
Tabbouleh recipe, 308
Tomato and Red Onion Salad recipe, 306
Yogurt Cucumber Salad recipe, 310
sirloin, 185
sirloin tip, 195
skewers, 30–31, 128
skirt steak, 187
slashing fish, 267
smoke, flavored, 14
smoked fish, 274–275
Smoked Salmon Fillet recipe, 275
smoker box, 18, 37–38, 47
smoking
dry, 15
with hardwood in gas grill, 46–47
overview, 14–15
soft-shell crabs, 280
Sonny Bryan's Smokehouse, 344
Soul Food Pork Ribs recipe, 160–161
Southern Soul Barbecue Sauce recipe, 162
Southwest marinade, 218
Soy-Marinated Pork Tenderloin with Asian-Flavored Vegetables recipe, 212–213
soy sauce, 59, 75
spare ribs. *See also* ribs
accordion-pleating, 176
overview, 152
spatula, 31
speed, 340
Spice Rub recipe, 171
spices, 70
Spicy Chili Butter recipe, 111
Spicy Chili Chicken Wings recipe, 237
Spicy Cinnamon and Soy Marinade recipe, 79
Spicy Soy and Cilantro Marinade recipe, 78–79
splitting Rock Cornish game hens, 255

spring lamb, 215
squab, 253
squash, 298–300
stainless steel insert thermometer, 32
steak-style leg of lamb, 224–225
storing grill, 40
Stuffed Summer Squash recipe, 299–300
sugar, brown, 64, 75
summer squash, 106, 299
Summer Squash Chutney recipe, 106
Summit S-670 gas grill (Weber), 22
Sun-Dried Tomato and Basil Mayonnaise recipe, 104
Sun-Dried Tomato and Mozzarella Cheese Pizza recipe, 313–314
sun-dried tomatoes, 61
Super Bowl of Brisket, 158
Sweet-and-Sour Shrimp Kebabs with Scallions recipe, 146–147
Sweet-Hickory Barbecue Sauce recipe, 159
sweet potatoes, 300–302
sweeteners, 63–64
Szechwan peppercorns, 236

• T •

T-bone, 185
Tabasco sauce, 61, 75, 287
Tabbouleh recipe, 308
table salt, 66
Tahini Dressing recipe, 99
tahini paste, 59
Tapenade recipe, 108
tarragon, 75, 286
Tarragon Sauce recipe, 96
temperature
  capabilities, 25
  gauge, 32
  maintenance, 25
  metric conversions, 347
  room, 19
tenderloin
  beef, 184, 195
  pork, 210–214
  turkey, 248-249
teriyaki marinade, 218
Teriyaki Sauce recipe, 100
Teriyaki Steak Kebabs recipe, 134–135
testing doneness, 339
Texas Beef Barbecue recipe, 191
Texas-style barbecue brush, 29
Thai fish sauce, 59
Thermador, 28
thermometers, 31–32
thighs (chicken), 243–244
thyme, 69, 75
Toasted Cashew and Brandy Butter recipe, 111
Tomato Bruschetta recipe, 315–316
Tomato Chutney recipe, 105
Tomato and Red Onion Salad recipe, 306
tomatoes
  overview, 122, 286, 302–303
  sun-dried, 61
tongs, 33
top loin (strip) steak, 184
toppings
  burgers, 121–122
  pizza, 312–313
  sausages, 125
torch light, 33
Tortilla Towers recipe, 320
transporting grills, 27
tri-tip roast, 195
trichinosis, 200
trussing chicken, 172
turkey
  Creole seasoning, 251
  Dale Curry's Hickory-Smoked Whole Turkey recipe, 250–251
  Grilled Turkey Tenderloins with Honey-Mustard Glaze recipe, 248–249
  overview, 247
  Turkey Burger recipe, 118
  rotisserie, 169
turmeric, 76

• U •

USDA Guide to Grilling and Smoking Food Safely (Web site), 18
utensils
  ash can, 38–39
  baskets, 34
  basting brushes/mops, 29
  charcoal divider, 36–37
  cleaning brush, 29
  drip pan, 36–37

fork, 29–30
grill cover, 30
grill topper, 34–35
grilling mitt, 30
knives, 30
motorized rotisserie, 38
overview, 28–29, 33
rib rack, 36
side burner, 38
skewers, 30–31
smoker box, 37–38
spatula, 31
thermometer/temperature gauge, 31–32
tongs, 33
torch light, 33
vegetable holder, 36
water bottle, 33
work table, 33

• V •

Vanns, 70
vegetable holder, 36
vegetables
artichokes, 288
Asian-Flavored Vegetables recipe, 213
asparagus, 289
Belgian endive, 290
broccoli, 290–291
Brussels sprouts, 291
carrots, 291
corn, 291–292
eggplant, 292–293
garlic, 293
Garlic-Grilled Portobellos recipe, 294–295
Grand Marnier Grilled Sweet Potatoes recipe, 301–302
Grilled New Potato Salad with Fresh Mint recipe, 298
Grilled Tomatoes with Cumin Butter recipe, 303
grilling techniques, 286
kebabs, 129–130
leeks, 293–294
Linguine with Goat Cheese and Grilled Asparagus recipe, 289–290
marinating, 286–287
mushrooms, 294–295
onions, 295–296
overview, 70–72, 285–286
parsnips, 296
peppers, 296–297
potatoes, 297–298
seasoning, 286–287
sides, cold, 306–310
sides, warm, 303–305
squash, 298–300
Stuffed Summer Squash recipe, 299–300
sweet potatoes, 300–302
tips, 287–288
tomatoes, 302–303
Veggie-Stuffed Burger recipe, 117
vent, 18
very rare, 189
very well-done, 189
Viking Range Corporation, 28
vinegar, 63
volume, metric conversions, 345–346

• W •

wagyu beef, 185
water bottle, 33
water smoking, 15
Web sites
About.com, 18
Arthur Bryant's, 341
Barbecue Wood Flavors Company, 45
Barbeques Galore, 28
Blue Smoke, 343
Bradley Smoker Inc., 28
The Brinkmann Corporation, 28
Broilmaster, 28
Carson's, 343
Char-Broil, Division of W.C. Bradley, 28
Charlie Vergos' Rendezvous, 341–342
D'Artagnan, 253
Ducane, 28
Fiesta, 28
Goode Company Texas Bar-B-Q, 342
The Holland Company, 28
Kreuz Market, 342
Lexington Barbecue No. 1, 343
Masterbuilt, 28
Mo Hotta Mo Betta, 70
The Monterey Bay Aquarium Seafood Web Watch, 260
Ono Hawaiian Foods, 344

Web sites *(continued)*
Penzeys, Ltd., 70
Sconyers Bar-B-Que, 244
Seafood Choices Alliance, 260
Sonny Bryan's Smokehouse, 344
Thermador, 28
USDA Guide to Grilling and Smoking Food Safely, 18
Vanns, 70
Viking Range Corporation, 28
Weber, 28
World Wide Weber, 18
Weber One-Touch Gold charcoal grill, 23, 28
Weber Summit S-670 gas grill, 22, 28
Weber's Char Q charcoal grill, 24, 28
weighing propane cylinder, 43
weight, metric conversions, 346
well-done, 189
West Indian rubs, 202
Western Beef Kebabs with Red Peppers and Onions recipe, 132–133
Western Lamb Steaks recipe, 224–225
wet aged beef, 183
wet smoking, 15
white wine, dry, 64–65, 75
white wine vinegar, 63
Whole Game Hens with Asian Flavors recipe, 256–257
whole-grain mustard, 61
Whole Grilled Trout with Thyme and Almond Butter Sauce recipe, 266–267
wild game birds, farm-raised game birds compared with, 251–252
wild pigs, 201
wines
basting, 64–65
fortified, 65
overview, 75
wings (chicken), 236–238
wood chips, 18, 249
wood chunks, 18
wood kindling, 51
wooden skewers, 128
Worcestershire sauce, 59, 75
work table, 33
World Championship Barbecue Cook-Off, 158
World Wide Weber (Web site), 18
wrapping ribs, 160

• Y •

yellow mustard, classic, 60
yellow onions, 72
yogurt, 76
Yogurt Cucumber Salad recipe, 310

INTERNET & DIGITAL MEDIA

AdWords For Dummies
978-0-470-15252-2

Blogging For Dummies, 2nd Edition
978-0-470-23017-6

Digital Photography All-in-One Desk Reference For Dummies, 3rd Edition
978-0-470-03743-0

Digital Photography For Dummies, 5th Edition
978-0-7645-9802-9

Digital SLR Cameras & Photography For Dummies, 2nd Edition
978-0-470-14927-0

eBay Business All-in-One Desk Reference For Dummies
978-0-7645-8438-1

eBay For Dummies, 5th Edition*
978-0-470-04529-9

eBay Listings That Sell For Dummies
978-0-471-78912-3

Facebook For Dummies
978-0-470-26273-3

The Internet For Dummies, 11th Edition
978-0-470-12174-0

Investing Online For Dummies, 5th Edition
978-0-7645-8456-5

iPod & iTunes For Dummies, 5th Edition
978-0-470-17474-6

MySpace For Dummies
978-0-470-09529-4

Podcasting For Dummies
978-0-471-74898-4

Search Engine Optimization For Dummies, 2nd Edition
978-0-471-97998-2

Second Life For Dummies
978-0-470-18025-9

Starting an eBay Business For Dummies, 3rd Edition†
978-0-470-14924-9

GRAPHICS, DESIGN & WEB DEVELOPMENT

Adobe Creative Suite 3 Design Premium All-in-One Desk Reference For Dummies
978-0-470-11724-8

Adobe Web Suite CS3 All-in-One Desk Reference For Dummies
978-0-470-12099-6

AutoCAD 2008 For Dummies
978-0-470-11650-0

Building a Web Site For Dummies, 3rd Edition
978-0-470-14928-7

Creating Web Pages All-in-One Desk Reference For Dummies, 3rd Edition
978-0-470-09629-1

Creating Web Pages For Dummies, 8th Edition
978-0-470-08030-6

Dreamweaver CS3 For Dummies
978-0-470-11490-2

Flash CS3 For Dummies
978-0-470-12100-9

Google SketchUp For Dummies
978-0-470-13744-4

InDesign CS3 For Dummies
978-0-470-11865-8

Photoshop CS3 All-in-One Desk Reference For Dummies
978-0-470-11195-6

Photoshop CS3 For Dummies
978-0-470-11193-2

Photoshop Elements 5 For Dummies
978-0-470-09810-3

SolidWorks For Dummies
978-0-7645-9555-4

Visio 2007 For Dummies
978-0-470-08983-5

Web Design For Dummies, 2nd Edition
978-0-471-78117-2

Web Sites Do-It-Yourself For Dummies
978-0-470-16903-2

Web Stores Do-It-Yourself For Dummies
978-0-470-17443-2

LANGUAGES, RELIGION & SPIRITUALITY

Arabic For Dummies
978-0-471-77270-5

Chinese For Dummies, Audio Set
978-0-470-12766-7

French For Dummies
978-0-7645-5193-2

German For Dummies
978-0-7645-5195-6

Hebrew For Dummies
978-0-7645-5489-6

Ingles Para Dummies
978-0-7645-5427-8

Italian For Dummies, Audio Set
978-0-470-09586-7

Italian Verbs For Dummies
978-0-471-77389-4

Japanese For Dummies
978-0-7645-5429-2

Latin For Dummies
978-0-7645-5431-5

Portuguese For Dummies
978-0-471-78738-9

Russian For Dummies
978-0-471-78001-4

Spanish Phrases For Dummies
978-0-7645-7204-3

Spanish For Dummies
978-0-7645-5194-9

Spanish For Dummies, Audio Set
978-0-470-09585-0

The Bible For Dummies
978-0-7645-5296-0

Catholicism For Dummies
978-0-7645-5391-2

The Historical Jesus For Dummies
978-0-470-16785-4

Islam For Dummies
978-0-7645-5503-9

Spirituality For Dummies, 2nd Edition
978-0-470-19142-2

NETWORKING AND PROGRAMMING

ASP.NET 3.5 For Dummies
978-0-470-19592-5

C# 2008 For Dummies
978-0-470-19109-5

Hacking For Dummies, 2nd Edition
978-0-470-05235-8

Home Networking For Dummies, 4th Edition
978-0-470-11806-1

Java For Dummies, 4th Edition
978-0-470-08716-9

Microsoft® SQL Server™ 2008 All-in-One Desk Reference For Dummies
978-0-470-17954-3

Networking All-in-One Desk Reference For Dummies, 2nd Edition
978-0-7645-9939-2

Networking For Dummies, 8th Edition
978-0-470-05620-2

SharePoint 2007 For Dummies
978-0-470-09941-4

Wireless Home Networking For Dummies, 2nd Edition
978-0-471-74940-0